IRISH
SPORT

1950 - 2000

EDITED BY IAN FOSTER

IRISH SPORT

1950-2000

An insight into
Irish sporting success

MANTICORE
BOOKS LIMITED

2002

First published in Great Britain in 2002 by Manticore Books Limited,
Silver Birches, Heronsgate, Rickmansworth, Herts. WD3 5DN
www.manticorebooks.com

British Library Cataloguing in Publication Data
A CIP record for this book is available from the British Library

ISBN 1 900887 08 8

The publisher thanks the various sporting bodies for
granting permission to use their logos on the cover of the book

Printed and bound in Great Britain by J.H.Haynes & Co. Ltd., Yeovil

MANTICORE
BOOKS LIMITED

CONTENTS

THIS BOOK IS DEDICATED TO

T.J. Fox and all sporting addicts

FOREWORD

Ian Foster was born in West Kirby in 1936 and educated at Mostyn House School Cheshire, St Martin's Middlesex and then at Leighton Park, Berkshire.

In 1956 he matriculated to Trinity College, Dublin and that autumn paid his very first visit to Ireland. Dublin and Trinity have greatly changed over the past fifty years. The ban on Catholic attendance at Trinity College was rigorously enforced in 1956 and the University attracted large numbers of students from the UK and further afield. Dublin was then one of the cheapest of European cities, now it is one of the most expensive, while the Trinity undergraduate population now more accurately mirrors that of the country as a whole.

Ian Foster read history at Trinity. Beside his enthusiasm for his subject, as an accomplished sportsman he was well placed to make the most of his undergraduate years in Dublin. Many of his colleagues from across the Irish sea were also excellent sportsmen: Chris Lea, Charlie Mulraine, Jonah Barrington, Algy Rice and Ian himself played games to international standard often in more than one discipline. They had the time of their lives in Trinity.

Upon graduation Ian joined the teaching profession, serving in England, New Zealand and in St Columba's College, Dublin. But, wherever he was based, Ireland, Irish sport and Irish sportsmen and women had captured his imagination and this book is a pietas for his sporting sojourn in Ireland and for the very many friendships cemented both on and off the field.

Together with an esoteric group including Gerard Siggins, Roly Meates, Colm Smith, Mike Halliday, Seamus King, John West, Ronnie Dawson, Cyril White, Michael Bowler, Mike Johnston and Ian Steepe he has compiled a book that expresses his sporting preferences, as indeed it should. Based primarily on rugby, golf, cricket and equine affairs it offers fascinating vignettes of athletics, hockey, soccer, motor racing, boxing and the Gaelic games. Not necessarily designed to be read from cover to cover, it presages many of the remarkable changes which have taken place in the very recent past in Irish sport – the primary one being a steady growth in the professionalisation of the major disciplines.

Professionalisation may, in the end, be neither a good or a bad thing, rather in today's TV driven world, it is probably inevitable; and we are grateful to Ian Foster and Friends for recalling a recent past in which Irish sporting achievements were less predictable but perhaps, for that very reason, even more exciting and we welcome with anticipation this fascinating compendium of modern Irish sport. ■

TREVOR WEST

■ Trevor West is professor of mathematics in Trinity where for 25 years he has been chairman of the Central Athletic Club administering university sport. He has represented the University in the Irish Senate, is a biographer of Sir Horace Plunkett (founder of the Irish Cooperative Movement) and author of 'The Bold Collegians, the Development of Sport in Trinity College, Dublin'.

PHOTOGRAPHIC CREDITS

Page	Credit
10	Lafayette, Dublin
12	Gavin Cawdwell and Portmarnock Golf Club
13	ICI Ltd courtesy Colin Shillington
14	Belfast Telegraph
15	Billy Stickland/Inpho
17	Moira McKelvey
19	Mike Halliday
20	Malcolm Thomas
21	Russell Orr and Malcolm Thomas
22	Bob Martin/Allsport
26	Seamus King
31-3	Seamus King
35	Justin Nelson and Seamus King
38	Devaney's Photos, Athlone
41	Seamus King
47-8	Seamus King
55	Seamus King
56	John Clarke
58	Seamus King
60	John Clarke and Seamus King
62	Seamus King
64	John Sheehan
65-6	Seamus King
72	H.S. O'Connor
74	New Zealand Herald
75-7	J.C. Murphy O'Connor
80	New Zealand Herald
81	Malcolm Thomas
82	Russell Orr, New Zealand Press Officer
88	Ray McManus/Sportsfile
91	Lorraine O'Sullivan/Inpho
93	Marriott Irons
95	Noel Traynor and London Irish R.F.C.
103	Independent Newspapers, Dublin and H.S. O'Connor
104	Eastern Mail and Echo, Cardiff and H.S. O'Connor
106	Lafayette, Dublin
112	Ronnie Dawson.
115	John West
125	Hulton Getty/Allsport
130	David Cannon/Allsport
132	Ray McManus/Sportsfile
136	David Maher/Sportsfile
137	Simon Bruty/Allsport
139	Michael Steele/Allsport
141	Clive Mason/Allsport
146	Antony Hallas
148-9	Ian Steepe
159	Ian Steepe
167	Lords Cricket Office
166	John Elder and the Irish Cricket Union
169-70	John Elder and the Irish Cricket Union
173	John Elder and the Irish Cricket Union
174	Mike Halliday
176	Mike Halliday
184	Tom Honan/Inpho
189	Hulton Getty/Allsport
190	The Secretary, Baltray Golf Club
182	David Beamish
194-5	The Secretary, Baltray Golf Club
196	Denis Bergin Photographs

Page	Credit
203	Bobbie Hopkins, Dublin
207	Steven Munday/Allsport
208	Allsport
209	Andrew Redington/Allsport
211	Allsport
212	Simon Bruty/Allsport
223	IOC/Allsport
226	Tony Duffy/Allsport
228	Billy Stickland/Inpho
229	Clive Brunskill/Allsport
231	Mary Peters
233	Mary Peters
233	G. Granham
233	Daily Mirror Photo Div.
236	Brendon Moran/Sportsfile
240-1	Micheal Johnston
244	Simon Newman and The Times Newspaper
249-50	Micheal Johnston
252	Micheal Johnston
255-6	Micheal Johnston
257	Craig Prentis/Allsport
264-5	Ray McManus/Sportsfile
266	Pat Maxwell Sports Pictures
268	Mel Christle
269	H.Y. Money
272	Mel Christle
274	David Maher/Sportsfile
276	David Maher/Sportsfile
280	Hulton Deutsch/Allsport
282	Henry Beeby, Doncaster Bloodstock Agency
283	Peter Mooney Photography
286	Bobbie Hopkins and Susan Hall
288-9	Susan Robinson
290	The Sun and Susan Robinson
291	W.W. Rouch and Susan Robinson
298-300	Bobby Burke
302	Ray Lohan/Sportsfile
303	Tom Honan/Inpho
304	Damien Eagers/Sportsfile
307	Billy Stickland/ Inpho
309	Patrick Bolger/Inpho
310	Tom Honan/Inpho
314	Heritage Motor Centre
315	Michael Bowler
321	Jaguar Daimler Heritage Trust
322	Jaguar Racing
324	Andew Redington/Allsport
327	Michael Bowler
330	Jaguar Daimler Heritage Trust
331	Autocar archive, Gordon Crosby painting
333	Jaguar Daimler Heritage Trust
338	Lorraine O'Sullivan/Inpho
340	Michael Bowler
344	Lorraine O'Sullivan/ Inpho
344	Brendan Moran/Sportsfile
345	Patrick Bolger/Inpho
345	Billy Stickland/Inpho
346	Billy Stickland/Inpho
348	Billy Stickland/Inpho
349	SquashPics.com

EDITOR'S ACKNOWLEDGEMENTS

Many people have helped with the production of this book. I am extremely grateful to the following contributors: Seamus King (Gaelic Sports), Micheal Johnston (Rowing), Ian Steepe (Hockey), Michael Halliday (Cricket), Michael Bowler (Motor Sports), Dr Cyril White (Athletics), Colm Smith (Golf) and Gerard Siggins (Soccer). I have written the chapters on Boxing, Rugby, Horse Racing and part of the Cricket; I have exercised my privilege as editor to write most of the captions for the illustrations and the biographies of the contributors that are to be found at the start of each chapter.

I have thanked those who contributed their own chapters and there are those who have written somewhat smaller pieces and in this context I would like to thank David Millar, Dr. Hubie O'Connor and Neil Durden-Smith OBE. Others have subjected themselves to interviews and have in many cases subsequently made suggestions as to improving the resulting pieces and I would like to thank Mel Christle, Malcolm Thomas, Roly Meates, Greg McCambridge, John West, Danny Hearn, Peter and Johnny McKeever, Brian Smith and Willie and Susan Robinson and Ronnie Dawson for their time and patience and knowledge of their sports. Also, I wish to thank Jim Murphy O'Connor, Malcolm Thomas, Jim Shackleton, Ted Woodward and Michael Lynagh who are members of Denham Golf Club for their memories of rugby.

The collecting of the photographs proved a happy task. I am very grateful to all who have supplied me with photographs: Henry Beeby of Doncaster Bloodstock agency, Dame Mary Peters DBE, The Secretary of Baltray Golf Club, Seamus King, Colin Shillington, Noel Traynor of London Irish, Marriott Irons, Gavin Cawdwell and Portmarnock Golf Club, Mel Christle, Willie and Susan Robinson, Dr Cyril White, Mike Halliday and John Elder (ICU), Peter Mooney, Ian Steepe, Michael Bowler, Malcolm Thomas, Jim Murphy O'Connor, Michael Westacott, Bobby Burke, Micheal Johnston; also David Maher (Sports File), Norman McLosky (Inpho) and Matt Holmes (Allsport) who have provided professional expertise. Others have supplied photographs and they are acknowledged elsewhere; the origins of some photographs have proved impossible to trace and I apologise for omissions.

This book would never have happened without the encouragement and support of many: I would like to mention in particular my sister, Gill Gibbins, who spent hours doing the typing, sorting out corrections, sending e-mails, looking through the internet for photographs. Gerard Siggins did the proof-read with efficiency and thoroughness. I am very grateful to him for spotting amongst other slips "...he was in bed by 9.00 p.m. and was rewarded by a memorable ride, witnessed by 49,000 spectators...", Barbara Hicks and Peter Waite helped with the editing, Gordon Templeton has scanned the photographs and Richard Warman has provided wise council and encouraged me to write this book. Many others, who deserve to be mentioned, are inadvertently omitted and I thank them too. ■

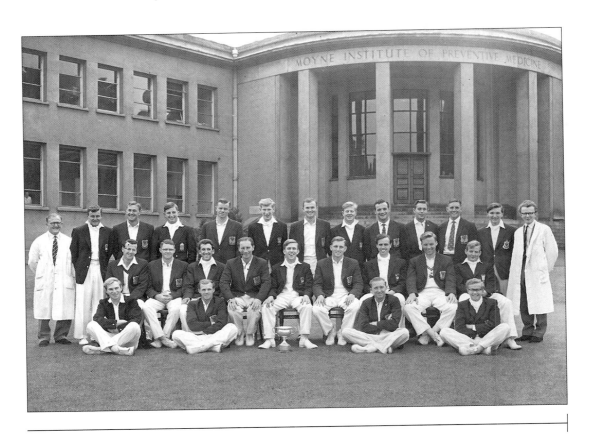

ABOVE ▪ July 1961. Dublin University Cricket Club v South African Fezela XI.
Back Row: Mr Lea, Tony Bradshaw, Colin Bland, John Fuller-Sessions, Peter Pollock, John West, Colin Rushmore, Chris Lea, Graham Bunyard, Denis Lindsay, Ray Gripper, Paddy Willis, Pat McAfee **Middle Row:** Jackie Botten, Peter Van de Merwe, Charlie Mulraine, Roy McLean, Ian Foster, Kim Elgie, Algy Rice, Chris Burger, Graham Guthrie.
Front Row: David Evans, L. Moly-Smith, Ian Fullerton, Billy Minns.

This introductory chapter is a collection of some personal recollections of people, events and places, in part an explanation of my support for all things to do with Irish sport. Many have asked why I am putting together a book on Irish Sport. After all, I am an Englishman born and bred. My only connection with Ireland was an uncle on my father's side, R.M. Foster, who attended St Columba's College in Dublin in the early 1900s, where he played cricket for the 1st XI.

My own support for Irish sport has given me great personal pleasure. I wrote to a number of people asking them to contribute an article on their sport. I stated that the book was to be basically about Irish sport between the years 1950 to 2000, that their article could cover school, club, provincial and international aspects of their sport; the form which it took was entirely up to them.

It has been a pleasure putting the book together; it has provided a chance of meeting old friends and acqaintances and making new ones. Dr Trevor West has put me up in his rooms in Trinity. Some contributors I have never met, some I have only spoken to on the phone, some I have wined and dined with and others are old friends and acquaintances.

The motivation for the book is to remember the past, enjoy the craic, wonder at the pride of the Irish, be disappointed at their near misses and approve of their attitude. Sport for the most part has overcome religion and the North/South divide. Athletics and soccer are the two sports to have been troubled by division. In the case of athletics this situation has been resolved. In soccer it suits to have a side from the Republic and a side from the North. The Republic has a side to be feared by all and the North hope for the emergence of another player with the footballing skills of George Best. In the Olympic Games at Sydney, Wayne McCullough, a Protestant from Belfast, proudly carried the Irish flag for all Ireland. In the year in which the British Embassy in Dublin was blown up and the sporting calm interrupted, Wales, Scotland and England declined to come to Dublin for their rugby matches; but France, having played Ireland in Paris, came to Lansdowne Road for a second match in that season.

Five years at Trinity College, Dublin, fuelled a passion for Ireland and its ways. College Park was an inspiring introduction to Irish sport. Lansdowne Road, with its intimate atmosphere, soon followed and then the golf courses – Portmarnock and Royal Dublin – beckoned. These were two exciting temples of the game; as students we could become University members. Harry Bradshaw reigned at Portmarnock and Christy O'Connor Senior was the doyen of Royal Dublin. As the desire to wander emerged, Lahinch and Rosses Point in the West of Ireland became favourite golf courses. Here they talked of Jimmy Bruen and Cecil Ewing. Back in Dublin a never-ending list of gems were to be found and played – Delgany, Baltray, The Island, Greystones to name a few.

ABOVE ■ Portmarnock – general ambience.

My own special interest is cricket. Cricket is played to a high standard in Dublin. The club grounds at Phoenix, Malahide, Rathmines, Pembroke and Clontarf compete with the very best and the characters of the late 1950s including of course my Trinity team-mates, were wonderful companions. Stanley Murphy the South African entrepreneur and millionaire sponsored the Fezelas. The object was to assemble a young side under the captaincy of a proven test player. Roy McLean, one of South Africa's greatest and most charismatic characters was chosen for the task.

Peter Van de Merwe would go on to captain South Africa on many occasions including the 1965 winning series in England. Others to represent South Africa with distinction included Colin Bland, Peter Pollock, Denis Lindsay, Jackie Botten and Eddie Barlow. Kim Elgie the vice-captain played rugby for Scotland and cricket for South Africa. The Fezelas won the cricket, lost the golf and halved the craic. Stanley Murphy wrote to say that the Fezelas' visit to Ireland had been one of the highlights of their tour. 'Fezela' in Afrikaans, means 'sting in the tail' and the rule was that if you scored a century you batted at the tail-end in the next match. In the match against Surrey, Roy McLean and Eddie Barlow, batting at number 10 and 11 respectively did not bat; the Fezelas had declared at 323 for three wickets.

It was not long before the other sports became part of my life. It was a privilege to watch racing at Fairyhouse, Punchestown, The Curragh and Phoenix Park. I had exciting experiences watching soccer at Tolka Park and the Gaelic Games at Croke Park.

LEFT ■ 1959/60 Colin Shillington just beats John Whetton competing for Great Britain against a combined Holland, Belgium and Luxembourg team.

Trinity sport in the late 1950s and early 1960s was of a high standard. Interest in hockey was inspired by the presence of David Judge and Ken Blackmore in the British Olympic team; they qualified for the team because of their Irish parentage since Ireland was part of the United Kingdom until 1921. Members of the Boxing Club were the elite amongst university sportsmen; you never argued with the boxers. The rowers always intrigued us – for half the year we never saw them and during the other half they were the socialites of the university; their home at the boat club in Islandbridge seemed a haven to us when we went out there. Athletics was transformed by Ronnie Delany's winning of the 1500 metres in the 1956 Olympics. Colin Shillington of Trinity was a great middle distance runner in his own right. Jonah Barrington, who just made the Trinity squash side, became world champion some years after graduation. A lifelong interest in all things to do with Irish sport was a natural progression for me.

ABOVE ■ Jim McKelvey in full flow!

As I came to put this book together, I thought about what it is that makes Irish sport so special, not just for the participants but also for the spectators. Perhaps it is the craic. Whatever the sport, it is played to win but then, importantly, it is also necessary to enjoy the game and to celebrate with one's opponents when the contest is over. Perhaps, it is the pride in playing for Ireland, province, club, university or school? There is nothing better than beating the English, but never rub salt in the wound – enjoy, but do not gloat. ■

The influence on Irish sport by all the universities has been particularly strong and beneficial. Ireland has a long tradition of the kind of personality that can mix academic and sporting ability. For example, Trinity provosts Mahaffy, Traill and Lyons, and the Trinity professors, father and son, A.A. and J.V. Luce. One has only to think of the likes of Oliver St John Gogarty, surgeon, senator, playwright, champion athlete and swimmer, author, wit and conversationalist, or his biographer Ulick O'Connor who has been a barrister, poet, playwright, diarist, first class rugby player, British universities' welterweight boxing champion and Irish record holder in the pole vault. This breed of sportsman maintained a gentleman's code of conduct that is still strong in Irish sport. I am reminded in golf of Padraig Harrington's

ABOVE ■ 1991 Rugby World Cup Australia v Ireland. Michael Lynagh's winning try.

disqualification at the 2000 Benson & Hedges International Open for failing to sign his card and his gracious acceptance of that decision; or the brave face to the hand of fate that has denied victory in soccer or rugby. For example, in soccer the injury time goals in Macedonia and Croatia which prevented Ireland qualifying for the 2000 European Soccer Championship and Michael Lynagh's winning try in the dying minutes of the quarter-finals of the 1991 Rugby World Cup at Lansdowne Road which gave Australia a 19-18 victory.

Irish sport has close links with English sport. I was watching England play rugby against Argentina on a wet miserable day in November 2000. England was giving the Argentinians a clinical beating. However, the day was enlivened when I realised Alan Lewis from Dublin was the referee. I remembered his father Ian, of Cork County and YMCA Dublin, being a fine batsman for his club and country. This was Alan's first match as a referee at Twickenham and he did this job with efficiency and authority. He comes from a rugby and cricketing background, having played for Old Wesley club as a fly-half and earning more caps than anyone for Ireland as an upper middle-order batsman. Alan is a man who has made an important contribution to Irish sport. His rugby commitments caused him to turn down the chance to represent Ireland at cricket in the World Cup qualifying tournament in Canada in 2001. Ian and Alan Lewis are examples of a generational theme in Irish sport which appears throughout this book.

Student days brought another family link; I played cricket against Jim McKelvey. He used to come with a Northern Ireland Cricket Club side, captained by Stuart Pollock to play in Trinity week against the university. Northern Ireland Cricket Club fixtures were always competitive and great craic. Jim McKelvey was one of those rare people, who was a dual international; playing for Ireland at cricket (two caps in 1954) and rugby (caps in 1956 against France and England). Perhaps of more note were the achievements of his wife's family. Moira McKelvey (nee Hopkins) played hockey for Ireland 22 times, but it was her sister, Thelma Hopkins, whose sporting career was the most remarkable. Thelma Hopkins was a dental student at Queen's University, Belfast. She was an outstanding exponent of the high jump. Whilst at school and before going to university, she came fourth in the 1952 Helsinki Olympics competing for Great Britain and Northern Ireland. In 1954 she won gold medals in the European Championships and the Empire Games. She set the world record (5 ft 8½ ins) for the high jump at the Queen's Grounds in Cherryvale in May 1956 and in the same year won a silver medal in the Melbourne Olympics. She played hockey 50 times for Ireland and represented Great Britain; she was also an Irish squash international. The family sporting prowess did not stop there. There were two cousins, who were brothers, one played hockey for Ireland and the other played hockey for Scotland (in those days Scotland required only a residential qualification) and a niece, Miriam Hopkins swam for Ireland.

ABOVE ▦ Thelma Hopkins shows her technique in the high jump, commonly referred to as the 'Frisby Flop'.
LEFT ▦ Thelma Hopkins vaults her garden fence.

Greg McCambridge, one time Leinster interprovincial golfer, sporting fanatic and companion on many a golfing outing in student days, was speaking at a dinner at the Kildare Street and University Club, on behalf of the Dublin University Golfing Society to celebrate the 75th anniversary of the foundation of the Dublin University Golfing Society (The Dublin University Golf Club was founded in 1894; the Dublin University Golfing Society was founded later). Those present included representatives from the Golfing Union of Ireland, from the Oxford and Cambridge Golfing Society, from the Royal & Ancient, from the Scottish and Welsh universities and the other universities in Ireland. There had been some fine and amusing speeches. When it came to Greg's turn to speak, after complimenting the previous speakers and after a rather lengthy speech given in his own inimitable drawl, he finally sat down. At which point Dr Grant, the UCD representative, stood up to reply and said, 'Thank you, Greg, for your speech in which there was neither a beginning, a middle or an end, but it certainly made winter much shorter'. And so the craic continued until the early hours of the morning.

I am sure the craic was just as good when Michael Hoey won the Amateur Championship over 36 holes at Prestwick in June 2001. He was the first Irishman to win the championship since Garth McGimpsey in 1985 and Joe Carr in 1953, 1958 and 1960. Michael's victory was some consolation to his father, Brian, who had lost the semi-final in 1970, when the Amateur was held at Newcastle, Co. Down, Northern Ireland. ▨

I wanted to include in the introduction three characters from the past to give a flavour for the book. Jimmy Boucher (cricket) and Andy Mulligan (rugby) played for their countries before their twentieth birthdays; Shergar recently celebrated the 20th anniversary of his Derby triumph. Sadly, all three have passed away, but each made a very special contribution to Irish sport.

Jimmy Boucher's education was at Belvedere College, the Jesuit Day School for boys in Dublin where they promoted the Anglicised games, rugby and cricket, rather than the Gaelic Games. Jimmy excelled at both rugby and cricket; he played scrum-half after leaving school for Old Belvedere but it was cricket that was his true forte. Albert Knight, formerly of Leicestershire, was the Belvedere coach and he recognised real talent in Jimmy. Boucher worked for the Central Electricity Board (later the ESB) throughout his life but his real devotion was to his mother, sister and cricket. In 1929, he played his first game for the Gentlemen of Ireland; they played the touring teams and the counties and some of their fixtures were recognised as being of first class status. Visitors to Ireland spoke in awe of J.C. Boucher, an off-spinner, who really turned the ball and bowled at a fast medium pace off a long run up. He headed the first class English averages in 1931, 1937 and 1948. Some examples of his remarkable figures were his six for 30

ABOVE ■ 1982 Cup Final. Jimmy Boucher and Stan Mitchell, captain of Phoenix, international and selector.

versus India in 1936 and in the next year, seven for 13 versus New Zealand. In 1937 he was invited by Lionel Tennyson to go on a tour of India; he declined. Had he gone, a place in the England Test team was a possibility, but his job, family and love for Ireland prevented him accepting the invitation. Perhaps also his fussy, earnest and anxious nature was another factor. In 1954, Jimmy, a legend in his own lifetime, retired from international cricket. He continued to play cricket for Phoenix until 1965 but his main duty was as Honorary Secretary of the Irish Cricket Union a post which he held until 1973. Irish cricket in the early 1950s was at low ebb; the Gentlemen of Ireland's first class status had been much diminished with only the annual fixture against Scotland remaining first class, but Jimmy Boucher's presence at Lord's kept Irish influence alive and respected. He died on Christmas Day 1995, aged 85. I was pleased to play cricket with and against Jimmy in the mid 1950s and early 1960s. He was a man to be admired.

Andy Mulligan is probably best remembered for his part in the only British Lions victory in the 1959 tour of New Zealand. He flew to New Zealand as replacement scrum-half for Stan Coughtrie. Mulligan was an outstanding rugby player. He received the first of his 22 caps in 1956 and retired from international rugby in 1961, having captained the Irish side when Ronnie Dawson was injured. He also played for London Irish and Wanderers but he was a versatile man. Mulligan was born in Kasauli (India) of Irish parents and was educated at Gresham's School, Holt and Magdalene College, Cambridge. His career embraced a wide variety of interests including journalism, authorship, work for the European Union and he established his own communications company. I remember him coming to Northwood Cricket Club with Tony O'Reilly; they had just started a ladies' lingerie company. He and O'Reilly were a famed double act known for their excellent mimicry of their fellow players to the accompaniment of Andy's guitar playing. Andy Mulligan died on 24th February 2001, aged 65 and a memorial service was held at the Chelsea Old Church, London. O'Reilly and Robin Roe, a former Chaplain General of the Armed Forces, gave addresses and the service was attended by a large congregation.

ABOVE ■ 1959 Lions Tour. Andy Mulligan (Guitar) and Tony O'Reilly lead the sing-song with Cliff Morgan, Malcolm Thomas and the boxer Howard Winstone.

ABOVE ■ 1959 Lions Tour. Lions on tour in New Zealand: J.R.C. Young (England), Kiwi keeper (Hawkes Bay), Malcolm Thomas (Wales), Ronnie Dawson (Ireland) and Alan Ashcroft (England).

Shergar, owned by the Aga Khan, trained by Sir Michael Stoute in England and ridden by Walter Swinburn, won the Derby in June 1981 by the biggest distance ever in the history of the Derby and he was being eased up. Lester Piggott on Shotgun was nowhere. In the words of Peter Bromley, the BBC Commentator, 'There's only one horse in it. You'll need a telescope to see the rest'. Eighteen months later Shergar was dead. He had returned to Ireland and retired after the 1981 season to the Ballymany stud. On 8th February 1983, Jim Fitzgerald the stud groom, was ordered at gunpoint by an IRA gang to lead them to Shergar; Shergar was put in a horsebox. It was the last time Fitzgerald saw Shergar. Fitzgerald was taken in a van and dumped 20 miles away. He says of Shergar that he was 'a grand, grand horse. He has to stand out as the best.' It was a monstrous cock-up by the IRA. Sean O'Callaghan, IRA member, in his autobiography The Informer says Shergar was killed within days of his kidnapping. He had thrown himself into a frenzy and had proved impossible to handle. However, to Walter Swinburn this version seemed unlikely as Shergar had an amazing temperament and 'he was the kindest horse I knew'. In any case the whole event brought discredit to the IRA. The bloodstock industry was threatened and the Irish love their horses. In Jim FitzGerald's eyes Shergar was a 'real gentle fella and a real champion'. His memory will live in the form of a bronze statue presented for the first time to the winner of the 2001 Derby. Appropriately the Epsom Derby 2001 was won by the Irish horse Galileo, sired by Sadler's Wells, owned by Mrs. John Magnier and Michael Tabor, trained at Ballydoyle by Aidan O'Brien and ridden by Michael Kinane. Jimmy Boucher, Andy Mulligan, and Shergar have made outstanding contributions to Irish sport. Their contributions are much admired on both sides of the Irish Sea. ▨

College Park, continues in summer or winter to be a peaceful and welcoming area, enlivened in the summer by Peter Ashe, a former London barrister and Oxford graduate, who keeps all on their toes and entertained with shouts from the boundary like 'Keep it tight, Trinity' or 'Very well done, Fergal Hoey; unusual for a C.Y. man'. A large crowd of undergraduates, in which the pretty girls are particularly noticeable, watch the sport with interest. Cricket is still

ABOVE ▨ Shergar 10 lengths clear beats the rest of the field to win the Derby at Epsom racecourse.

played to a high standard. Ed Joyce, Ireland and Middlesex, is a very promising left-handed batsman in a good Trinity side. Joyce's batting technique and temperament has been compared to David Gower and Graeme Pollock and he has been encouraged to take a four-year qualification for English residency to enable him to be considered for selection for the England Test team. He follows in the footsteps of nine other Irishmen who have played for Middlesex, the most recent being Dermott Monteith (1981-82). Earlier, Eddie Ingram played 12 games for the county either side of the Second World War captaining the county on at least one occasion. I remember Eddie as captain of Ealing Cricket Club in the late 1950s. He worked for the Guinness Brewery at Park Royal, he was a large man in girth but he was a remarkably agile fielder, particularly in the slips. He was a very good bowler, bowling quickish off-breaks or medium pace in swings and a hard-hitting batsman, but above all he was a welcoming, smiling host both on the field and at his house to many Trinity sides. Leslie Compton (Enfield), Ian Bedford (Finchley) and Bob Pipe (Wembley) offered similar hospitality to Trinity touring teams.

Rugby finds Trinity in the echelons of the lower divisions but when I saw them in early 2001, I was impressed. They were well coached and they played with skill, flair and spirit. However, the modern era of professionalism has arrived and left university sport behind. For example Brian O'Driscoll and Denis Hickie formerly UCD students have been forced to abandon their studies to keep pace with the demands of professionalism. At international, interprovincial, university, school and club level, Ireland competes with pride, with passion and with success.

Half a century of Irish sport represents a period of change and progress. The Unions and Associations of the individual sports supported by the provincial, university, club and school structure continue to exert a major influence in organisation, coaching and finance. The most popular spectator sports – soccer, racing, rugby and the Gaelic games, hurling and football continue to attract large crowds to improved facilities and to perform to world-class standards. Golf is a sport that welcomes all; Irish golf is renowned throughout the world and its courses and players are much respected. New courses, new players and the allocation of the Ryder Cup for 2006 is testimony to golf's popularity and standing.

Rowing, boxing, cricket, motor racing, athletics and hockey as the following chapters reflect, have produced their moments of glory and disappointment. Gone at the international level are the days of unprofessionalism; no longer for instance, will you be able to tell when a rugby season has started by the sound of heavy feet pounding the streets of Dublin City in the evening trying to get fit. Even the cricketers are being subjected to new fitness and skill regimes. However, there still remains the attitude of sportsmanship, the craic, low levels of violence and a happy mixture of rival fans at major events.

At all levels, the Irish Sports Council and the Sports Council for Northern Ireland are important influences. The Irish Sports Council, founded in 1999, plays a vital role in Irish sport, by not only its financial support but also its commitment and encouragement to all levels of sport. The Irish Sports Council emphasizes: 'We want more people to participate in more sport for longer. We want them to enjoy it. We want every participant to reach the maximum of his or her potential fairly. We want to ensure that our talented athletes are given every opportunity to succeed at the highest level'.

The Sports Council for Northern Ireland was founded in 1973 and although older than its southern Irish compatriot, it is clear that there are disparities in sporting opportunities available between the North and South. Sport in the North has had its problems but the Sports Council for Northern Ireland is now in a stronger position with the establishment of an Assembly in Northern Ireland and the possibility of lottery funding to increase its financial support to sport. The aims of the Sports Council for Northern Ireland are to increase and sustain committed participation especially among young people, to raise the standards of sporting excellence and to promote the good reputation and efficient administration of sport. The Council's aims will be achieved by developing the competences of its staff who are dedicated to optimising the use of its resources.

Thus the governments in both parts of Ireland are committed to sport as a means of making a significant contribution to peace, to building a stable society, to creating sporting excellence and to the enjoyment of sport by all. However, sport in the South is in a better financial position. The economy in the South has boomed; it has been suggested that in the region of IR£450 million has been committed to sports by the government, private sponsors and other sources. The Sports Council for Northern Ireland has in the region of £8 million to finance its sport. Gus Connelly, at the Sports Council for Northern Ireland points out that they are a small organisation with eighty-seven sporting bodies, thirty-five of which are all-Ireland. The link between the North and South in most major sports is important and helps Ireland to compete at world standard.

And so my motivation for compiling this book is to remember the past, to enjoy the memories of Irish sport and to look forward to the future.

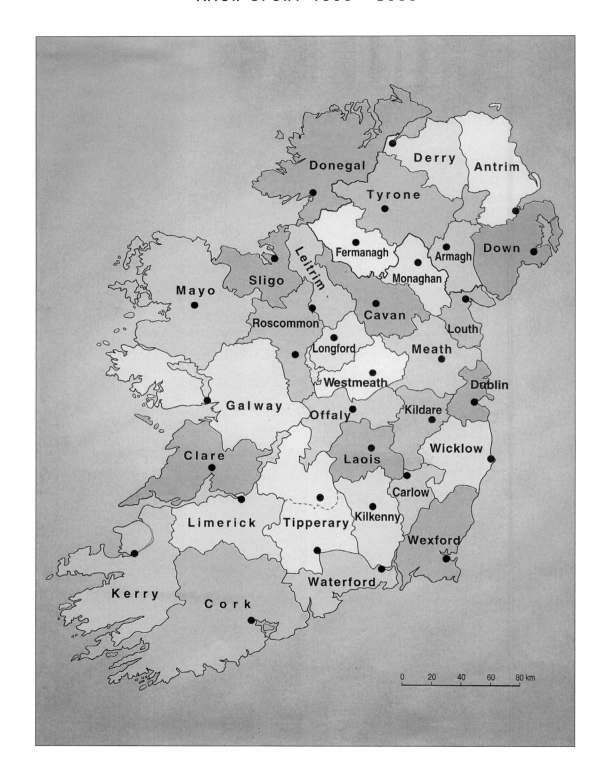

Seamus J. King, a native of Lorrha, Co. Tipperary has been living in Cashel since 1965, where he works as a teacher at Rockwell College. After his early education at Redwood N.S., he spent five years in St Flannan's College, Ennis, where he played on the Dean Ryan and Harty Cup hurling teams. He was a member of Lorrha team, which won the North Tipperary senior hurling championship in 1956. After attending university at Cork and Dublin, he spent four years abroad before returning to work at Cashel. He has a long involvement with Cashel King Cormacs GAA club, including eight years as chairman, and is currently president of the club. He has been writing on GAA matters for many years and his books include club histories of Lorrha GAA club and Cashel King Cormacs: County Tipperary GAA History, 1935-1984: County Tipperary Bord na nOg History: A History of Hurling: The Clash of the Ash in Foreign Field: Hurling Abroad and History of the GAA in the North Tipperary Division. He was a joint author of the recently published Tipperary's GAA Ballads. He is currently chairman of the County Tipperary GAA Yearbook Committee. Married to Margaret, they have three adult children, Sharon, Aidan and Ruadhan. ■

LEFT ▨ The 32 Counties of Ireland.

The Rules

Hurling is a field game played between two teams of fifteen players each. The players line out as follows: a goalkeeper, three full-backs, three half-backs, two centrefield players, three half-forwards and three full-forwards.

The two fundamental requirements for the game are a hurley or caman and a ball or sliothar. The Irish word for hurley – caman, recognises its nature by incorporating the Irish word for crooked – cam. And that is what a hurley literally is, a crooked stick, made from ash wood, about 13 centimetres wide at the striking point and 75 centimetres long. Ash has always been regarded as the ideal wood for the making of hurleys because the timber has a pliability that is necessary to withstand the impact of two hurleys coming in contact with one another. The sliothar or ball weighs about 120 grams and has a diameter of about 7.6 centimetres. It contains a core of cork, covered in layers of thread and cased in pigskin leather. The thread around the cork is very important as it prevents the cork breaking up. If this were to happen the ball's pressure would be reduced and its resilience suffer. The leather casing is held togther by wax stitching and coated in a water-resistent protection.

A game of hurling lasts for 70 minutes, divided into equal halves with an interval of 15 minutes. The length of the playing surface is 150 metres and the width 75 metres. At each end of the field are two goal posts with a crossbar approximately 2.15 metres high. The aim of the game is to get the ball between the goalposts. When the ball goes under the crossbar it is a goal and when it goes over it is a point. One goal equals three points. If a player puts the ball over his end line wide of the posts, a 65 metre free is awarded to the opposing team. When a player puts the ball over the sideline, a free strike from the sideline is granted to his opponent in which the sliothar has to be struck from the ground. Frees are awarded for picking the ball off the ground with the hand, for carrying the ball too far in the hand, for pushing the opponent in the back, for holding an opponent and for rough and dangerous play.

All frees are taken by rising the ball with the hurley and striking it without catching it in the hand. In normal play it is permitted to catch the ball in the hand from the air or raise it to the hand from the ground with the hurley. Each team is allowed five substitutes during the course of the game.

The referee has six officials to help him control the game. At each set of goalposts there are two umpires, one to decide on goals and a second on points. When a goal is scored, a green flag is waved and a white flag is waved in the event of a point. As well, there are two linesmen who decide which side has put the ball over the sideline and to award the free shot to the other side.

The game demands a degree of courage. To the uninitiated, it can appear dangerous but to properly trained players it is not. Anyone brought up with the game learns to defend himself instinctively and protect himself with the hurley. The most common injuries are skinned knuckles, or cuts and bruises to the head. It is a very fast game with the ball moving from end to end of the field at a great pace. It can be a very exciting game when the ball is moving fast and the players are well-trained in the skills of the game. A variation of hurling called Camogie, with slightly different rules, is played by women.

Gaelic Athletic Association

The relationship between the Gaelic Athletic Association and other sports has not always been good but since 1971, an amicable working relationship with most sporting bodies has been established. Trevor West, in his book *The Bold Collegians*, says, 'The GAA ban prohibiting members of the association from playing in, or watching, "foreign" games was formally revoked in 1971. Given the links, in 1884, of the Protestant athletic establishment with unionism and of the GAA with nationalism, some such dichotomy was probably inevitable; the tragedy is that the ban so long outlasted the conditions that gave rise to it'. Michael Cusack founded the GAA in 1884 with the purpose of encouraging the Gaelic games; Cusack was an excellent club cricketer and rugby player and favoured all sports. It was the second generation of GAA administrators, in the 1890s, that developed 'the ban' mentality.

The first mention of hurling in Ireland is a literary reference dated 1272 BC. By the 18th century hurling had grown in popularity and that century is sometimes called 'the golden age of hurling'. During this time it was patronised by landlords, who sponsored teams and organised games for wagers with neighbouring landlords. However, by the 19th century, hurling had begun to decline in popularity; the French revolution created an atmosphere of uncertainty – landlords withdrew their patronage, the Catholic Church frowned on Sunday games, the middle class disassociated themselves from many forms of popular culture and the Great Famine (1846-49) had its influence too.

By 1880 the game was in a perilous state. As one authority stated, hurling could 'now be said to be not only dead and buried but in several localities to be entirely forgotten and unknown . . .' but in 1884 Michael Cusack founded the Gaelic Athletic Association and it set out to restore Gaelic pastimes, athletics, hurling, football and handball. The GAA was successful in its ambition and today hurling is the third most common game in Ireland.

By 1950 hurling was well administered with a clear set of rules and organised with competitions for different age levels. The ambition of every player is to be a senior player, be picked for his county and win an All-Ireland final. This is achieved by playing for a county and winning the intercounty competition of his province, Ulster, Munster, Leinster or Connacht. The four champion counties from each province then play the All-Ireland semi-finals with the winners contesting the All-Ireland final. The final is played at Croke Park, Dublin on the second Sunday of September. In 1954, 80,000 watched the All-Ireland final. In the early part of the last century attendances were small but in the 1920s 30,000, in the 1930s 50,000 and 1940s, 60,000 were common attendance figures. More recently numbers have declined below the 1954 crowd as improved facilities were developed which reduced capacity, and health and safety requirements had to be met. At the present time Croke Park is being developed and, when it is completed, will have a capacity of 80,000.

The Gaelic Athletic Association was more than a sporting organisation; it also had a cultural dimension as it became involved in the revival of the Irish language, Irish dancing and other aspects of Irish culture. There was a political dimension in that it identified with the separatist wing of the Nationalist Ireland movement. Michael Cusack, although a keen supporter and player of the Anglicised games, saw them as a threat to the development of the national game, but Archbishop Croke of Cashel, who was the patron of the association influenced for a moderate view. However in 1904, written into the GAA rule book was the following: 'Any member of the Association who plays or encourages in any way rugby, football, hockey or any imported game which is calculated to injuriously affect our National Pastimes, is suspended from the Association'. The rule was to remain on the books until 1971.

A related rule was Rule 21, which prohibited members of the Royal Irish Constabulary (later, the Royal Ulster Constabulary) and British defence forces from participating in Gaelic games. It also forbade GAA members from attending social functions hosted by the RUC or British forces. This rule was revoked at a special congress of the GAA at the end of 2001.

By 1950 Tipperary (14 wins), Cork (16 wins) and Kilkenny (13 wins) had established themselves as the strongest hurling teams. London, in 1901, caused a major surprise when they won the final, and Dublin won the All-Ireland final six times before 1938. Geographically, the game established itself in the south-east and in an irregular swathe westward across Ireland, and in isolated pockets such as North Kerry, the Glens of Antrim and the Ards Peninsula in County Down.

The winning team in the All-Ireland senior hurling championship receives the MacCarthy Cup. It was presented to the GAA in 1922 by William, later more commonly known as Liam,

ABOVE ■ Michael Collins, Paddy Dunphy and Harry Boland at a hurling final in Croke Park circa 1920. Later Collins and Boland were to take opposite sides in the Civil War.

MacCarthy. He was the first treasurer of the London County Board of the GAA, which was formed in 1896, and later president. He was also involved in the Gaelic League. A man of great character, proud of his Irish roots, he is regarded among his compatriots as the 'Father of the London GAA'. He died in 1928 and is buried in Dulwich cemetery, London. The cup was first presented to Bob McConkey, captain of the victorious Limerick team in 1922. ■

During the first half of the century the game produced many fine players, who became heroes to their clubs and their counties and were feared by opponents. One of the greatest was Cork player, Christy Ring (1920-1979), who played in ten All-Ireland finals, winning eight of them. He captained three of the winning teams. He was the outstanding forward in the game, playing at senior county level from 1939-1962. Another outstanding player was Mick Mackey, Limerick (1912-1982). His best position was centre half-forward and his achievements with his club, Ahane, and Limerick are legendary. His senior playing career stretched from 1930-1947.

By the middle of the 20th century the Gaelic Athletic Association had established itself very firmly in the mind of the Irish people. It was one of the integral parts of Irish society and culture, together with the political party of De Valera, Fianna Fail, and the Catholic Church. At a time of economic misery and large-scale emigration, the GAA provided an opportunity for people to express themselves and celebrate sporting achievements. Hurling was a major outlet. Cork, (12 wins), Kilkenny (13 wins), Tipperary (10 wins) in the period 1950 to 2000 have continued to dominate the All-Ireland finals but Waterford, Limerick, Galway, Offaly and Clare have also achieved success.

The early '50s were dominated by Tipperary-Cork rivalry. Tipperary won the All-Irelands in 1949, 1950 and 1951 after many breathtaking encounters with their old rivals. Cork duly came along in the following three years and captured the three titles after equally enthralling contests with the men from Tipperary. These encounters took place within the framework of the Munster championship but such was the dominance of Munster hurling at the time, that in all the six years, the Munster champions went on to claim All-Ireland honours.

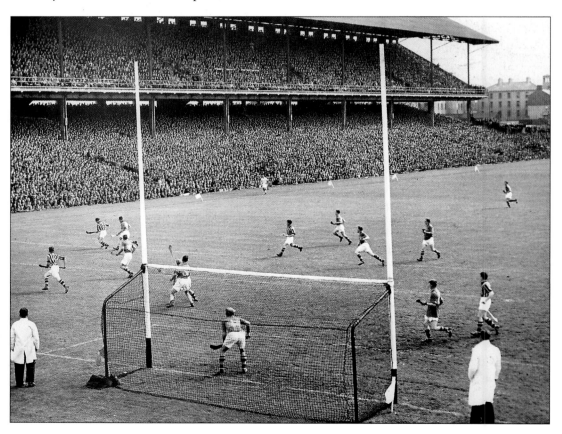

A halt was put to this dominance in the middle of the century by the men of Wexford. This county was originally a football stronghold and its hurling prospects at the beginning of the decade were anything but promising. There was gradual improvement and they reached the All-Ireland final against Cork in 1954. A record number of people for a hurling final, 84,856 saw Cork victorious in an epic game. The winners were captained by the inimitable Christy Ring but the Wexford side had their collosi in the three Rackard brothers, Nicky, who played full-forward, Billy, who played centre-back and Bobbie, who played cornerback. Wexford came back in the following two years to win All-Irelands and they won a third in 1960.

Brendan Fullam in his book *Giants of the Ash* describes one of Bobbie Rackard's greatest games. The moment of greatness came for Bobbie Rackard in the 1954 All-Ireland final against Cork. With about 20 minutes remaining, Nick O'Donnell, the great Wexford full-back, broke his collar-bone and had to leave the field. Wexford reshuffled their team and took Bobbie Rackard to full-back. He proceeded to give a power-packed and impeccable display of defensive hurling

ABOVE ■ 1955 All-Ireland Final. Dr Kinane the Archbishop of Cashel and Patron of the GAA throws in the ball to start the final between Wexford and Galway. This had been the practice since 1884 but ceased in the 1970s; from then on, the only players present for the throw-in are those at centrefield. **LEFT** ■ 1950 All-Ireland Final. Tipperary beat Kilkenny 1-9 to 1-8 before 68,599 spectators. Jimmy Langton (Kilkenny, No 12) threatens the Tipperary goal.

that will forever have a special place in hurling history and will be talked about whenever great feats of individual brilliance are recalled.

The Wexford teams were immensely popular with the public and this was shown in the huge numbers who came to see them play. In the 1955 final against Galway, 72,854 spectators turned up, the eighth largest attendance at an All-Ireland. In the National League final against Tipperary in May 1956, the attendance of 45,902 constitutes a record. The record for a hurling All-Ireland was set in 1954 and the second largest crowd attended the 1956 final, when 83,096 saw Wexford defeat Cork. The fourth and fifth biggest crowds were present in 1960, when Wexford beat Tipperary, and in 1962, when Tipperary reversed the result.

Wexford had something special to offer. Physically they were big men but allied to their size was a high level of skill. They were noted sportsmen, renowned for performances that sometimes approached chivalry. Many of them revealed qualities of leadership that set them apart from the rank and file of humanity: there was a romance, an energy and an excitement about them that made them larger than life; they appeared to step out of the pages of the heroic past of myths and legends. Many hurlers have ballads and tributes written of them. One of the finest to be written was on the death of Nicky Rackard, the chorus of which said:

> *We watched you on September's fields*
> *And lightning was the drive*
> *You were the one Cuchulainn's son*
> *In nineteen-fifty-five.*

One of the contributing factors for the increased popularity of hurling was the radio. Radio Eireann, the national broadcasting station, may not have been a very exciting media experience during the fifties, but its one claim to fame was the coverage of Gaelic games. In this it was fortunate in having one of the most popular broadcasters of all time, Micheal O'Hehir. Beginning in 1938 he soon established himself as an outstanding broadcaster. He had a distinctive voice, a great knowledge of the game and was an intimate acquaintance of the players and the little-known villages and townslands they came from. On Sunday afternoons his voice was to be heard in kitchens and living rooms, in pubs and shops, in public parks and on beaches, bringing his exciting account of a Munster or Leinster final or All-Ireland day to people far and near. His voice was also carried to Irish emigrants abroad through radio link-ups. He gave remote places a national platform and made unknown players household names. When television arrived he transferred successfully to it but he will always be remembered as the radio broadcaster who could paint a picture of the game and make it live as vividly as if one were present.

Towards the end of the '50s another team came on the scene to challenge for hurling honours. Waterford made their first breakthrough to All-Ireland glory in 1948, when a star-studded team defeated Dublin in the All-Ireland. The success was greeted by a welcoming-home crowd of 25,000 people and six bands. Waterford didn't capitalise on the victory and failed to qualify for an All-Ireland again until 1957, when they were beaten by Kilkenny, who were returning to glory after ten years in the wilderness.

Waterford got their revenge in 1959 when they came through Munster and qualified for the All-Ireland against Kilkenny. The game attracted a crowd of over 73,000 and was rated one of the greatest finals ever; a tense and thrilling contest played at a furious pace. For a long time it appeared to be going Waterford's way, and they led by five points at the interval, but Kilkenny came back to snatch a draw. The replay attracted nearly 78,000. Waterford had learned most from the drawn game and, after another superb encounter, victory went their way by 3-12 to 1-10. There were some marvellous displays for Waterford from their captain, Frankie Walsh, and their centre-forward, Tom Cheasty. A big, strong player and a most unorthodox striker of the ball, his forte was cutting through the centre, making straight for the goal and palming the ball over the bar.

LEFT ■ 30th June 1957. The Munster semi-final between Cork and Tipperary at Limerick which Cork won by 5-2 to 1-11. In the second half Christy Ring went off with a broken wrist. Mick Mackey, who was doing umpire for referee Mick Hayes of Clare, says something to Christy Ring as he leaves the field.

The sides met for a third time in seven years in the 1963 All-Ireland. Waterford shocked Tipperary in the Munster final and Kilkenny defeated Wexford in Leinster. The game was a record-breaker in that the combined scores created new figures for a 60-minute final, Kilkenny 4-17, Waterford 6-8. The Kilkenny victory was due to some outstanding displays, from Eddie Keher, who scored fourteen points in the game, and Seamus Cleere, who played a captain's part. ▪

The '50s will also be remembered for the Railway Cup competition, the interprovincial competition, which began in 1926. It reached the height of its popularity during this decade and the final, which was always played at Croke Park on St Patrick's Day, used to attract over 40,000 people. The competition gave countrywide exposure to great players from less successful hurling counties who otherwise had little chance of national exposure. Players like Jimmy Smyth of Clare and Jobber McGrath of Westmeath come quickly to mind. At the same time it gave better-known players the opportunity to show off their brilliance. The competition was dominated by Christy Ring for over two decades during which he won an incredible eighteen finals with Munster! For a host of reasons the Railway Cup began to decline in popularity in the late seventies and, even though it is still played, it is but a shadow of its former self.

The 1960s were dominated by Tipperary. Of the ten All-Irelands between 1960-1969, the county played in seven, winning four and losing three. The team was regarded as the greatest that ever wore the blue and gold. It began to show its potential when winning the 1958 All-Ireland, beating Galway after accounting for Kilkenny in the semi-final. Its progress was halted when unexpectedly beaten by Wexford in the 1960 All-Ireland. The defeat was attributed to fatigue after an extremely strenuous encounter with Cork in that year's Munster final.

Success came in 1961 when Dublin were defeated in the final. What was expected to be a relatively easy encounter turned out to be an extremely difficult battle. Dublin nearly surprised everyone by snatching victory and might have done so but for the sending off of Lar Foley in the second half and the saving of a certain goal by Tipperary goalkeeper Donal O'Brien. The defeat was a misfortune from which Dublin never recovered. They were badly beaten in the following year's Leinster championship and have never since reached an All-Ireland final.

In contrast Tipperary went on to more victories. They defeated Wexford by 3-10 to 2-11 in a thrilling encounter in the 1962 All-Ireland, which saw outstanding displays from Donal O'Brien, John Doyle, Tony Wall, Tom Ryan and 'Mackey' McKenna for Tipperary, as well Tom Neville, Pat Nolan, Phil Wilson and Ned Wheeler of Wexford. Tipperary set their sights on a third in a row in 1963 but they were halted in their tracks by Waterford in the Munster championship. However, they came back the following year to take the Munster championship, defeating Cork by 3-13 to 1-5 and the All-Ireland by defeating Kilkenny by 5-13 to 2-8. They were to repeat the success in 1965, crushing Cork by 4-11 to 0-5 in the Munster final, and defeating Wexford by 2-16 to 0-10 in the All-Ireland.

The Tipperary team of 1964-65 is generally regarded as one of the greatest hurling forces that ever took the field. Traditionally Tipperary teams had shone in their back players but this team also had a fluent attack. Every one of the forwards was a match-winner in his own right. With Jimmy Doyle and 'Babs' Keating on the wings, Donie Nealon and Sean McLoughlin in the corners, and Larry Kiely and Mackey McKenna providing the backbone, Tipperary had a forward line that was unrivalled in its brilliance. At the other end of the field, John O'Donoghue between the posts received magnificent cover from John Doyle, Michael Maher and Kieran Carey. John Doyle won his eighth All-Ireland in 1965, bringing him equal to Christy Ring with the record of having won the greatest number of All-Irelands on the field of play. Further out Mick Burns, Tony Wall, Michael Murphy in 1964 and Len Gaynor in 1965, were outstanding and the team was completed by Theo English and Mick Roche in the centre of the field. Even the best of teams reach a peak. This seems to have happened to Tipperary in 1965. A chink appeared in their mantle of invincibility in 1966 when they lost the National League 'home' final to Kilkenny. This was more than a mere defeat. It was a huge psychological victory for the Kilkenny men, their first defeat of Tipperary in major competition since 1922!

After the league defeat, Tipperary made a few changes for the championship. It was expected they would be forewarned but they didn't learn anything in either physical or mental readiness. Their opponents, Limerick, showed themselves a team of fire and dash and Tipperary just couldn't cope with their super-fitness and were well-beaten, 4-12 to 2-9. Unfortunately Limerick were unable to capitalise on their significant victory and were beaten by Cork in the Munster semi-final. Cork went on to beat Waterford in the final. Kilkenny were Cork's opponents in the All-Ireland final and were widely tipped to win but they were out-hurled and out-manoeuvered on the day and were beaten by 3-9 to 1-10. Cork were greatly helped by a quartet of splendid players from the under-21 side, three McCarthys, Gerald, Charlie and Justin, and Seanie Barry. It was twelve years since Cork had won an All-Ireland and there were unprecedented scenes of joy when the final whistle sounded.

If Tipperary were poor in 1966 they had a brilliant Munster campaign in 1967. They pushed Waterford, who had put Cork out of the championship in the first round, aside in the semi-final and Clare in the final. Tipperary's opponents in the All-Ireland were Kilkenny. On a blustery day Tipperary had the breeze in their favour in the first half and led by double scores at half-time. But, they were totally eclipsed by Kilkenny after the interval and lost by 3-8 to 2-7.

ABOVE ■ John Doyle, winner of eight All-Ireland senior hurling championship medals in a career stretching from 1949 to 1967 is acclaimed by Tipperary supporters.

It was a disappointing result for John Doyle who was going for his ninth All-Ireland. It was his last year to play for Tipperary. For 19 seasons between 1949 and 1967 he had played senior hurling for his county. During these years he had never failed to turn out in a championship game and he never retired injured during a game. Starting at left cornerback, his career got a new lease of life in 1958 when he lined out at left-wing back, and he finished his hurling days at right cornerback. He played in ten All-Irelands and won eight of them. He also holds the record for National League victories, 11 in all. His ability and his longevity at the top were recognised when he received a decisive vote for the left cornerback position in the 1984 Team of the Century and the 2000 An Post Millennium Team.

A namesake of his, Jimmy, was one of the most brilliant forwards of the period. Playing in thirteen All-Irelands between 1954 and 1971, he won nine of them. Four of them were in minor finals of which he won three, in 1955, 1956 and 1957. At the senior level he played in nine finals, winning six. He captained the minor team to victory in 1957, and the senior team in 1962 and 1965. He was also picked on the teams of the century and the millennium.

In his article on Jimmy Doyle in *Hurling Giants*, Brendan Fullam had this to say: 'Among the great thrills of his early days was to hear a man shout "Congratulations" to him as he walked back to school with his bag on his back. "What for?" said Jimmy and the reply was "You have been selected on the Munster Railway Cup team." He travelled to Belfast accompanied by Christy Ring. Coming off the train Ring donned a cap and pulled it down over his eyes. Jimmy was a bit baffled and asked Ring why he was wearing the cap in that manner. "Ah", said Christy, "I don't want to be recognised." There were occasions when Ring liked privacy and as time passed Jimmy was to learn and understand for himself the significance of Ring's feelings. Even to this day there are times when Jimmy wishes he could operate incognito.'

As well as John Doyle, Kieran Carey, Tony Wall and Theo English had disappeared from the hurling scene when Tipperary faced into the 1968 championship. They had an easy victory over Cork in the Munster final and came up against Wexford in the All-Ireland. Wexford trailed by 1-11 to 1-3 at the interval but staged a great rally in the second half. Inspired by newcomers Tony Doran, Tom Neville and John Quigley, plus a great half-back line of Vinny Staples, Dan Quigley and Willie Murphy, they transformed the interval deficit into a final victory score of 5-8 to 3-12. It was a sad day for Tipperary captain, Michael Roche, who was captaining his team to a second All-Ireland defeat. Tipperary's greatest period of hurling dominance came to an end with this defeat. There was to be one brief flash of brilliance in 1971 before the county settled down to a long spell in the hurling wilderness. After the riches of the '50s and '60s, the famine of the '70s and '80s was difficult for the county's supporters to bear, and when it came to an end in 1989 there were unprecedented scenes of joy and euphoria throughout the county.

Cork and Kilkenny reigned supreme in the 1970s. The best way to view the period 1969-79 is via the statistics. 22 teams contested the eleven All-Irelands during the period. Kilkenny appeared in eight finals, five times as winners. Cork had six appearances, four of them victorious. Wexford made three unsuccessful appearances and Galway made two. Limerick had one success and one failure, and Tipperary made one successful appearance. So, between them, Kilkenny and Cork won nine of the eleven All-Irelands. Another feature of their supremacy is the way they dominated their respective provincial championships. Kilkenny won the Leinster championship eight times during the period, including five in a row from 1971-75. Cork also won eight Munster championships at the same time and their successes included a five in a row from 1975 to 1979.

Cork defeated Tipperary in three major competitions during 1969, a year that probably marks the turning point in Munster hurling from Tipperary dominance of the 1960s to Cork supremacy of the 1970s. Cork defeated Tipperary in the Munster final, their first championship success over this opposition in 12 years. In the All-Ireland against Kilkenny, although the game was even enough in the first half, Cork appeared to have the edge. After the interval Kilkenny put in a storming performance and ended up easy winners by 2-15 to 2-9.

In 1970 the playing time for provincial finals and All-Ireland semi-finals and finals was increased to 80 from 60 minutes for all senior championship games. It was to remain so until 1975, when the 75 minute final was introduced and this has been the duration of finals in these competitions since.

Another development was the re-introduction of All-Ireland semi-finals. They were played until 1958 after which Galway made their debut in the Munster championship. Up to then Galway, as representatives of Connaght, used to meet the Leinster or Munster champions in rotation, in the All-Ireland semi-final. From 1970 onwards, Galway played in the All-Ireland semi-final.

Cork came out of Munster after an exciting game with Tipperary in the 1970 Munster championship. In Leinster, Wexford surprised Kilkenny, who were without Eddie Keher for most of the game. They defeated Galway in the All-Ireland semi-final and played Cork in the final. It was a poor game of bad temper and rough play at the end of which Cork had a 14 point margin of victory on a scoreline of 6-21 to 5-10.

Limerick were the form team going into the 1971 Munster championship, having beaten Tipperary in the National League final. In the Munster semi-final they recorded their first championship win in 31 years over Cork. In the Munster final they came up against Tipperary at Killarney and lost by a point in a thriller. In Leinster, Kilkenny were back in the winning frame again and defeated Wexford in the final. Tipperary accounted for Galway in the All-Ireland semi-final. The final was the first to be televised in colour and it attracted the smallest attendance for a final since 1958. In an epic tussle Tipperary came out on top, winning by 5-17 to 5-14.

The All-Star scheme was introduced in 1971. Under this scheme the top 15 players of the year were chosen by a committee of sports journalists and GAA officials and were given a trip to the USA. The intention behind the trip was to encourage and promote the organisation and playing of hurling among Irish exiles across America. A sponsor was required and the Irish tobacco company, P. J. Carroll and Co., came on board. They remained as sponsors until 1979, when Bank of Ireland took over. Powerscreen International took over in 1994 and they were succeeded by Eircell in 1997. There have been a number of changes in the scheme over the years and foreign trips have become rarer. The award of an All-Star remains the ambition of most hurlers.

ABOVE ▪ Cork v Tipperary in a Munster championship game, circa 1970.

Kilkenny were rank outsiders against Cork in the 1972 All-Ireland. Cork, who defeated Tipperary in the Munster semi-final replay, had the easiest of victories against Clare in the final. Kilkenny defeated Wexford in a replayed Leinster final and accounted for Galway in the All-Ireland semi-final. It was expected that the 80 minute All-Ireland would suit the younger Cork side but it was the older and more experienced Kilkenny players who were the sprightliest at the finish. Cork led by eight points with 22 minutes remaining but Kilkenny scored 2-9, without reply from Cork, and transformed the eight point deficit into a seven point lead with a score of 3-24 to 5-11.

Limerick's turn eventually arrived in 1973. They had been threatening since 1971 and they made it through Munster with victories over Clare and Tipperary. Their opponents were Kilkenny, who defeated Wexford in the Leinster final. It was the first time since 1940 that Kilkenny and Limerick met in an All-Ireland final. Kilkenny were handicapped by injuries and Limerick won their first All-Ireland in 33 years.

Limerick came through Munster again in 1974, beating Clare in the final. The Leinster final between Kilkenny and Wexford was one of the most fantastic matches ever seen at Croke Park, with Kilkenny victorious by 6-13 to 2-24. They beat Galway in the All-Ireland semi-final and came up against Limerick in the final. In a repeat of the previous year, Kilkenny were never under pressure and won convincingly by 3-19 to 1-13. Eddie Keher scored 1-11 for the winners and Pat Henderson gave an inspired performance at centre-back.

Eddie Keher was one of the all-time great hurling forwards. His senior career spanned the period from 1959-1977 during which time he played in 11 finals, winning six. He also won nine Railway Cup medals and three National Leagues. After the All-Star system was introduced in 1971, he won five awards. He probably scored more than any other forward in the game, including 2 goals and 11 points in the 1971 All-Ireland final, which makes him the second highest scorer on record. His name fits comfortably in the company of Christy Ring, Mick Mackey, Nicky Rackard and Jimmy Doyle. In an interview with Brendan Fullam in *Giants of the Ash* Eddie Keher said: 'I enjoy everything about the game, watching, playing, training, practising. Whereas All-Irelands are the glamorous occasions, some of my greatest memories are from club championship or tournament games. I suppose "firsts" are inclined to be memories, and my first school, county medal in 1952 (under 14) is high on the list. My first appearance with Kilkenny in 1959, my first win, 1963, captain of a winning team in 1959; my first and only county championship with Rower Inistioge in 1968 – all have their own significance. 1972 against Cork was probably the best 80 minutes of hurling I have had the pleasure of playing in.'

The big surprise in the 1975 championship was the defeat of Cork, who accounted for Limerick in the Munster final, by Galway in the All-Ireland semi-final. It was Galway's first time to qualify for the All-Ireland since 1958. Their success against Cork was anticipated by their victory over Tipperary in the National League final, their first victory in this competition in 24 years. They were expected to do well against Kilkenny, who defeated Wexford in the Leinster final, but their performance on the day was a complete disappointment and they lost to Kilkenny by 2-22 to 2-10.

Cork won three titles in a row in 1976, 1977 and 1978. They beat Limerick in the 1976 Munster final and came up against Wexford, who trounced Kilkenny in the Leinster final and beat Galway in a replayed All-Ireland semi-final. In an even contest Cork came out victorious in the end, by 2-21 to 4-11, as a result of some well-taken points by Jimmy Barry Murphy. The same two teams qualified for the 1977 All-Ireland. Cork came through Munster with victories over Waterford and Clare. During the latter game there was an armed robbery of £24,000 of the day's takings from under the stand at Thurles. Cork defeated Galway in the All-Ireland semi-final. Wexford successfully defended their Leinster title, defeating Kilkenny in the final. This was Eddie Keher's last championship game for Kilkenny. Cork gave a great display in the final with Denis Coughlan and Gerald McCarthy particularly outstanding and won by 1-17 to 3-8 for Wexford, who never really played up to expectations.

In 1978 Cork made it three in a row when they beat Kilkenny by four points in the All-Ireland final. Cork again defeated Clare in the Munster final while Kilkenny overcame Wexford by a goal in a thrilling Leinster final. The Leinster men defeated Galway in the All-Ireland semi-final. The final was expected to be a classic but it didn't fulfil its promise and Cork were in front by 1-15 to 2-8 at the final whistle. Cork won their fifth Munster final in a row in 1979 at Thurles when they beat a disappointing Limerick who were without Pat Hartigan their star player. They looked good for a fourth All-Ireland in a row but their plans came unstuck against Galway in the All-Ireland semi-final. Kilkenny were Galway's opponents in the All-Ireland, having defeated Wexford in another exciting Leinster final. The Connacht men had considerable expectations but they failed to deliver on the day and were beaten by 2-12 to 1-8. It was Kilkenny's 21st title.

One of the outstanding developments of the 1970s was the introduction of a senior club championship. The club, based on the parish and with strong family loyalties, has always been the backbone of the Gaelic Athletic Association. In the very early years of the Association, the club represented the county in the All-Ireland championship. In the course of time it was allowed to include players from the rest of the county and the team gradually evolved into a representative county side. In 1970 it was decided to start a new championship for the club teams which won their respective county titles. The club championship was born and it has gone from strength to strength. It is played late in the year with the final taking place on St Patrick's Day and it gives an excitement and purpose to the clubs involved at a time of year when the other championships have been completed. It generates as much interest and enthusiasm as the Railway Cup competition used to do in its heyday. Its strength lies in the way it has levelled the playing pitch somewhat, giving clubs from weaker counties a chance of achieving greatness.

The last two decades of the 20th century saw the arrival of three new teams as contenders for All-Ireland honours. Galway, who had a lone All-Ireland senior championship to their credit, dating back to 1923, became a force in hurling and captured three titles. Offaly, whose previous achievement was confined to two junior titles in 1923 and 1929, broke through the psychological and traditional barriers to win senior championships for the first time. Clare had a lone All-Ireland dating back to 1914 and they overcame decades of sickening defeats when they won two All-Irelands in the nineties and established themselves as meaningful members of the hurling establishment. Galway's victory in the 1980 All-Ireland was received with tremendous enthusiasm, not only in Galway but much further afield. The estimated 30,000 supporters who greeted the team in Eyre Square were probably more enthusiastic and emotional than any crowd that came out anywhere in Ireland to welcome home an All-Ireland side. The wait had been so long and the disappointments so many that the crowd wallowed in the joy and pride of it all.

During the previous decade there were signs that Galway hurling was turning a corner. There were still upsets and disappointments, as in the 1975 and 1979 All-Irelands, but they were important straws in the wind. Galway were now managed by Cyril Farrell, one of the new brand of managers who were making names for themselves on more and more county teams. In the All-Ireland semi-final, Galway played Offaly, who had won their first ever Leinster senior title with a victory over Kilkenny, and won by two points. In the Munster final, Galway came up against Limerick, who upset the odds when beating Cork who were going for their sixth successive Munster title,. The pairing of Galway and Limerick in the All-Ireland was unique. Limerick were favourites on the basis of their league performance and their defeat of Cork in the Munster championship. They also had one of the best forward lines in the game with Eamon Cregan, Joe McKenna and Ollie O'Connor on the inside line. On the day Limerick failed to produce their best form and Galway did to win by 2-15 to 3-9.

Backboning the Galway team in the historic victory of 1980, were the Connolly brothers, John, Michael and Joe, with Padraic as a sub. In fact seven brothers were on the Castlegar team that won the All-Ireland club championship in 1980. In a piece he wrote for Brendan Fullam in Giants of the Ash, John described how the family bonded: 'It was also a tradition of ours, even after us getting married with our own homes, we would all meet in our old home place the morning of a match, known to everybody in Galway as Mamo's, which was an old name for Grandmother. We would chat about the game, and without realising it, we built up a kind of spirit that stood to us on the field. Then as we left Mamo's she would shake the bottle of holy water on us, saying: "Mind yourselves and don't be fighting, and don't come back here if ye lose". Of course we had many a fight and we lost plenty of times, but we were always welcomed home.'

It was to be Offaly's turn in 1981. They defeated Wexford in the Leinster final. Limerick came out of Munster but lost the All-Ireland semi-final to Galway after a replay. They were dogged by misfortune and injury and despite their defeat, won many friends for the tremendous courage and tenacity shown in the face of misfortune. Galway were undoubtedly favourites for the All-Ireland and looked even more so at half-time with a comfortable lead. But Offaly refused to buckle, gradually reduced the lead and snatched victory from the jaws of defeat with a great goal by Johnny O'Flaherty about five minutes from time.

Kilkenny were back in the frame in 1982 and 1983. They defeated Offaly in the Leinster final as a result of a controversial goal and Galway in the All-Ireland semi-final. Their opponents in the final were Cork, who had come through Munster with ease, defeating Waterford in the final. Kilkenny were devastating, defeating Cork by 3-18 to 1-13, with the man of the match award going to Christy Heffernan, who scored 2-3 for the winners. Kilkenny created a record for the county in 1983, when they won the league and the championship for the second year in a row. They beat Offaly in an exciting Leinster final and came up against Cork in the All-Ireland for the second year in a row. Cork scored an easy victory over Waterford in the Munster final and had a comprehensive victory over Galway in the All-Ireland semi-final. The final was a disappointment, marred by a strong wind, and, although there were only two points between the sides in the end, Kilkenny were never really in danger. For Kilkenny goalkeeper, Noel Skehan, the victory brought a record ninth All-Ireland senior medal. Although the number is greater than that won by Christy Ring and John Doyle, it does not carry the same distinction as three of them – 1963, 1967 and 1969 – were won as a sub to Ollie Walsh. The remaining six were won on the field of play in 1972 (as captain), 1974, 1975, 1979, 1982, 1983. ▪

The year 1984 was the centenary year of the founding of the Gaelic Athletic Association at Thurles and it was decided to play the All-Ireland final in the town. Offaly and Cork qualified for the final. Offaly won in Leinster as a result of beating Wexford in the final. Cork won out in Munster following a dramatic victory over Tipperary in the final. For the first time since 1954 there were two All-Ireland semi-finals, with Antrim representing Ulster, where hurling is very much a minority sport. Offaly defeated Galway and Cork defeated Antrim in the semi-finals. The final was a major disappointment as Offaly played way below form and were beaten by 3-16 to 1-12 by Cork.

Offaly were very disappointed with their performance but came back to win the 1985 All-Ireland. They had an easy victory over Laois in the Leinster final. Cork came through in Munster, beating Tipperary in the final, but were shocked by Galway in the All-Ireland semi-final. Galway were favourites as a result but in a closely contested final, they were beaten by Offaly on a scoreline of 2-11 to 1-12.

Offaly failed to get out of Leinster in 1986 as they were defeated by Kilkenny in the Leinster final. Cork came out of Munster after victory over Clare in the final. Kilkenny were well-beaten by Galway in the All-Ireland semi-final and Cork were nearly shocked by Antrim. Galway were favourites for the final but the tactics which proved successful against Kilkenny, backfired against Cork, and they were beaten by 4-13 to 2-15.

It was a case of third time lucky for Galway in 1987. In Leinster, Kilkenny were victorious after a brilliant contest with Offaly. Tipperary won out in Munster for the first time since 1971 after an epic tussle with Cork, which went to a replay and extra time. Galway defeated Tipperary in the All-Ireland semi-final, which attracted the biggest crowd, over 49,000, since the semi-final in 1958. Kilkenny defeated Antrim after a struggle. The All-Ireland was a tough game played in a tense atmosphere and Galway were victorious by 1-12 to 0-9 for Kilkenny. Galway made it two in a row in 1988, beating Tipperary in the All-Ireland. Tipperary defeated Cork in the Munster final and Offaly defeated Wexford in Leinster. Galway defeated Offaly and Tipperary defeated Antrim in the All-Ireland semi-finals. The final was a much publicised affair as each team was managed by high profile managers, Galway by Cyril Farrell and Tipperary by Babs Keating. In the end victory went to Galway by 1-15 to 0-14.

The advent of team managers was one of the developments of the '80s. There had always been managers, or at least spokesmen for bands of selectors, but the '80s saw the rise of a new phenomenon, the arrival of the manager with a higher profile than any of the players. In many cases a former outstanding player, who was given almost complete control over the preparation of his team. He became the sole spokesperson for the players. He made all the decisions on the field and was given a distinctive bib, which identified him as he paced the sidelines during a game. In many cases he was well paid, was attributed God-like genius in the event of his team's victory and resigned when they were defeated. He was the centre of the media's attention and his every utterance quoted. His arrival signalled a growing professionalism in the preparation of teams.

Tipperary made it back to the winner's enclosure in 1989 against such unlikely opponents as Antrim. The latter beat Offaly, who came out of Leinster, sensationally in the All-Ireland semi-final. In the other semi-final, Tipperary, who won in Munster for the third year in a row, beat Galway in a tense game. Antrim were really no match for Tipperary in the final, which saw the winner's star forward, Nicky English, establish a scoring record for an All-Ireland hurling final of 2 goals and 12 points.

Cork deprived Tipperary of four in a row in Munster in 1990. Offaly won out in Leinster but were beaten by Galway in the All-Ireland semi-final. Cork won the other semi-final against Antrim. Galway were favourites for the final but in a thrilling contest Cork came out on top to win by 5-15 to 2-21.

Tipperary came back to take the 1991 All-Ireland. They came out of Munster after a couple of epic games with Cork. Kilkenny won out in Leinster and qualified for the All-Ireland with victory over Antrim in the All-Ireland semi-final. Tipperary defeated Galway in the other semi-final and went on to defeat Kilkenny in the final.

Kilkenny won in 1992 and 1993 defeating Cork and Galway respectively. In 1994, Offaly came back in dramatic fashion to snatch victory from defeat. Their opponents were Limerick, who scored a comprehensive victory over Clare in the Munster final. Offaly were five points down with as many minutes to go but, in a dramatic turn of events, they scored 11 points during the period to win by six points from a hapless Limerick side.

Clare came through in dramatic fashion in 1995. They had given warning the previous year when they beat Tipperary, reversing an 18 point drubbing by the same side in 1993. They beat Cork in the Munster semi-final and Limerick in the final at Thurles. The scenes of joy after this victory were unbelievable. Motivated and driven by a committed manager, Ger Loughnane, the team went all the way, beating Galway in the All-Ireland semi-final and Offaly in the final. Thus

ABOVE An action shot from the 1991 All-Ireland semi-final between Galway and Tipperary.

the cup returned to Munster and Leinster's recent apparent dominance was halted. Clare brought a new dimension to the game. They reached new heights of physical fitness, psyched themselves up with convictions of certainty and were led by a Messiah-like figure in Loughnane who inspired them with a blinding purpose. Above all the team included some of the most exciting players to appear on the scene for a long time and they served up a brand of direct, skilful and aggressive hurling, which swept opponents off their feet.

Ger Loughnane was Millennium Manager of the Century at the end of 2000. It was a major award and an indication of his gigantic stature in the history of managers. An outstanding player in his own right, he was a member of the Munster Railway Cup team for seven years in a row from 1975 onwards. His playing years spanned 16 years at senior county level. The Clare team of the period was an exceptional team that probably never got the reward it deserved – an All-Ireland title. Two National League titles were won in 1977 and 1978. The failure to win an All-Ireland must have rankled with Loughnane and must have been the dominating motivation when he took over as manager of Clare in 1994. The team had not won an All-Ireland in 80 years. Brendan Fullam in *Legends of the Ash* describes his success: 'His exuberance and infectious

ABOVE ▨ 1995 The Clare senior hurling team that made the breakthrough to win their first All-Ireland since 1914. **Back row:** Brian Lohan, Michael O'Halloran, Frank Lohan, Conor Clancy, David Fitzgerald, Sean McMahon, Ger O'Loughlin. **Front row:** Liam Doyle, P.J. O'Connell, Ollie Baker, Anthony Daly, James O'Connor, Fergal Hegarty, Fergus Tuohy, Stephen McNamara.

enthusiasm spilled over onto the players. His approach, befitting his teaching profession, was hortative. He urged and encouraged; he praised and drove. He was a generator of confidence, a moulder of spirit. A man of unshakeable faith in the potential of his panel and players, he imbued in them a deep pride in the jersey they wore, in the county they represented, in the game they played. He bred the winning mentality.'

If Clare were responsible for the excitement of 1995 it was Wexford that brought out the colour and excitement of 1996. Inspired by their impressive manager Liam Griffin, they swept through Leinster, defeated Galway in the All-Ireland semi-final and Offaly in the final. As with Clare this Wexford victory gave hurling a new lease of life, brought out the supporters in their thousands, blanketed the stadia with masses of colour and made it great to be alive. Clare were back again in 1997, beating Tipperary in the Munster final and the same opposition in the All-Ireland final. This came about as the result of a change in the running of the All-Ireland series. Under the new scheme the beaten finalists in Leinster and Munster entered the All-Ireland series, meeting the winners in Ulster and Connacht at the quarter-final stage. This system had an unexpected result in 1998 when Offaly, beaten in the Leinster final, went on to beat their Leinster conquerors, Kilkenny, in the All-Ireland final. This year saw the re-emergence of Waterford as a force in Munster hurling. It was hoped the county could deliver on its promise as the arrival of new teams or the re-emergence of old ones give a great fillip to the game and increases its support.

Cork were back in winning mode in the 1999 All-Ireland, beating Kilkenny in the final. In the year 2000, after losing two years in a row, Kilkenny came back to take the All-Ireland title in no uncertain terms with a comprehensive victory over Offaly in the final. The latter team had sensationally defeated Cork in the semi-final. One of the stars of the Kilkenny team was DJ Carey, one of the most exciting players in the game at the end of the second Millennium. An outstanding forward he illustrates all the skills of hurling with a brilliant turn of speed. ■

At the beginning of the third Millennium the game of hurling is in a reasonably strong position. The support for the game at intercounty level is stronger than ever. The televising of all the major games over the summer months has given it increased exposure and attracted more followers. The training of teams has become more and more important and counties are spending enormous sums of money preparing teams for the championship. The demands on players and the sacrifices they must make are very strenuous. More and more players are looking for rewards for their labours and this is where the question of professionalism arises. At the moment it would seem that players are not interested in hurling as a professional game but would like to get more generous expenses for their commitment. Whether this will lead to professionalism or semi-professionalism down the line remains to be seen. ■

Gaelic Football cannot claim the antiquity of hurling, but it is by far the most popular of Irish sports today. The first direct reference to the game is to be found in the Statutes of Galway in 1527, which forbade citizens to play football and under the Sunday Observance Act of 1865 the game was again forbidden. The laws failed to suppress the game. In Kerry, one of the strongholds of the game, there were two forms of the game: field caid, which was confined to one field with goals at each end, and cross-country caid, in which the object was to take the ball from one parish to another. However, by the late 19th century, as with hurling, the game was in danger of extinction because of reasons already mentioned and also because of the lack of proper organisation and proper rules. Rugby and soccer were better organised.

The foundation of the Gaelic Athletic Association in 1884 improved matters. In January 1885, Michael Davin, the first President of the Association, instigated the adoption of a set of rules. These rules were the first codification of the playing of the game. Numerous changes in the rules were to occur over the years. Perhaps the most important being the introduction of point posts, goal nets and the reduction of players from 21 to 15.

Competition has always been an important feature in the sport. Initially there was the senior championship which was played between the respective county champions. The first All-Ireland championship was played in 1887, and in the 1920s the Sam Maguire Cup was presented to the winners of the All-Ireland senior football final. The Railway Shield for interprovincial competitions was introduced in 1906, the Croke Cup for the defeated provincial finalists in 1909 and the Sigerson Cup for the inter-university championship in 1911. The junior All-Ireland championship, for players who were not up to senior standard, was introduced in 1912. The National Football League began in 1925 and Laois became the first champions. The first

The Rules

The following rules were the first codification of the playing rules of the game. They laid the basis of the game that was to become the most popular in the country. The first recorded game under GAA rules was that between Callan and Kilkenny on February 15, 1885.
At that time the rules were as follows:

1) There shall not be less than fourteen or more than twenty-one players a side;

2) There shall be two umpires and a referee. Where the umpires disagree the referee's decision shall be final;

3) The ground shall be at least 120 yards long by 80 in breadth, and properly marked by boundary lines. Boundary lines must be at least five yards from fences;

4) The goal posts shall stand at each end in the centre of the goal line. They shall be 15 feet apart, with a cross-bar 8 feet from the ground;

5) The captains of each team shall toss for choice of sides before commencing play, and the players shall stand in two ranks opposite each other until the ball is thrown up, each man holding the hand of one of the other side;

6) Pushing or tripping from behind, holding from behind, or butting with the head, shall be deemed foul, and the players so offending shall be ordered to stand aside, and may not afterwards take part in the match, nor can his side substitute another man;

7) The time of actual play shall be one hour. Sides to be changed only at half-time;

8) The match shall be decided by the greater number of goals. If no goal is kicked the match shall be deemed a draw. A goal is when the ball is kicked through the goal posts under the cross-bar.

9) When the ball is kicked over the side line it shall be thrown back by a player of the opposite side to him who kicked it over. If kicked over the goal line by a player whose goal line it is, it shall be thrown back in any direction by a player of the other side. If kicked over the goal line by a player of the other side the goal keeper whose line it crosses shall have a free kick. No player of the other side to approach nearer 25 yards of him 'till the ball is kicked;

10) The umpires and referee shall have during the match full powers to disqualify any player, or order him to stand aside and discontinue play for any act which they may consider unfair, as set out in rule 6. No nails or iron tips on the boots. (Strips of leather fastened on the soles will prevent slipping). The dress for hurling and football to be knee-breeches and stockings and boots or shoes. It would be well if each player was provided with two jerseys, one white and the other some dark colour. The colours of his club could be worn on each. Then when a match was made, it could be decided the colours each side should wear.

Numerous changes in the rules were to occur over the years. In 1886 wrestling and hand grips between players were prohibited. Point posts, as still obtain in Australian football, were introduced. Points were to count only if no goals were scored but no number of points was to equal a goal. Balls going over the sideline were to be thrown in by umpires or the referee. Two years later the referee was recommended to use a whistle. Forfeit points, which were given if a player put the ball over his own end line, were replaced by a fifty yard free.

More important changes were made in 1892. The maximum number of players on a team was reduced from twenty-one to seventeen, and this number was to be reduced to fifteen in 1913. The county champions, who represented their county in the All-Ireland championship, were now given the right to select players from other clubs. Five points were declared to be the equivalent of one goal, and the number of points was reduced to three in 1895. The following year the cross-bar was lowered from ten and a half feet to eight feet. In 1910 the point side posts were abolished. Goal nets were introduced. Three years later the backs took up their positions before the ball was thrown in. Prior to then all the players remained in the centre of the field for the throw-in. From 1914 the All-Ireland final was played on the fourth Sunday of September.

Railway Cup competition, for provincial teams, began in 1928, with Leinster becoming the first champions. A minor All-Ireland championship, for under-18 players, was introduced in 1929 and Clare became the first champions. An under-21 championship began in 1964 with the first final won by Kerry. A club championship, for county senior football champions, began in 1971, with East Kerry becoming the first champions. Championships for secondary schools were introduced in 1918.

Games were badly disrupted between 1919 and 1923 because of the Irish War of Independence and the Civil War. In one game during the period, between Dublin and Tipperary on November 21, 1920, British soldiers entered Croke Park and began shooting into the crowd. Thirteen people were killed, including Tipperary player, Michael Hogan, whose name is commemorated in a stand named after him in the stadium. The shooting was in retaliation for the killing of a number of British Secret Service agents by the Irish Republican leadership in Dublin that morning. ■

The 1920s saw the introduction of a new skill peculiar to Gaelic football, the solo run or toe-to-hand. The year was 1921 and the player was Sean Lavan from County Mayo. In a game against Dublin at Croke Park having got possession of the ball he set off for goal at speed, playing the ball from toe to hand and then shooting a point. It was the first time the skill was seen and ever since it has been an important part of the repertory of skills of the Gaelic footballer. It is the only legitimate way to carry the ball in Gaelic football.

Kerry with 16 wins, followed closely by Dublin with 15 wins dominated the All-Ireland championships and finals in the pre 1950 period; Wexford, Tipperary, Kildare, Galway and Cork each had three or more wins in this period; the 1947 final was unique in that it was the only All-Ireland final to be played outside Ireland. The decision to play the final in the Polo Grounds, New York was taken to revive interest in the game in the USA where it had declined during the war years and to commemorate the centenary of the Great Famine which had been responsible for creating the large Irish population in the USA. The decision generated great interest in the championship and Cavan and Kerry emerged to contest the final in New York on September 14. An attendance of 35,000 saw Cavan win by 2-11 to 2-7.

Kerry was again the dominant side of the 1950s, but others were to challenge their position. One of the strongest footballing counties of today is Meath but they were late winning their first All-Ireland. The year was 1949 and they had to play Louth three times in the Leinster semi-final before coming through. These contests captured the imagination of the public and gave the victors a high profile. Westmeath were beaten in the Leinster final, Mayo in the All-Ireland semi-final and there was huge excitement in the county when Cavan were conquered in the final. Meath lost two successive finals in 1951 and 1952 before winning again in 1954, beating hot favourites Kerry well in the final. The victorious side included eight of the 1949 team, among them such stalwarts as Paddy O'Brien at full-back, the two corner men, Mick O'Brien and Kevin McConnell, and Brian Smyth and Peter McDermott in the forward line. It was to be ten years before Meath came out of their province again, and thirteen before another All-Ireland was won.

Mayo had been a great team during the thirties but went through a barren stretch during the forties. Their fortunes began to improve late in the decade as a result of a new approach to training and team selection. They were narrowly beaten by Cavan in the 1948 All-Ireland, lost to Meath in the semi-final the following year and came through for two All-Ireland victories in 1950 and 1951. Louth were defeated in 1950 and Meath the following year. The team included players whose names became legends in households around the country, players such as Sean Flanagan, who captained the two winning teams, Henry Dixon at centreback, Eamonn Mongey, who was an outstanding midfielder, Padhraic Carney and Tom Langan. After that it was to be lean times for the county. Mayo didn't win in Connacht for some time after that. There was a single success in 1955, followed by defeat in an All-Ireland semi-final replay, and the county had to wait until the late sixties before their graph began to rise again.

ABOVE ▪ 1952 All-Ireland semi-final – Cork v Cavan.

According to Jack Mahon in A History of Gaelic Football, Eamonn Mongey tells a good story against himself. Soon after retirement he gave a pair of football boots to be sold in a fund-raising sale. They were bought by a publican in Tobercurry. 'A few years ago, after heart surgery, my wife and I journeyed west for a holiday during my convalescence, and we decided to visit Killoran's and see the old boots again. On entering we ordered coffee and enquired of the man at the bar about the boots and who owned them. He told us they belonged to a fellow named Mongey, who won All-Irelands with Mayo about 50 years before. He then added: "You know, the same Mongey looked old when he was playing and often wore a cap to hide his baldness, and I do believe the so-and-so is still alive." Now what could I do but laugh.'

Kerry recorded three victories in 1953, 1955 and 1959. In the first of these years they defeated Armagh, who were making an attempt to bring the Sam Maguire across the border to Northern

ABOVE ▦ 1954 Meath – All-Ireland Champions. **Back Row:** P. Brady, E. Durnin, R. Mee, J. Farrell, B. Smith, K. McConnell, M. Grace, P. Connell, T. Moriarity, B. Flanagan, F. Byrne, G. Smith, P. O'Brien. **Front Row:** P. Ratty, J. Reilly, K. Lenehan, T. O'Brien, M. McDonnell, Peter McDermott (captain), P. Meegan, P. McGearty, W. Rattigan, L. O'Brien, J. Clarke, M. O'Brien.

Ireland for the first time. In fact many would regard it as the best Armagh team of all times. In a game which will be long remembered for its excitement and football skills, for brilliant individual performances and for sportsmanship which has seldom been bettered over the years, Kerry won by 0-13 to 1-6. Armagh missed a penalty at a vital time of the game. In the 1955 final they beat Dublin. The latter had been in the football doldrums since 1942 but were a rising force in the game at this time. Many of the players were products of the great St Vincent's club, which was hugely successful at this time. In the history of the club there is reference to 1955: 'All-Ireland final day 1955 is remembered as one of the most colourful and emotion filled days in All-Ireland history. It was the day that for the first time Hill 16 (the Railway end terrace in Croke Park) became the undisputed property of Dublin supporters. To have stood on the Hill that day is to boast of a singular honour and to lay claim to have been part of one of Ireland's great sporting occasions.' A crowd of nearly 90,000 watched the game which the more seasoned and more wily Kerry side won by 0-12 to 1-6. Kerry's third victory in 1959 was against Galway, who were an emerging force in the late fifties. The score was level going into the final quarter of the game but Kerry, inspired by Sean Murphy, Tom Long and Mick O'Dwyer, subsequently one of the great coaches in the game, dominated the final stages to win decisively by 3-7 to 1-4.

Galway had an impressive run of success in the Connacht championship in the fifties, winning five finals between 1954 and 1959. During the same period they had one All-Ireland success, in 1956, when they defeated Cork. It was a success long cherished in the county and in particular, the displays of Sean Purcell, Jack Mangan and Frank Stockwell, who scored 2-5 from play. It was a great team that deserved more success. Cork lost the 1957 All-Ireland also, this time to Louth, the smallest county in the country. The winners were captained by Dermot O'Brien, who became famous as a musician. Louth had won two All-Irelands in 1910 and 1912 and this was to be their last victory to date. The victory was received with tremendous excitement in the county and 40,000 fans lined the streets of Drogheda to welcome home the team. Dublin achieved All-Ireland success in 1958, beating Derry in the final. The latter had won their first ever Ulster final that year and were inspired by two great players, Sean O'Connell and Jim McKeever. They beat Kerry in the All-Ireland semi-final but lost to an able and experienced Dublin side, which was captained by Kevin Heffernan and had talented players like Ollie Freaney and Dessie Ferguson, among others. ∎

The '60s saw the emergence of Down for the first time as a football power. The first year the county came to the notice of the public was in 1958 when they reached the Ulster final, only to be beaten by Derry. The following year they won their first Ulster title but were beaten by Galway in the All-Ireland semi-final. In 1960 they went one better to claim All-Ireland success, defeating Kerry in the final. Down's success was due to an extremely talented side, which included such players as Sean O'Neill, James McCartan, Kevin Mussen (capt.) and Joe Lennon, allied to a very professional management team. They were the first county to bring the Sam Maguire across the border into Northern Ireland and the success was greeted with incredible outpourings of joy and celebration. Down repeated the success in 1961, beating Offaly in the All-Ireland. This game attracted a massive crowd of 91,000 to Croke Park, the greatest attendance ever at an Irish sports fixture. Down had further successes in Ulster in 1963, 1965, 1966 and 1968. In the latter year they won their third All-Ireland, beating Kerry in the final. In doing so they established a unique record of never losing an All-Ireland final, a tradition they were to continue when they won in 1991 and 1994.

Galway were the other exciting team of the sixties, also winning three All-Irelands. They won out in Connacht six times during the decade but the high point were the years 1963 to 1966, when they played in four All-Irelands. In the first of these years they lost to Dublin. Galway led at half-time by two points but Dublin, inspired by Des Foley, Mickey Whelan, Paddy Downey

ABOVE ■ 1960 All-Ireland final. Kevin Mussen, Down and Paudie Sheehy, Kerry with referee John Dowling, Offaly before the start of the game. Down won by 2-10 to 0-8 and became the first county from Northern Ireland to take the Sam Maguire Cup across the border.

and John Timmons, took over and won by 1-9 to 0-10. The experience was to serve Galway well the following year. Their opponents in the final were Kerry. Galway were on top at all times, led at half-time by four points and had five to spare at the final whistle. Kerry were defeated again in the 1965 final, this time by three points. Galway's opponents in the 1966 All-Ireland were Meath. They were well ahead at half-time, 1-6 to 0-1, and even though their margin of victory in the end was only six points, their superiority was much greater than the score would indicate.

In all 10 players took part in all three winning finals. Mattie McDonagh became the first Connacht man to win four All-Ireland senior football championship medals, as well as the only Connacht man to win ten Connacht senior football championship medals. Goalkeeper Johnny Geraghty did not concede a goal in any of the three victorious All-Ireland finals. From these dizzy heights of success Galway and Connacht went into decline and it was to be 32 years before an All-Ireland senior football title was won again by a team from across the River Shannon.

Kerry added two further All-Ireland titles during the sixties, in 1962 and 1969. In the former year they beat Roscommon in the final. The Connacht side made a brief resurgence in 1961 and 1962, losing the first year to Offaly in the All-Ireland semi-final and beating Cavan the second year. In 1969 Kerry defeated Offaly in the final after narrowly overcoming Mayo in the All-Ireland semi-final.

Mick O'Connell, who shone for Kerry in the '60s, was probably the greatest footballer of all time. He was a perfectionist in eveything he did, in his preparation and in his play. In his autobiography *A Kerry Footballer* he states: 'I practised several self-devised exercises to improve agility and pliability. One was to simulate the blockdown first on one side and then quickly across to the other side. This twisting and turning, when continued on for a while, was a great workout for the midriff section. Hurdling rows of wire fencing, approximately three feet high, which were dividing the field next to where I trained, was another exercise that I relied a lot on. Allowing myself only a very short run-up, I repeated this jump rapidly over and back several times. This served the purpose of strengthening the jumping muscles.'

Meath won the All-Ireland in 1967 after a lapse of 23 years. The county had been a force for some time but were unfortunate to have to contend with brilliant Galway during the period. They beat Cork in the 1967 final and the team included well-known stars like Jack Quinn, Pat Collier, Bertie Cunningham and Matt Kerrigan. It was Cork's third All-Ireland defeat since their last victory in 1945.

Attempts were made from early in the 20th century to establish an international dimension to Gaelic football. From the 1920s, teams from Ireland began to travel to the UK and the USA to play selections picked from among the Irish diaspora in these countries. In the early sixties the Central Council of the Gaelic Athletic Association agreed to issue an invitation to an Australian Rules football team to play a game in Ireland. There was a belief that the development of Australian football owed much to the influence of emigrant Irishmen. The two games are similar in their methods of catching, screening, running with the ball, punting and passing. In the Australian game the ball is oval, the game is played on a round pitch, the ball is lifted from the ground, the play is in quarters rather than halves, the tackle is different and the game uses point posts similar to those used by the GAA until 1913. In 1967 an Australian team from Victoria State, called the Galahs, organised by Harry Beitzel, came to Ireland and played the newly crowned All-Ireland champions, Meath. The sole concession granted to the Australians was being allowed to pick the ball off the ground; otherwise it was GAA rules all the way. The men from Australia took Meath apart with a display of high fielding and long kicking. Meath, stung by the defeat, set about organising a trip to Australia the following year. The trip was an outstanding success and Meath recovered their honour. Since then there have been other trips between the two countries. In 1984 a set of compromise rules was drawn up for games between the two countries. Since then these rules have been perfected and compromise rules games between the two countries have now become part of the GAA calendar. These games have given international dimension to Gaelic football. ▪

The '70s were a really exciting decade because of the great rivalry between Dublin and Kerry. The latter began the decade in grand style, defeating Meath in the All-Ireland final. However, they had to play second fiddle to Offaly for a few years after that. Offaly were a new force in football. They never won out in Leinster until 1960, when they lost the All-Ireland semi-final to Down in a replay. The following year they lost out to the same opposition in the All-Ireland final. The county was unlucky to have come up against a great Down team.

ABOVE ▪ 1971. The Offaly team that captured the county's first ever All-Ireland senior title by defeating Galway 1-14 to 2-8. **Back row:** Paddy McCormack, Mick O'Rourke, Murt Connor, Kieran Claffey, Nicholas Clavin, Sean Evans, Martin Furlong, Mick Ryan, Kevin Kilmurray.
Front row: Johnny Cooney, Tony McTague, Willie Bryan, Eugene Mulligan, Martin Heavey, Jody Gunning.

All these defeats were forgotten with the successes of 1971 and 1972. In the former year they defeated Galway in the All-Ireland final and repeated the success against Kerry in the replayed final of 1972. The successful teams included players who have entered the folk history of the county, legends like Paddy McCormack, Willie Bryan, Tony McTague, Murt Connor, to name a few.

Cork eventually came good in 1973 when they beat Galway in the All-Ireland final. The team included Jimmy Barry-Murphy, who was the minor sensation of 1972. He was as good at hurling as he was at football and other players on the victorious side, like Brian Murphy, Denis Coughlan and Ray Cummins, were equally adept in both codes. The captain of the side was goalkeeper, Billy Morgan, an inspiring figure for club and county. The great Dublin-Kerry rivalry began in 1975. Dublin won glory in 1974, beating Cork in the All-Ireland semi-final and Galway in the final. They qualified for the All-Ireland again the following year but were well beaten by Kerry. When the sides met in the 1976 final, Dublin reversed the result. The following year Dublin defeated Kerry in the All-Ireland semi-final and went on to defeat Armagh in the final. Kerry then took over to win four All-Irelands in a row, beating Dublin in 1978 and 1979, Roscommon in 1980 and Offaly in 1981.

One of the most talked-about incidents in Gaelic football was an incident that took place in the 1978 All-Ireland. Dublin dominated the game for the first 20 minutes and seemed destined for victory, when they went five points ahead. But against the run of play, Kerry came back to draw level. Then three minutes before half-time, the referee, Seamus Aldridge of Kildare, awarded a free to Kerry after the Dublin goalkeeper, Paddy Cullen, had cleared the ball. While Cullen argued with the referee about the free, his goal was left unguarded. Mikey Sheehy was handed the ball by a Dublin player and, instantly seeing an opportunity, took a quick free. At the last minute Cullen realised the danger. He made a desperate effort to back-track to the goals but the ball floated over his head into the net and he backed into the side of the netting. The goal was allowed; the incident was replayed again and again on the television screens and Paddy Cullen must have had waking nightmares for years afterwards. Dublin never recovered from the setback and were well beaten.

Kerry were going for a record fifth in a row in 1982 when they met Offaly in a repeat of the 1981 final. They appeared to be heading for victory and were two points up with about five minutes remaining. A long ball was floated in to the Offaly left corner-forward, Seamus Darby, who had come in as a substitute shortly before and was told by his manager, Eugene McGee, to stay near the goal. He beat his man to the ball, turned, and scored a goal to give his side a one-point lead, which they held onto for the remaining minutes. It was a sensational victory for Offaly and a hugely disappointing result for Kerry, who seemed to be on the brink of creating

ABOVE ■ 1970s Kerry v Dublin. Sean Walsh, Kerry and Brian Mullins, Dublin display the skill of fielding the high ball.

history. That Kerry team, which was to win three more All-Irelands in the mid-eighties, is regarded as the greatest football team of all time. Wherever football is spoken the names of Mikey Sheehy, Pat Spillane, Ger Power, Jack O'Shea and others will be mentioned. The strength of the team was in its scoring power. No other team, either then or since, had such capacity for putting the ball between the posts. The longevity of the side was also impressive. Most of them came into the side in 1974 and lasted until 1987, four of them winning as many as eight All-Irelands each. Of great importance to the side was the influence of manager, Mick O'Dwyer, who came into the position in late 1974, after Kerry's defeat by Cork in that year's Munster final at Killarney. ■

Any account of the '80s has to take account of another manager, Kevin Heffernan, who came in as manager of Dublin in 1973 for a three-year period. His objective was to restore Dublin's senior football pride by gathering a group of players who would give total commitment to this objective. A group of players gathered together over a period of time and the new manager set about developing a team by improving individual skills, achieving maximum fitness and developing field tactics suitable to the team. The result was a very successful period for Dublin football and the winning of three All-Irelands. As a result of this period of rivalry between Kerry and Dublin, and between O'Dwyer and Heffernan, managers began to play a bigger part in Gaelic football. They were responsible for a growing professionalism in the approach to the preparation and training of teams. They were given almost absolute control over teams and became centres of media attention. Until 1970 the duration of an All-Ireland final was 60 minutes. In 1970 the first 80-minute final was introduced and this was to be the case until 1974. The 75-minute final was introduced in 1975 and has been the case since.

After the disappointment of 1982, Kerry suffered further defeat in 1983 when they were beaten with a last-minute goal by Cork in the Munster final. Kerry were seeking their ninth successive Munster title. Cork lost to Dublin in a replayed All-Ireland semi-final and Dublin went on to defeat Galway in the final.But Kerry were far from finished. They came back to win the next three All-Ireland titles. In 1984, the centenary of the foundation of the Gaelic Athletic Association, they outclassed Dublin to win the final. In 1985 they beat the same opposition by a smaller margin, but still very convincingly. In 1986 their victims were Tyrone, who were seeking their first All-Ireland. Until early in the second half it appeared that Tyrone might be good enough but Kerry took over and won easily in the end. For five of the players, Paidi O'Shea, Ogie Moran, Pat Spillane, Mikey Sheehy and Ger Power, it was their eighth All-Ireland title. O'Shea and Moran had been on the starting fifteen in every final. Spillane came on as a substitute in the 1981 final. Moran had the distinction of playing in the same position, centre-forward, on all the winning teams. Nobody anticipated after the victory in 1986 that it would be eleven years before Kerry won another All-Ireland.

ABOVE ■ 1985 All-Ireland final Kerry v Dublin. Ambrose O'Donovan, Kerry punches a high ball away from the Dublin midfielders.

One of the greatest Kerry footballers of the glorious team of the '70s and '80s was Pat Spillane. In his autobiography Shooting from the Hip, he said: 'I am amused nowadays when I read about team managers banning their players from giving interviews or reading newspapers before a big game. Throughout my career I made a point of reading as many papers and listening to as many interviews on radio and television about the big games I was involved in. It helped that I am the most positive thinker imaginable. I wasn't the greatest footballer of all time. But, I believed I was much better than my opponent, even if I had no solid ground to back my argument. The day you go out thinking your opponent is better than you – you're in trouble. I never lacked confidence and I had the capacity to take positive meaning out of anything that was written about me. If a journalist wrote that I was the best footballer in Ireland I would be pleased, but also anxious to prove it was correct. On the other hand, if somebody suggested I was past it – then I would go out and try to prove them wrong.'

The team that succeeded Kerry for All-Ireland honours was Meath. The county got a new manager in 1982, when Sean Boylan took over, and he has been with them over the intervening years. Meath won out in Leinster in 1986 but went down to Kerry in the All-Ireland semi-final. The experience was to stand to them the following year. Meath hadn't been in an All-Ireland since 1970 and Cork were their opponents. After a bright start Cork were pegged back and Meath ran out easy winners with six points to spare. Cork were again their opponents in the 1988 final. The game ended in a draw as a result of a late Meath point from a free. The replay was a tough encounter at the end of which Meath had a point to spare, 0-13 to 0-12. Cork got their own back in the following two years. In 1989 they defeated Mayo in the final, after accounting for Dublin who had beaten Meath in Leinster in the All-Ireland semi-final. Cork won their second title in 1990, beating Meath in the final. The team included players, who became national figures. Such were Niall Cahalane, Stephen O'Brien, Larry Tompkins, Shay Fahy and Teddy McCarthy. The latter had the distinction in 1990 of winning a hurling as well as a football All-Ireland. ◾

ABOVE ◾ 1985 All-Ireland Final. The determination of Jack O'Shea, Kerry.

ABOVE ■ 1985 All-Ireland Semi-final. Pat Spillane, Kerry showing fierce determination. Pat, who won eight All-Ireland medals, is regarded as one of the greatest footballers of all time.

The first half of the '90s will be remembered for what has been called the 'Northern Renaissance', a succession of four All-Ireland victories by teams from Ulster. Down started the pattern in 1991. Since the glory days of the '60s, when three All-Irelands were won, the county had not much in the line of success. There were victories in Ulster in 1971, 1978 and 1981 but no advancement beyond the All-Ireland semi-final. At the beginning of 1991 the county's expectations weren't great. However, the team won through to the provincial final, which was won easily against Donegal. Down's opponents in the All-Ireland semi-final were old rivals, Kerry, who had never yet beaten the northerners in a senior football championship game. Down came through the encounter, easily in the end, and qualified to play Meath in the final. Down were ahead by eleven points with sixteen minutes to go but Meath made a dramatic fight back and got within two points by the final whistle. Down had kept their All-Ireland final record complete.

Donegal were the successful team in 1992 when they won the All-Ireland for the first time. Even though there was a long tradition of football in the county, the first Ulster title wasn't won until 1972. The county's resurgence continued after that with further provincial titles in 1974, 1983 and 1990. All these four successes had been followed by All-Ireland semi-final defeats. The 1992 campaign began with a draw in the first round but it gathered momentum along the way. Derry were defeated in the Ulster final. The next test was against Mayo in the All-Ireland semi-final which Donegal won despite playing badly. So, it was into their first All-Ireland against the experience and tradition of Dublin. After a nervous start Donegal got into their stride and thoroughly deserved their four point victory.

Derry won their first ever All-Ireland the following year. Somewhat like Donegal, Derry were late winning their first Ulster title. That was in 1958 and further titles were won in 1970, 1975, 1976 and 1987. The county got to the All-Ireland in 1958 only to be beaten by Dublin, but lost the other four All-Ireland semi-finals. In the 1993 Ulster final they defeated Donegal, their conquerors of the previous year. Dublin were their opponents in the All-Ireland semi-final and, after a very close game, they won through by a point. In the final against Cork, Derry started badly and were 1-2 down after six minutes. They came well into the game after that and led by three points at half-time. Cork went ahead in the second half but Derry kept plugging away and had three points to spare at the final whistle. The victory was a very emotional one not only for the team but for all their loyal supporters down the years. Down came back to win again in 1994 and make it four out of four for northern counties. After the victory in 1991 Down fell to Derry in the 1992 and 1993 Ulster championships. They overcame the same opposition in 1994 and went on to beat Tyrone in the Ulster final. Down decisively beat Cork in the All-Ireland semi-final and preserved their 100% record in All-Ireland finals when they defeated Dublin by two points.

By seven o'clock on Tuesday morning after the 1991 All-Ireland final, Paddy O'Rourke, the victorious Down captain, had had enough, according to Jerome Quinn in *Ulster Football and Hurling*: 'Thirty-eight unforgettable but exhausting hours after winning Sam (the Sam Maguire Cup), it's time to take leave of the celebrations at his Burren club and take the Cup home.

Dozens of cars block the road, their owners still in party mood, so the Down captain improvises by taking the short cut he had taken as a young boy, over Burren hill. It was the most idyllic setting, dawn breaking over the beautiful Burren valley and rabbits scurrying for cover as the local hero climbed to the top of the hill. At the summit he paused for breath, turning and looking down at the clubrooms he had just left. Some happy faces caught sight of him, others were called to the windows and, as they cheered, O'Rourke lifted the Cup and shook it vigorously above his head, as he had done at Croke Park. "It all came home to me at the moment, 20 years of hard work to achieve the ultimate goal of bringing Sam Maguire to my county and my people." '

Two other teams from these years deserve mention. Clare made it out of Munster in 1992 for the first time since 1917 and Leitrim won out in Connacht in 1994 for the first time since 1927. Neither team progressed beyond the All-Ireland semi-final stage but their provincial successes bred hope in every other unsuccessful county and generated fresh enthusiasm.

In 1995 Tyrone came out of Ulster and hoped to emulate the achievement of the other successful Ulster counties and win their first senior football All-Ireland. Although the county made it to the All-Ireland final, having beaten Galway in the semi-final, they failed against Dublin. The latter came out of Leinster for the fourth successive year and, after failing to win on three of the occasions, were determined to succeed. Meath had played second fiddle to Dublin in Leinster since 1991 but eventually succeeded in 1996. They beat Tyrone in the All-Ireland semi-final and met Mayo in the final. The latter came to Croke Park with great expectations, having beaten Kerry in the semi-final and they did everything but win. They dominated for great stretches of the game but due to poor scoring ability and the undying spirit of Meath, they could only draw. The replay was a controversial affair in which the verdict was uncertain until the very end but it was Meath that had the point advantage at the final whistle to take their fifth All-Ireland title.

Mayo were back again in 1997 and qualified for the final when they defeated Offaly in the All-Ireland semi-final. Their opponents were Kerry, who defeated Cavan in the other semi-final. Mayo played poorly, didn't score until the 23rd minute and were led by five points at the interval. They did improve in the second half but were always struggling and Kerry had three points to spare in the end. It was their first All-Ireland title since 1986. Galway and Kildare brought great excitement to the 1998 championship. The Galwaymen hadn't won since 1966 and beat Roscommon in a replayed Connacht final. They beat Derry in the All-Ireland semi-final and came up against Kildare in the final. The latter defeated Kerry in the other semi-final and there was great expectation that they were going to win their first final since 1928. Since

1990, when the former Kerry manager, Mick O'Dwyer, had taken them over, there had been a resurgence in the county. They led Galway by a goal at half-time but an outstanding performance by the Connacht men in the second half put paid to Kildare's hopes and dreams.

Meath were back in the winners' enclosure in 1999. They beat Dublin in the Leinster final and accounted for Armagh in the All-Ireland semi-final. Mayo came out of Connacht again but were beaten by Cork in the second semi-final. Meath were favourites to take the title and duly obliged, beating Cork by three points. It was their seventh All-Ireland crown and was won on the 50th anniversary of their first in 1949. It was also the 17th year for the fortunes of the county to be guided by Sean Boylan, who had been elected manager for the first time in 1982.

The Millennium All-Ireland was won by Kerry. Having won their 67th provincial title when they beat Clare in the Munster final, Kerry took two games to defeat Armagh in the All-Ireland semi-final. Many believed the northerners left victory behind them in the drawn game. Their opponents in the final were Galway, who won their 40th provincial title when they defeated Leitrim in the Connacht final, and who then beat Kildare in the All-Ireland semi-final. Galway opened very badly in the final and trailed by seven points after 25 minutes. But they made a great recovery and with 20 minutes to go were within a point of Kerry. At this point they looked like winning but in the remaining time could manage only a point to draw level and the game ended at fourteen points each. Kerry claimed their 32nd All-Ireland title two weeks later when they won the replay by 0-17 to 1-10.

The game of Gaelic football has changed over the past 50 years. There have been a number of significant changes in the rules in Gaelic football in the period since 1950. For instance the number of substitutes is now set at five, no stoppages are allowed for injured players, goalkeepers must wear distinctive jerseys and are allowed to pick the ball from off the ground and may not be charged within a triangle 15 by five yards and there are rules in regard to dissent, free kicks, throw-ins and sideline kicks. Prior to the '70s the game was much more free-flowing with the traditional skills of catching and kicking and solo running very much to the fore. A change came about at that time with the evolution of the running game in which possession became more and more important. Short passing became a feature. The game became much tighter and this led to an increase in frees as pull and drag tactics were employed to halt the movement of the play. With this development there was the need for a top class place kicker to convert frees. Tony MacTague of Offaly was one of the first. The game became more professional and players more cynical, with the resulting development of negative tactics to counteract the strengths of the opposing team. The advent of managers, with a fierce desire to prove themselves and pressure to win, aggravated many of these developments.

Sponsorship and live television coverage have given the game a higher profile. Attendance at games has increased. Coverage of the sport in newspapers has expanded. Personality reporting and dramatic action shots have become commonplace. Another development has been the spread of women's Gaelic football, the fastest growing sport in the country at the present. The promotion of the game at underage level in the clubs and the schools, the creation of many competitions at secondary school and third level have contributed to the general popularity of the game.

But everything in the game in not as it should be. There is massive competition from other sports for the loyalty of young players, who pick and choose from a supermarket shelf of choices. The dropout rate at an early age, as students concentrate on examinations or prefer the easier option of vicarious experience from the television set, is alarming. The game itself is in difficulty. The hand pass is not clearly defined. The traditional skill of the toe pick-up of the ball has almost disappeared. There is no effective way of tackling the player in possession of the ball. Positional play has largely been eliminated by the running game. Refereeing is a serious problem because of the wide difference in the interpretation of rules.

Despite these problems, Gaelic Football remains one of Ireland's most popular and supported sport. In 1961, 90,000 spectators attended the All-Ireland senior Gaelic Football final and equally in comparison, in the 2001 final when Galway defeated Meath, the game was played before a capacity crowd. The pride in Ireland's traditional native sports, Hurling and Gaelic Football, will ensure their position as the country's premier sports. ▪

I t was September 1956 that I arrived in Dublin to start my studies for an honours degree in history at Trinity College. It was not long before I was in College Park watching the University XV. Thus began a lifelong interest in Trinity rugby, and Irish rugby at university, club, interprovincial and particularly at international level. The international side has given me great pleasure; I suppose I must have watched every home international from the 1956/57 season to the 1960/61 season and then I was fortunate enough to be teaching at St Columba's, Rathfarnham between 1st September 1981 and 1st September 1983; years which included Ireland winning the Triple Crown and Five Nations Championship. In recent years there have been visits to Dublin with my friends the Foxes and Pat Lingwood, trips to Cardiff Arms Park with Dr Derek Browne, to Twickenham and the lunch parties with friends to watch Ireland on television.

The glorious uncertainty of Irish rugby has been a constant theme; the dull, sure, confident victory has been uncommon. There have been glorious victories, defeat when victory was almost there, but never a dull moment and always in defeat or victory, a triumph for the game of rugby and the true spirit of sport. This chapter looks at Irish rugby through the eyes of a Trinity undergraduate and later a graduate who lived and worked mostly outside Ireland. More recently Denham Golf Club has provided an interesting International link with Irish rugby.

Trinity rugby in the 1950s and early 1960s was strong; good enough to win the Leinster Cup on one occasion and to defeat Oxford and Cambridge and University College, Dublin in the annual Colours match at Lansdowne Road. The Colours match commenced in 1952. Up to that time rugby Colours were awarded to members of the side that played against Oxford or Cambridge in the home fixture. Trinity and UCD had enjoyed many a stirring encounter, particularly since 1919 when UCD became a senior club. In 1948 the two universities met in the Leinster cup final and in an exciting match played before a large crowd at Lansdowne Road, UCD won narrowly. It was this game that prompted Harry Thrift (DUFC) and Sarsfield Hogan (UCD), both of whom were Irish delegates on the International Rugby Football Board, to propose the idea of an annual Inter-Varsity match at Lansdowne Road on the basis of which each club would award its colours.

ABOVE ■ Dublin University defeated Oxford University 14-9 in the 1952/53 season. It was Hubie O'Connor's first match for the university. There were ten, past, current or future internationals in the two sides of which Trinity claimed seven; the Trinity players gained 42 caps between them. The Oxford University side included the Scottish internationals J.H. Henderson, B.E. Thomson and E.A.J. Fergusson (the future British Ambassador in Paris).

This was the era with a strong worldwide influence particularly South Africans and Rhodesians, for example, Jock Mostert, Peter Sang, Nick de Wet, Micky Dawson and George Patrikios. There was also British element which included Tony Reid-Smith, Tony Endall, Chris Lea, Danny Hearn, Bob Read, Martin Rees and a strong Irish element from both sides of the border which included the internationals: J.T. Gaston, J.I. Brennan, Larry L'Estrange, H. O'Connor and Robin Roe and many others such as Peter Dowse, Bud McMullen, the Bielenberg brothers, D.J. Fitzpatrick, J.R. Fullerton, C.C. Powell, T.P. Smyth and W.G. Taylor.

The formation of the Irish Universities Rugby Union in 1950-51 did much to strengthen Irish university rugby; there had been earlier examples of Trinity and UCD fielding combined sides and a Combined Universities of Ireland XV had enjoyed fixtures since 1933, but on an irregular basis. The goal of all university players was to play for the Combined Universities XV. On Tuesday April 6th, 1965 at Thomond Park, Limerick, the Combined Universities XV defeated the South Africans 12-10. It was the first win over a touring South African side by an Irish team. The Universities' side included two current internationals – Jerry Walsh (University College, Cork) and Henry Wall (University College, Dublin) and former internationals in Al Moroney (UCD) John Murray (UCD), Mick Leahy (UCC) and Eamon McGuire (University College, Galway), but it was an outstanding team effort (see Statistics) which won the day for the red-shirted University side. The pitch was greasy after heavy rain; the Springboks monopolized the ball but could do little with it as the red shirts swarmed everywhere tackling anything that moved. McGuire and Mick Grimshaw scored tries, Tony Hickie kicked a penalty goal and John Murray whose defensive kicking was outstanding that day, kicked a magnificent left-footed drop goal from 40 yards. The Springboks' scores came from two converted Tommy Bedford tries. Even more remarkable was the fact that the Universities side was without Tom Kiernan, Roger Young, Pat McGrath, Ken Kennedy, Ray McLoughlin and Bill Mulcahy who were playing for Ireland on the Saturday. Jerry Walsh, who played in the international, was allowed to play as he was the Universities' captain and Henry Wall had been dropped for Ronnie Lamont. The Combined Universities have played many memorable matches and achieved some outstanding victories, but few have compared with this famous victory.

On the international front, Ireland began the 1950s inauspiciously with only one win that season against Scotland at Lansdowne Road 21-0, but in the 1950/51 season they only failed to win the Grand Slam and Triple Crown because of a 3-3 draw at Cardiff Arms Park. The last time Ireland had won the Grand Slam and Triple Crown was in 1947/48 and prior to that was 1899. Karl Mullen, the hooker, was captain; he was to captain the British Lions tour of 1950 in Australia. He was a good captain and Ireland had a well-balanced pack but the strength of the Irish side lay in an outstanding pair of halves in Jack Kyle, who was brilliant in attack and defence, and John O'Meara who won the first of his 22 caps against France. A student at University College Cork, he qualified as a solicitor. During his career O'Meara partnered Kyle on 19 occasions to equal the record established by Eugene Davy and Mark Sugden between the wars. George Norton was an immaculate full-back; his catching and tackling were superb, but a shoulder injury in the Scottish match ended his career and left Ireland one short, but good defence by the backs and Kyle's flair led to a narrow victory.

The mid 1950s saw Irish rugby at a low ebb. In the span January 1954 to mid-February 1956, Ireland's international record read: played 11, won one, drawn one, lost nine. The only victory

ABOVE ■ 1950 Lions in Auckland – Karl Mullen with the ball.

came in 1954 at Ravenhill, Belfast. This was the last match played in Belfast by the international side. The results might have appeared poor, but in the 1954/55 season it was suggested after an excellent performance against France, that Ireland were Triple Crown contenders. A young pack had played well and A.J.F. O'Reilly in his debut game was an exciting prospect but uncertainty at half-back (Kyle and O'Meara were dropped for the Scottish game) and 'a lack of direction up front' led to Ireland finishing with the wooden spoon. Despite this, Robin Thompson, a fine forward either as a lock or No. 8 and Ireland's captain, was honoured with the captaincy of the 1955 Lions to South Africa. He was to play one more game for Ireland before joining Warrington Rugby League Club.

During this period, two Denham golf club members, Doctor J. Murphy O'Connor and J.S. Ritchie were capped. Jim Murphy O'Connor, an affable giant, played against England as No 8 on 13th February 1954 at Twickenham. Also earning his first cap for Ireland was Gordon Wood; the two debutants roomed together in the team hotel at the Richmond Hill Hotel. It was Jim's only cap, although he was picked for the next game against Scotland at Lansdowne Road but a back injury prevented him from playing. Ireland lost 3-14 to England but Jim kicked a long distance penalty goal. Ted Woodward, another Denham member, capped 16 times for England and lifelong friend of Jim, was playing in the centre, remembers that: 'Jim was carried off in the match; it was rather a bizarre sight. Jim was too big for the stretchers of those days and his legs were hanging limply over one end, while his arms dangled incongruously over the other end and the St John's Ambulance men were struggling to keep Jim on the stretcher'.

For the Irish matches versus France and England at the start of 1956, Jimmy Ritchie, a Belfast born engineer, charismatic leader and highly regarded flanker for London Irish was brought in to captain the side in Paris and at Twickenham in his only two matches for his country. Only

ABOVE ▪ 1954 England v Ireland at Twickenham. Gordon Wood (3), father of the Irish hooker and 2001 Irish captain Keith Wood passes the ball to John O'Meara, the scrum-half. Keith is more inclined to run with the ball.

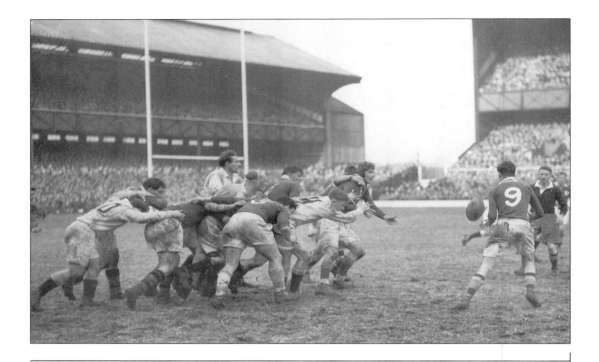

ABOVE ▪ 1954 Ireland v England at Twickenham. Jim Murphy O'Connor passes the ball to John O'Meara.

H.G. Cook in 1884 similarly had captained Ireland on his debut although Rob Saunders emulated the feat in the 1990s. Noel Henderson, the big centre, succeeded Jimmy Ritchie as captain and led Ireland to victory at Lansdowne Road in the last two matches of the season over Scotland and Wales. The 1957 season began with expectations high; a fine set of backs in P.J. Berkery, A.J.F. O'Reilly, N.J. Henderson (captain), A.C. Pedlow, N.H. Brophy (his first season), J.W. Kyle and A.A. Mulligan but a largely unproven pack, although Gordon Wood, a strong Garryowen prop and Robin Roe, the hooker, had played in all the matches the previous year, but there were new caps in H.S. O'Connor and P.J.A. O'Sullivan in the back row.

The opening match of the season was against France at Lansdowne Road on 26th January 1957. I remember it well; it was the first time I had been to Lansdowne Road. As students we gathered at the Lincoln Inn and then began the two-mile walk to the ground – the streets were full of Irish and French supporters, shouting good natured abuse at each other. The journey took longer than it should for there were numerous 'watering holes' to be tested, but we arrived in good time. The atmosphere was special and Lansdowne Road a magnificent theatre. I became a fanatical

ABOVE ▦ 1954 England v Ireland at Twickenham. **From back left**: R. Roe, G. Wood, F.E. Anderson, P.J. Lawlor, R.H. Thomson, G. Reidy, A.C. Pedlow, J.C. Murphy O'Connor, R.J. Gregg, J.S. McCarthy (captain), M. Mortell, J.T. Gaston, N.J. Henderson, W.J. Hewitt, J.A. O'Meara.

Irish supporter from that moment onwards – perhaps I was lucky, it was a wonderful game; Ireland won 11-6. Jack Kyle scored one of the best tries of his long career. He received the ball on the French 25, swerved and dodged and scored to the left of the uprights at the far end (that's how I remember the try, almost half a century later!). Niall Brophy from University College Dublin scored a try on his debut, whilst Cecil Pedlow converted Kyle's try and kicked a penalty goal. A memorable match and Ireland were to have a good season, winning narrowly at Murrayfield and losing in close matches to England and Wales.

The 1950s ended with two good seasons but unlucky defeats cost the side championships. In the 1958 season Ireland picked six new caps for the match with Australia: D. Hewitt, A.R. Dawson, J.B. Stevenson, A. Mulcahy, J.A. Donaldson, N.A.A. Murphy. David Hewitt was a young and elusive centre who went on to gain 18 caps. The other five new caps were forwards, three of them were to become household names in Irish rugby. Ronnie Dawson was an expert hooker whose qualities as a leader earned him the captaincy of the 1959 Lions to Australasia and 27 caps, Bill Mulcahy was a medical student at University College Dublin who gained 35 caps and Noel Murphy played 41 times in the back row, before returning to international rugby as the Irish team coach. The other two, J.B. Stevenson (5 caps) who partnered Bill Mulcahy in the second row and the flanker J.A. Donaldson (4 caps), were only to play for that season but the rest of the side were very experienced (see Statistics).

Ireland's victory over Australia 9-6 was their first victory over a touring side and was achieved as full time approached; a towering kick by Henderson led to the debutant Dawson following up at speed to touch down for a try. On the resumption of play, Hewitt, another debutant, made an interception and sent the 'big man' Henderson on a long and thrilling run to win the match with a glorious try. Earlier Pedlow had kicked a penalty goal to Australia's two unconverted tries and thus they had led 9-6 in wet and windy conditions before the memorable climax. Kyle's last match was at Lansdowne Road against Scotland. Ireland won 12-6 with two tries by Pedlow playing on the wing and two penalty goals by Berkery and Henderson respectively. History has judged Jack Kyle well. He qualified as a doctor from Queen's University, Belfast and played for Ireland between 1947 and 1958, winning 46 caps and scored seven tries and one drop goal for his country. He was one of the outstanding players on the Lions tour to Australia and New Zealand in 1950. Bill McLaren, writing in 2001, picks Kyle as one of the great fly-halves of all time and describes him as: 'a beautifully balanced runner who seemed to float rather than run and who had the ability suddenly, to find another gear that enabled him to escape opponents. Although he wasn't a big man, he was brave and resolute in defence. He was an astute tactician and a dangerous attacker.'

The other match in the 1958 season at Lansdowne Road was lost to Wales 9-6; unfortunately the matches against England (0-6) and France (6-11) were also lost. Three great matches and tremendous fun for the young student The 1958/59 season was disappointing only in that Ireland lost two matches they could have won. Ronnie Dawson had succeeded Noel Henderson as captain. Henderson was to play his last season at full-back. The two matches at Lansdowne Road were exciting affairs. Ireland was unlucky to lose the first match against England, the forwards earned plenty of good possession but the backs' sole objective appeared to be to give the ball to O'Reilly playing at centre and let him score, but the English defence was too disciplined.

However, in the final match of the 1950s, the champions France, were defeated by an Irish side playing with great spirit. Niall Brophy scored a try, Mick English dropped a goal and D. Hewitt kicked a penalty goal. In the meanwhile Scotland had been defeated 8-3 at Murrayfield and Wales had won 6-8 at Cardiff Arms Park due to two late tries and a conversion. Ireland were unlucky not to score a try in the opening seconds of the game. In a sensational start, Henderson kicked off to the left, away from the forwards, Brophy picked up the ball at full speed and ran deep into the Welsh half. As Brophy was tackled by C. Ashton the fly-half, he passed inwards to Murphy who appeared to score a try. But the referee G. Burrell (Scotland) ordered a line-out and this despite the fact that the touch judge had not raised his flag. Malcolm Thomas (Denham Golf Club) was playing in the centre for Wales.

Malcolm Thomas won 27 caps for Wales as a wing, centre or fly-half and went on two British Lions tours in 1950 and 1959 in Australasia. He knew the Irish players well, not only as opponents for he played six times against them being on the winning side four times, but also as colleagues on Lions tours. Perhaps his most memorable match against Ireland was his first. The match was played at Ravenhill, Belfast 11th March 1950 and Wales would take the Triple Crown if they won. There were barely a couple of minutes to go before the whistle and the score was 3-3, when Thomas, 21 years old and playing on the left wing, received a good long pass from Lewis Jones. He had 15 yards to go to the line and the Irish cover defence to beat. Norton the full-back tackled the diving Welshman. The corner flag was knocked over, the crown seemed lost to Wales but Ossie Glasgow the Irish touch judge on the spot, set off to run behind the posts signalling that Wales had scored the winning try. ▪

I t was just over 50 years later that I went to see Malcolm Thomas, a long time Denham golf club member, at his home in Beaconsfield, Bucks. He recalled: 'I remember the try well, it was my second try for Wales and perhaps the most important one in my career. I played my first international for Wales in 1949 against France and my last game was also against France in 1959. Both matches were at the Stades Colombes. It was always great fun playing against Ireland and with them as colleagues on two Lions tours; they always played with great passion and loved a story and a sing-song – great tourists. On my first Lions tour in 1950 we went by boat through the Suez Canal to New Zealand and then to Australia – the whole trip took six months. We lost the tests against New Zealand 3-0 with one drawn; they were just too big and fit, out-scrummaging us in the forwards and too efficient in the rucks in the second phase, but our backs won great acclaim for their willingness to play open, attacking rugby.

'We won the two Test matches of the Australian section comfortably and in fact scored 150 points in six matches in Australia. The Irishmen on that tour, as far as I remember were: George Norton who was a full-back and a very fine kicker – one of the best goal kickers at that time – he didn't play in the Tests. M.F. Lane, a wing who played well over 20-odd times for Ireland but

I don't believe he ever scored a try for Ireland – he played in two Tests. Noel Henderson who was a fairly wild, big strong centre played in one Test. Jackie Kyle was world-renowned as one of the finest outside halves and everybody thought so – he played in all six Tests. Clifford who was a dustman from Limerick, a very lovely man, big strong chap as front row forward – he played in five Tests. Karl Mullen was captain, the hooker and a very good player – he played in three Tests. Jimmy Nelson, a great big second row forward – he played one Test. J.W. McKay a wing-forward, extraordinarily fit very quick and very, very good in his position – he played in all six Tests. McCarthy the wing-forward who really because of the size of the New Zealand players was rarely able to throw his weight about and use his speed. He didn't play in the Tests. Those were the nine Irishmen. Although we failed to win a Test in New Zealand the results were always close: Dunedin 9-9, Christchurch 0-8, Wellington 3-8, Auckland 8-11. I think it was the coaching at all levels which made the difference. Their players always knew what to do, after all they had done it since childhood. We were just as talented though.

'On the 1959 tour to Australasia I was lucky to be picked; I had had a good game against Ireland. In fact I was considered with Jeff Butterfield (England) for the captaincy but Ronnie Dawson, the Irishman was picked as captain. All three Lions tours in the 1950s were captained by

ABOVE ■ 1950 Noel Henderson with Lions Tour in Greymouth, New Zealand.

ABOVE ▓ 1959 Lions tour to New Zealand. David Hewitt watches Tony O'Reilly make a tackle.

Irishmen: Karl Mullen in 1950, Robin Thompson in 1955 in the drawn series against South Africa and Ronnie Dawson in 1959. This time the tour started in Australia, we won the tests there (17-6 and 24-3) but again the All Black pack was too strong and we lost that series three matches to one. We lost the first Test in Dunedin 17-18 despite the fact we scored four tries. We converted one try and one penalty goal to their six penalties all kicked by Don Clarke. We won the final Test at Eden Park, Auckland 9-6. Andy Mulligan flew in as a replacement for Stan Coughtrie the injured Scottish scrum-half. In fact he played in a dozen tour games and was picked for the Auckland Test instead of Dickie Jeeps; he played quite brilliantly. Peter Jackson, Bev Risman and Tony O'Reilly scored tries to make up the Lions nine points to the New Zealanders' two penalty goals. Tony O'Reilly's try, together with his try in the Dunedin Test and his two tries in the Australia Test and his two tries in the 1955 tour of South Africa created a record for the Lions. On the 1959 tour he scored 22 tries and he was the outstanding player of that tour. Of the other Irish players, David Hewitt was a quite brilliant centre (five Tests);

Gordon Wood (prop) played in two Tests – he was always very fit and a great character. He spent a lot of his spare time fishing. Sid Millar was a very strong front row forward (two Tests); Noel Murphy, (three Tests) was a very good wing-forward. Ronnie Dawson led the side well in all six Tests – he was very very fit and a fine player. Ossie Glasgow the touch judge of 1950 fame and international referee managed the side and completed the Irish contingent which made such a valuable contribution to the overall success of the 1959 tour.'

The 1950s was a lovely period in Irish rugby, perhaps not achieving the championships or grand slams that the talent of the players warranted, but always the Irish enjoyed their rugby, gave pleasure to their supporters and were recognized as players of ability by the British Lions. ▪

ABOVE ▪ June 1959. Gordon Wood enjoys his favourite hobby at the Fish Farm, Greenmeadows, Napier, New Zealand.

The 1960s were a mixed decade for Irish rugby. The early 1960s were disappointing from the results point of view and this despite having a large number of current and future British Lions players in their teams: T.J. Kiernan, A.C. Pedlow, N.H. Brophy, D. Hewitt, A.J.F. O'Reilly, A.A. Mulligan, S. Millar, A.R. Dawson, B.G.M. Wood, W.A. Mulcahy and N.A.A. Murphy. In the 1959/60 season Ronnie Dawson was injured until the final match and all the games were lost for the first time since 1920. Three of the defeats were by very narrow margins 5-8 at Twickenham, 5-6 to Scotland and 9-10 to Wales both at Lansdowne Road, but there was a heavy defeat in Paris 6-23. The 1960/61 season saw a more promising start. In December, Ireland only lost in injury time to the South Africans because of a pushover try and in the first match of the Championship, England were defeated at Lansdowne Road by 11-8. However, defeats at the hands of the Scots 8-16, the Welsh 0-9 and the French 3-15 left the Irish once again with the wooden spoon. The last match of the season against France was disappointing. France were undefeated and the Irish pack was outplayed; J.T. Nesdale, who replaced Bill Mulcahy and D. Scott were playing in their first matches and C.J. Dick was only playing his second game. It was a sad day for me too, as it was the last game I was to see as an undergraduate, but happily my support for Ireland was to continue.

The 1961/62 season was another poor one. There were nine new caps for the lost game 0-16 to England at Twickenham, but two of them Bill McBride and Ray McLoughlin were to become amongst Ireland's all time great forwards. Ronnie Dawson lost the captaincy and my Trinity colleague, L.P.F. L'Estrange gained his one cap on the wing. The 1962/63 and 1963/64 seasons saw victories against Wales and England only, but in December 1963 the All Blacks were very nearly defeated. Johnny Fortune a speedy but erratic winger scored a spectacular try which was converted by T.J. Kiernan. It was only in the closing minutes that the All Blacks kicked a penalty to put them in the lead 6-5 points. However it was at Twickenham in February that the young Trinity (and at that stage Cambridge) undergraduate C.M.H. Gibson burst on to the international scene with 'a scintillating display of dashing fly-half play'. Ireland scored three very good back line tries – P.J. Casey and M.K. Flynn (2). Noel Murphy also scored a try to record an 18-5 victory. However, injuries to key players were to upset the momentum of that victory.

At last in the 1964/65 season Ireland played to its potential only losing to Wales, with good victories over England 5-0, Scotland at Murrayfield 16-6. J.A.P. Shackleton (Denham Golf Club) played in the centre for Scotland and remembers that 'Ireland were much the better side'. A win against South Africa 9-6 and a draw with France 3-3 made them runners-up in the Championship. Five new caps were awarded for the opening game against France; Roger Young, a dental student went on to play 26 games as a scrum-half for Ireland. In the forwards, S. McHale, K.W. Kennedy, M.G. Doyle and R.A. Lamont gained their first caps. Doyle scored a fine try and became a regular for the next four seasons; Ray McLoughlin was promoted to the captaincy. He was a deep thinker, a forceful motivator and a solid scrummager.

The rest of the decade was to see Ireland competing with more success. The 1966 season began with a narrow defeat in Paris 6-11 to a brilliant French side. Dr Mick Molloy gained his first cap in this match and was to form a successful partnership with Bill McBride as Ireland's second row combination for 26 matches. A 6-6 draw at Twickenham, a loss to Scotland 3-11 and a victory over Wales 9-6 followed. By now I was teaching at King's College, Auckland, New Zealand. I was at Eden Park on Saturday 10th September 1966 to see the All Blacks defeat the British Lions 24-11. A.J.W. Hinselwood and C.W. McFadyean scored tries with Stewart Wilson (Denham Golf Club) adding the remaining points. Ireland was represented in this match by C.M.H. Gibson, K.W. Kennedy, R.J. McLoughlin, W.J. McBride and R.A. Lamont. I remember Mike Gibson making two long runs up the middle of the field and deep into All Black territory, but there was no one in support to carry on the runs.

Also I think back to Ken Kennedy, coming to morning assembly at King's on the Monday before the match and talking to the whole school and staff about the Lions and Irish rugby. I was only a new member of staff but it was a happy moment to introduce Ken Kennedy. He was to earn 45 caps for Ireland over ten seasons and played three times in Tests for the Lions. He was a member of the 1974 victorious Lions squad to South African and he was recognised as a hooker with exceptional technical skills in the tradition of Ronnie Dawson, Robin Roe and Karl Mullen. However, the British touring team lost every Test against New Zealand. It was clear that scrummaging and rucking techniques were not good enough and that in general, coaching and fitness levels had to be improved.

In the 1966/67 season, Ireland was deprived of a share of the Five Nations Championship by losing 6-11 to France at Lansdowne Road in the last match of the season. However, earlier in January, Australia had been defeated by 15-8. 'Mike Gibson had played with outstanding poise, he tackled and covered ubiquitously in defence, distributed the ball sensibly in attack and contributed two drop goals and a brilliant individual try to Ireland's score.' His overall control at fly-half was due to an excellent forward effort in which Kennedy and Murphy were the heroes but also O'Callaghan, Moroney, McBride, Molloy, Doyle and Goodall had played very well. The first match of the championship was lost 3-8 to England at Lansdowne Road. Ironically one of the English heroes was really an Irishman; his name was Danny Hearn.

In 1967 Danny played four matches for England, but missed the match against Australia. In the game against Ireland in Dublin, he was named as the reserve but played in the centre. It was a tight game, but the match turned when Tom Kiernan in a broad Cork accent said he was coming into the line but only Hearn in the English side understood what Kiernan was saying. Hearn made a devastating tackle, the ball popped out and into the hands of McFadyean the English wing, who scored under the posts. Danny spent the evening at the Lincoln Inn with his Trinity mates; a renegade welcomed home, Ireland had lost but the man of the moment was really Irish! Ireland won their next matches at Murrayfield and Cardiff Arms Park and might have won the Triple Crown if it had not been for Danny's tackle.

The 1967/68 and 1968/69 seasons were marked by a remarkable unbeaten sequence of seven matches between February 1968 and March 1969. There was a 9-9 draw against England at Twickenham, Scotland (14-6) and Wales (9-7). Australia (10-3) and England (17-15) were beaten at Lansdowne Road and in 1969 France (17-9). Scotland was outplayed at Murrayfield (16-0) with Ireland scoring four tries. Some argue that the side that represented Ireland against England in 1969 at Lansdowne Road was the best ever with T.J. Kiernan, full-back and captain; A.T.A. Duggan and J.C.M. Moroney, wings; F.P.K. Bresnihan and C.M.H. Gibson, centres; B.J. McGann and R.N. Young, half-backs; S. Millar, K.W. Kennedy, P.O'Callaghan, W.J. McBride, M.G. Molloy, J.C. Davidson, K.G. Goodall and N.A.A Murphy constituted the forwards (see Statistics).

I was teaching at Worksop College at the time. Dr N.M. Hall (St Mary's Hospital and England) had a son there and I remember that staff and boys were not pleased when I used to point out that in the 1960s Ireland's record against England now read: played 10, won 4, drawn 3, lost 3. Despite this sequence of victories, losses to France in 1969 and to Wales in 1969 meant Ireland finished runners-up in both these seasons in the Championship. ■

The 1970s was a mixed decade. Until the mid 1970s, success continued with an Irish side based on the experience of Ray McLoughlin, Bill McBride, Mike Gibson, Ken Kennedy and Fergus Slattery. In 1974 the side became champions for the first time since 1951, but the retirement of McBride, Kennedy and McLoughlin at the end of the 1975 season and injuries to Dick Milliken and Slattery led to a poor 1976 championship season; only England was beaten 13-12 at Twickenham. It was in this environment that Roly Meates was appointed coach to the Irish side. His first task was to take Ireland on its first tour of New Zealand in the summer of 1976.

I talked with Roly on Thursday 10th August 2000 at the Kildare Street Club. We remembered that tour since I was back in New Zealand teaching at King's College, Auckland: 'The tour went extremely well. We played seven matches in New Zealand and on the way home stopped off in Fiji. It was great to have two Trinity men in the squad: John Robbie and Philip Orr, they both played in the Test match at Wellington. In New Zealand we won four games and lost two to provincial sides and lost the Test 11-13. Incidentally your King's College, Auckland boy, Ian Kirkpatrick scored one of their tries; H.H. MacDonald, another King's boy, played in the second row for the All Blacks. The Irish pack particularly Moss Keane and Willie Duggan played with aggression and great spirit. I have always felt that with more experience and awareness that we could have won the Test. You know, Ireland had not played an international-board country overseas since 1967 against Australia in Sydney when we beat them 11-5. Many players developed well on the New Zealand tour. I think of Tony Ensor, Stuart McKinney, John Robbie; also Moss Keane made a significant contribution to making the tour a success, as of course did Mike Gibson. It is exciting to remember the relative disregard of the New Zealanders when we arrived and the respect we had earned by the end of the tour. Sadly my period as Ireland's coach did not produce the results I might have hoped for. We lost all the matches of the 1977 season narrowly and Noel Murphy took over the coaching of the Irish side until he was succeeded at the end of the 1980 season by Tom Kiernan.'

In 1978 Ireland defeated Scotland at Lansdowne Road 12-9, but lost narrowly on a frozen-hard pitch in Paris 9-10. The matches against Wales and England were lost. However Tony Ward playing in his first international season scored a then remarkable 38 points. The 1979 season saw Ireland recognized as the most improved team in the championship. This was followed in the summer by a tour of Australia. Ireland won both the Test matches 27-12 in Brisbane and 9-3 in Sydney; Ollie Campbell controversially replaced Tony Ward not only as the fly-half but also 'Mr Boot', scoring 28 points in the two Tests. In the 1980 Five Nations season, Ireland won two, lost narrowly to France 18-19 at the Parc des Princes and lost 9-24 to England at Twickenham. Ireland scored 70 points in that season, six tries and 46 points to the trusty boot of Campbell. Ciaran Fitzgerald in the match in Paris appeared to score a perfectly legitimate try in the closing minutes but this made the Irish more determined to beat the Welsh in the last game of the season; the Welsh were defeated 21-7 at Lansdowne Road by a fitter, faster and more motivated side. This time Ciaran Fitzgerald was rewarded with a fine opportunist try. ■

I was back in England in 1980. My first game was to go to Cardiff Arms Park in November for the centenary match Wales v the All Blacks. Ireland was represented by John West, the referee. I had obtained two tickets from Bret Codlin and Bret Wilson who were former pupils at King's and members of the New Zealand touring party but not picked for the Test team. Tim Fox took me in his Ford Grenada and we watched the All Blacks win comfortably 23-3. Nicky Allen (ex Auckland Grammar School) playing at fly-half scored a fine try. I remember the try well – Allen almost certainly touched the ball down inches short of the try line but the movement deserved a try and West, a former colleague at Trinity was not going to spoil a great piece of play.

The 1981 season began with a new coach Tom Kiernan, and Ireland were favourites to win the Championship. They lost all their games. However despite the defeats: 13-19 France, 8-9 to Wales, 6-10 to England and 9-10 to Scotland, there were plus points from the season. Hugo MacNeill made his debut at full-back and was hailed the discovery of the season. An experienced pack had played well and the experiment of playing Ward at fly-half and Campbell in the centre had looked promising. A tour to South Africa in the summer led to opposition from within Ireland for political and ecclesiastical reasons and many of the squad were forced to resign from their jobs when their employers refused to grant leave of absence. The two Tests were lost 15-23 and 10-12 but in the last Test in Durban, Ireland had led 10-6 until two late drop goals by the South African fly-half H.E. Botha.

The 1981/82 season began in November with a narrow loss to Australia. It was the 17th time that Fergus Slattery had captained Ireland. Ward kicked four penalty goals, but it was Ireland's seventh successive defeat. Things did not augur well for the Championship but the appointment of an army officer Ciaran Fitzgerald as captain, infused an experienced side with fresh enthusiasm. Only Trevor Ringland, Donal Lenihan (the manager of the 2001 Lions side to Australia), Keith Crossan and Ronan Kearney were new caps, and the Triple Crown was won for the first time since 1949. Wales was defeated 20-12 at Lansdowne Road; England lost at Twickenham 15-16 and Scotland lost 21-12 at Lansdowne Road but the French had a commanding victory 22-9 at the Parc des Princes. The French had lost every match in that championship but the return of R. Paparemborde and P. Dospital to the front row transformed their pack and this combined with the brilliance of their backs: Gabernet, Fabre, Mesny, Belascain, Blanco, Lescarboura and Berbizier led to the overwhelming of the Irish side. I remember in particular being fearful for the safety of the Irish pack. Ollie Campbell equalled his own record by kicking 46 points in the championship; he also scored all Ireland's points against Scotland, six penalties and one drop goal.

In 1983, Ireland shared the championship with France, who they beat 22-16 at Lansdowne Road with Moss Finn scoring two tries, but a loss to Wales 9-23 at Cardiff Arms Park denied them the Grand Slam. However, Scotland (15-13) and England (25-15) were both beaten. Against England Ollie Campbell kicked five penalty goals, scored a try which he converted and Fergus Slattery also scored a try. Campbell scored 52 points in the Championship. For the first time in Irish rugby history the same 15 players were picked in the four championship matches (see Statistics). Ciaran Fitzgerald's leadership qualities were recognized by the Lions who made him skipper for the tour to New Zealand.

The 1984 season was not a good one; the pack for the first match of the season in Paris was playing together for the eighth time, but was crushed by the powerful French forwards and the season ended with a 9-32 defeat to Scotland at Lansdowne Road, which meant a whitewash of defeats. However, in 1985 Mick Doyle replaced Bill McBride as coach and Ireland won the Triple Crown and Championship. In the course of the season Brendan Mullin (centre), Michael Bradley (scrum-half) and Willie Anderson, Philip Matthews, Willie Sexton, Brian Spillane and Nigel Carr in the forwards gained their first caps. Michael Kiernan scored 47 points and a leading Irish rugby critic, Sean Diffley, regarded the side as 'the most highly skilled all-round team ever produced by Ireland'. The team beat England at Lansdowne Road by a late drop goal by M.J. Kiernan. Three Trinity men – MacNeill, Mullin and Orr were on this side.

The 1986 season was a great disappointment; all matches were lost despite twelve of the previous year's championship side being available for selection. The year 1987 was better with Donal Lenihan replacing Ciaran Fitzgerald as captain; he was generally regarded as the best line-out

ABOVE ■ 30th March 1985 Five Nations Championship, Lansdowne Road. The Ireland Rugby team that beat England in the Triple Crown. **Back row:** Mick Cuddy, Chairman of the Selection Committee, Phil Orr, Philip Matthews, Donal Lenihan, Willie Anderson, Hugo MacNeill, Nigel Carr and Jim McCoy. **Front row:** Michael Bradley, Paul Dean, Trevor Ringland, Michael Carroll, President IRFU, Ciaran Fitzgerald, Michael Kiernan (capt) Keith Crossan, Brendan Mullin and Mike Doyle.

jumper in the British Isles. England were defeated 17-0 at Lansdowne Road with tries by M.J. Kiernan, K.D. Crossan and P.M. Matthews but defeats to Scotland and France, before a 15-11 victory at Cardiff Arms Park followed. The 1980s ended with two rather lacklustre seasons with only victories against Wales (1989) and Scotland (1988) being achieved. ▦

The 1990s proved difficult years for Irish rugby. Their record reads – against France: played ten, lost 10; against Scotland: played 10, lost 9, drawn one; against England: played 10, won two, lost eight; against Wales: won six, lost three, drawn one. There were also losses to Italy and Samoa. However, I like to remember the 1990s for Ireland's victory 17-3 over England at Lansdowne Road in 1993. I had travelled to Dublin with my friends Tim and Sue Fox and Pat Lingwood. We had made the long journey from Chorleywood to Holyhead by car and ferry to Dun Laoghaire and after a guided tour round the large car park there, 'this is to get you in practice for driving in Ireland', we arrived in Blackrock for the night. The match was in the words of Edmund Van Esbeck, the rugby correspondent of the Irish Times for thirty years 'one of the great Irish displays of the modern era'.

The 1993 season had begun inauspiciously. Australia had defeated Ireland 17-42 at Lansdowne Road and Ciaran Fitzgerald had resigned as coach to be succeeded by Gerry Murphy, a fine all-round sportsman and graduate of Trinity College. Convincing defeats by Scotland and France were to follow, but in the French match Ireland had put up a spirited performance. The Irish had not won a Five Nations match since March 1990 when they played Wales, and Wales were defeated again 19-14 at Cardiff Arms Park. England were the last opponents of the season and were expected to win comfortably but a number of factors hinted at a possible upset. Willie Anderson, an outstanding second row forward from Dungannon and international between 1984 and 1990, had been asked to assist in coaching the forwards. Eric Elwood was now installed as a fly-half after a successful debut against Wales. The same side which had played well against Wales was picked. The Irish 'A' side had put up a good performance against the England 'A' side before losing 23-18 at Donneybrook and apparent English arrogance further stiffened Irish resolve.

Gerry Murphy remembers 'we were very, very determined'. There followed one of the very best of Irish victories when the pack played with ferocity and skill. Michael Bradley, captain and scrum-half had the game of his life, his tactical play and brilliant defence were enhanced by a great back row of Pat O'Hara, Brian Robinson and Denis McBride, who hunted, chased and harassed the opposition with unrelenting determination. The potentially dangerous English back line was deprived of the ball and when they got it, they were tackled unmercifully. The score was 3-3 at half-time. If the Irish had played well in the first half, they played even better in the second half. Elwood kicked an early penalty and then scored a superb drop goal to give Ireland a 9-3 lead. With five minutes to go Elwood scored another drop goal after good play by the forwards. England now saw defeat looming and tried to run the ball through their backs. Will Carling was hit by a devastating tackle, Elwood picked up the loose ball, passed to Mick Galwey who drove for the line to score a try which was greeted with a great cheer by the capacity crowd – a magnificent victory. After the excitement of the game we were soon engulfed in chaos; a train had stopped, the level crossing gates were closed, the crowd wanted to move forward and the ladies were not feeling comfortable but some large Irishmen stood their ground to ensure everyone's safety. Great fun and part of watching rugby in Ireland!

And also I remember well, 1st February 1997 which saw me travelling with Dr Derek Browne to Cardiff Arms Park. This was the last match played in the old Cardiff Arms Park Stadium. Brian Ashton, an Englishman and the successful coach of Bath, was now Ireland's coach. Ireland was without the injured Keith Wood who was replaced by Ross Nesdale, a New Zealander with Irish blood who won his first cap. Denis Hickie, another debutant, playing in the wing, scored a try. His uncle had played for Ireland in the forwards in the early 1970s as a No. 8 and his father had been a final trialist. Jonathan Bell and Eric Miller also scored tries, but again Eric Elwood's boot was to play an important role, kicking 11 points. Ireland appeared to be heading for a comfortable victory but a late Welsh rally ended with the narrowest of Irish victories 26-25. The rest of the decade and century saw only a solitary victory in the Five Nations Championship against Wales, 29-23 at Wembley Stadium in February 1999.

However, the new century, with Warren Gatland, the former All Black hooker as coach, began with splendid victories over France 27-25 at the Stade de France, Scotland 44-22 and Italy 60-13 (now making it the Six Nations Championship), both at Lansdowne Road but losses to Wales and England spoilt any chance of Ireland winning the Championship.

The 2001 season started well with victories over Italy 41-22 and France 22-15. Tickets, accommodation and the flight were organised for the Ireland v England game, but the Irish government took the wise precaution that the English match scheduled for 24th March at Lansdowne Road should be postponed due to the outbreak of foot and mouth in the British Isles. The momentum of success was halted but a mood of optimism prevailed, the international side was doing well. Munster, Ulster, Leinster and to an encouraging extent Connaught, were producing outstanding performances in the Heineken European Cup. To add to the grounds of optimism was the improvement in coaching, in playing standards at all levels of rugby in Ireland and in players with Irish qualifications performing well for English clubs. After attempts in April and May had failed, the 2001 Six Nations Championship was completed in the Autumn. Ireland finished the season with mixed feelings: a fantastic performance against England, preceded by a good win against Wales, but a lacklustre match against Scotland earlier deprived Ireland of the Grand Slam, Triple Crown and the Championship.

I was in Dublin for the England game. Saturday 20th October produced a bright, sunny day and the walk from Trinity to Lansdowne Road took me back nearly half a century; the atmosphere on the morning of an international is electric and for a match against their oldest rival (1875) the atmosphere is even more tense. There had been suggestions that Ireland should have been made to play their matches in Paris and that the postponed matches had no meaning. The bookmakers gave Ireland no chance, but England were without two key players Martin Johnson and Lawrence Dallaglio and had had no warm up game of international standard.

ABOVE ■ 20th October 2001 Six Nations Championship. Keith Wood scores a try during the match between Ireland and England at Lansdowne Road, Dublin.

A capacity crowd at Lansdowne Road, the roar that greeted the Irish XV, a Keith Wood try and the disciplined, fervent play of the whole Irish side brought England down to reality and put an Irish victory very much on the cards. David Humphreys' line and tactical kicking was brilliant; in contrast, especially during the first 20 minutes, Johnny Wilkinson's kicking showed a lack of tactical awareness. However, Humphreys missed a number of penalty kicks and Ireland went into half-time with an 11-6 lead. Keith Wood's try came in the sixteenth minute – Ireland elected to go for a lineout in the right corner of the England 22, rather than take points from a penalty. Wood took a superb high take, peeled away to the back of the lineout and with a burst on an arcing run he managed to barge his way over for a try. The roar of acclamation would have been heard in the distant Wicklow mountains. Humphreys missed the conversion but managed to kick two penalties which were matched by Johnny Wilkinson.

Kyran Bracken replaced England's captain Mat Dawson as scrum-half for the second half. The turning point in the half came after both sides had scored penalties when Peter Stringer, Ireland's diminutive scrum-half, ankle-tapped Dan Luger as he appeared with a spectacular run from the halfway line to have a try under the posts at his mercy. Ronan O'Gara's first act and participation in replacing the injured Humphreys, was to kick a 35 metre penalty and his second penalty, from the right touchline, seemed to seal victory. With Ireland leading 20-9 and only five minutes to go Austin Healey scored in the corner and injury time seemed to go on for ever. Healey knocked on with a try a possibility but the whistle went and Ireland had won a famous victory – equal in merit to that of 1993.

England had won the Championship on points difference from Ireland but had failed to win the Grand Slam or Triple Crown. However, after Ireland's narrow loss to New Zealand, the 2001 season ended with the dismissal of Warren Gatland. The removal of Gatland amazed many but the relationship between Eddie O'Sullivan the back coach and Gatland had not been good for some time. Eddie O'Sullivan became Warren Gatland's assistant in 1999 when he brought a new incisiveness and creativity to Ireland's back play and results improved. Under Gatland, Ireland's record had read: seven wins and 11 losses, but with O'Sullivan in charge of the backs, Ireland's record was: won 11 and lost six. The new coaching team of Eddie O'Sullivan and the Munster pair of Declan Kidney and Niall O'Donovan, supported by Mike Ford the defensive coach from Oldham Rugby League club, will find Irish rugby in good heart. They will be endeavouring to build on the recent successes of the international side, the outstanding play of the provincial sides in the Celtic League and the achievements in the Heineken Cup.

London Irish Rugby Football Club *Founded 1898*

In his book Passion in Exile - 100 Years of London Irish RFC, Peter Bills paints a picture of wonderful characters, loyal servants and warm-hearted folk who have all contributed to the rich fabric of one of the world's most charismatic rugby clubs.

ABOVE ■ The London Irish XV 1959/60 **Back Row:** R.M. Johnston, J. T. Bamber, W. Grahan, J.P. MacDonnell, M.A. O'Flaherty, M.A. Byrne, D.W.M. Irons, N. Feddis, T. Tranter **Seated:** V.A. Poole, J.L.A. Brown, A.A. Mulligan (captain), W. Morgan (President), S.J. McDermott (vice-captain), R.J. McCarten, A.T. Pearce **Front Row:** G.W. Hackett, J. Moore. Absent: B. O'Hart, S.T. Jones.

Played 35 – Won 30 – Drawn 3 – Lost 2 – Points For: 491. Points Against: 163.

One of the very best London Irish sides was the 1959/60 side. It lost only two matches 9-16 to Lansdowne in Dublin and its very last match in England, 5-10 to a Northampton side which contained seven internationals. London Irish had agreed to play Northampton in a re-arranged fixture, the earlier one being cancelled due to fog. The London Irish squad (18 players) included two ex-Irish internationals: N Feddis (one cap 1956), S.J. McDermott (two caps, 1955), one future Irish international R.J. McCarten (three caps, 1961) and one current international, A.A. Mulligan (22 caps 1956-61). Mulligan, the captain played in only nine of the 35 matches played that season. The success of the side was built around a settled side, tremendous team spirit and the supreme fitness of the players under the guidance of Ted Hammond at the Duke of York's H.Q., which enabled a mediocre side to play with typical Irish fierceness, to be very mobile and show remarkable ball handling skills. Mulligan described it as 'the great Corinthian period of rugby'.

Few London Irish sides have come close to emulating the 1959/60 successes; Ken Kennedy in the late 1960s and early 1970s, both as a player and coach, instigated and organised disciplined hardness. The 1980s saw the club enjoy enormous playing talent: Hugo MacNeill, Neil Francis, Brendan Mullin, Michael Gibson, John O'Driscoll, Simon Geoghegan, John Hewitt, Hugh Condon, Jim Staples and many others, but results were never as good as they should have been. In the 1980s the club was struggling to grasp the realities and consequences of semi-professionalism. One problem was the choosing of a team which was constantly disrupted by the demands of interprovincial matches in Ireland and the international programme. Relationships with the IRFU were not always good but London Irish was a fun club, a home away from home for Irish players and their families. Everyone wanted to go to Sunbury, watch the rugby and enjoy the post-match craic.

The 1990s and early years of the 21st century have seen their triumphs, disasters and difficulties. The decade started with optimism. There was a fine set of backs in the club including the internationals Rob Saunders (12 caps, five as captain 1991-94) which included his debut game, David Curtis (14 caps 1991-92), Simon Geoghegan (22 caps 1991-96) and Jim Staples (24 caps 1991-97) but the 1993/94 season saw them relegated from Division One of the League and the departure of players to other clubs. For instance, Simon Geoghegan went to Bath and Jim Staples went to Harlequins. 1995/96 season saw them promoted again and their position in Division One has been cemented by the recruitment of non Irish qualified players, particularly from the southern hemisphere. The difficulty of expanding the Sunbury ground has led to the transference of most of its major matches to the Madejski Stadium, Reading. Its value to Irish rugby may have diminished but the club will remain a meeting place of the Irish.

TOP ▧ Simon Geoghegan. London Irish, Bath and Ireland. Ireland 36 caps
ABOVE LEFT ▧ Jim Staples. London Irish. Harlequins 1991-97, 27 caps
ABOVE RIGHT ▧ Hugo MacNeill. Dublin University, Oxford University, Blackrock College.
Ireland 1981-88, 38 caps.

This chapter has evolved through talking to five friends from university days: H.S. O'Connor, A.R. Dawson, T.W.R. Meates, J.R. West and R.D. Hearn. Each has made a remarkable contribution to rugby and in their careers, to life in Ireland or in England. It has been included because it illustrates many of the qualities mentioned in the book: dedication, pride and expertise and not just in a sporting environment.

It seems appropriate that my first interview for this book on Irish Sport should have been with Danny Hearn. He was born in Ireland, educated in England and Ireland, played rugby for and schoolmastered in England and has a house in the West of Ireland to which he retired at the end of 2000. Danny was educated at public school in England at Cheltenham attending both the junior school and college. Many southern Irish Protestant families sent their sons to Protestant schools in England. Cheltenham was a popular choice as it was readily accessible via the ferries from Ireland and then by rail or car. The Irish influence in the educational world in England was complimented by an influx of English into the Irish universities, particularly Trinity College, Dublin. The attraction to Trinity for overseas students not only those from the British Isles but also the Commonwealth countries, was particularly strong in the early and middle years of the 20th century. The late 1960s saw the end of English grants to students to study at Trinity, the troubles in the north escalated, the ban on Catholic students attending Trinity was abolished and Trinity became largely a university for the Irish of all religious denominations. This led to a decline in overseas students. ▪

Danny went to Trinity and read economics and political science between the years 1960 and 1964. Amongst other old boys from Cheltenham at Trinity around the same time were Martin Rees (scrum-half and Welsh trialist) and Jonah Barrington (later world squash champion). Post-war Dublin offered a marked contrast between the professional middle class, the student and the poor. Most students could afford the pleasures of the then unspoilt Georgian Dublin. It was a wonderful place to be a student. Danny came from a well-known Cork family, his grandfather was Bishop of Cork and his father played scrum-half for Cork Constitution. Danny quickly established himself in a good Trinity side, which had an outstanding back-line: Rees, Reid, Hearn and for a time Gibson. Martin Rees (the captain) and Bob Reid (who was to play for England) were the established half-back partnership. Michael Gibson was denied his favoured fly-half position and chose to join and play for Wanderers, one of Dublin's best club sides. Gibson was to complete his university career at Cambridge where he gained a blue and was to go on to play for Ireland and the Lions with outstanding success. Danny Hearn earned his reputation as a hard tackler; it was this characteristic which was to lead to fame and sad misfortune. In one match for Trinity against Instonians, having beaten David Hewitt on the outside, he was crunched by the two opposition wings arriving at the same time, and he ended up in Paddy Dun's Hospital with a dislocated hip, which kept him out of rugby for a while.

Soon interprovincial rugby beckoned and a trial for Munster at Limerick in which he found himself marking Jerry Walsh (an Irish international and a doctor). Danny was not selected. After graduating from Trinity, he went to Oxford University. In 1965 he was selected for the Irish Universities to play South Africa, but, in a previous match in making a tackle, his finger caught in the pocket of his opposition centre; he broke his finger and was unable to play against the South Africans. In the annual Oxford and Cambridge match of 1965 the Irish selectors came to watch and to assess those with Irish qualifications; namely, Craig, Dorman, Houston, Hearn. Danny was very much in the Irish selectors' eyes but England were interested in him as well – Danny was a realist, he knew other centres in Ireland were strong (Walsh, Gibson, Casey, Bresnihan) and that his English taint was a problem. He had been sent to Cheltenham to get rid of his Irish accent. Danny was playing club rugby for Bedford. He was eligible for both Ireland and England since his mother was English and his father Irish. An offer for an Irish trial came, but the whisper was he would be picked for England if he publicly turned down the offer of an Irish trial. Danny opted to play for England and was selected for the match v France in Paris in February 1966. He was chosen for his tackling ability, he remembers the game for being short-arm tackled by the French centre, and Wynne Walters, the diminutive referee who always wore a blazer or jersey to referee, saying 'that he would have done something about it if he had not got up'. He also played in the last match of the 1966 season against Scotland at Murrayfield.

As I sat watching cricket – Haileybury v Oundle at Haileybury on a sunny early summer's day, Danny began to eagerly reminisce: 'Lansdowne Road is the oldest international ground; still unspoilt. They will sell it for development and build a new stadium outside the city. You know the two teams used to share the same baths and toilets. England players were allowed to keep their jerseys after each match but the Irish side was allowed only to keep two jerseys for the four matches of the home internationals. The Scots had to buy their own jerseys. I remember in 1953 watching Oxford University playing Major Stanley's XV at Iffley Road. Jackie Kyle played; he was my hero.' I thought back to 1957–Ireland v France; it was the first time I had been to Lansdowne Road. Kyle scored a great try in the 11-6 victory.

'Great Irish players of my era were Ronnie Dawson, an outstanding hooker and captain of the British Lions in 1959.' I remembered meeting Ronnie at Jammets with the South Africans: Mostert, Sang, Dawson and de Wet. Jammets was a favourite restaurant amongst the undergraduates and their friends. Here Eamon and his colleagues used to serve pea soup, prawn cocktail, and large tender and thick steaks and a Gaelic coffee for the princely sum of £1.

'Noel Murphy, flanker for Cork Constitution and Ireland, taught me about back row play, he was a great reader of the game. The modern game is very different, the players take such a battering and they are all so strong, skilful and quick. The chest hits particularly on the fly-halves and centre are awesome. The back-up team, for the English tour to South Africa, is almost equivalent in numbers to the players; there are physiotherapists, dentists, doctors, fitness, forward, back and kicking experts. It's not so much fun these days; winning is all important, evenings out are rare and boredom is a real factor on a tour. Many players do not survive the demands. Eric Miller the Irish back row player in the 1998 and 1999 seasons may be an example of a young player "burnt out" before his day. You know, when the great All Black side of 1962 came to Ireland, I watched them practice in College Park and was very disappointed that all they did was to play soccer. Actually, they almost lost the international; Johnny Fortune, who was known for being blind, caught a long pass and scored.

'You know, Ireland in the 1960's was very poor and almost backward. The West of Ireland was particularly isolated and poor. The 1990's have seen huge changes; a swagger and confidence has appeared; emigration has declined and many Irish are now returning. Europe has been the answer, and increased prosperity and confidence has been achieved "not on the coats of England". I boxed for Trinity. Trinity boxing was very strong – they won the British University Championships on many occasions in the 1950's and 1960's. Fred Tiedt who won a silver medal in the 1953 Olympics and Frankie Kerr, a tailor by trade were the trainer and the coach; a marvellous pair who created many a champion in the old Trinity gym. I could go on and on but I would like to end with some of my memories. We played for fun, losing was not the end of the world; now rugby is big business. After my injury I was confined to a wheelchair and for many years I coached the Haileybury XV. It was great fun. The Haileybury connection with

Ireland is completed by the fact that Dr. Stevenson, an old Haileyburian, won 42 caps for Ireland.' Danny Hearn received his paralysing injury in making a tackle against the touring New Zealander side in 1967 – he has not allowed the injury to deter his interest in rugby or his zest for life. ■

Hubie S. O'Connor played in all the Five Nations matches of the 1957 season and has been an eminent doctor in Dublin for many years. Hubert Stephen O'Connor was born in Merrion Square, Dublin. His father, a doctor, moved when Hubie was five to County Sligo where he set up practice in the small village of Enniscrone. At the age of twelve Hubie was sent to Terenure College in Dublin; bullying was prevalent and the only way to overcome the problem was to take up rugby. Soon he became a member of an excellent Terenure College 1st XV, which won the Leinster Senior Schools Cup (1952) the first Terenure side to achieve this feat. Hubie also played Gaelic football for the County Sligo minor team.

Hubie's ambition was to be a doctor, but having failed Irish in the School's Leaving Certificate, he knew he would be unable to attend the Catholic UCD but Trinity was a possibility despite the fact that he was a Catholic, provided the Archbishop of Dublin (John Charles McQuaid) would give his permission – Hubie's father insisted on this. Permission was granted on the understanding that he did not become a member of the Philosophical or Historical Societies or play rugby for the University. Hubie did join the Philosophical and Historical Societies and an invitation from Robin Roe, an international and Divinity student and future Chaplain General of the British Forces to play rugby for the university proved too difficult to refuse.

Hubie O'Connor went on to tell me: 'The following year I was invited to play interprovincial rugby for Connaught. We somehow seemed to beat Ulster on every occasion. We were also the first Connaught side ever to beat Leinster at Lansdowne Road. I played in five Irish trials. Eventually, in 1957, I was capped to play in all four internationals as open side wing forward. Like everyone else who gets a cap for the first time I felt I did not deserve it. I was too young (22) I was too light (13 stone) and I felt I was not ready for it!

'My first international match was at Lansdowne Road against France. The atmosphere in the Lansdowne Pavilion was quiet but tense. Everyone appeared to be getting psychologically prepared for the match. The locker room was no different to any other but on this occasion there was something special. The green jerseys were laid out in numerical order around the square room with its cold cement floor. We each walked towards our own number. I picked mine up. The number 6 seemed to fill the whole back of the jersey. I caught Jackie Kyle's eye – he smiled and gave me an assuring wink. Tony O'Reilly quietly shook my hand – he said nothing. There was no need to; we had played with and against each one another during our school days. Cecil Pedlow whispered, "Welcome to the most exclusive club in the country" and then Andy Mulligan, always smiling, came over. He shook my hand and said quietly, "Well, we made it." I was so pleased he included me in the "we".

'I remembered our first meeting in Cambridge almost a year before. We had an excellent match, Trinity going down by 14-12. I was most impressed by the Cambridge scrum-half. He was by far the best player on their side. Following a long hot soak in a bathtub (only Oxford and Cambridge appeared to have individual bathtubs) we met up in the Hawks Club. Andy came over to me with a large enamel jug full of rather insipid beer. I congratulated him on his excellent game and said: "Andy, with a name like yours, you must have some Irish ancestry. Where were you born?" "I was born in India (pronounced Indria). But I do believe Grandpapa was born in Ireland (pronounced Ahland), Bally–something or other", he replied in his faultless Oxbridge accent. "Andy, would you like to play for Ireland?" I asked. "Rather! Where is it?" he replied showing all of his 32 perfect white teeth.

'On my return to Dublin I reported my new discovery to Cyril Boyle, one of the Irish selectors. It was an excellent excuse for all five selectors to attend the Varsity match in Twickenham the following week. Andy had a great game. Apparently "Grandpapa" came from Ballymena. He soon played for Ulster and, within six weeks of our conversation Andrew Armstrong Mulligan was playing scrum-half for Ireland. We were now ready to play against France, but there were some delays. We went outside for our photographs and then back into the pavilion. We warmed ourselves jumping up and down – our metal studs making a deafening clatter on the cement floors. Officials and selectors kept coming in and out. Every time the door opened there was a huge roar from the crowd; they sounded happy. The clatter of studs suddenly stopped. There was silence in the room. Our captain Noel Henderson gave a short speech. The air was thick with the smell of oil, sweat and wintergreen. He ended his speech by welcoming the four new caps – there was more backslapping and then another long wait. The French team must go out first. Eventually the door opened. "Right lads, good luck!"

'We clattered out onto the hard path, through a small gate and onto the pitch. The mowed soft grass was wet. Andy fired a "torpedo pass" at me. It was hard as a rock. It is going to be slippery I thought. I had reached the middle of the pitch before I realised that I had missed the welcoming roar of 50,000 fanatical supporters. All my life I had waited for this great moment – and I had missed it! Concentration seems to overcome the roar of the crowd. We lined up to meet the President, His Excellency Sean T. O'Kelly. He was tiny. He wore a yellow Crombie coat with a belt. He wished me well, shook my hand and walked on.

'Only now I became aware of my opposite number. The French wing forward was nodding at me. I nodded back and smiled. He kept nodding and eventually smiled. All his teeth were metal. He looked about 40 years of age. He was only five feet tall and almost five feet broad. He had bulging muscles everywhere. His jet-black hair was going slightly grey. He rolled up his sleeves, showed a tattoo on his bronze bulging arms. He looked like a small heavyweight boxer (I was later to find out that he actually was a boxer). Suddenly the National Anthem was played. I stood straight and looked at the Irish flag. I was prepared to die, and die I almost did. Just after the first scrum as I was peeling off someone said "Scusi". I turned and almost said "Yes" but this was cut off by a sickening hammer blow into my liver. I don't think I had ever felt so much sickening pain. I just collapsed. I was eventually able to get up. No one had seen the incident. The ball had gone into touch. There was a merciful delay. I staggered over to the line-out. Ronnie Kavanagh asked: "Hugh, are you all right?" I nodded. I could not speak. "Never mind, I will get him", he said. Somehow or other I staggered through the match. Ronnie did get our boxing friend. Our revenge was made sweeter by a good victory. We won 11-6. Jackie Kyle was at his mercurial best scoring a great try in the second half.

'The team remained unchanged for the next match against England. On the morning of the match I had an exam (I had missed so many tests that this one was obligatory). So I rushed through the exam and about an hour before the finish, I left the exam hall and rode on my bicycle up to The Shelbourne Hotel. I put my bike up against the railing at Stephen's Green and walked over to the large crowd which was endeavouring to get in. A tall and imposing doorman was adamant "No one else is getting in. All the tickets are gone", he explained. I firmly stated that I had to get in, but he refused "No more will get in", he declared. "But, I am actually playing!" I said rather frantically. Cyril Boyle, a selector, saw me and I was eventually admitted.

' "Jaysus", said the green-clad custodian of the now firmly closed door. "I am sorry about dat. Is there anything I can do for you?" I replied: "It's all right, it's not your fault, but yes you can do me a favour. Could you please keep an eye on my bicycle, that's it over there leaning against the railings." Some three days later I picked up my bicycle, still in the same place.

'We went to Lansdowne Road by bus – just 15 of us; it felt very empty. The roads were packed with thousands of people all walking to see us play. I hoped sincerely that we would not let them down. We were again in the same pavilion. Once we had changed there were more photographs. The most senior members of the team would sit in chairs. The newer and younger members would stand behind. Tony O'Reilly said to me, "Hubie would you stand beside me for this photograph?" "Of course" I replied, rather pleased and walked behind one of the chairs. He followed and said, "Move down". So I moved. "More" he said; I moved again. "More" he demanded and I moved right down to the very end. I now found myself standing in a hole. "Hey Tony I am standing in a hole", I said. "Quiet, they are taking the photographs", he replied. I was about to protest when I heard the ripple of rugby boot studs. "Hold it", came the order. "Smile everyone" and umpteen photographs were taken. Too late I became aware that the standing group beside me were all on their toes. My head was at the level of Tony's elbow – he was grinning like a Cheshire cat. This photograph shows 14 strong fine Irish men, and a midget at one end! Many years later people would still come up to me and say, "Do you know you are much bigger than I thought!"

'The match was fairly uneventful apart from the fact that Jackson – possibly the fastest man playing rugby at that time scored a try against us. This was the only try we conceded all that year. Sadly our excellent wing three-quarter Niall Brophy broke his ankle. There were no substitutes allowed in those days, so I had to leave the scrum and play on the wing for the very first time in my life! I had great fun out there and almost scored on one occasion from Tony's cross kick, but Jackson beat me to the touchdown.

ABOVE ▧ 1957 England v Ireland at Twickenham. H.S. O'Connor with the ball supported by Jack Kyle.

'Towards the end of the match came my one great moment. I followed up a long cross kick, again from Tony. I ran as fast as I could but Jackson beat me to it. He gathered up the ball, turned, and sidestepped. There was no one in the English half of the field apart from Jackson and myself. It was a very lonely place out there. He sidestepped again but I hung on to him. If the Gods were with me he might try again – one sidestep more and I would have him. He did. I hammered in a good tackle and he dropped the ball. I can still hear the roar of the crowd. We were most unfortunate not to score. As I got up, Jackson gave me an approving pat on the head. "Well done," he said. That was the way rugby was so many years ago!

'We flew to Scotland in an old rusty Dakota. It seemed to take half a day to get to Edinburgh. Now I felt an "old hand". At long last I was one of the team. We played in a snowstorm – the pitch was nothing more than frozen mud. I was able to tackle their out-half every time he got

ABOVE ■ In the 1950s the Irish sides used to fly by Aer Lingus Dakotas for away matches. Cardiff for instance took one and a half hours. Tony O'Reilly took the opportunity to give a running commentary on the landing. Included in this photograph are A.R. Dawson, then a reserve to Robin Roe; P.J. Berkery, Gordon Wood and in the front row H.S. O'Connor, J.R. Kavanagh, A.J.F. O'Reilly, P.J.A. O'Sullivan and two selectors.

the ball. He was eventually switched into centre for the second half. I felt that was a most wonderful compliment. I was well satisfied with the match. We won. To get our boots off we all had to cut our shoelaces open with a penknife since they had been frozen over!

'Our last match was against Wales in Cardiff. After the photographs we were asked to come onto the pitch from "the other side of the ground". Wales would come in from the cricket side. So the Irish team set off on the long walk around the outside of the stadium. We came in with thousands of red-scarved Welsh supporters. One burly man came up and hit me quite hard – it didn't hurt, I smiled – he looked embarrassed. As we stood in the centre of the field, listening to Bread of Heaven the skies opened. There was a torrential downpour. Soon I was standing in a pool of water. Good, I thought, I will be able to get Cliff Morgan in this wet!

'It would be my last and best game for Ireland. I was so fit I could run forever. It was impossible to hold the ball, so I had a field day against the great Welsh Wizard. There was mud everywhere. Following a Welsh line-out, the ball was whisked to Cliff Morgan under his posts. Like Jackson he tried to sidestep me twice. I caught him. He tried to hand me off and his thumb almost excised my left eye. At the same time he dropped the ball and Ronnie Kavanagh fell on it. We were five points up at half-time. In the second half the referee had to stop the match. There was so much mud on everyone he could not distinguish the Welsh from the Irish Players. One team would have to go off and change. As the visiting team, we were given the first option. Noel Henderson said, rather unwisely, "We came on in green and we will go off in green!" I just wondered did we have another set of green jerseys. So the delighted Welsh team disappeared for quite some time, while we ran around trying to keep warm in our wet muddy jerseys which now weighed almost a ton. Eventually the Welsh side reappeared in clean white togs and red jerseys without numbers. They all smelt of brandy. They pinned us down to our line for the rest of the match. They got a penalty – it was now 5-3. We were well into extra time when again one of our backs was caught offside; another penalty, and we lost 6-5.

'I returned to Dublin saddened but immensely satisfied. I had now nine months of medicine to catch up with. I put away my boots, forgot my rugby and began to study. I eventually qualified and was offered the post of house surgeon to Mr Nigel Kinnear at the Adelaide Hospital, a most excellent teaching hospital. When I reminded Mr Kinnear that I was a Roman Catholic he replied briskly: "Never mind, it is time we had a change".'

In November 1957 together with his great rugby-playing friend, Peter Dowse, Hubie was offered a scholarship to the University of Lyon provided that they played rugby for ASUL–the Academie Sociale University of Lyon. The idea of going to Oxford was forgotten. In a remarkable rugby season ASUL became the Champions of France with two Irish doctors being their outstanding players. There followed a career in gynaecology and obstetrics; firstly at the Rotunda Hospital (Dublin), then twelve years in London where he played for London Irish before a broken finger forced his retirement from the game and finally Hubie returned to Dublin to set up practice. H.S. O'Connor has reached the pinnacle in rugby and in his chosen profession of medicine.

A R.Dawson has had a glittering career in rugby; captain of Ireland 11 times, 27 international caps, coach and administrator at all levels and a career in architecture with the Bank of Ireland. I met Ronnie in Dublin on Wednesday 21st March 2001 and on other occasions later in the year. We talked about Irish rugby. Ronnie believes that the inconsistencies of the international match results in the 1980s follow a pattern which existed for many years and were carried on into the 1990s, but that the most striking event was the announcement at the 1995 Paris meeting of the International Rugby Board which declared the game 'open' or professional. It was perhaps an inevitable decision; there was too much pressure on the international players who were amateur. They were expected to play matches at all levels: international, interprovincial and club, together with out of season tours and Rugby World Cup and all the necessary training and preparation.

LEFT ▪ Ronnie Dawson: Captain of the 1959 Lions.

Ronnie told me: 'The World Cup commenced in 1987 and it was the first tournament to put the greatest pressure on the players. The next World Cup in 1991 continued the trend; pressure was increased by the media and commercial companies and many of the players responded by what could be loosely called "regarding rugby as a freelance professional occupation". Thus the players had the best of both worlds; they could continue to do their day-to-day work and be rewarded for playing rugby football – a sort of "shamateurism". There was an obvious need to review the amateur regulations. The Unions were canvassed as to their opinion and many wished to hold on to the amateur ethos but pressure from television, the media and the players themselves made this difficult.

'The situation in Ireland was that rugby was relatively well-structured but still totally amateur and the Irish Rugby Football Union was in favour of retaining this position. Rugby football is played at all levels throughout Ireland, North and South and there is a sound pyramid structure from school to youth, to club, to interprovincial, to international. Rugby is the fourth game of consequence in Ireland behind the two Gaelic Games and Soccer. Thus there are only about 15,000 adult players to pick the international side from. By comparison, England has over 350,000 adult players. New Zealand has a population similar in size to Ireland's four million, but rugby football has a long tradition there as the national game and a large proportion of adults play the sport. Irish rugby has over the years depended to a great extent on the schools – the well-established secondary schools both North and South have retained a great tradition of rugby football. In the past the dedication of schoolmasters in coaching the game has been the key factor, but this influence has diminished somewhat in recent years although the schools' competition in each of the provinces is still looked upon with great interest and continues to provide excellent players to the higher levels. The Irish Schools international team has competed very successfully since the introduction of Schools international matches.

'Following the declaration of professionalism in 1995, many Irish players left to play for the leading clubs in Britain and in France. Although it did not favour a professional game, the IRFU reacted quickly to the situation. It was seen that the domestic game and international team would suffer if an exit of top players was allowed to continue. The IRFU invested heavily in the provincial structure and also at national level; a committee was formed to negotiate with and encourage the Irish players playing outside Ireland to return home and become contracted to the IRFU. It was considered that the Irish club and provincial structures would be more suited to their needs as professionals. Most players who went to Britain and France did return, but some stayed, most notably Keith Wood and Jeremy Davidson. Keith Wood was contracted with Harlequins but he did arrange for the 2000 season to take a year out in order to play for Munster; memorably they reached the final of the European Cup. Following the Lions Tour to Australia in 2001 Jeremy Davidson decided to return to play for Ulster.

'Other things were happening too. Italy joined the Home Unions and France to make the Six Nations Championship (2000) and the European Rugby Cup was brought into place. Tom Kiernan and Dr Syd Millar were prime movers in the establishment of the European Rugby Cup. Because of friction between the larger English clubs, the Rugby Football Union and the European Cup Committee, English clubs did not take part in the first year of this competition. The successes of Ulster who won the competition, Munster who were beaten finalists, to a lesser extent Leinster and also Connacht's performance in the European Shield since the inauguration of the competitions, have been a great boost for the improvement and development of rugby in Ireland.

'This success has been mainly due to the financial injection into the game by the IRFU and the establishment of off-field support structures. For instance the investment in players and coaches now stands at over IR£8 million a year; the Union has 150 contracted players, but the IRFU, through good management of its affairs over the last two decades, has a fund which stands at over IR£20 million. The salaries for international players abroad may well be more attractive but the policy of the Irish Union to try to curtail the number of matches in any one season played is aimed to reduce the pressure and is welcomed by the players. A new competition, the Celtic League involving Irish, Welsh and Scottish teams has been introduced. This, together with all other existing international commitments will mean that contracted professional players will not be in a position to play many, if any, matches for their clubs. In a contact game, with tackles and commitment harder than at any time in the history of the game, there has to be time for rest and recovery and the IRFU advise that no more than 25 to 30 games should be played. In England players play many more games than this.

'The IRFU has a good relationship with its players. For instance medical and training resources are financed by the Irish Union through the pyramid structure from school to international level but club rugby has suffered with the arrival of professionalism; the IRFU priorities have to be with the international and provincial squads. The clubs need to recognise this and to continue to build and develop club rugby, in most cases on an amateur basis, for the continued enjoyment to all involved at this level and with some financial support from the IRFU.

'In regard to coaching, Ireland has had some excellent contributors. Perhaps outstanding amongst these has been Tom Kiernan whose successes with Munster and the Irish side have been exceptional. In recent years the IRFU have engaged coaches from overseas to coach the national side. Murray Kidd, a New Zealander (1995-97), Brian Ashton, an Englishman (1997-98) and Warren Gatland, a New Zealander (1998-2001) have coached the Irish squad. The coach has a full support staff on the fitness, playing and medical sides in order to ensure that the international teams achieve their best against opponents and to ensure that injuries are treated early and properly. Each provincial squad has a similar set up. With all this expertise the Irish side has improved, but so have the other rugby nations. Ireland with its small numbers to select from may well continue to be inconsistent in its international results. For progress to be sustained it is vital that the Irish provincial teams continue to compete in the final stages of the European Cup as this will provide the best opportunity for growth at national level. Such progress and success is vital to the ongoing financial and developmental stability of the Irish Rugby Football Union.

'The Munster provincial side has over the years made a tremendous contribution to Irish rugby; support for the Munster side stems from the cities of Limerick and Cork and all over the province they will and roar their side to success. Munster provides a high proportion of the Irish side. Outstanding amongst these are Mick Galwey, Peter Clohessy, and the half-back pairing of Ronan O'Gara and Peter Stringer is excellent, who together with Leinster's Brian O'Driscoll and Denis Hickie, make as good an Irish back line as seen for some time. The "A" team is also playing with skill and ability and thus Ireland has a quality reserve side.

'The disruption of the 2001 international season, due to enforced restrictions because of the serious outbreak of foot and mouth disease in Britain, was most unfortunate. Who knows what would have happened had the continuity of the first two wins of 2001 been allowed to continue? However, there are still problems; the set scrums don't look as steady as they might and there are lapses in concentration and decision-making, but this will always happen. Another encouragement has been the excellent results of Ireland's under-age teams in recent years.

'Since the advent of professional Rugby Union the game has become more structured. Defences have become more sophisticated and the influence of Rugby League is very apparent in this area. Referees often seem to ignore the requirement to put the ball straight into the set scrum and since the introduction of lifting support for the jumper in the line-out, primary possession at these two phases of play has become utterly predictable. The desire to make international rugby an entertainment event may have merit, but the fact that the laws relate to the game and players at all levels, amateur as well as professional, must not be overlooked. The safety of players must remain a priority.

'Lansdowne Road is the oldest rugby ground in the world, the IRFU are proud of it and it has been developed within the financial limits of the resources of the IRFU. It has many attractions, being easily reached by road and rail and by foot from the city centre but there are difficulties. It is bounded by Lansdowne Road, a railway line, the River Dodder and listed buildings. A new stadium was considered but there is not the space to accommodate the safety regulations which go with an international ground. To give themselves another option, the IRFU did purchase land on the west side of Dublin near the M50 motorway, but in excess of IR£200 million is required to build a stadium which poses financial questions especially with the high costs of running a professional game. However, the Irish Government proposes to build a Campus Ireland at Abbotstown that will include a number of sporting facilities, one of which is a state-of-the-art international stadium which could be used for international rugby matches. The IRFU are in negotiation with the Government with a view to being one of the tenants of the new stadium. Lansdowne Road will certainly, in the near future, be retained as a rugby ground; it has a capacity for a 49,500 crowd but there is seating for only 24,000. The stadium could be developed with a lower all-seated capacity, with more facilities for patrons and needs of corporate entertainment would have to be looked at, but it has a very special atmosphere. The IRFU has also been involved with the improvement of the provincial grounds. Major development has taken place at Musgrave Park, Cork, Thomond Park, Limerick and Ravenhill Park, Belfast and top quality floodlighting has been installed at Lansdowne Road and four provincial grounds.

'I served as one of Ireland's two representatives on the International Rugby Board for 20 years. The International Board originally consisted of two representatives from each of the foundation members' unions: England, Scotland, Ireland, Wales, Australia, New Zealand, South Africa and France. More recently the Board has expanded to include Argentina, Canada, Italy and Japan and FIRA. Since the declaration of an "open game" in 1995 the Board has changed its structure. Formerly the executive council was charged with the responsibility of governing rugby worldwide but with one honorary secretary. These days the IRB offices are located in Dublin with a staff of over 30 people. The Executive Council, under the Chairmanship of Mr Vernon Pugh QC, has representatives from each of the Unions formerly mentioned. The Council divides its work into Committees, for instance, Policy, Laws, Game Regulations, Anti-Doping, Referees, International Matches and Tours, Finance, Medical, Women's Rugby Advisory and so on. I was Chairman of the International Matches and the Tours committees for a number of years. This was an interesting task; the main considerations were to ensure that there was a relatively equal balance between tours by the southern hemisphere unions to the northern hemisphere unions and to incorporate the long established unions, such as the United States, Canada, Japan, Argentina, Samoa and Fiji into a regular tour schedule. The basic problem now is that rugby is now virtually a 12 month game and the physical demands on the players are too great and, as previously stated, the maximum number of games played by international players during a year must be reduced.'

Ronnie Dawson's career lasted between 1950 and 1965. He played for Wanderers in Dublin, Leinster, Ireland, the Barbarians and the Lions. It was a magnificent career, capped by captaining each of these sides and being involved in some memorable matches. He played for the Barbarians before receiving his first cap for Ireland. Robin Roe was the Irish hooker between 1952 and 1957. Ronnie's first cap was in January 1958 in the 9-6 victory over Australia at Lansdowne Road. Before that he played for the Barbarians on the Easter tour of 1956 and the tour to South Africa in 1957. The South African tour was very successful. The Barbarians always play the last match of the major incoming touring team's games. Thus in 1958, Ronnie played against the Australians and captained the side in the games against South Africa (1961) and New Zealand (1964).

Ronnie continued: 'We were the only side to beat the 1961 Springboks. It was an extraordinarily dirty day in the old Cardiff Arms Park; it was an appallingly muddy ground that didn't particularly suit the South Africans. I lost the toss with Avril Malan, the South African captain and he chose to play against a very considerable wind. I thought at the time that our best chance of winning was to score first and try to hang on to our lead. We did score first and managed to hold on to win the match. A significant fact was an enormous tackle which our full-back, Haydn Mainwaring made on a South African player as he was going for the line. It was a boneshaker. It was probably the most important event of that match. The 1964 match against New Zealand ended in us being badly beaten. It was a fine New Zealand side captained by Wilson Whineray and amongst those in the New Zealand touring party who were unbeaten in their internationals were Don Clarke, Ken Gray, Colin Meads and a great back row of Waka Nathan, Kel Tremain and John Graham. Ireland lost their match with the New Zealanders to a late penalty.

'I have fond memories of my first international for Ireland. It was against Australia in 1958. I scored a try but the match was best remembered for the great try that Noel Henderson scored to win the match. George Leech, the ageing Irish Times photographer, summed the try up beautifully by saying: "Well Noel, I got your photograph when you took the pass from David Hewitt on the Irish 25 and I was round behind the goal line to 'snap' you touch it down." That was an indication of Noel's reducing pace at the end of his career. A great player, a great administrator and a great friend who alas is no longer with us.'

Ronnie Dawson not only had a magnificent career as a player but also as a coach and administrator. He has been president of his club, province and national union and has been selector and coach at all levels including the British Lions. He has also served on committees for the Barbarians, Six Nations International Rugby Board, The Wanderers Club, Leinster Branch IRFU and the Irish Rugby Football Union. A career associated with senior rugby lasting from 1950 to 1994. ■

ABOVE ▪ Ronnie Dawson with George Leech outside the Wanderers Club House at Lansdowne Road in the early 1970s. George Leech served in the Royal Flying Corps and was for many years a photographer with the Irish Times.

Roly Meates has had a distinguished career in rugby, particularly as a coach, and he is a prominent dentist in Dublin. I asked Roly how he had become so involved with coaching. He replied: 'I played for the 1st XV for the High School in Dublin. I was very keen but not an outstanding player and so when I entered Trinity to study dentistry in 1956, I knew it would be hard to get on the Trinity 1st XV. I therefore played a season for the Wanderers 2nd XV as a prop. The next year I was picked for Trinity and thus began a long association with the university rugby side. It was a good era in the history of Trinity rugby; we won the Leinster Senior Cup for the first time for 35 years under the excellent captaincy of Tony Reid-Smith. He went on to play in an Irish trial. Other outstanding Trinity players of the 1950s and early 1960s were Peter Dowse, Hubie O'Connor and George Patrikios. The university played an adventurous style and it was great fun.

'I also played for Leinster, the Combined Irish Universities and the Wolfhounds (the Irish equivalent of the Barbarians). Some of my playing colleagues on the Irish Universities side were: Tom Kiernan, Jerry Walsh, Ray McLoughlin, Bud McMullen, Caleb Powell, Frank Byrne, Billy Mulcahy, George Patrikios. I went on to play for Wanderers for about six seasons with amongst others, Mike Gibson, Gerry Culliton, Ronnie Dawson, Wally Borneman, Andy Mulligan and Ronnie Kavanagh. At one stage I was captain of Wanderers, but after an injury and mindful of recurrence of an eye injury which could affect my career as a dentist, I decided to stop playing. I was at a loose end, still young and fit and keen to put something into rugby. It was then that Cyril Boyle, a member of the Trinity rugby hierarchy, asked me to come and help with the Trinity side. At first it was just the training sessions but soon it was a proper coaching regime with the 1966/67 Trinity team captained by David Buchanan. Trinity had gone through a lean period since the early 1960s despite having players of the calibre of Martin Rees (Wales reserve scrum-half), Bob Reid (England) and Danny Hearn (England). They had only won the Colours match with UCD once. However, a number of excellent players came into Trinity from the late 1960s; some were good enough to go on and play for Ireland. Amongst these were Billy McCombe, Paddy Johns, Gerry Murphy, Phil Orr, Hugo MacNeill, Donal Spring, Brendan Mullin, Des Fitzgerald, Harry McKibben, Frank Ellis, Fergus Dunlea, John Sexton (he had not played much rugby until he came to Trinity). Then, of course, Chris Hawksworth got four blues at Oxford and Mike Roberts was capped for Wales and the Lions.

'It was always great fun coaching Trinity sides. Generally most of the players were 20 to 22 years of age and they had a tremendous appetite and enthusiasm for the game. We tried to play positively, sometimes we were not so good but, overall, it was a very satisfying task. In fact I only stopped coaching the Trinity side in 1995 but I still take an interest. I like to take an interest with the players by individual contact. I am particularly interested in the technicalities, not only of the front and second row but also of the backs. Trinity has produced a number of very talented backs.

'I was invited to coach the Leinster side in 1970 and did this for five seasons before coaching the Irish side between 1976 and 1977. The tour to New Zealand in the summer of 1976 was a success but we lost all our championship games of 1977 and in 1978 with Noel Murphy coaching the side, only defeated Scotland. However, in 1979 and in 1980, with Tom Kiernan as coach, we did well. Against the All Blacks in November 1978 we lost to an injury time try but in the Championship matches we were generally regarded as the most improved side, only losing narrowly to Wales 21-24 at Cardiff Arms Park but defeating England 12-7 at Lansdowne Road. This meant in the 1970s, Ireland had beaten England six times with four losses. I like to think I had some part in the development of these more successful sides.

'When I look back on the many players it has been my good fortune to encounter during my coaching days, I think that probably in the earlier days, Mike Gibson would have been the outstanding individual. My memories of him would be of absolute attention to detail in his pursuit of excellence, particularly in the tour to New Zealand in 1976. I remember his tremendous commitment to supporting those around him. A top class player, if he is to play well, must have those around him playing well. Again on that tour Tom Grace was a quite outstanding leader and captain. I much admired his unrelenting pursuit of success; he was under tremendous pressure but never flagged in his efforts to ensure a successful tour. Phil Orr and Des Fitzgerald were outstanding props. Brendan Mullin was a centre of rare expertise – he had the ability to swerve and run on to a ball; John Sexton never played rugby until university days but he had intelligence, balance and pace; Paddy Johns just plays with passion and skill and so I could go on…

'Of the coaches of my time J.J. Stewart, the New Zealander, was quite tremendous; all his sides played with total commitment and utter dedication. They were helped by a common pattern of play in their rugby from schoolboy to university, to club, to provincial, to international level, based on Position, Pace and Possession together with knowledgeable coaching at every level. The Welsh used to try to convince us that their coaching structure was just as good and that they could produce players such as Barry John and Gareth Edwards for ever. They didn't lose, I think I am right in saying, a Five Nations game at Cardiff Arms Park in the 1970s but I am convinced it was because their teams consisted of a large number of outstanding players. For instance the 1970s sides contained: Gareth Edwards, J.J. and J.P.R. Williams, Mervyn Davies, Morris the Shadow and the rugged Pontypool front row of Tony Faulkner, Bobby Windsor and Graham Price.' One of Roly Meates major interests in life has been rugby. ∎

John West has been recognised as one of the world's top referees; he has also made successful contributions in the administration field. He has been a dedicated and respected schoolmaster. John was born in Midleton, Co Cork. He came to Trinity in the last 1950s and played rugby for the Trinity 3rd team. He became secretary of the DUFC and after an operation on his neck took up refereeing. 'I was very young for a referee. My very first game came under unusual circumstances. Trinity and Wanderers were both playing in the North of Ireland and as they met at the station which is Amiens Street, now called Connolly Street, there was a phone call to say, "Don't travel north there is black ice there – no matches are going to be played north of Dundalk". The two teams agreed to play in College Park but they suddenly realised they had no referee. I think I was in bed after a party or something or other and was hauled out to referee this match. I remember it was good fun. I can still remember the pace of the game was faster than I was used to, but as I was going off the field Dickie Hartford, the Regius Professor of Divinity, the Right Hon R.R. Hartford DD came up to me and he said, "Well done

John, I thought you refereed extremely well. You only made one mistake and since it led directly to a Trinity try, it was of no consequence." That was the first time I refereed a senior match.'

On leaving Trinity John West joined the teaching staff at King's Hospital where Caleb Powell, an ex Trinity rugby captain, was influential in furthering John's career as a referee. John refereed school matches and after a year was encouraged to join the Referees Association. 'You are watched by two assessors; you start at the very bottom of the pile and you gradually slowly claw your way upwards. You are watched and people report on you to say whether things are going well or not and you are marked; the rugby then was in grades. The highest level of course was the international panel, then just below that was the interprovincial panel. Below that was the Senior Cup panel. It was great to get a Senior Cup game, it meant you had really arrived as a referee and then there was Senior 1 and Senior Junior and so on, right down. The problem was to be watched. One day I had a lucky break. The referee for the Lansdowne and St Mary's match broke his leg and I was asked if I would do the game because they had heard the good report of the game I had refereed recently. Again, frost had a bearing on this. There was quite thick frost in Dublin and almost all matches were off. Now Lansdowne Road had lush grass and the surface was definitely playable and both sides were keen to play, even though it was only a friendly match. So we went along to the game and I found that because all the other games were cancelled and everybody was fed up with the Christmas season and wanted to get away from their wives and the children, they all turned up for the match. So I, who maybe had had two assessors in four years, found I had six assessors for this match! The game went well for me and that established that I was on the move upwards.

'Then a few years later I got on the interprovincial panel and my first interprovincial was in Cork. It was Munster and Connaught. Connaught were good at the time because they had Ray McLoughlin, his brother Felim and Mick Molloy who were all internationals playing in the pack. Cork Constitution, one of the leading clubs in Munster, provided a few of the less quiet members of Irish rugby: "Noisy" Murphy and Tommy Kiernan. I anticipated problems. My good friends Roly Meates and Caleb Powell said, "When you give a penalty against Munster, what is going to happen is that Tom Kiernan is going to walk 50 yards up to you and ask, 'Can you justify it' and Murphy is going to be in your ear at the same time. The only thing we are saying to you is, make sure you get the first penalty right, otherwise you are in real trouble!" Kiernan was captain and "Noisy" Noel was his usual "What was that for Ref?" I was prepared and the game went reasonably well. I can remember Ray McLoughlin at the post-match dinner, after thanking the referee, saying that "He didn't mind John West penalising him for stepping on his opposite number but he did object to the way he grinned maliciously when he penalised him." This would be around 1972.

'In the Centenary year of the IRFU (1973), the President Charlie Conroy from UCD, nominated me as the touch judge for the match at Murrayfield. It was wonderful to travel with the Irish team. The referee was Ron Lewis from Wales. I had done touch judging and I didn't think it was going to be that difficult. The game started in a most peculiar way. There was a kick-off to my side of the pitch and Peter Brown the Scottish second row, jumped up and headed the ball 30 yards forward directly into touch. You couldn't kick the ball directly into touch from outside the 22 but he hadn't kicked it – he had headed it. He was, of course, a soccer player, so I had to decide if it was a line-out, was it going to be level with him or where the ball went in the first time? That was my very first decision in the match. Fortunately I got that one right, and then I got into a controversy. There was a kick at goal by the Scottish scrum-half Duggie Morgan. The Murrayfield posts, which are now enormous things, were then little dumpy ones, the ball swirled as it was coming and it looked as though it was going completely wide but I thought at the last minute it was going over, so I put up my flag to see my opposite number, who was a Scottish international referee, Eric Grierson, shaking wildly to indicate that it wasn't. So there was one touch judge with the flag up and one touch judge saying "not" and the referee who was in no position to see because he was directly in front of the posts and hadn't followed the flight of the ball. He gave the decision with me – that was another very frightening experience. The next controversy involved Tom Kiernan. It was Tom's last game for Ireland; he scored in the corner and as he scored Alistair McHarg dived across to tackle him and knocked the corner post. It was in fact the defender who knocked the post but on television it looked very much as if Tom Kiernan had knocked it before he scored, which of course would have negated the try. There was a great outcry by the locals. In fact there was a very good photograph showing that Kiernan had touched the ball down before the corner flag was knocked but it wasn't clear on television – it looked very much the other way round. So I had no illusions that life was going to be a bed of roses even in the touch judging scenario. I never enjoyed touch judging anything like as much as the refereeing.

'In 1974 I refereed my first international: England v Wales and in 1975 I refereed the Scotland v Wales match at Murrayfield. It was the last not-all-ticket match in Scotland and a crowd of 104,000 was recorded, which was a world record crowd attendance for a rugby match until the Olympic Stadium in Australia clocked 109,000 spectators. 104,000 may have watched the match in 1975 but there was another 14,000, many with tickets, left angry outside the ground.

'Then in 1976 I refereed Wales v France at Cardiff Arms Park. It was the last game of the championship – Wales won a terrific match, which was played at tremendous speed. Also I refereed the 1976 Australia touring side when they played the club sides Cardiff and West Wales, and their international against Wales. I refereed the All Blacks nine times – I think six of these were internationals. In 1978 I refereed the All Blacks twice, once in Rodney Parade, Newport and I also did the Test Match against Scotland in Murrayfield. In 1979 I was chosen to go out to New Zealand. The story there was that New Zealand and France had a very bad record for discipline in New Zealand. France said that they needed a non New Zealand referee and New Zealand said they objected strongly to this idea. So the French said in their civilised, uncompromising way "OK, if we don't have a neutral referee we won't travel". The New Zealanders with very bad grace gave way, and I got a splendid letter from the secretary of the New Zealand Referees saying: "Dear Mr West. My Committee has instructed me to write and congratulate you on your appointment to the two internationals. Although we disagree most vigorously with the idea of having a referee from outside our country coming to do these matches, this will in no way affect your personal welcome." Well it didn't; in fact the referees were very good to me there. They were very encouraging and I got on well with them and the two Test matches were terrific.

'I remember I refereed a warm-up match in Wellington when I arrived, but I hadn't refereed for about eight weeks since it was our summer. I was pretty fit but you need the match sharpness as well. On the way to the ground I asked the driver if he could tell me about the game. I knew it

ABOVE ■ 1977 Toulouse. All Blacks v France, John West refereeing.

was a game between Wellington Athletic and one of the local sides. I asked "What sort of a game is it – is it a serious game or is it a friendly?" "Friendly!" he exclaimed, "there is no such game in New Zealand." The first Test match was in Lancaster Park, Christchurch and I think the score was 23-9 to the All Blacks. You wouldn't have put a penny on the French turning things round in a week's time. You would have given them no chance of coming back to win the one in Eden Park, Auckland which was a super game – absolutely magnificent and the French won it 24-19. There were some wonderful tries. There were ten tries scored in those two matches. The second game ended with the All Blacks attacking and kicking ahead into goal. Three All Blacks were on side with no French men in sight, but Costes the little French wing ran across, caught the ball on the full and put it into touch. That was the last move of the game. Both had won one and lost one and they won and lost with great grace.

'There were some wonderful players in the two teams; in the All Blacks, I think particularly of in the backs: B.W. Wilson, Stuart Wilson, B.J.Robertson and M.W. Donaldson and in the forwards, Andy Haden, Gary Seear, Frank Oliver and Brad Johnstone. Graham Mourie was their captain and a very good one. It was the French backs: Aguirre, Averous, Codorniu, Mesny and Costes, who caught my eye and Jean Pierre Rives was an outstanding wing-forward and captain.

'The Welsh Centenary was in 1980 and they invited New Zealand to play four games prior to the Test match. They selected a referee from each of the "Home Nations" countries to come and referee the four games: Welsby, Hosie, Palmade and myself were the four referees and the All Blacks had the choosing of a referee for the Centenary Test. Happily they selected me! In fact it was a good game and the All Blacks played smashing rugby. However, their kicker Doug Rollerson was a poor place-kicker; he could have won the match easily for New Zealand had all his kicks gone over. Mourie got a marvellous try on the right hand side, following a movement which could have been a Welsh try when Dai Richards broke away and should have scored. I think his legs ran out on him, but the Blacks re-grouped and attacked, the field was wide open and Mourie scored. Bruce Robertson was one of the stars of that lot – they were a very good side. Mourie, Mexted and Shaw were the back row; Shaw and Mexted were very strong. Mourie was a super player, a very good captain and a very good bloke.

'Nicky Allen was the fly-half. He was a bit undisciplined but very gifted. He had a lot of talent. Actually he was involved in a somewhat dubious try as to whether he touched it down or not; I thought he did. Later, sadly, he was killed in a club game in New South Wales. Dave Loveridge was the scrum-half. He was a super player, he was terrific. Wilson and Fraser were on the wings and they had a big pack; Andy Dalton was the hooker. They were a magnificent side and very well disciplined. I like the All Blacks. As I say, I refereed in 20 countries but not necessarily internationals in all countries. In 1985, after the Romania v France match I retired from international refereeing.

'I have always refereed in Trinity socks and it was a proud moment when in 1999 I was elected President of the DUFC. I have been involved with a number of aspects of Irish rugby including the Irish Universities Rugby Union. My brother Trevor had been secretary of the IURU for eleven years before I took over from him. The IURU have been on two tours recently – South Africa in 1994 and Australia in 1997 – where much good rugby has been played and has shown university sport at its best. Also I took over from Roly Meates as the Trinity representative on the Leinster Branch of the IRFU. In 2001, by rotation, I became the President of the Leinster RFU.

'A new role for me has emerged: Citing Commissioner for internationals, whose job it is to report violence undetected by the referee. I was the first Commissioner to view a game; it was Italy and Scotland in Rome 2000 and I have been Citing Commissioner three times. Also, I have been Liaison Officer for visiting rugby sides. I was with the Australian World Cup winning side for six weeks in 1999; a superb bunch, excellently organised on and off the field and worthy world champions – another wonderful experience. Rugby has given me so many wonderful experiences.'

Gerard Siggins was educated at Marian College, Dublin and obtained a history degree at Trinity College, Dublin. Apart from his interest in music and history, he has maintained a keen interest in all things to do with sport, particularly rugby, association football and cricket. He is a great nephew of Con Martin who was an Irish soccer international. From 1989 to 1995 he was Sports Editor of the Sunday Tribune and was an NUJ card-carrying member of Jack's Army in Dalymount Park, Lansdowne Road, Tolka Park, the RDS, Cagliari, Latvia and Hanover and covered the 1990 and 1994 World Cups. He also covered World Cups in cricket and rugby. He is now assistant editor of the Sunday Tribune. He was editor of the Irish Cricket magazine between 1984 and 1987 and president of the Dublin University Cricket Club 1992-97. ■

SEVEN MATCHES THAT SHAPED THE GAME

When Irish soccer hit the halfway point of the 20th century it was only with optimism for the future. We had just achieved the greatest result since the birth of the state when beating England 2-0 at Goodison Park – England's first defeat on home soil at the hands of a foreign nation – and although we had failed to qualify for a play-off for a place in the World Cup finals in Brazil, there were many positives to be taken from the campaign and narrow exit. However, it would be another 40 years before Ireland would reach the world stage as rapid advances in the international game left us far behind. The hope of 1949 disappeared as our status slipped with successive failures to qualify for the big tournaments. We had our near misses, of course, but it was not until the Football Association of Ireland hired an Englishman, World Cup winner in 1966, Jack Charlton, that the national side started to compete at the top level. It was a bleak future that wouldn't have been countenanced in 1949. One of the proudest boasts of our near neighbours was of their eminence in international football, and how they never lost a game at home to 'foreign' opposition until Puskas's Magical Magyars whopped them 6-3 at Wembley in 1953. That statistic has been a sore irritation on this side of the Irish sea for more than half a century – ever since the 21st of September 1949 when a team of Irishmen beat England 2-0 at Goodison.

Ireland was, by then, an extremely foreign entity. All the stages of disengagement from Britain had been passed in the previous 30 years – rebellion, war, treaty and independence. The Republic had been declared the year before and the last link with the Commonwealth sundered. It was an extremely inexperienced Irish side that lined out in Liverpool that Wednesday. Only four men had played more than 10 internationals, and Johnny Carey, with 22 caps, had almost twice as many as the next man – indeed there were only 74 caps between them before kick-off. The main reason for that, of course, was the World War that interrupted football for seven years.

The Irish side came to Goodison with confidence high; two weeks before they had beaten Finland 3-0 to record their first ever World Cup win. The England selectors were keen to try out a few new players in advance of the Home International Championship, which was to serve as a qualifying group for the 1950 World Cup. Three new caps were picked, with Stanley Matthews and Stan Mortensen dropped to accommodate two new forwards: Jesse Pye of Wolves and Peter Harris of Portsmouth. Pye never played again, and Harris only once five years later, so their memories of international football were to be humiliating – they were part of the first England team to lose on home soil to 'foreign' opposition. While those two were sunk without trace, it would not be fair to presume that Ireland caught a weak side cold – they also featured two of the greatest English forwards of all time in Wilf Mannion and Tom Finney.

The home press were certainly refusing to countenance defeat – Henry Rose of the Daily Express suggested a 'brains test' for anyone who might consider Ireland to have a chance of winning. Nine of the Irish side played for clubs in England, so only the Shamrock Rovers pair of Tommy Godwin and Tommy O'Connor travelled over on the mailboat on Sunday night with trainer Billy Lord. The English-based players checked into the hotel in Birkdale on Monday, where they discovered they were a mere 11; the FAI reckoned that there was no need for reserves in those pre-substitution days. Only seven turned up for training at Southport the next day as the train from Birmingham, carrying Con Martin (Aston Villa) and Davy Walsh (WBA) was late, while the Everton pair of Peter Corr and Peter Farrell trained with their own club. There was no such thing as a manager in those days so it was left to captain Johnny Carey to devise the tactics. Godwin had been struggling for Ireland and Rovers, so Carey gave him particular attention. The Manchester United back stood inside the penalty area and threw more than 100 balls at Godwin, testing him in every part of the goal. Watching the exhausted, sweating Godwin didn't inspire confidence in Carey.

The home side attacked in waves for the first 30 minutes, and reports expressed incredulity that they failed to beat Godwin even once. Pye missed two sitters in that time, and was also foiled when Tommy "Bud" Aherne of Luton made a crucial interception. Five Irishmen lined across the field, tackling anything that moved and Godwin kept out anything that slipped through. Carey decided to lay-off Finney, who persisted in trying to beat a man before passing and the result was a drop in tempo in the English attack as by the time Finney crossed, Ireland had the extra men back. Just after the half-hour, O'Connor released Peter Desmond who advanced on the angle of the penalty area. Mozley was beaten for pace and tripped the Middlesbrough inside forward from behind. Con Martin stepped up to take the penalty kick in his usual effective fashion – he galloped up and launched the ball so hard – just a yard to the right of Williams so that, although he got his hands to the shot, the sheer power of Martin's boot bent his fingers back and carried the ball into the net.

Ireland came more into the game after the first goal, and Walsh and Desmond both had chances to score before the interval. After half-time England went flat out for the equaliser – Billy Wright drew a full length save out of Godwin, who later denied Harris (with the help of the crossbar) and Morris. Centre half Martin was back on two occasions to clear the ball off the line. While England pressured, Ireland broke and in the 85th minute made sure of their historic victory before a disbelieving crowd of 51,047.

From the breakdown of an English attack Tommy O'Connor broke away with Peter Farrell keeping pace with him. O'Connor drew two defenders wide before slipping the ball to the Everton man who lobbed the advancing English 'keeper. Within a week Godwin was back in England signing for Leicester City, while Middlesbrough reserve Desmond had made his league debut. The English press did not take the defeat well and refused to accept that their precious home record had been broken. One wrote thus: 'Not only is Ireland part of the British Isles, but only two of the Eire team do not play for English League clubs. How can players like Carey and Martin be regarded as "foreign".'

The teams that lined up that day were as follows:

ENGLAND: (2-3-5) Bert Williams (Wolves), Bert Mozley (Derby), Johnny Aston (Manchester United), Billy Wright (Wolves), Neil Franklin (Stoke), Jimmy Dickinson (Portsmouth), Peter Harris (Portsmouth), Johnny Morris (Derby), Jesse Pye (Wolves), Wilf Mannion (Middlesbrough), Tom Finney (Preston).

IRELAND: (2-3-5) Tommy Godwin (Shamrock Rovers), Johnny Carey (Manchester United), Tommy 'Bud' Aherne (Luton Town), Willie Walsh (Manchester City), Con Martin (Aston Villa), Tommy Moroney (West Ham), Peter Corr (Everton), Peter Farrell (Everton), Davy Walsh (WBA), Peter Desmond (Middlesbrough), Tommy O'Connor (Shamrock Rovers).

Although Ireland failed to qualify for the 1954 and 1958 World Cups, that decade was not the worst we suffered. Only three out of 17 home games were lost, to Argentina, France and Yugoslavia and some notable scalps were claimed, including West Germany, Austria and Holland (4-1 in Amsterdam). But there some awful hammerings: back-to-back 6-0 defeats in Vienna and Madrid, and a 5-1 pasting in Wembley. The return game against England which Ireland needed to win to claim a place in the 1958 World Cup finals, was a famous, epic encounter which saw Ireland lead for 87 minutes through an early Alf Ringstead goal. With injury time running out and the 'Dalymount roar' at crescendo point, a Tom Finney cross was headed in by John Atyeo and, as one reporter famously put it 'the silence was heard in O'Connell Street'. Five of the players that day: Roger Byrne, Duncan Edwards, David Pegg and Tommy Taylor of England, and Ireland's Liam Whelan were dead within the year, perishing on a wintry night in Munich when their Manchester United flight crashed.

On the first day of November 1959, a new era dawned for Irish soccer when a 19 year-old from Blackhall Place in Dublin pulled on the Irish jersey for the first time in the dressing room under the stand at Dalymount Park. Michael John Giles was one of three new caps in an inexperienced line-up, travelling over on the mailboat with his friend, Manchester United colleague and fellow debutant Joe Carolan. Giles was so small that the shorts he was given ended nearer his ankles than his knees. Sweden, beaten in the World Cup final by Brazil the year before, were the opposition, fresh from a 3-2 win over England at Wembley and rapidly took a two-goal lead through Borgesson (7 minutes) and Berndtsson (12 minutes); but the visitors' lead would not last another 12 minutes. Fionan Fagan speculatively lobbed the ball towards the Swedish penalty area, from where the clearance was knocked out to him again. This time he sent in a curling cross which was headed clear, straight to Giles who stood a full 30 yards out. Before the ball fell to earth, Giles volleyed it straight into the top of the net. Many reports stated unequivocally that

Noel Cantwell

Noel Cantwell one of Ireland's most popular sportsmen, was a dual international: cricket and soccer. He played cricket for Cork County and soccer for a number of clubs. In 1952 aged 18, he signed for West Ham, was transferred to Manchester United in 1960 for £29,500, a record for a full-back. He subsequently became player-manager and later, manager at Peterborough. He also served as a manager to Coventry and in the USA. He currently runs a pub in Peterborough.

ABOVE ■ 25th May 1963 at Wembley. Noel Cantwell, skipper of Manchester United, throws the FA Cup into the air as his team-mates look on. United beat Leicester 3-1.

it was the finest goal ever seen at Dalymount and there are many old and middle-aged men who still testify to that. Dermot Curtis equalised shortly afterwards and scored the winner early in the second half. The 40,250 Irish fans went home happy, enthusing about this startling new inside forward that had been uncovered in Manchester United's reserves. He was just two months short of his 20th birthday that day, when he won the first of his 59 caps.

IRELAND (2-3-5): Noel Dwyer (West Ham), Joe Carolan (Man United), Noel Cantwell (West Ham), Mick McGrath (Blackburn), Charlie Hurley (Sunderland), Pat Saward (Aston Villa), Fionan Fagan (Man City), Johnny Giles (Man United), Dermot Curtis (Ipswich), George Cummins (Luton), Joe Haverty (Arsenal).

Although Giles played 59 times for his country, the demands of his club managers meant he missed out on 43 more caps before his retirement in 1979. Ireland's habit of playing internationals on Sundays was not popular with the top English managers and it became routine for Don Revie of Leeds to invent an injury that would prevent Giles travelling. At that time, Noel Cantwell was playing for West Ham. He went on to lead Manchester United in the 1963 FA Cup win, beating Leicester 3-1 at Wembley. ▪

On the 10th November 1965, at the old rugby ground at Stade Colombes in Paris, Ireland arrived at another crossroads in our football history. At stake was qualification for the World Cup finals the next summer, to be held in England. Television had just taken root in Ireland and the prospect of an international event taking part close at hand with an Irish team involved would have given the game an enormous boost. However, it was not to be. We had been reasonably lucky with the draw, ending in a three-team group with Spain and Syria. The Syrians withdrew leaving a head-to-head with the Spaniards, the current European champions. Ireland triumphed 1-0 at Dalymount, but despite taking the lead in Seville, went down 4-1. Aggregate or goal difference was not considered – the tie-breaker was to be another game. London and Paris were offered as venues but when the Spaniards suggested that Ireland could keep all the gate money if the game was held in Paris, the cash-strapped FAI jumped at the offer. More than 30,000 Spaniards swarmed over the border and Colombes resembled a home game for Spain.

Although Charlie Hurley and Alan Kelly were injured, Johnny Giles was available for the game, and was in the thick of it as Ireland created several good chances in the first half. Spain gradually got on top however, and Ireland was forced to rely on the occasional breakaway. Pat Dunne made some notable saves before Spain finally broke through with just 11 minutes left. The incomparable Luis Suarez put Pereda clear, the winger beating Tony Dunne before crossing for Suarez, who missed the ball, which then ran free to the unmarked Ufarte who netted. It was another night of disappointment, made all the harder to take by the controversy over the venue, which contained very few Irish fans – a lone tricolour was spotted among a sea of red and gold in an official attendance of 35,731. The greatest of all Irish football commentators, Philip Greene, remembered the night thus: 'There have been other great results and even victories. The Goodison win in '49, the agonising draw with England in the World Cup, the League of Ireland's terrific win over the Football League in Dalymount – these were great, but the performance in Paris, even though ending in defeat, was the greatest of all. Playing in a foreign field with penny whistle support muted by the engulfing orchestra of Spain, against this all the odds of their opponents' greater endowments and inducements, these modern Wild Geese fought like men possessed with valour and with skill. Nobody who saw them can ever forget them. They can walk tall now and forever.'

IRELAND: Pat Dunne (Man United), Shay Brennan (Man United), Tony Dunne (Man United), Theo Foley (Northampton), Noel Cantwell (Man United), Mick Meagan (Huddersfield), Frank O'Neill (Shamrock Rovers), Eamon Dunphy (York), Andy McEvoy (Blackburn), Johnny Giles (Leeds), Joe Haverty (Shelbourne). ▪

The 1966 World Cup came and went and although it did lead to a huge upsurge in interest in soccer in Ireland, it is still a matter of some regret that the Irish team was not there to play a full part. They weren't in Mexico either and failure to qualify for the 1970 finals persuaded the players that it was time to force the FAI to appoint a national team manager with full control over selection and tactics. The old Everton half-back Mick Meagan was given the job and told to get on with it. His period in charge coincided with a limited range of players to choose from and unprecedented conflict between the squad and the FAI. Meagan ended his twelve games as manager with three draws and nine defeats.

Liam Tuohy took over and his first game, in October 1971, saw a team hit by withdrawals and containing ten League of Ireland players humiliated 6-0 by Austria. The situation improved however under the astute former Shamrock Rovers winger, and the results in the 1974 World Cup qualifiers were indicative of that improvement: beating France 2-1 in Dublin and getting a 1-1 draw in Paris, losing 2-1 and 1-0 to the USSR.

In October 1973 Giles took over as manager, and his first game was a notable 1-0 win over the Poland team that had just knocked England out of the World Cup. Twelve months later, Giles gave a first international cap to Liam Brady in a European Championship qualifier against the Soviet Union. One of the greatest Irish players of all time, Brady, was to go on to win a then record 71 caps. He was a few months younger on debut than Giles, who was by then player-manager of the Irish side. Sporting a mass of hair in the then fashionable Afro style, Brady was instantly taken under Giles's wing and had an assured first cap. The highlight for him was a 30 yard shot which was saved by Pilgui, for an instant taking many observers back 15 years to Giles's own debut.

In his first, ineptly ghosted autobiography *So Far So Good...* (1980), Brady described the scene: 'The place was absolutely electric, it made my blood pump fast and my scalp tingle. The dressing room was a babble of happy voices – jokers, boasters, justifiably proud Irishmen who were determined not to let the moment slip away from them.' Brady's memory had obviously faded a bit, as he went on to describe 'that October night', when it was played on a Wednesday afternoon. Giles described the new star's entry: 'Young Brady was a revelation. He has all the ability in the world and if he applies himself I have no hesitation in nominating him as one of the most successful players of the future.' And while Brady certainly made his mark, it was Don Givens who was the hero of the day, scoring all the goals in a stunning 3-0 win. It was probably Ireland's greatest win since Goodison 25 years before, and the best up to then in a competitive international.

Givens and Brady, like Giles, had emerged from the great Dublin schoolboy nurseries of Rangers and St Kevin's respectively (Giles played for Stella Maris). Givens had promised much, starting his English league career at Manchester United, but like Giles he was to find much greater success when he moved away. He played for Ireland before he ever played for United, but he never made the breakthrough there. Those five years saw him play six times for Ireland and eight times for the club. He moved on to Luton Town for £15,000 and in July 1972 signed for Queen's Park Rangers. It was at Loftus Road that he enjoyed the best period of his career, helping the club to promotion in his first season and to second place in the League behind Liverpool in 1976.

Ireland had done well in the qualifiers for the 1974 World Cup, scoring a win and a draw over France and losing by one-goal margins to the Soviet Union home and away. The USSR was drawn to play Ireland again in the 1976 European Championships, alongside Turkey and Switzerland. In the opening match in the group Ireland, attacked from the outset, with newspaper reports claiming that we could have scored thrice in the first 15 minutes, two of the chances falling to Givens. The QPR man did not take long to make amends, nipping in between two defenders to convert a Kinnear cross after 23 minutes and hooking in a Treacy pass seven minutes later. In the second half, the USSR pressed hard and goalkeeper Paddy Roche made a string of fine saves. The Ringsender is unfairly labelled as an abysmal goalkeeper thanks to a couple of high profile blunders in televised games for Manchester United; his record for Ireland was good and he never let his country down. (After conceding six on debut in 1971, he only let in four in seven games between 1974 and 1976). Givens completed his hat-trick – only the third ever for Ireland – when he headed home a Giles free kick in the 70th minute.

IRELAND: (4-3-3) Paddy Roche (Man United), Joe Kinnear (Tottenham), Paddy Mulligan (Crystal Palace), Terry Mancini (Arsenal), Jimmy Holmes (Coventry), Mick Martin (Man United), Johnny Giles (Leeds), Liam Brady (Arsenal), Steve Heighway (Liverpool), Ray Treacy (Preston), Don Givens (QPR).

Ireland went on to pick up a point in Turkey and beat the Swiss at home, but all chance of qualification ended in a disastrous week in May 1975 when we lost by a single goal in Kiev and Berne. The campaign came to a conclusion, with a place in the finals eventually just one point away, at home to Turkey. Almost one year to the day after the defeat of the Soviets, Givens emulated his incredible feat, scoring all four goals against the Turks.

Ireland warmed up for the next World Cup campaign with a good 1-1 draw in Wembley, but only one of the four games was won – France going down to a magnificent individual goal from Liam Brady at Lansdowne. Giles' last stab at reaching the finals of a major competition was to be the 1980 European Championships. In their opening tie in Copenhagen Ireland led 3-1 with ten minutes to play but ended up having to share the points after a stunning 30 yard drive from Soren Lerby. A tense 0-0 draw was the almost inevitable result of the historic first game against Northern Ireland and a third draw was the result when England visited Lansdowne Road. Denmark was overcome in Dublin but again a trip to Sofia ended in defeat. When Bulgaria came over for the return they were hammered 3-0, but the campaign fizzled out with defeats in Belfast and Wembley.

Giles took Ireland into the new World Cup campaign, which began six weeks later, but bowed out having served up a 3-2 win in Cyprus. His era had introduced a greater degree of professionalism to the Irish side but his frustration with Merrion Square politics led him to quit, ostensibly to concentrate on managing Shamrock Rovers. Eoin Hand inherited a well-organised side, adorned with the blossoming talents such as Brady, Mark Lawrenson and Frank Stapleton. Ireland kicked off with a notable 2-1 win over Holland, the previous World Cup beaten finalists, but followed with a home point dropped to Belgium and a defeat in Paris. Cyprus was hammered before the turning point of the campaign in Brussels. Ireland had a perfectly good Frank Stapleton goal disallowed and then the home side scored from a wrongly awarded free kick with just three minutes left. Hand confronted the referee at the final whistle and called him 'a disgrace and a cheat.' The feeling of having suffered an injustice was to be carried for many years. A point was won in Holland and France beaten 3-2 in Dublin, but the French were eventually to squeeze Ireland out on goal difference and eventually reach the semi-finals.

The next European campaign was unsuccessful, Ireland losing their 11-year unbeaten home record in competition when going down 3-2 to Holland, but finished on a high with a record 8-0 thrashing of Malta. Hand's next – and last – 16 games would only yield eight more. The 1984 World Cup campaign kicked off when the USSR was beaten by a Mick Robinson goal at Lansdowne, but defeat in Oslo and Copenhagen meant the chance of qualification was almost gone. Norway then stole a point in Dublin before Hand won some respite from the now strident critics with a 3-0 home win over the Swiss. Defeat in Moscow was followed by a 4-1 thrashing at home to Denmark and the game was up for Hand. Just 15,000 fans rattled around Lansdowne, a far cry from the situation a couple of years later when Charlton mania took hold.

The appointment of the former England and Leeds centre half was actually an accident. In a process conducted with typical FAI ineptness and nasty politicking, with late candidates

ABOVE ▓ September 1984 Liam Brady in action during the World Cup qualifying match against USSR at Lansdowne Road, Dublin. Ireland won the match 1-0

emerging and votes being switched, Charlton eventually triumphed over ex-Liverpool boss Bob Paisley, the favoured local candidate Liam Tuohy, and Giles. Tuohy wryly pointed out that he entered the meeting in a two-horse race and ended up finishing fourth. Charlton inherited a quality bunch of players, but he was wary of some of the more established stars, particularly the trio who started at Arsenal: Liam Brady, Frank Stapleton and David O'Leary. All three were the feel the wrath of Charlton after very public rows.

The qualification rounds for the European Championship kicked off with a point earned in Brussels thanks to a late Brady penalty. Scotland drew 0-0 in Dublin and disaster loomed when an injury-weakened side travelled to Hampden Park. Forced to play midfielders Ronnie Whelan and Paul McGrath at fullback, the new formation allowed Mark Lawrenson to get forward in the middle and was from such a move that the only goal was scored in the sixth minute. Still, things were not looking good with defeat in Bulgaria and another home point dropped to Belgium. Two wins over Luxembourg and another against Bulgaria ended the campaign, but the Bulgars only needed a point at home to Scotland to qualify. Astonishingly, a goal two minutes from the end by substitute Gary Mackay was to send Ireland into its first major tournament. Mackay became a minor celebrity in Ireland and was much in demand by sponsors and advertisers for a while.

Liam Brady, who had been sent off in the home win over Bulgaria, was handed a four match ban because he gave the referee a 'stiff extended right arm salute' and would therefore miss the first two games in Germany. Charlton clearly didn't want to bring the gifted midfielder – there was a clear clash of footballing cultures and Brady was a powerful figure in the dressing room – but the manager came under enormous media pressure to select him. As it turned out Brady was injured, and one of Ireland's greatest players missed our first step onto the major stage. ▪

Euro 88 pitted just eight teams against each other, and Ireland was drawn in a formidable group alongside England, the Soviet Union and Holland. On Sunday 12 June 1988, in the Neckar Stadium, Stuttgart, Ireland entered the big time. And with fitting irony, England were the first opponents. After eight minutes a Tony Galvin cross was mis-kicked by Kenny Sansom and John Aldridge headed it on to Ray Houghton who looped his header over Peter Shilton into the net. The next 82 minutes were to pass as slowly as any in Irish history, but when the final whistle went there was an outpouring of delight. A stunned BBC presenter put it to Bobby Charlton that he must be suffering mixed emotions, to which he replied 'Nah, blood is thicker than water. I'm delighted!' His brother Jack, who hadn't even had the courtesy of a letter of acknowledgement when he applied for the England manager's job some years before, savoured a bitter revenge.

ENGLAND: Peter Shilton, Gary Stevens, Mark Wright, Tony Adams, Kenny Sansom, Neil Webb, Bryan Robson, Chris Waddle, Peter Beardsley, Gary Lineker, John Barnes. Subs: Glenn Hoddle for Webb (60m), Mark Hateley for Beardsley (82m).

IRELAND (4-4-2): Packie Bonner (Celtic), Chris Morris (Celtic), Mick McCarthy (Celtic), Kevin Moran (Man United), Chris Hughton (Tottenham), Ray Houghton (Liverpool), Paul McGrath (Man United), Ronnie Whelan (Liverpool), Tony Galvin (Sheff Wed), Frank Stapleton (Derby), John Aldridge (Liverpool). Subs: Niall Quinn (Arsenal) for Stapleton (63m), Kevin Sheedy (Everton) for Galvin (76m).

The Irish caravan, augmented by an enormous, good-humoured horde of fans who styled themselves as Jack's Army, moved to Hanover to play the Soviet Union. A stunning goal from Ronnie Whelan, volleyed in from 20 yards following a Mick McCarthy long throw, earned Ireland a 1-1 draw. There we were, on top of the group with three points from two games, needing just a draw against the Dutch to go through to the semi-finals. Sadly, that wasn't to be as the eventual champions dominated a tense game and snatched a late winner through Wim Kieft.

ABOVE ■ June 1988 Ray Houghton celebrates scoring Ireland's winning goal in the European finals against England at Stuttgart, Germany.

Ireland ended Euro 88 with a renewed confidence in our ability to mix with the football élite, and a new respect by those countries, particularly England. If Ireland had lost all three matches in Germany, it would still have been a significant, but soon forgotten competition. To beat England, of all teams, led to previously undreamed of support flocking to the team from throughout the country and transformed how soccer was perceived here to this day. Charlton's football wasn't always pretty, based on putting the opposition players under pressure and liberal use of the long ball, but it was very effective in maximising limited resources. The improved results led to an improved seeding for major tournaments, which in turn increased the chances of qualification.

As it turned out, Ireland had quite a comfortable passage to the 1990 World Cup finals, four home wins and draws in Hungary and Belfast were enough to see them qualify behind Spain. The run-up to the finals was marked with controversy over the players' sponsorship deals and Charlton's attitude to the waning talents of Brady and Stapleton. Brady retired before the finals after being humiliatingly withdrawn after 20 minutes of a friendly against Germany, and although Stapleton was brought along at the expense of the 23rd man, Gary Waddock, he was not to play in Italy. As fate would have it, Ireland's first game in a World Cup final was again against England. On Monday 11th of June 1990 an enormous travelling support thronged to the Stadio Sant'Elia in the Sardinian capital, Cagliari. There was much concern over the behaviour of England's notorious fans, but the ground and town was flooded with police – I had my asthma inhaler confiscated at the turnstiles as a potential weapon – and there was just one arrest all night.

Of the team that played England in 1988, only Tony Galvin wasn't in the squad, although Houghton, Whelan and Stapleton were no longer in the starting XI. Charlton had conducted a vigorous campaign of recruiting second generation Irishmen who were playing in Britain. Many of the Irishmen who built Britain's motorways in the 1950s stayed behind and raised families. Those boys were now in their twenties and dozens of them were professional footballers. Of the team that played in Stuttgart, only four were born in Ireland, and that figure was down to three by the game in Cagliari. There was much criticism in England of this exploitation of what was dismissively called the 'granny rule', with jibes that FAI stood for 'Find An Irishman'. It rankled with the English that they had missed players of the calibre of Andy Townsend and Mark Lawrenson, but the truth is that most of those that did opt for Ireland were not good enough to play for England. Anyway, pointed out the Irish press, wasn't John Barnes born in Jamaica and Terry Butcher in Hong Kong?

There was more debate when the game began, but the Irish fans were silenced after eight minutes as England took the lead when Gary Lineker bundled the ball into Packie Bonner's net. An unseasonable thunderstorm broke out at half-time and the sturm und drang continued on and off the pitch for the next 45 minutes. With just 18 minutes left, Bonner launched one of his trademark long, high kicks into the English half where it was collected by Kevin Sheedy. England substitute Steve McMahon, who ironically was one who could have played for Ireland but didn't, gathered but was then harried off the ball by Townsend; the ball ran to Sheedy who fired a low drive into the far corner.

ENGLAND: Peter Shilton, Gary Stevens, Des Walker, Terry Butcher, Stuart Pearce, Chris Waddle, Paul Gascoigne, Bryan Robson, John Barnes, Peter Beardsley, Gary Lineker. Subs: Steve McMahon for Beardsley (69m), Steve Bull for Lineker (83m).

IRELAND (4-4-2): Packie Bonner (Celtic), Chris Morris (Celtic), Mick McCarthy (Millwall), Kevin Moran (Blackburn), Steve Staunton (Liverpool), Ray Houghton (Liverpool), Paul McGrath (Aston Villa), Andy Townsend (Norwich), Kevin Sheedy (Everton), Tony Cascarino (Aston Villa), John Aldridge (Réal Sociedad). Subs: Alan McLoughlin for Aldridge (64m). ▪

A dismal 0-0 draw with Egypt followed which caused controversy back home when TV pundit Eamon Dunphy was misquoted as saying he was 'ashamed to be Irish' and there was concern that the last group game was again against the Dutch. But Holland were not in the same you-or-us position as they were two years before, and once Niall Quinn equalised Ruud Gullit's early lead goal – again from a Bonner missile – a certain inertia fell over the game as a draw would ensure both teams progressed. With time running out the two captains seemed to 'agree' on a draw, as both would go through. According to Irish captain Mick McCarthy the referee told him to 'play football'. With Ireland passing the ball around to each other McCarthy replied: 'this is the most football we've ever played!'

The second round forced the swelling support to travel to Genoa where Romania was the opposition. A gripping match in sapping heat failed to produce any goals, as did the 30 minutes of extra time. A penalty shoot-out ensued, a flawed way of sorting out football's tiebreak, but one which was to facilitate Irish progress. Packie Bonner was superb, guessing which side each penalty-taker aimed for, but although he got his fingertips to a couple, couldn't keep any out. After four kicks, the score was 4-4, but Bonner brilliantly saved the last kick by Daniel Timofte and Ireland turned to substitute David O'Leary. Charlton had frozen O'Leary out of the Irish side for three years after he refused to cancel a family holiday to play in a 'mickey mouse' tournament in Iceland. But Charlton brought him back into the squad in time for Italia '90 and the Arsenal centre half rewarded the manager with a resolute display when he came on in this, the only World Cup match he was to play in his long career.

However, stopping people scoring was his main job, he had never taken a penalty before. Up he stepped and blasted the ball to Lung's left. 'My only mistake was to stay where I was', he revealed afterwards, ruing the scrum of more than 20 other players and officials who formed on top of him.

Next stop was the Olympic Stadium in Rome and a tough quarter-final encounter with the hosts. The entire nation was consumed with football at this stage and there was a crazy scramble for tickets and flights to Italy. The Taoiseach, Charles Haughey, flew out as he always did when there was a bit of reflected glory to be stolen. Italy was put under typical pressure, but Ireland rarely threatened to score – two first half headers by McGrath and Quinn was the sum of efforts on target. Home hero Toto Schillaci – recently used in an advertising campaign in Ireland – nipped into score before half-time and was only denied by the woodwork in the second half. Time ran out and it was time to go home. There was an enormous open-topped bus parade through Dublin and an emotional party to honour the players, but it was soon down to business for the 1992 European qualifiers.

This was to prove Charlton's first failure to qualify: four draws against England and Poland meant we lost out to 'the old enemy'. The 1994 World Cup was scheduled for the United States and the prospect of a trip to the land where at least 50 million people call themselves Irish American was an exciting one. Three good home wins and draws in Spain and Denmark set us up nicely, but a point was dropped at home to the Danes before three more wins away to the group 'minnows'. As qualification loomed, we suffered a damaging 3-1 defeat to Spain at Lansdowne Road and it became necessary to earn at least a point in the last group game in Belfast. On an emotional night – it was the middle of a particularly nasty period of the Troubles – the home team took the lead. The Northern Ireland manager Billy Bingham clearly enjoyed Jimmy Quinn's goal as he danced a jig and exhorted the crowd to chant 'there's only one team in Ireland' in retaliation for the Lansdowne Road crowd first using that inane chant the year before. An increasingly nervous performance was settled when substitute Alan McLoughlin fired through a sea of legs to earn the crucial point. The national broadcaster switched to Barcelona where Spain were leading Denmark 1-0 and we watched in unbearable tension as they hung on to ensure we stayed ahead of the Danes.

As the nation spent the winter recultivating a relationship with every long-lost Aunt and Uncle in Boston and the Bronx, Charlton and the squad again became bogged down in financial difficulties as sponsors piled in to be associated with an Irish success story. The media interest became greater, too, as none of the four UK teams had made it to the finals. Ireland shaped up very well and Charlton wasn't afraid to introduce new players to his squad. Two stunning results in friendly games meant Ireland were not going to be underestimated. Holland were beaten 1-0 in Tilburg and Germany 2-0 in Hanover. Come June 1994, however, and the focus was on Giants Stadium in New Jersey, where Ireland was to play another great European nation who had helped build America. There was a bit of a personal element to the tie as well, because our opponents were Italy.

ABOVE ■ 18th June 1994 Ray Houghton scores Ireland's winning goal against Italy in the 1994 World Cup Finals at Giants Stadium, New Jersey.

IRELAND (4-5-1): Packie Bonner (Celtic), Denis Irwin (Man United), Phil Babb (Coventry), Paul McGrath (Aston Villa), Terry Phelan (Man City), Ray Houghton (Aston Villa), Roy Keane (Man United), John Sheridan (Sheffield Wednesday), Andy Townsend (Aston Villa), Steve Staunton (Aston Villa), Tommy Coyne (Motherwell). Subs: Jason McAteer (Bolton) for Houghton; John Aldridge (Tranmere) for Coyne.

ITALY: Pagliuca, Tassoti, Baresi, Costacurta, Maldini, Donadoni, Dino Baggio, Albertini, Evani, Roberto Baggio, Signori. Subs: Masoro for Evani, Berti for Signori.

On to the searing 100 degree heat in Orlando, where Mexico were far more at home than the Irish and won with two goals from Luis Garcia to a late consolation from John Aldridge. That goal was to prove vital when the final game, back in Giants Stadium against Norway, was a dour 0-0 draw. The result meant that the group table ended with all four teams on four points and a neutral goal difference, but Mexico (3 goals), Italy and Ireland (2 each) progressed on goals scored, over the hapless Norwegians who scored just one. Ireland's win over Italy broke that tie but the prize was another trip to Orlando and a game against Holland. The temperature was mercifully down on the previous visit, but that was no help when defensive blunders led to Holland taking the lead through Bergkamp after 11 minutes. The Dutch rampaged upfield for the rest of the half and were unlucky not to score until four minutes before the break when Bonner missed a speculative drive from Wim Jonk. The big Celtic keeper hammered the ground with his fists but there was no recovery from that position and the adventure was over.

And as a fictional countryman of those opponents famously said, 'revenge is a dish best eaten cold'. In an eerie reprise of Stuttgart in 1988, Ireland took an early lead through Ray Houghton – this time a spectacular lobbed shot – and hung on. Charlton's initial reaction to the goal was 'We've gone and scored too early! There's a whole bloody game to get through yet.' But get through it they did, with the Italians rarely threatening in the second half, and another stunning

ABOVE ■ 18th June 1994 Giants Stadium, New Jersey. Roy Keane and Guiseppe Signori dual for the ball during the World Cup game.

win against a world power was ours. Holland, Germany and now Italy had been despatched in rapid succession, and without losing a single goal; Ireland's odds for the trophy were slashed from 25-1 to 16-1.

We had reached the second phase in two World Cups. Scotland didn't make it past the group stage in six successive finals, but arguably it was the dour, efficient but unadventurous football that prevented us going even further. Ireland's nine games at two memorable World Cups actually saw just one win, over Italy. There were three defeats and five draws, but only four goals. ■

The 1996 European Championships were held in England, but again a chance to visit our nearest neighbours was thwarted in a playoff. Ireland finished a distant second to Portugal in the qualifiers, but pipped Northern Ireland to the playoff spot. Again the Dutch were the opponents in Liverpool and again they saw us off with a 2-0 win. Charlton folded his tent after Anfield, and his most loyal captain and fellow native of the north of England, Mick McCarthy, who had been managing Millwall of the English first division, took over. The Irish fans were keen that we qualify for our third successive World Cup finals due to be held in easily-accessible France in 1998. Sadly, with a transitional team it was another case of being shaded at the last, this time by Belgium. Ireland finished second to Romania, whose only dropped point in ten games came in Dublin. Ireland dropped ten points more than that, most disastrously when going down 3-2 in Macedonia. The playoff in Dublin ended 1-1 but we slipped to a 2-1 defeat in Brussels.

Ireland missed out on the 2000 European Championship as well, again ruing the vagaries of the play-off system. Drawn in a tough, tiring section which also included Yugoslavia, Croatia, Macedonia and Malta, four home wins put us in the box seat, but patchy away form meant Yugoslavia pipped us for the automatic qualification spot. The failure could be directly attributed to a failure of concentration in Croatia, when Davor Suker won the match with an injury time goal; and again nightmarishly in the final game in Skopje. Ahead thanks to a Niall Quinn goal, Ireland again succumbed deep into injury time and gifted Macedonia an equaliser. Instead of a direct ticket to the co-hosted finals in Holland and Belgium, Ireland had to face yet another tense play-off.

Drawn to play Turkey, Robbie Keane scored with just 11 minutes left of the first leg in Dublin, but a penalty four minutes later gave the visitors a vital advantage. The second leg was fixed away from the capital, in the tiny and hostile ground in Bursa. Needing to score, Ireland persevered but there was no way through and defeat on the away goals rule was a bitter medicine to keep down. With his critics growing more vocal, McCarthy was given a mountain to climb with the draw for the 2002 World Cup qualifiers – Holland, Portugal, Estonia, Andorra and Cyprus. The fixtures didn't look too promising, with visits to the top two teams in the Autumn of 2000. Stunningly, Ireland took a 2-0 lead against the Dutch, and although that was hauled back in the last quarter, an away point was a huge bonus. When that was also the result of the trip to Lisbon, the old confidence returned and the dream of another World Cup finals, this time in Japan and Kore, began to be talked about. After two facile wins away to Cyprus and Andorra, Ireland got a fright at home to the Pyrenean principality when Lima gave them the lead before three Irish goals restored respectability to the scoreline. An awesome Roy Keane performance capped with the lead goal, saw honours shared when World Footballer of the Year Luis Figo netted with 12 minutes left.

The entire campaign wound up with a death-or-glory encounter with the Dutch at Lansdowne Road. A win or draw would guarantee Ireland at least a play-off spot, while defeat would end our interest. The sublimely talented Dutch team looked set to overrun Ireland in the first half but failed to make their chances count. When Gary Kelly was sent off early in the second half it looked impossible that we might hold out. Then a nippy run by young full-back Steve Finnan led to a cross deep into the box which sailed over the defence and fell to Jason McAteer who

ABOVE ■ 10th November 2001 World Cup playoff at Lansdowne Road, Dublin v Iran. Robbie Keane takes the ball past Rahmna Rezaei.

drove home and the play-off place was secured. The virtual formality of a home win over Cyprus was duly sealed by 4-0. For several weeks, inordinate interest was taken in the Asia qualifying campaign after we were drawn to meet the side that finished third in that region which turned out to be Iran. Goals by Ian Harte (from a penalty) and Robbie Keane were enough to give us a useful two-goal advantage, confirmed thanks to Shay Given who made some important saves.

The final step on the road to Korea and Japan was taken in front of 80,000 fans in the National Stadium in Tehran. Shorn of the talismanic Roy Keane and leading goalscorer Niall Quinn, Ireland were under pressure for much of the game. Iran eventually broke the deadlock one minute into injury time at the end of the game. There was unbearable tension for a couple of minutes in many Irish homes, bars and workplaces but when the final whistle blew a third trip to the World Cup had been assured. Qualification this time is be arguably a greater achievement than any of Charltons qualifications. A tightening up of the parentage rules has dried up a very important source of players and, bar Manchester United's Roy Keane, none of the Irish squad could be considered as world-class players.

Regulations have also been introduced which will slow the export of Irish boys to England. While the local clubs have welcomed this, the semi-professional National League has been irrelevant to the international story for many years as the most promising schoolboy players are hauled across to England as 15 year-olds. The last player from a local club to win a full cap was Pat Byrne in 1986 in Charlton's fourth game. The league is an economic basket case as the crowds that support the national team direct their energies and money towards following English soccer. That said, there are no countries with a population of 3.5 million that can support a fully professional league. Even countries as successful internationally as the Dutch, Danes and world champions France export their best players to Spain, England and Italy. When you consider that Ireland's tiny pool is further reduced by the numbers playing the two more popular indigenous games of hurling and Gaelic football – and a decent chunk playing rugby too – it is extraordinary that we can compete successfully against nations like Holland and Portugal which have professional leagues and no major competing sports.

Ireland's soccer story has been one of immense commitment and passion allied to a decent level of skill. Players like Giles, Brady, McGrath, O'Leary and Keane were among the best in the world at their peak. Others will follow, too, and as long as our resources are maximised, we'll have a few more days in the sun. ▪

ABOVE Jordan-Honda boss Eddie Jordan (centre) poses with Paul McGrath (left) and current captain of Manchester United Roy Keane before the French Formula One Grand Prix held in Magny Cours, France 1st July 2001.

Ian Steepe was educated at Villers, Limerick, St Columba's College, Dublin and Dublin University. Whilst at university (1955-61), he was a member of an outstanding Trinity side that included internationals in David Judge, Ken Blackmore, John Lavan and Ian himself as well as a number of interprovincial players. Ian captained Trinity in 1959 and 1960 and was capped by Ireland 31 times between 1961 and 1972. He played interprovincial hockey for Munster and club hockey for a number of sides including Three Rock Rovers, YMCA (Dublin), Instonians (Belfast) and Hounslow (England). He coached the Irish Men's Hockey side between 1975 and 1978 and the Irish Ladies Hockey side from 1981 to 1988. Both sides qualified for the World Cup. He is currently teaching at Drogheda Grammar School. ∎

It was an afternoon of dreadful heat and humidity in Kuala Lumpur, scene of the 1983 Intercontinental Cup and the World Cup Women's hockey tournaments. Uniquely, both tournaments ran concurrently and in the same city. Controversially the FIH (International Hockey Federation) had selected Ireland for the 'lesser' tournament, the Intercontinental Cup, a qualifying tournament for the following World Cup in 1986. Ireland's opponents on that steamy afternoon in Kuala Lumpur were South Korea, newcomers to the international scene. The Koreans were in the early stages of preparing a women's team to compete in the Seoul Olympic Games five years later. Most of the Irish players on the pitch were looking despairingly towards their coach – sitting under a parasol – begging to be substituted, while those on the bench were not showing their usual keenness to be sent onto the field! A combination of skill, luck and greater experience saw Ireland record an important victory

143

(3-1) on the way towards winning the Intercontinental Cup one week later. In 1988 South Korea, as host nation, duly competed in Seoul; in fact Korea reached the Olympic Final against Australia and became the Olympic silver medallists. The point to note in all of this is that Korea, with no club structure in their country, could achieve so much in such a short period of time. The contrast with Ireland could not be more pronounced. Hockey has been played on this island for more than 100 years and Irish teams, women's and men's have never qualified for Olympic hockey tournaments. Yet the popularity of, and enthusiasm for, hockey in Ireland at club level is indisputable.

Leaving aside the huge cultural differences between our respective societies, Korea and Ireland, this raises the question, should our long-established club structure, and our fondness for league and cup competitions, produce more successful national teams, or is it the very importance of hockey at club level which militates against success at international level? In a survey carried out in 1998 by the then Irish Hockey Union (Men's), it was ascertained that approximately 6,000 were playing in 66 schools, and 4,300 men and 2,400 boys were playing in 75 clubs. The Irish Ladies Hockey Union conducted its own census one year earlier. At that time between 7,000 and 7,500 women and girls were registered to 126 clubs. Of the just over 3,000 women players under 21 years of age, approximately 2,000 were playing in schools and colleges.

Three years after Kuala Lumpur a situation arose which encapsulated for me the conflicting and apparently incompatible demands of club and country. As part of our preparations for the women's World Cup in Amsterdam in August 1986 – for which we had qualified by winning the Intercontinental Cup in Kuala Lumpur – the Ireland squad travelled to Holland at Easter for an international festival event. Ireland reached the final on the Monday afternoon and then proceeded to win the tournament by virtue of a victory over the full England squad, in a wonderful game of hockey. The Irish squad flew back to Belfast on the following afternoon. Cars were waiting at the airport that Tuesday evening to bring the Leinster-based players back to Dublin, not least to ensure that they could play for their clubs in the days that followed. In Holland I had urged the players to rest during the following 7 or 8 days, prior to our departure for Largs in Scotland to play England and Wales on successive days as part of the Four Nations (Home Countries) Championship. Most of the players acknowledged the need for a break; they had, after all, been playing on four successive days in Holland. But with no directive from the ILHU, their strong club loyalties came to the fore; if their clubs insisted that they play, then they felt they had to do so. And so, arriving in Largs, Ireland faced England with a number of tired and over-played team members; the Ulster players had also succumbed to pressure and had represented their clubs during the nine days between Holland and Scotland.

The matter of the playing surface was also a crucial factor. The dearth of artificial, synthetic playing surfaces in Ireland in the mid 1980s, made it imperative to travel to places such as Holland to prepare for the Amsterdam World Cup. The Largs matches were also played on a synthetic pitch. So, by playing club hockey in the interim, our international players were returning to play on bumpy, end of season, grass and 'all weather' surfaces. Imagine a tennis player, having come from a clay court tournament in Monte Carlo or Rome, preparing for the next clay court event, at Roland Garros, say, by spending a few days practising on grass! In the event a somewhat depleted and re-organised Irish team lost to England (2-1), going 2-0 down in the opening 10 minutes to a tigerish England side eager to erase memories not only of Easter but of the two previous years' encounters; in 1984 Ireland beat England 1-0 on the grass of Wembley Stadium, and the following year defeated England, also by 1-0, on the new superturf pitch at Grange Road, Dublin. A year after Largs, Ireland defeated England again, in Gateshead, winning the Triple Crown that year as well. Three victories over England in four seasons – this represents an unrivalled period of success for Ireland in over 100 years of competition between Ireland and England (incidentally, Ireland has not recorded a victory over England in the men's game since 1949!). ▪

The FIH had been founded back in 1924; in 1938 Ireland made a decision against joining. By 1949, Ireland was 'the only significant hockey-playing country which had not affiliated … in January 1950 the IHU agreed unanimously to apply for membership of the FIH in view of the prospect of more and more matches against Continental opponents. Ireland's affiliation was approved at a meeting of the FIH in Barcelona during November 1950.' (*90 Years of the Irish Hockey Union:* T.A. Wynne and Chris Glennon, 1986). The IFWHA (Women's Federation) was founded in 1927; Ireland was a founder member. 'In 1982, after many years of discussion between the IFWHA. and the FIH, the two federations merged and the responsibility for all hockey matters at World and Olympic level was assumed by the FIH with headquarters in Brussels. The first official FIH tournament in which Ireland's women took part was the first Intercontinental Cup in Kuala Lumpur, in 1983'. (*First 100 Years, a Centenary History:* ILHU, 1996) Thus, in 1950 (men's) and in 1982 (women's) decisions were made which were to have profound effects on the international match programmes of Irish teams. The traditional fixtures against England, Scotland and Wales gradually were augmented, and later replaced, by matches against 'foreign' countries. Dermot Ashmore, in The Irish Times in April 1975, wrote: 'It is hard to grasp the reality that this is the last Home Countries Championship, 80 years after the first international match between Ireland and Wales at Rhyl. The remarkable modernisation of hockey and its subsequent demands rule out, it seems, the regular continuance of the annual games with our neighbours and the voyages of character to Inverness or midnight revelry in Carlow.'

This reference to 'voyages of character' and 'midnight revelry' recall for me occasions like the visit of Ireland's men's team to North Wales to play Wales in 1966. An away match in North Wales; in terms of proximity to Ireland, who could ask for better than that? The Ulster players, making their own travel arrangements, came first to Dublin. The sea crossing from Dun Laoghaire to Holyhead allowed us, the 12 players, to renew acquaintances and to introduce new faces! We waited in Holyhead for our chartered bus to arrive, which it did – eventually. And so we trundled across Anglesey in the small hours of the morning. A few hours sleep, a late breakfast, a stroll through the streets of Bangor, lunch, transport to the pitch (situated in the middle of an exposed expanse of playing fields), the conviviality of the post-match dinner with the Welsh players and officials, then, some time around midnight, the journey back to Ireland began. We waited on the platform of Bangor station for the London - Holyhead express, the Irish Mail! An impromptu game of hockey, lit by the station lamps, ensued; the disappointment of losing the international match a few hours earlier was eased a little as we played a game of 'gaining ground', inebriated players smashing the ball back and forth the length of the platform!

ABOVE ▨ October 1963 Ireland v England at Trent Bridge, Nottingham (1-1).
Back Row: Ian Steepe, Pat Hade, Derek Hennessy John Lavan, Dixon Rose, Derek Shaw.
Front Row: Reg Treacy, Billy Walsh, Ken Blackmore, Harry Cahill, David Judge.

I place alongside this remembered weekend, the memory of another March day, almost exactly 12 years later. 16 Irish players, plus a manager, a coach and a trainer, arrived in Buenos Aires in a torrential downpour, after a journey that had taken us from Dublin to London, London to Geneva, and then Geneva to Buenos Aires, via Dakar, Sao Paolo and Rio de Janeiro. Incredibly, David Judge, who had played on that far distant weekend in Bangor, was still a member of the Irish team which had come to Argentina to play in the World Cup in 1978. In fact his 21-year playing career had begun in Inverness, back in 1957!

These two memories encapsulate for me the extraordinary expansion that took place in Irish hockey during the 1970s, the broadening of our horizons, the ever-increasing challenge of trying to compete globally at international level. From 'Seasick at Holyhead' to 'Jet lagged in Buenos Aires' in the space of a few short, momentous years! There have been exceptions, but too often Irish teams, men's and women's, produce their best performances and results in the early stages of a tournament; then there follows the loss of a vital pool game by a slender margin and in the final classification matches, Irish teams slump to seemingly inevitable defeat. The performances of the Irish men's team in the Intercontinental Cup in Barcelona in October 1985 are a dramatic illustration of this unhappy trend.

As stated in the book, *90 Years of the IHU*: 'With the decision to play the 1986 World Cup in London, Ireland was more than normally enthusiastic about the prospects of qualifying for the finals'. The cost of sending the national team to London would be considerably less than to other far-flung venues. In fact Ireland had to qualify even for the Intercontinental Cup itself; in a 'sub-qualifier' in Dublin, Ireland defeated Italy 2-1 and 2-0. Then, in a European final play-off, Ireland defeated Scotland (2-1) and Belgium (3-2). These victories, on successive days in Amsterdam, augured well for Ireland's chances of success a month later in Barcelona where the Irish team began its campaign with a 2-0 victory over South Korea. A facile win over Zimbabwe followed (9-0). In the third pool match, Ireland played Poland, which had already defeated Argentina (3-1) and Korea (4-2). With ten minutes of the Ireland v Poland game remaining, Ireland led 3-0; the final score was 3-3! Carl Anderson, writing in World Hockey said that: 'Ireland folded in the face of a late, desperate Polish onslaught – perhaps three matches on three hot days took their toll on Ireland'. In their two remaining pool matches, Ireland lost 3-1 to New Zealand, the pool winners and defeated Argentina (3-1). The top two teams in each pool qualified automatically for the London World Cup finals. Poland and Ireland finished joint second, but Poland qualified due to a superior goal difference. Had Poland lost to Ireland, then Ireland would have played in London. Still, all was not lost – Ireland, Kenya, Malaysia and Argentina had to play off for the fifth qualifying place. Ireland defeated Kenya (1-0), Argentina dispatched Malaysia (3-0) and so Ireland and Argentina met again, with the prize of a World

Cup place for the winners. This time the result of the Pool match was reversed, with Ireland losing 2-0! 'Ireland', wrote Anderson, 'were left to rue their earlier indiscretions.'

I only read about the Barcelona tournament, but my own first-hand experience of what might have been came in the sixth Women's World Cup played in Amsterdam in August 1986, for which Ireland had qualified for this tournament by winning in Kuala Lumpur in 1983. Controversy dogged this tournament before ever a ball was struck. Until six or seven months earlier, the venue was to be Vancouver. Then the Canadian organisers informed the FIH that they were unable to run the tournament. Luckily the Netherlands Hockey Association volunteered to act as hosts, but stipulated that the entire programme of 42 matches would have to be compressed into just ten days, instead of the usual 12 days. Thus there was the extraordinary anomaly that the Men's World Cup in London – two months later – was played

ABOVE ■ Women's Hockey. Ireland v England. Grange Road, Dublin March 1985.
Irish players (white tops) left to right. Jacqui Potter, Joanne Menown (dribbling), Jackie Burns (nee McWilliams), behind Menown.

ABOVE ■ Irish Ladies Hockey Team. World Cup, the Netherlands 1986.
Back Row: Mary Costello (physiotherapist), Mary Nugent, Margaret Sloan, Glynnis Taylor, Caroline Fusco, Margaret Gleghorne, Mary Barnwell, Jackie Burns, Rionach Tierney, Ian Steepe (coach). **Front Row:** Jo Dwyer (manager), Orla Galvin, Joanne Menown, Sandra Drum, Margaret Brown, Noelle Branagan (captain), Rose Nagle, Jacqui Potter, Deidre Courtney.

over twelve days, and the women had to complete an identical schedule in two days less! The match programme in Holland presumably approved by the FIH also scheduled just two matches, the final and the third to fourth place match, for the last day, thus eight of the 12 competing nations had to play their seven matches in the space of nine days!

When this match programme was announcd, just three to four months prior to the tournament, I wrote an article for World Hockey magazine, pleading that the organisers extend the tournament, citing factors such as insufficient time for recovery between matches, that the schedule could not but have a detrimental effect upon the standard of play, etc. The coaches of England and Scotland 'seconded' this report but the Editor of World Hockey was asked by the FIH not to publish the article.

And so to the tournament itself. On the final day of the pool matches, victory for Ireland over New Zealand would have brought Ireland to the semi-final of the World Cup. In the event, defeat by the narrowest margin (4-3) was followed by successive defeats in the two classification matches and a final ranking of 12th, last place, in the tournament! Before the New Zealand encounter, Ireland had played four matches, against West Germany, the USSR, the USA and Argentina. A scoreless draw with the Germans included a missed penalty stroke awarded when the German goalkeeper swept the ball away with her hand after a thunderous penalty corner shot from Mary Barnwell had rebounded from the left-hand post. A scintillating performance by the Irish against the Soviets, in a marvellous contest, produced a 3-3 draw. A rest day followed, and then Ireland became embroiled in the most controversial – and brutal – hockey match I have ever witnessed. The USA had lost their first two matches and victory over Ireland was imperative if they were to retain any further interest in the tournament. The scoreline, 2-0 to the USA, tells nothing of the drama of that awful afternoon.

Patricia Ward, the Editor of Hockey Field, the official magazine of the All England Women's Hockey Association, had this to say: 'From the start the States were in uncompromising mood… Joanne Menown, this so talented young player, showed her skills and spelt danger to the US defence almost everytime she touched the ball. Five minutes into the game, and Jackie Burns, the busy Irish right-midfielder, received her first injury when the ball flew high from a fierce hit, catching her full in the face. After treatment, she bravely continued… The States seemed frantic in attack, desperate in defence during this period, though this uncontrolled play went almost unrecognised, apart from the awarding of free hits, by the umpires… Diane Bracalente was lucky to receive only a green card warning five minutes into the second half, for a slashing stick tackle which left Noelle Branagan, the Irish sweeper and captain, with badly bruised fingers. Only minutes later, Jackie Burns received yet another blow in the face and had to leave the field for a while for treatment (six stitches). This robust, forceful but frantic play from the States still failed to stop Ireland as they again tried to find the equaliser, which with Menown around was still quite possible (the two US goals were scored in the 33rd and 56th minutes)… Still more tragedy was in store for the Irish; first Mary Barnwell was caught in the midriff, then Joanne Menown received a bone-breaking hand-high tackle from Megan Donnelly, who was given a yellow card and a spell in the sin bin, but was allowed to return to the field of play later. For Joanne it meant a trip to hospital and the end of her World Cup appearances.'

The Hockey Field editorial (27th September 1986) had this to say of the Amsterdam World Cup: 'The matches provided us with shocks, deep disappointments, high excitement, amazement, sheer delight and – alas – horror, the last reaction caused by the apparent policy "to take out key players" used by the USA side in their match against Ireland. This was one of the saddest days in women's international hockey history, many spectators not being able to believe the carnage they watched. Ireland's top five players were the recipients of harsh contact, leaving them all injured, some seriously, one unable to play again in the tournament…

This match overshadowed the tournament; I felt the umpires on the day were open to criticism for allowing such tactics to occur, but in the first place the use of those tactics must be called into question.'

The ILHU officials chose not to protest at what they had seen. The tournament officials sitting at the Technical Delegates table took no action. The FIH remained silent. Imagine a match of such controversy taking place in the football World Cup finals, played out in the full glare of media coverage; what a furore there would be then! The crowded playing schedule meant that Ireland's women had to play their two remaining pool matches on the two days following the US debacle, making a total of three matches in three days. A goal down to Argentina at half-time, the Irish girls turned in a spirited second half performance to win 3-1; now the points position in the Pool was such that victory over New Zealand would ensure a place in the semi-final, a draw would mean playing for places five to eight, while defeat would mean that Ireland would be relegated to playing for the last four places. As stated earlier, Ireland lost 4-3. Ireland was awarded just three penalty corners in the entire match; Mary Barnwell scored from all three! Had Joanne Menown been fit to play, I must believe that the corner tally would have been much, much higher. The sight of Joanne, slightly built and an outstandingly gifted player, her arm in a sling, a forlorn figure walking the corridors of our hotel or watching her team's gallant efforts, is my saddest memory from the ten years I spent watching more than 100 international matches as coach to Ireland's men's and women's hockey teams.

In 1996, the ILHU produced an attractive 80-page book entitled *The First Hundred Years, 1894 – 1994 A Centenary History*. It is easy to criticise a book's omissions, but Ireland's participation in Amsterdam was dismissed in three lines: 'Sadly, injuries took their toll on this occasion, and the team finished twelfth. It was a bonus, however, to receive the Fair Play Trophy'. I have tried to put Ireland's performances in Amsterdam into perspective; the players who strove so hard there, eventually surrendering to exhaustion and near despair deserved a better fate and certainly their achievements deserve to be recognised by future generations. As I write, this is still the only time that an Ireland women's team has qualified for the World Cup Finals. Ireland did also participate in the eighth World Cup Finals in Dublin in 1994, but as host nation, did not have to qualify.

The credit for gaining qualification for the World Cup is due, of course, to the Intercontinental Cup-winning squad in Kuala Lumpur in 1983 and this achievement certainly did receive much media coverage and acclaim at that time (and since). On Thursday night, 21st April, 1983, in the Merdeka Stadium, Ireland defeated Spain in the final of the first-ever Intercontinental Cup competition (2-1 after extra time). Three days earlier, Ireland defeated the host nation, Malaysia, in a tense semi-final (1-0) and thus qualified for the 1986 World Cup Finals. In the space of 13 days, Ireland played seven matches, winning six and drawing the other, surely one of the outstanding achievements in the history of Irish team sports.

Yet the supreme irony is that Ireland should never have had to compete in the Intercontinental Cup at all. Throughout 1982 it was thought that Ireland would be competing in the World Cup tournament to be held concurrently and in the same city, Kuala Lumpur. It was thought that the playing records of all four Home Countries were good enough to ensure their participation in the 12-nation World Cup. England, Scotland and Wales were duly chosen, but Ireland was ranked 19th in the world by the FIH seeding committee, who thus expected Ireland to finish seventh in the Intercontinental Cup. Just two months prior to the FIH decision, Ireland had travelled to Durham, drawing all three matches, with the USA, Belgium and New Zealand; the USA and New Zealand were selected for the World Cup. Thus it was a very determined Irish party that set out for Malaysia on 1st April wanting to prove a point by significantly improving on our seeding. It should also be added that had Ireland been selected for the World Cup and played on the astroturfed surface of the Razak Stadium, we would have gone there totally unprepared because there was not a single artificial pitch in Ireland at that time (with perfect timing, Grange Road opened just a few months later, enabling us to prepare for the 1986 World Cup on the Three Rock Rovers super-turf pitch). The Intercontinental Cup tournament, however, was played on bumpy grass pitches, a surface with which the Irish players were very familiar. ▪

The opening match against Japan remains a vivid memory. Presumably this was the first time that the Irish women's team had to be roused at 5 o'clock in the morning in order to be wide enough awake to start a match at 7.30! At the start, the omens were not good – the bus taking us to the ground did not arrive on time so our warm-up had to be curtailed. Just before the start, the sky began to lighten and the sight of the Japanese flag reminded us that we were about to play against The Land of the Rising Sun. For the first 15 minutes it seemed inevitable that Japan would win, as nine or ten small and agile players swarmed around the Irish circle. But they committed hockey hari kiri; in their eagerness to attack, they forgot to defend. Ireland's first attack let to a penalty corner and Laura Dobbs scored. Two further corners in the first half saw her complete her hat-trick; Japan scored a consolation goal in the second half. Three penalty corner goals from three attempts within a space of 15 minutes – everything about that memorable morning was unreal.

The next day, Sunday, Ireland played South Korea at the more familiar – but far more dangerous – time of 4.30 in the afternoon. At this hour in Kuala Lumpur the heat and humidity are at their worst, often culminating in a violent storm. This day the rains did not come and even breathing was not easy. The score 3-1, flattered us – the South Koreans, talking incessantly, replied to our early goal, then dominated the game in the second half as we wilted in the heat; then we managed a breakaway goal and scored again in the final minute. A rest day followed then Ireland had another afternoon encounter, though this time with European opponents, Austria. Again the final score (4-1) does not tell the whole story. Ireland went behind the 13th minute – a penalty stroke and equalised just seconds before half-time. The second half saw Ireland establish control. Two rest days followed. Then came another 7.30 am fixture against our weakest opposition, Hong Kong. We strolled to a 4-0 victory. Our final pool game against Belgium, was played under floodlights in the Merdeka Stadium where we were to return for the semi-final and final, and ended in a 2-2 draw. Thus Ireland headed the pool, with nine points out of ten and an impressive goal tally of 16-5.

Ireland well-deserved the semi-final victory over Malaysia (1-0). To defeat the host nation, playing in front of their partisan supporters was a great achievement. We were helped by the fact that this match was played in the vast national soccer stadium, because there the vociferous home crowd was seated well back from the playing area. The final, three days later against Spain, was in a sense an anti-climax (qualification for the World Cup was achieved with the win over Malaysia). Until the last ten minutes of normal playing time, Ireland did not play well: nervousness, tiredness and tight marking took their toll on most of the players on both teams. In extra time, Eilish Macken converted a penalty stroke awarded when Joanne Menown's penalty corner shot was stopped on the line by a defender's foot. A few minutes later, exactly the same situation occurred, but this time Marie Crawford, who had come on during the second half, missed the stroke. She made amends in the second period of extra time by scoring from open play. Spain's goal, never hit by a Spanish player inside the Irish circle, came in the final seconds.

Barbara Fitzgerald was the only Irish journalist with the squad, and it was her articles in The Irish Times and match reports on RTE Radio and Television which created a mood of excitement and euphoria back in Ireland. 'Victory after victory soon had the ears of Ireland tuned… It was difficult (in Kuala Lumpur) to appreciate the impact the team's string of successes made on people back home, but from all accounts, every butcher, busker, schoolgirl and executive knew that the Irish team was winning – time after time.' She also captured the incredible moments that followed the final final whistle! 'Exhaustion was forgotten and exuberance carried the players on their last piece of "official exercise" the lap of honour. The magic of the moment of the whole tour had to be when the huge scoreboard flashed the results – "First: Ireland!" It was chilling and fantastic. I won't forget the privilege of being one of the few "natives" present when the Irish became champions. It's a privilege rare to Irish sportswriters…' In the world of team sports, very rare indeed.

In the same chapter, from the *Seven Up Book of Irish Sport (1983)*, Ms Fitzgerald also describes one of the more light-hearted moments of the tour. After Malaysia, the squad spent three days in Singapore before travelling on for three 'friendly' matches in Pakistan. It was in the luxurious Intercontinental Hotel in Karachi that one of the Irish midfield players encountered the hotel laundry man 'She stepped out of the bathroom one evening. She was without clothes, as are most when they come out from the shower. Bending down to plug in the television, she was disturbed by the laundry man. Facing him, still naked, she ordered him from the room and covered herself with one of the large white hotel towels. She then summoned the man back to the room and asked him his business. Blushing in true Pakistani fashion, he answered cheekily that he was sorry but that he had come to collect the towels!' ▪

Eight years after Amsterdam, Ireland's women played in their second World Cup tournament. The ILHU had asked, in 1990, to host the World Cup in Dublin in 1994, appropriately the year that marked the centenary of women's hockey in Ireland. The FIH voted to accept Ireland's application. A relatively inexperienced Irish team struggled to make their mark in such exalted company. Their five pool matches produced just one goal, as Ireland lost to Argentina (0-3), Korea (0-2) and Australia (0-4); the two remaining matches were drawn, with Spain (1-1) and Russia (0-0). The first two classification matches for ninth to twelfth places had the incentive for the winners of claiming the last places in the Olympic qualifying tournament in Cape Town. In a tense, dramatic match with England, Ireland drew 1-1, so the match was decided on penalty strokes. Ireland failed to score from their five attempts, England scored just twice. Canada defeated Russia, also on penalty strokes and so won the other Olympic qualifying tournament place; such is the narrow dividing line between success and failure! On the final day in Dublin at 8.00 am, Ireland faced Russia in the match to determine 11th and 12th positions. Happily, Ireland won 3-2. The organisation of this tournament was superb; many visiting officials, media personnel, etc. regarded this World Cup as the best ever staged, and the weather was perfect for players and spectators alike.

Ireland's women's great achievement in winning the Intercontinental Cup in Kuala Lumpur in 1983 was preceded by the men's team's success in reaching the final of the Intercontinental Cup in Rome six years earlier. Carl Anderson rated the players as 'the best Ireland squad I have ever seen'. Ireland went into the final with a six-match unbeaten record, having beaten Italy 1-0, Mexico 3-0, Japan 6-2 and drawn 3-3 with Belgium and 2-2 with Nigeria. A 2-1 semi-final victory over the USSR was an outstanding performance. A controversial umpiring decision – the award of a dubious penalty stroke to Poland with just five minutes remaining – decided the final. Anderson described the result as a 'completely unjust 2-1 defeat'. Still, for the first time in the history of men's hockey, Ireland had qualified to compete in a major international competition.

Unfortunately, the preparation for Argentina left much to be desired. Between Rome in September 1977 and Buenos Aires in March 1978, Ireland played not a single international match. Some administrators – and players – seemed to think that the achievement of finishing second in Rome would lead to further success in Buenos Aires. Some players were not as fit as they should have been and this was only discovered during the tournament. A trainer, who accompanied the squad to Argentina, was appointed just two weeks before our departure from Ireland! 14 countries competed in Argentina; Ireland lost narrowly to the host country and then were routed by the magnificent Pakistanis. A narrow defeat by Spain followed, then came a draw with Malaysia and a win over Italy (taking the place of the USSR). The final pool game was lost to the Netherlands. Ireland then played Poland in the first classification game; the victors would qualify automatically for the 1982 World Cup in Bombay. At full-time the score was 1-1; a further 15 minutes of 'sudden death' did not produce a goal, and so the match was decided on penalty strokes. Poland scored from all five penalties, Ireland converted their first four, but the fifth effort sailed over the crossbar! A tired and dispirited Irish team lost again the following morning to Canada. Ireland had travelled to Argentina with a world ranking of 11; the loss to Canada meant that Ireland finished the World Cup tournament just one place below their ranking.

Twelve years after Rome, Ireland again qualified for the World Cup. In Madison, USA, the top five teams in the Intercontinental Cup won the right to play in the World Cup in Lahore the following year (1990). Ireland finished fifth. In their pool matches Ireland lost to the Netherlands, defeated Zimbabwe and the USA and drew with both Canada and Malaysia. This meant that Ireland, Malaysia, New Zealand and Poland had to play off for the crucial fifth place in the tournament. Ireland went a goal down to Poland but came back to win 2-1 after extra time; Malaysia defeated New Zealand 5-4, also after extra time. The next day Ireland defeated the more fancied Malaysians. They moved 3-1 ahead after 19 minutes and then shut up shop. For Ireland to finish fifth behind the Netherlands, Canada, India and France was a considerable achievement.

Success in Rome was followed by perceived failure in Buenos Aires; after Madison came 'failure' in Lahore. Ireland did not win even one of their seven World Cup matches in Pakistan. A 1-1 draw with Canada was the only consolation: Ireland lost to England, Pakistan, Germany and Spain. Then in the 'cross over' matches, Argentine defeated Ireland 4-1 and, sadly, Ireland lost their final match to Canada 3-0, thus finishing the tournament in 12th and last position. ■

To compete in the World Cup or the Olympic Games must be the ultimate goal for sportsmen and women. Qualification for the Olympic hockey tournament has, so far, proved beyond the capabilities of successive Irish teams. It is ironic that the year when perhaps the strongest likelihood of Ireland receiving an invitation to the Olympics – there was no pre-Olympic qualifying tournament then – came in 1971, coinciding with a time of terrible violence and extreme unrest in Northern Ireland. 'That was the year of the Munich bother,' wrote the Irish poet, Patrick Kavanagh, but he was alluding to events in the 1930s! In the context of hockey in Ireland, the year of the Munich crisis was 1971; a formal application to enter for the Olympics had to be made by the end of that year.

The Executive Committee were in favour of applying for entry, but 'it became apparent that the Ulster Branch Council would find difficulty in supporting the Ireland team entering for the games' (*90 Years of Irish Hockey*). The financial implications were a concern, but it was the issues raised by flags and anthems that threatened to divide the IHU. In Brussels in 1970, the four provinces flag and Danny Boy had proved acceptable, but apparently at the Olympic Games, national flags and anthems had to be used. 'In the final analysis, the unity of Irish hockey was probably the dominant factor. The vote on a secret ballot resulted in a defeat by 27-25 for the motion that an application should be made' (*90 Years of Irish Hockey*). Five weeks later, a Special General Meeting was convened by the Leinster Branch, 'to reconsider and, if thought fit, to rescind the motion passed in October. The outcome of the ballot was 27 in favour of the motion to rescind, with 21 against. As there was not a two-thirds majority, required to reverse a previous decision, the motion was lost. Ireland would not be entering for the Munich Olympic after all' (*90 Years of Irish Hockey*).

In 1980 the Olympic Games were held in Moscow and a number of countries boycotted the Games because of the Soviets' invasion of Afghanistan. Ireland was asked to stand by. The Executive declined, not least on the reasonable grounds that the team would not have adequate time to prepare, but their decision again raised the issue of the IHU's policy with regard to Olympic participation. A case of 'The Munich bother' revisited! In May 1981 the IHU proposed a motion that the FIH be informed of Ireland's intention to apply for the Los Angeles Olympics (1984). After another secret ballot, this motion too was defeated. I was living and working in Belfast at the time of the Munich controversy, so I could well understand the depth of feeling behind the 'anti-Olympic participation' lobby. On the other hand, as a member of the Irish team, I desperately wanted to play in the 1972 Munich Olympic hockey tournament.

Ireland's participation in the first European Cup in Brussels (1970) was seen as an essential part of the preparation for Munich. But the legacy of the build-up towards Brussels persists to the present day. The challenge of sending an Irish team to Brussels led to a fundamental restructuring of the way that the national team was prepared; the selection of a squad of players, regular training weekends under the guidance of the national coach and, just prior to the selection of the 16 players for Brussels, a week spent living together in Tollymore Forest Park in

Co. Down, attempting (with varying degrees of success) to master the basic skills of canoeing in Newcastle Harbour, rock climbing, orienteering, running up sand dunes and on the beach, and taking turns at cooking the meals for everyone!

Nineteen countries took part in the Brussels tournament; Ireland finished ninth overall, despite losing just once in their six matches. Ireland's men's teams have taken part in all the subsequent European Nations tournaments; Madrid (1974), eleventh; Hanover (1978), eighth; Amsterdam (1983), tenth; Moscow (1987), sixth; Paris (1991), seventh. In 1995 the venue for the European Cup was Dublin and like the Women's World Cup the previous summer, Belfield was the venue for another splendidly run event. Ireland made the most of home advantage, achieving fifth, their highest ever ranking. In 1999 Ireland travelled to Padua and fared very poorly; all five pool matches and the first classification match were lost. Ireland finished 11th and as a consequence failed to qualify for the World Cup Qualifying Tournament in Edinburgh in 2001. Ireland's women's teams have also competed in every European Nations Cup, beginning in Lille in 1984. Their highest placing came in that very first competition, also fifth. In London in 1987, Ireland finished seventh, while in Brussels (1991) and in Amsterdam (1995), Ireland finished in eighth place. Perhaps some time in the 21st century a team representing Ireland – men or women – will qualify for, and participate in the Olympic Games, but at the present time it would appear to be a distance dream. More and more countries are emerging as serious contenders, mainly because of state funding which enables players to become full-time professionals. In the meantime Ireland's priority must be to qualify for every European Nations Tournament and to finish in the first six or eight places. ▪

The profile of hockey in Ireland has suffered from a lack of media exposure; the exception was the superb television coverage – by RTE and of the Women's World and Men's European Cups in 1994 and 1995. In the print media, men's hockey owes most to Carl Anderson in Belfast and Dermot Ashmore in Dublin. Carl Anderson tells of how he declined the offer to become rugby correspondent of The Belfast Telegraph. His sports editor was astonished at this decision. 'But rugby's a high profile sport, hockey is a minor sport.' Anderson admits that his decision was selfishly motivated, 'I was attracted by the prospect of travel. At that time (1970) hockey seemed to be a street ahead of rugby in its planning for future development; a reasonably well-organised hockey nation could look forward to two or three major tournaments, each lasting 10-12 days, inside a four-year cycle, with other international competitions needed to provide the build up. It's only comparatively recently that rugby has introduced a World Cup and in general terms their speed of innovation has lagged badly behind hockey. This is not an attempt to say hockey is a better sport than rugby. It's not and lacks the resources ever to make that claim, but I reckon hockey is the sport to be in if you want to travel the world.'

I, too, have relished the opportunity to travel to countries that I would surely otherwise never have visited. In my time as National Coach: Men's, 1975-78; Women's, 1981-88 I visited Argentina, Malaysia, Singapore and Pakistan; while as an FIH trainer I assisted in the running of coaching courses for coaches in Zimbabwe, the USA, Ghana and Oman. This list does not include the various European countries visited. At the start of this chapter I referred to the clash of loyalties that can arise between club and country, as seen from the National Coach's perspective. For the majority of Irish hockey players however, such issues are irrelevant, club hockey is the bedrock, the life blood, of the game in Ireland whether it be the fiercely contested league and cup competitions or the festival events where action off the pitch is every bit as important as what happens on the field of play.

Mary Hannigan, the women's hockey correspondent of The Irish Times in an article written after Ireland's most capped international player – Mary Logue – had announced her retirement, splendidly captures the spirit of club hockey in Ireland. The dilemma of being a minority sport in a world where the values of the market place are increasingly all important, and where women's sport is still regarded with some condescension by macho males – that is, if it isn't ignored altogether! 'If she'd been a rugby or football international she'd have had a Late Late Show devoted to her by now, shampoo, crisps and breakfast cereal advertising contracts to her name and maybe even the freedom of Cork City, her home place, devoted to her. God knows, she might have even had her own chat show by now, or at least her name held up as an example to the nation's youth by your average party leader at your average ard fheis. After all, over 12 years of her life, she played 153 times for Ireland, readily forfeiting a normal social life and jeopardising her working career along the way because she was born with a sublime sporting talent and she was determined to put to good use, and one she was honoured to put at the disposal of her country. For no return of course – an amateur in the old sense of the word. But a professional in every other aspect, except the financial one. Twelve years of looking at bank statements and concluding: "Christ, unpaid leave so that I can represent my country is all very well, but is that the bailiffs I hear knocking on my font door?" When she announced her international retirement at the age of 33, the news was a mere footnote on most sports pages, the few that even chose to mention her at all. Mind you, if she'd received the tributes and recognition she deserved the shock might have left her in need of rescuscitation... for her sport was filed under "minority" and her gender "not a lad – the other one! Why would we be wanting to hear anything about hockey? It's only what the girls do to fill their hours, while the lads are playing rugby, football or hurling."

'Yes, hockey. The game played by thousands upon thousands of kids and adults of every class, gender and religious persuasion in every corner of this country, at schools and club level. Some claim it is the biggest female sport in Ireland. So, every week shy, introverted, withdrawn young girls go out onto pitches from Bandon to Ballymoney and leave them reborn because in the course of the previous 50, 60 or 70 minutes they've learnt they've a whole lot more in them than they ever imagined. Maybe it was just one, single crucial tackle that earned them a congratulatory slap on the back from two or three of their team-mates, but it made them feel they weren't so ordinary after all and made them feel they were part of something, belonged to a team. So they go home smiling, buoyed by their new found self-belief, one, with the help of a higher power, they'll carry into every other area of their lives. That, we used to believe, is what sport is about. Whether it's hockey or another sport, it doesn't matter, so long as it gives kids the blank canvas to express themselves.'

RIGHT ■ Terry Gregg was, in the words of ex-internationals Freddie Martin and Ian Barrett, 'an outstanding centre forward'. Gregg played his first international at schoolboy level in 1968 and by 1981 he had achieved his 100th full international cap for Ireland. He was vice-captain of the Great Britain and Northern Ireland hockey side which won the bronze medal at the 1972 Munich Olympics. More recently he has coached the Lisnagavey Club side to seven successive Ireland wins and the club has won its league championship on many occasions under his tutelage. His latest position was to coach the Irish Ladies Senior International team. Billy McConnell, Steve Martin and Jimmy Kirkwood, like Terry Gregg, born and bred in the North of Ireland, have in more recent times been selected for Great Britain and Northern Ireland Olympic squads.

There is one development at club level that is not helpful in terms of improving the overall standard of play. Increasingly, the players who comprise the national squads are coming from fewer and fewer clubs. This is because the very best players follow one another to just a handful of clubs – clubs which aim to compete in one of the two European Club Championships for league winners and cup winners respectively. One could argue that the national squads' standards will improve with greater understanding amongst groups of players, but this trend is more likely to have a detrimental effect, in women's hockey in particular. One or two clubs in Leinster and in Ulster are proving far too strong for all the rest, making for far too many one-sided matches – or mismatches! – with the elite clubs recording too many facile victories, often winning by five or even ten goal margins. In Ireland there are never very many players of international standard, potential or actual and to have so many of the best players in just a couple of clubs cannot be good for the game's development. This situation militates against the raising of skill levels, reduces the tempo at which games should be played and blunts that competitive edge on which the best players thrive.

Considerations of space prevent me from writing about the splendid achievement of Ireland's U16 and U18 teams, male and female and the part played by the traditional, hockey-playing schools and universities and, increasingly, by those far-sighted clubs which are introducing young people to the game through the organisation of colts and junior teams; obviously the future development of hockey in Ireland depends upon these young players. ▪

Michael Halliday went to school at Wesley College and is currently on the staff of Wesley. He is a graduate of Dublin University where he played for the university cricket XI between 1968 and 1972, captaining the XI in 1970 and 1971. He went on to play cricket for Ireland 93 times between 1970 and 1989 and captained the side 25 times. He followed in Jimmy Boucher's footsteps as a very talented off-break bowler and during this time playing for Ireland, he took 192 wickets at an average of 30.30. Michael has been an Irish selector and a stalwart of Phoenix Cricket Club and was co-author of A History of Dublin University Cricket Club. ∎

The editor reflects: My special interest is cricket. A background of preparatory and public school cricket, Chorleywood and Northwood cricket clubs and services cricket led to university cricket. I was thrilled when in the team sheet posted at the front gate, my name appeared to represent Dublin University in the first league match of the 1957 season. I think I played in every match played by the university between 1957 and 1961.

A bumptious young English undergraduate was soon brought down to size; the wickets were slower than in England but did favour the cut and hook, and the opposition apart from its skill, knew how to exploit the conditions. Every Dublin club side had its gentle medium pacer and apparently innocuous spin bowler. All bowled just outside the off stump to well-set fields – the drive on the off side required concentrated execution. There were the exceptional bowlers who come quickly to mind, to name a few, Alec O'Riordan bowled quick-ish left arm over, Rodney Bernstein and Ernie Bodell bowled quickly, Jimmy Boucher and Ken Hope bowled off-breaks and Gerry Duffy with his flighted leg-breaks deceived many an unwary batsman. Of the batsmen, Stanley Bergin, a left-handed player seemed to score runs every time he played against Trinity. There were a number of quality batsmen, good enough to have played the best club cricket or minor county cricket in England; I think of players like Joe Caprani, Jack Notley, Louis Jacobson, Paddy Neville, Jimmy Gill, Kevin Quinn, David Pigott and Bill Haughton. Paddy Neville and Bill Haughton were big men, multi-talented sportsmen with tremendous eyes for the ball. Jack Notley and Kevin Quinn represented Ireland at both cricket and rugby.

Trinity sides were strong in this period, often with a predominance of overseas students from South Africa, Rhodesia and England, but due to term dates and the percentage system, found it difficult to win the league. But the Leinster Cup was won in 1961, for the first time since 1952, when they defeated Railway Union captained by Derek Scott in the final. The 1961 Trinity side were wonderful companions and good cricketers – a tidy bowling side, reliable batting, some very good fielders and an excellent wicketkeeper.

However, my special memories apart from the cut and thrust of the league and cup were the visits in Trinity week, of a side from the North of Ireland captained by Stuart Pollock including cricketers such as Jim McKelvey, Larry Warke, Willie Webb, Ray Hunter and Stanley Hewitt. Trips to Cork and in particular matches against Cork County at the Mardyke were unforgettable. Cork County sides were generally captained by Jim Kiernan or Ian Lewis and included in their side Tom Keirnan, Noel Cantwell, Des Cashell, Pat Riordan, Niall McConnell and Pat Dineen.

A highlight of the season was a one-week tour to England. Here the London clubs, Ealing, Enfield, North Middlesex, Finchley and London University welcomed us. The hard, fast, beautifully manicured pitches seemed to suit us and despite the presence of Eddie Ingram and Allan Coxon at Ealing, Ian Bedford and 'Josh' Levy at Finchley, Leslie Compton at North Middlesex and Bob Pipe and John Price at Wembley, we usually won! I should add that Ian Bedford who played cricket for Middlesex, was the Finchley captain for a while and England wanted him to be available for selection. Sadly he died young. I remember Donald Pratt, a left-hander and multi-gifted sportsman used to hit Ian Bedford's leg spin all over the ground. Most mortals found Ian Bedford too good and even impossible to establish bat on ball.

Very special memories include playing cricket at Halverstown with Paddy Boland, at Headfort School and at St Columba's (1954-86) with the Leprechauns. Norman Lush, deputy warden and master in charge of cricket at St Columba's (1954-86) with his enthusiasm and dedication produced some fine schoolboy sides. Also, perhaps less auspiciously, I remember circling under a high and important catch in a league game and, I fear, not only dropping it but also disappearing into a ditch on the boundary. I remember too the engine of my Morris Minor falling through the floor whilst on tour in Devon and Cornwall and a friendly conversation with the Garda on the way back to Trinity after the 1961 Cup triumph. I remember coming to Trinity in 1970 to play in the cricket week. I was about to return to New Zealand after a sabbatical at Worksop College, Nottinghamshire. It was a two-day game, a great reunion and I am afraid I failed to trouble the scorer in either innings. Ken Orme, who never gave me out in student days, gave me out twice, lbw, I like to think dubiously, but it was worth it for the craic of the after match celebrations. To the undergraduate, Irish cricket was tremendous fun and very competitive. Nearly half a century later, it remains in good heart, played enthusiastically and with skill particularly in the centres of Dublin, Belfast and Cork as well as other pockets. Irish cricket is below Test-playing standards; the immediate ambition is to qualify for the World Cup and it is keenly supported.

Cricket in Ireland has always been a minority sport, imported by British settlers, landlords and the army. This is, of course, true of all parts of the world where cricket is played, and the same can be said of other sports which originated in Britain and were given an organised format for the first time in the 19th century. The oldest club still playing in Ireland is probably Phoenix, founded in 1830 and its colours reflect this. The green and red are the colours of British regiments stationed in Dublin at the time and the black represents the black soil of the Phoenix Park. This British connection was to have a negative effect on the development of the game after the extremely successful foundation of the GAA in 1884. Cricket was categorised, along with Football, Rugby and Hockey as a 'foreign game' and those who played it were seen as somehow less Irish than those who wielded the hurley or played the Gaelic version of football. It was not until 1971 that the GAA dropped its ban on its members playing these imported games.

The narrowness and insularity of the brand of Irish nationalism that developed as the 20th century progressed tended to exclude from membership of the Irish nation anyone who could be tainted with things British. That could include Protestants, players of foreign games, or even such notable writers as Yeats and Synge who refused to conform to the stereotype demanded by the nationalist critics of their day. Thus, one day in August 1978, in an Ireland fixture at the North of Ireland Cricket Club in Ormeau, Belfast, I was forced to ponder the incongruity of fleeing from a hail of stones and being described as an 'Orange Bastard' while representing my country and wearing the shamrock proudly on my sweater. The fact that cricket is one of the games that brings all 32 counties together in one team would be lost on the youths who were firing the stones and those who a few years ago torched the clubhouse. Downpatrick Cricket Club also lost their pavilion three years ago. It is also fair to add that GAA clubs in the North of Ireland have suffered similar abuse – and worse – in recent times from those who see the GAA as some sort of threat to their British identity.

Despite this rather grim picture, cricket does play its part in bringing people of all classes and creeds together in the modern Ireland. Politics is successfully relegated to the recycle bin when sport takes over centre stage. This was well illustrated by the warm welcome afforded to the thousands of supporters draped in Ulster flags who made their way to Dublin for the final of rugby's European Cup in 1999. In all the time I have been involved, as a player, manager or recently as a selector, I have come across no efforts to select or overlook players because of where they came from. Whether or not Ireland selects the best team available is always a matter for argument, but politics does not play a part. ▪

The story of Irish cricket since the Second World War falls neatly into two chapters, the pre-overs cricket period, which comes to an end with the entry into the Gillette Cup in 1980, and the last 20 years which saw the expansion of the fixture list and the appearance of a number of overs competitions. The most important of these is the International Cricket Council Trophy for those nations ranked one rung below the test-playing nations. This is played every four years and (usually) the sides that finish in the top three in that competition play in the next World Cup alongside the best sides in the world. That is what Ireland aspires to, as it would raise the profile of the game in the country and attract much larger funding and sponsorship. In 1999, Ireland was within 30 runs of qualifying for the last World Cup, but missed out to Scotland. Predictably Scotland found the going pretty tough in the competition and there was a very heavy burden on their amateur players. However the structure and money in the game has improved as a result. Expectations were high that Ireland would qualify for the 2003 World Cup in South Africa through the ICC tournament held in Toronto in July 2001, but Ireland finished a terribly disappointing eighth. The problem for the Irish Cricket Union and the players is coming to terms with this challenge and deciding how best to prepare. The goal, outlined in a recently produced strategic three-year plan, is to achieve One Day International status. Kenya has recently been accorded this standing. Bangladesh has recently become a test-playing nation and the International Cricket Council is very supportive of any country which sets its sights as high as is reasonably possible. Included in this new plan is the provision of two offices in the North and South for the administration of the game and the appointment of a Chief Executive and appropriate staff. These officers would support, rather than replace, voluntary participation in ICU affairs.

The first sign that the Irish Cricket Union was serious in its efforts to keep pace with other second division cricketing nations was the appointment in 1995 of the first professional coach, Mike Hendrick, the former Notts, Derby and England seam bowler. Mike introduced a much more professional approach to preparation and attitude in the national team and developed a series of promising fast bowlers. He found the amateur ethic ingrained in the Irish game quite hard to come to terms with, and was frequently frustrated with unavailability and players who perhaps didn't want to make the commitment that he demanded. Winning the Triple Crown and the European Cup were the highlights of his spell in charge. In 2000 he was replaced with ex-New Zealand captain, Ken Rutherford. It was hoped that Ken, being mainly a batting coach, would mend the main weakness in the Irish team which is inconsistent and unreliable batting. It has been interesting to watch the different approach of two successful test players in dealing with a disparate group of amateurs. Management skills are vital in this job and to mould a happy and successful side is not an easy task. Rutherford resigned after the debacle of Toronto.

In an effort to give Irish players the chance to learn from some of the best test players, The Irish Independent, owned by Sir Anthony O'Reilly, of British and Irish Lions and baked bean fame, has sponsored a guest player for three weeks over the past few years. Hansie Cronje, Steve Waugh, Jonty Rhodes and Mark Waugh have spent time in the country, playing, coaching and helping promote the game. What they thought of their time here would be an interesting appendix to this chapter. The lowest point of their collective experiences was when Jonty discovered that one of his Irish team mates had been suspended for indulging in a bout of fisticuffs with his opening bowler at three in the morning. The high point came during Hansie's Irish sabbatical and that will be mentioned later. A story that Steve Waugh recounted involved his batting partner whom he encountered in the middle of the wicket between overs in a match ironically against the Australian 'A' team. Waugh was of the opinion that maybe it was time to accelerate the run rate. 'Off you go then', said the amateur Irish batsman, 'you're the one getting paid'.

The standing of Irish cricket as a minority sport is reflected in the annual grant awarded to the ICU by the Irish Sports Council, the body charged with developing sport in The Republic. In 2001 that amounts to £43,968 and includes money designated for the Irish Women's Cricket Union, which has recently amalgamated with the ICU. The Northern Ireland Sports Council grant to the Union is £60,000. In October 2000 the Irish Women had to make a large personal contribution to enable them to travel to New Zealand for the World Cup. If one was to judge the importance of a particular sport in the eyes of the Irish Sports Council by the size of grants, you would come to the conclusion that the following are more worthy recipients of funding: Handball (£62,000), Table Tennis (£58,000), Mountaineering (£44,000), Pitch and Putt (£50,000), Volleyball (£72,000). I have no gripes with any of these sports receiving these grants and good luck to them. I am sure they could do with far more. In world cricket terms Ireland may be a minnow, but we are in the top eighteen in the world and are striving to improve our standing. Money is needed to improve infrastructure, coaching, pitches and for the payment of players at the top level. I am not suggesting that taxpayers' money should go towards paying players – that could be covered by sponsorship and the three-year plan envisages a massive expansion in private and corporate finance in the game. The Ireland squad needs a reliable core of semi and full-time professionals if the status and standards of the game are to improve, and they are an absolute necessity if Ireland is to aspire to being a One Day International team.

Major weaknesses in the Irish game are the relatively low standards in club cricket, which means that the better players are not being sufficiently tested week in, week out, and the generally poor condition of many Irish pitches, which inhibits the development of confident batsmen and good, accurate, line and length bowling. However there are many strengths in the game in Ireland, notably in the successes of the under age sides and the enthusiasm of younger players. It is when the inevitable compromises, inherent in a purely amateur game, become evident – usually in the early twenties age group – that progress slows and availability becomes a problem. In the English game, many of the better under age players will be contracted to a county side at that stage. In Ireland this is very rare, although in recent times we have had four young players try their luck across the water. Ed Joyce of Middlesex is the best known scoring two hundred at the end of the 2001 summer. The two Patterson brothers, Mark and Andy tried their luck with

ABOVE ■ Ed Joyce as an undergraduate plays a powerful shot in Dublin league cricket and his talents warrant a career in the professional game.

MARYLEBONE CRICKET CLUB

LORD'S GROUND

CricInfo Championship

30p **MIDDLESEX v. WARWICKSHIRE** 30p

Wednesday, Thursday, Friday & Saturday, August 22, 23, 24 & 25, 2001 (4-day Match)

	MIDDLESEX	First Innings		Second Innings
1	A. J. Strauss	b Dagnall	14	
2	M. J. Brown	b Drakes	0	
3	O. A. Shah	c Piper b Dagnall	17	
4	S. P. Fleming	c Piper b Brown	102	
5	E. C. Joyce	run out	104	
6	P. N. Weekes			
*7	D. C. Nash			
8	J. W. M. Dalrymple			
9	S. J. Cook			
†10	A. R. C. Fraser			
11	T. F. Bloomfield			
	Bonus Points	B , l-b , w , n-b ,		B , l-b , w , n-b ,
		Total		Total

FALL OF THE WICKETS

1—0 2—32 3—33 4—252 5—268 6— 7— 8— 9— 10—

1— 2— 3— 4— 5— 6— 7— 8— 9— 10—

ANALYSIS OF BOWLING

Name	1st Innings						2nd Innings					
	O.	M.	R.	W.	Wd.	N-b	O.	M.	R.	W.	Wd.	N-b
Dagnall	...	...	...	...	...	...	...	...	...	...	...	...
Drakes	...	...	...	...	...	...	...	...	...	...	...	...
Brown	...	...	...	...	...	...	...	...	...	...	...	...
Richardson	...	...	...	...	...	...	...	...	...	...	...	...
Spires	...	...	...	...	...	...	...	...	...	...	...	...
Wagh	...	...	...	...	...	...	...	...	...	...	...	...

MATCH BALLS SPONSORED BY DAVENPORT LYONS

	WARWICKSHIRE	First Innings	Second Innings
1	N. V. Knight		
†2	M. J. Powell		
3	M. A. Wagh		
4	I. R. Bell		
5	D. L. Hemp		
6	D. R. Brown		
*7	K. J. Piper		
8	V. C. Drakes		
9	C. E. Dagnall		
10	J. A. Spires		
11	A. Richardson		
	Bonus Points	B , l-b , w , n-b ,	B , l-b , w , n-b ,
		Total	Total

FALL OF THE WICKETS

1— 2— 3— 4— 5— 6— 7— 8— 9— 10—

1— 2— 3— 4— 5— 6— 7— 8— 9— 10—

ANALYSIS OF BOWLING

Name	1st Innings						2nd Innings					
	O.	M.	R.	W.	Wd.	N-b	O.	M.	R.	W.	Wd.	N-b
	...	...	...	...	...	...	...	...	...	...	...	...
	...	...	...	...	...	...	...	...	...	...	...	...
	...	...	...	...	...	...	...	...	...	...	...	...
	...	...	...	...	...	...	...	...	...	...	...	...
	...	...	...	...	...	...	...	...	...	...	...	...
	...	...	...	...	...	...	...	...	...	...	...	...

Umpires—G. Sharp & R. A. White   Scorers—M. J. Smith & D. E. Wainwright
†Captain   *Wicket-keeper

Play begins at 11.00 each day. Luncheon Interval 1st, 2nd & 3rd days 1.15—1.55, 4th day 1.00—1.40
Tea Interval 1st, 2nd & 3rd days 4.10—4.30, or when 32 overs remain to be bowled,
whichever is the later. 4th day 3.40—4.00.
Stumps drawn 1st, 2nd & 3rd days at 6.30, or after 104 overs have been bowled; 4th
day at 6.00 or after 96 overs have been bowled. The captains may agree to end the
match at 5.30 on the 4th day if there is no prospect of a result.
If play is suspended for any reason the minimum number of overs to be bowled in the
day shall be reduced by one over for each 3¾ minutes of play lost.

Middlesex won the toss

ABOVE ▧ 22nd August 2001 Middlesex v Warwickshire. Ed Joyce scores his first century for Middlesex and shares a partnership of 219 with Stephen Fleming, the New Zealand Captain and is run out at the close of play on the first day.

Surrey and Sussex, while a bad injury cut short Ryan Eagleson's career with Derbyshire, at least for the time being. Over the years the question of which Irish cricketers would have been successful in the professional game has frequently been asked. In 1981/82, at a late stage in his career, Dermott Monteith had a short but successful spell with Middlesex and there are many players who would have been a success if they had decided to try. However most of the top-ranking cricketers were career driven and to many the idea of becoming a professional did not warrant a second thought.

The best known of all was the Phoenix off spinner, Jimmy Boucher, whose career lasted from 1929 until 1954. His control and sharpish off spin could have seen him play for England. Alec O'Riordan, of Old Belvedere, fast left arm and right-hand bat also fits into this category. Ivan Anderson, of Waringstown, would have graced any county ground. In a two-day match v MCC at Lord's, Ivan was denied two centuries in the same match by the South African Clive Rice, who bowled two overs of bouncers to prevent an Irish win and Ivan's second century. Alf Masood, who was close to playing for Pakistan before he left the country, has easily the best batting average of an Irish player. The hard-hitting Masood was once dismissed at Lord's, ten minutes before lunch on the first day, for 136. His interprovincial batting average is 69; the next best is 41! Dermott Monteith was a gifted slow left arm bowler and captain whose supreme self-confidence made him always an interesting companion, both on and off the field. On one occasion I was not only rooming with him but the two of us were both 0 not out overnight. The game was against Worcester at New Road. Rooming is not quite the correct word as Dermott seldom used bedrooms. That night was no exception, and as the bleary-eyed Monty and I set out to face Norman Gifford at 10 am I did not give Ireland much chance of saving the match. Half an hour later I was still 0 not out but Monty had reached 40 not out!

A hit and run driver finished his career in 1985 but he is still active as an Irish selector and was President of the ICU in 1999. He was a captain who was not afraid to take chances, such as deciding to bat first at Lord's against Middlesex in Ireland's first ever game in the Gillette Cup in 1980. There was no thought of damage limitation when he was confronted with teams full of test players. He firmly believed he was the third best slow left arm bowler in the world in 1977. When he saw Dilip Doshi in action against Ireland that year he promptly moved himself up the pecking order to second. He was willing to allow Bishen Bedi the pole position; his team talks were direct and to the point and he would not speak for half an hour if one minute would do. On one occasion, before taking the field at Rathmines against the West Indies, his urgings to his side amounted to an instruction to 'Consider yourselves whipped up'. Monty's rival for the character of the era was undoubtedly Ossie Colhoun, the wicketkeeper from Sion Mills. Apart from having a superbly fast pair of hands, he had the quickest line in repartee. It was extremely fortunate that the opposition had a pretty limited understanding of what he was saying, delivered as it was in a form of North West Jive. His greatest moment came in 1969 when he kept wicket at Sion against the West Indies on the famous occasion when Ireland dismissed the side – who had just drawn the Second Test at Lord's – for 25. Ossie is a singer of note, fronting his own band with a mixture of middle-of-the-road pop and country. He was also Ireland's nightwatchman for many years, although the first time that I saw him in this role, against Scotland at Perth in 1970, he was run out going for a third run! ■

t is invidious to make lists of great players from any era but some others should be mentioned. Stanley Bergin, from Pembroke; Scott Huey, from Eglinton; Alec O'Riordan from Old Belvedere; Jack Short, from Leinster CC and Cork County; Simon Corlett and Paul Jackson from North; Dougie Goodwin from Malahide; Alan Lewis and Angus Dunlop from YMCA and Stephen Warke from Woodvale would get into anyone's list. In looking for the highlights of these last 50 years in international cricket, the dismissal of the West Indies for 25 and the subsequent 9 wickets victory has to be the most talked about. When the teams went on to play a two-day match at Ormeau, in Belfast, Ireland held out for a draw. Thus it could be claimed that Ireland

ABOVE ■ 1994 ICC Trophy Nairobi Kenya. Alan Lewis – Rugby Referee and Cricketer – is run out for 50 v Papua New Guinea.

ABOVE ▪ 1987 Ireland v Leicester. Paul Jackson, Ireland's equal most capped wicketkeeper with Ossie Colhoun, plays a forcing stroke off his legs in a limited overs match.

won the series! The game was a triumph for two of Ireland's long-serving opening bowlers, O'Riordan and Goodwin. It was claimed by some that the opposition had succumbed to Irish hospitality prior to the game. However the truth is that a soft, green wicket, excellent bowling and a few careless shots were the cause of this astonishing scorecard. A film of this remarkable day for Irish cricket has survived, with a commentary by a young Neil Durden-Smith. More than 30 years later Neil Durden-Smith OBE remembers the match well: 'I have to admit to feeling partly responsible for the West Indies being bowled out for by far the lowest score in their history. Let me explain: In my time as a broadcaster I was quite often invited to go to Ireland to be the commentator for the BBC's Outside Broadcasts, on both television and radio. In the summer of 1969 I was asked to cover the historic televised inaugural one-day cricket match between Ireland and the West Indies at Sion Mills, a tiny Ulster town in Co. Derry. How historic it turned out to be!

'Tuesday 1st July was the last day of the Lord's Test and England batted all day, Boycott scoring 106 and Sharpe 86. I was in the Test Match Special team in those days alongside John Arlott and Brian Johnson and that evening I went to Heathrow with the West Indies party from St

John's Wood to catch the flight to Belfast. We were met at Aldergrove by a fleet of cars and driven to a hotel in Londonderry where we were to spend the night. After dropping our bags off, we all went out to have dinner in a Chinese restaurant. I remember thinking then it was slightly incongruous being with a collection of cricketers from the Caribbean tucking into sweet and sour pork and fried rice in a Chinese restaurant in the Emerald Isle, having completed a Test Match at Lord's that very afternoon!

'The following morning, Wednesday 2nd July 1969 – a day destined to go down in Irish sporting folklore – dawned cloudless and sunny. Garry Sobers, captain of the touring side, had decided in his wisdom to take a few days off to go racing and Lance Gibbs, the vice-captain, had bowled 41 overs in England's second innings at Lord's and his spinning finger resembled a piece of raw steak, so there was no way he could play. Basil Butcher, the next senior player, was appointed captain for the match and Clyde Walcott, the manager, was pressed into service (not a bad former player to have in your side!). I travelled to the ground in the same car as Butcher, Gibbs and Walcott and Basil asked me en route what he should do if he won the toss. "You must bat", said I, "because if you field first and bowl Ireland out before lunch there won't be a match worth watching". I was not to know that my pearls of wisdom were to lead to utter disaster for the West Indies!

'The beautiful Sion Mills ground, with a river running down one side of it, was absolutely packed. The outfield looked immaculate and, due to some overnight rain, the wicket was fittingly emerald green and slightly damp to boot. That didn't stop Butcher electing to bat after he had won the toss and at 11.30 Steve Camacho and Joey Carew duly walked out to open the innings. In Dougie Goodwin, the captain, and Alec O'Riordan, Ireland had a pair of opening bowlers good enough to have played first-class cricket had they been interested. They bowled brilliantly, so brilliantly that after 40 minutes the West Indies: Butcher, Lloyd, Foster, Walcott, Shepherd et al were 12 for 9! At that point a little known fast bowler called Blair came in at No 11 to join Shillingford. Together they scythed at every ball and somehow they managed to score another 13 runs between them, easily the highest partnership of the innings with Shillingford's 9 not out, the highest score. So the mighty West Indies had been humbled for 25, Goodwin taking 5 for 6 and O'Riordan 4 for 18, with one bye. It could so easily have been 12 all out! Ireland duly won by 9 wickets and the West Indies sportingly agreed to carry on and play a beer match for the benefit of the huge crown jammed into the idyllic little ground. They made many friends by doing so and they took their defeat with great charm and good humour. How it must have hurt though!

'On a personal note I will never forget my day at Sion Mills. The commentary box was just that: a box perched dangerously high up on top of a Heath Robinson contraption, sometimes known as scaffolding. The only way up was via a flimsy ladder – rather like going up the north face of the Eiger I imagine. There was just room in the box for one other person, the Producer. The scorer was a lady sitting in a deck chair at ground level and the bowling figures (there weren't many runs) had to be hauled up to me at the end of each over in a bucket on the end of a piece of rope! I thanked my lucky stars for my strong bladder because I was stuck up in that box for hours doing pieces into seemingly endless radio and television programmes. It was even the lead story on all the one o'clock news bulletins! My days of proffering advice to touring teams on how to proceed when winning the toss are definitely over.'

The second most memorable match in this period was Ireland's first victory over professional opposition in a competitive game. This was the win over Middlesex in the Benson and Hedges Cup at Clontarf in 1997. Assisted by the bookies' friend, Hansie Cronje, Ireland made 281 for 4, with Cronje making 94*, but with notable contributions from other home-bred players, especially man of the match Decker Curry who hit a rapid 75. Middlesex replied with 235 all out. This victory was preceded by an Irish triumph in the first ever European Cup in Copenhagen in 1996. But there has been little of note to happen since.

I would pick the win over Sussex in a three-day match at Pagham in 1977 as another significant milestone. It was Imran Khan's first game for Sussex, and at that stage he was vying for the title of best all-rounder in the world. In 1977 he was also being described as the fastest bowler in the world. Ireland bowled Sussex out twice and won chasing 200 in the last innings. Jack Short made 99, Chris Harte 49 and the great memory of the game was a duel between Imran and Podge Hughes, the Irish seam bowler, who came in to bat at number 9. In bad light, wearing spectacles but no helmet, Podge backed away and slashed Imran over cover, over the slips, over the wicketkeeper. Instead of trying to bowl him, which would not have been difficult as Podge was standing in the vicinity of the Square Leg Umpire, Imran tried to hit him. He succeeded but the ball went for 4 leg byes off the middle of the Clontarf man's back. Eventually Imran was warned and taken off by the Sussex captain, Peter Graves. These unorthodox runs kept us in the game with a chance of winning.

A ground-breaking tour to the USA and Canada was undertaken in 1973, visiting places as diverse as Louisville, Kentucky; Washington Park, Chicago and Palo Alto, San Francisco. Zimbabwe has been visited three times. The first being in 1986, when a 19 year-old called Graeme Hick made 309 in the three-day game. He was famously dropped by John Prior when on 16, not a particularly difficult chance. John himself made 0 and 1 in the match so he reckons he came out of the game with a deficit of 292! It was during one of his spells bowling at Hick in this match that the author of this piece had his first experience of homesickness. Prior may not have had his best game in Harare but it would be wrong to gloss over his career. The most

ABOVE ■ Ireland team prior to the tour to USA and Canada 1973. **Back Row:** Derek Scott (Asst. Sec. ICU), Alfie Lenihan, 'Ginger' O'Brien, Chris Harte, Gerry Duffy, John Elder, Mike Halliday, Roy Torrens, David Pigot, Ian Lewis, Jim Harrison. **Front Row:** Jimmy Boucher (Sec. ICU), Ossie Colhoun, Alec O'Riordan, Tony Robertson (President ICU), Dougie Goodwin, Ivan Anderson, Billy Ritchie (selector). Also in the squad – P. Dineen and A. Linehan.

memorable sight I ever had in an Irish cricket ground was when John hit a century in 51 balls against Warwickshire at Rathmines in 1982. Gladstone Small, attempting to break into the English Test XI, was brought back to quieten things down and remove John from the crease when he had reached 93. He then hit Gladstone for five successive fours to go to 113. ■

One great advantage of having the honour to play cricket for Ireland was that you got the chance to play against the best players in the world. Despite being an amateur team from a minority sport in a small country, all the test-playing countries included Ireland in their itinerary from time to time, and generally they were delighted to come as a welcome break in the middle of a test series in England. Of the thousands of talented club cricketers throughout the world, I got the chance to meet and play against household names like Colin Cowdrey, Sunil Gavaskar, Allan Border, Joel Garner, Viv Richards, Courtney Walsh, Mike Brearley and Geoffrey

Boycott – and just because I was lucky enough to be an Irish cricketer. It is also important to acknowledge the role of a succession of excellent cricket administrators in the Irish game who helped make these fixtures happen. Foremost in this role was Derek Scott, secretary from 1974-98, who, apart from his untiring work for Irish cricket, became a respected committee man at the TCCB and President of the ICU in 2001.

There are four regional unions in Ireland and about 150 clubs throughout the country. The majority are situated in Northern Ireland in the Northern Cricket Union area, centred around Belfast and in the North West Cricket Union area centred around Derry. Dublin has 16 senior clubs in the Leinster Cricket Union, while there are only a handful of clubs in the Munster Cricket Union. Munster play in the Second Division of the Leinster League, however there is a long history of cricket in Cork at the beautiful Mardyke ground and many of the best memories

ABOVE ■ 1982 Ireland v India at Ormeau. Mike Halliday (captain of Ireland) and Sunil Gavaskar (captain of India) stand with their teams.

of Irish cricketers surround trips to the 'Dyke' and nights which ended in the Westpoint Guest House. While there are many rural clubs in the North, there are only a few junior clubs outside Dublin and Cork in the South. However there are teams to be found in Galway, Limerick, Tralee, Waterford, Co. Mayo, Lismore, Wexford and Ballyeighon, Co. Tipperary and in some midland areas. Touring sides frequently find their way to picturesque grounds such as Mount Juliet, slightly better known for its golf course, Bagenalstown, Mullingar, Halverstown and Headfort, the home of County Meath. It is said that the barrister and author Charles Lysaght made a big impression on Cambridge captain Mike Brearley when he arrived at nets at Fenner's. He told Brearley that he played county cricket, omitting the fact that it was for County Meath. Unfortunately Charles didn't talk his way to a blue, but achieved the next best thing, Presidency of the Cambridge Union.

The most successful clubs of the period have been Waringstown in the Northern Cricket Union, Phoenix in Leinster, Donemana and Limavady in the North West and Cork County in Munster. Waringstown is a picturesque village, probably best known for its cricket club. The Harrison family dominated the team and cricket in the NCU throughout the '70s and '80s. Four Harrison brothers played for Ireland, Roy, Jim, Deryck and Garfield, a record that will take some beating. Phoenix won the Leinster Cup five years in a row in the '70s and the superiority of Ulster clubs is emphasised by the fact that Phoenix are still the only southern club to have won the Irish Senior Cup, a feat achieved in 1986. Donemana and Limavady have extraordinary records in the recent past with the former winning nine league titles in a row in the North West only to be replaced in the last seven years by Limavady.

By far the most fanatical cricketers are to be found in the North West, where one could say there is a separate cricketing republic. There are parallels here with rugby in Limerick, whose sporting public is not only the most knowledgeable but the most partisan followers imaginable. There is a general belief in these two areas that their sporting sons are the most gifted and the most hard-done-by. Players from Belfast or Dublin are pathetic wimps in comparison. In Yorkshire there would be a similar healthy disregard for those wearing a Middlesex sweater. It is only in the counties of Derry and Tyrone that you can find large enthusiastic crowds attending a club match, urging the batsmen to 'Gi'er the lang handle in the heel o the evenin', or 'Gi'er a drink'. (There might be a river over the midwicket boundary) There are plenty of 'incidents' in the North West League, probably more than in the rest of the country put together, and there is fierce rivalry between clubs such as the above mentioned Donemana and Limavady along with their main challengers Brigade, Eglinton, Sion Mills and Strabane. My first experience of playing in the North West came in 1968, just as the "Troubles" were beginning. I was travelling to Strabane late on a Friday night with three other Dublin cricketers when the car with its southern

ABOVE ▓ 1982 Cup Final. David Pigot and Alf Masood open the batting for Phoenix v Malahide at Clontarf.

plates was stopped somewhere in rural Tyrone by the 'B' Specials, the soon-to-be-disbanded armed police reserve. We were lined up and searched in what could be described as a rather threatening manner. They relented somewhat when they found we were in possession of cricket bats but when I asked them did they know Ossie Colhoun, we changed dramatically from being 'Fenians from the Free State' to red carpet visitors. We were given a motor cycle escort straight to the Fir Trees Hotel, Strabane.

My favourite on-field story with a North West provenance involves Big Roy Torrens, the well known Brigade fast bowler, Derry City footballer and magician. Ireland was playing Surrey at the Oval and the Irish team had taken a dislike to the Kiwi Geoff Howarth, who had visibly and orally indicated that he was less than pleased at being asked to play in such a match, especially as he had just been told he was surplus to Surrey's requirements the following season. It was coming to the end of the Irish innings and I, as captain, asked Roy to go in and throw the bat and score a few quick runs. Roy faced his first ball that was a good length outside the off stump. He launched into an extravagant drive, missed the ball, followed through and the bat flew from his hands in the direction of Howarth, who happened to be standing beside the square leg umpire. Luckily for both men the bat sailed over their heads. Much mirth ensued in the middle. When Roy returned to the visitors changing room he announced that the 'skipper told me to throw the bat'. We knew that it was no accident that it was the hapless Kiwi that was in most danger. In the same game Roy was taking a bit of a pasting from the Surrey openers, Alan Butcher and Duncan Pauline. In the third over of the innings as we hastily reset the field with slips disappearing to all parts of the Oval, Roy hesitated at the end of his run up and shouted out that he would like 'Jacko' to move to extra cover on the boundary. This would not normally be strange but for the fact that 'Jacko' was the wicketkeeper. In recent years Roy has become a larger than life character in the administration of Irish Cricket. Having been a selector for a number of seasons he was President of the Union in the Millennium season. The sight of himself and 'Monty' (Dermott Monteith) walking around the boundary at an international match, or sitting in a hotel lobby at two in the morning in the company of a Famous Grouse is one of the great spectacles of modern Irish cricket administration.

In the Belfast area, as in the North West, cricket is widely played and reported. The profile of the game in Dublin is not as high. This is partly due to the limited space apportioned to the game in Dublin and also to the odd fact that apart from Trinity, Phoenix and perhaps Malahide there are no senior grounds that are visible to casual passers-by. Most are down laneways or behind high walls. Many cricketers have come to live and work in Dublin and have taken a couple of years to discover that cricket was played in Ireland. In fact many Irish people are only vaguely aware of its existence. Lord Killanin, the Irish ex-President of the International Olympic Committee, once famously announced that cricket was not played in Ireland!

College Park, in Trinity, was the home for Irish matches in Dublin until 1963, when the West Indies were played on a dodgy rain-affected wicket. Sadly the venue was dropped after that. It is the only ground that approximates to an English county ground, in size and setting. There was always a large crowd in attendance for internationals and I can remember the crowd being five deep all around the ground for that game in 1963, and for the game against the Australians in 1961. Stories abound about matches at the ground. Leslie Webb, a cricket fanatic who used to score for Trinity said that he couldn't walk down the promenade without imagining his hero, Victor Trumper, making 47 for Australia against Trinity Past and Present in 1905. He would also wistfully recall the fact that Frank Browning of Trinity, made two half centuries in that match. Browning later became President of the IRFU and was killed during the 1916 Rising in Dublin. He was a reservist in the army out on a training march, not realising that a rebellion had begun in central Dublin, when his group were hit by sniper fire. W.G. Grace played there nine times and the crowds were even bigger then. Staging internationals there is not easy for the ICU as a university club does not have the manpower and know-how when it comes to staging a big match and taking a 'gate' is problematical with so many points of access. But they are problems that should be addressed as the game's profile would increase with the big games being staged in a highly attractive central location. Clontarf is Dublin's major international ground and staged a game between the West Indies and Bangladesh in the last World Cup. Rathmines, (Leinster C.C.) and Malahide are the two other designated international grounds in Dublin, while in the North it is hoped that Civil Service C.C. at Stormont will become the regular ground used in Belfast with Waringstown and Lurgan as back up. In the North West, Eglinton and Brigade are the main venues.

University cricket is greatly hampered by the exam season in May and June. Trinity and University College Cork are the only universities to play in senior leagues in the country. Indeed, Queen's University Belfast are the only other college side to play in any league and that is in Division Two in the Northern Cricket Union. However the latest sad news is that Queen's have disbanded as an NCU league side. It is to be hoped that this is a temporary measure. Other colleges put together teams for an Irish Universities Championship in June and an Irish XI plays every year in the British Universities tournament. They have won this competition on three occasions. Student cricket continues to be fun, but also intensive. A promising player in Trinity could play up to 25 games before the end of June. This involves a huge commitment in time, both on and off the field and in the bar.

Schools cricket is much bigger in the North of Ireland where the summer term continues to the last week in June. In Dublin the schools close at the beginning of June so there is frequently a season of only six or seven weeks. In these circumstances the clubs are very important in running under age cricket. Senior schools sides in Dublin play in a league, with a cup final. These games are played on Wednesdays and are only 35 over matches. On Saturdays the better players are usually absent playing for their clubs. Every year Ulster Schools play a Southern Schools XI and an Irish team is chosen following that game. Interprovincials are played at Under 13, 15 and 17 level, usually in July. Irish under age teams have done well in recent seasons, winning the European trophy at Under 19 level in 1999 and the European Under 15 Championship in 2000. The most promising 18 year-olds will then be drafted into an Irish Cricket Union Development squad, which will tour, usually in England, most summers. Apart from providing opposition of a higher quality than is available at home and experience on more reliable wickets, these tours are vital in preparing young players for important tournaments in the future. Who is a good tourist? Who has the stamina to play consistently well over a number of games, often without a rest day? Who is prone to homesickness? Who can't be trusted to discipline themselves when they are away from home? Who is good at taking responsibility for their own performance? Who has pride in pulling on an Irish sweater? Who will encourage the less experienced and younger players? Captaincy is probably more important in cricket than in any other game I know and it is on tour that captaincy skills are honed and developed. Irish players must tour more often and that demands more finance than is available at the moment. ▨

What brings an Irishman, or woman, to be a cricketer? The answer is a bit different in the north of Ireland to the south. In the south the majority will not have started their cricket in school and will be drawn to the game through a family connection or friends. Television will have played its part in the making of many cricketers and BBC coverage which first arrived on the east coast in the '60s is hugely influential. At the present time Channel 4 and Sky coverage is watched by a surprisingly high number of Irish people, considering the game's profile. Sport and its competitive nature has a huge following in Ireland and the number of people who take an interest in cricket far outnumbers the number of people who actually play. It is, after all, a very difficult game and the process of organising yourself to play, buying gear and practising is a major effort compared to many other pursuits. The length of time it takes to play a game is another reason why more numbers do not play. So who does play, and why? The social aspect of cricket is a major consideration here as it is in most Irish sport, and cricket clubs are excellent social centres, often dominating clubs that have far more members in their tennis or bowling sections. Being a summer team game is an attraction to many who enjoy the craic in a changing room or bar. In Dublin cricketers are mainly from a middle class background, as is the case in the Belfast area. In the north county area of Dublin and in the north west there is a much wider social profile with players drawn from all sections of the community. The attraction of clubs to young players is paramount. Parents are always delighted when their children are taken off the street for long periods in the summer and cricket is a game which is very difficult to adapt to if you have not had a grounding as a schoolboy or girl in a club. The ICU strategic plan hopes to increase the number of primary schools playing KWIK cricket by 10% in each of the next three years and rather optimistically hopes that the number of secondary schools playing increases by 25% each year.

The average club cricketer is about 26, has a good job, practices once a week and if he is keen to do well in his club is probably highly annoyed by the number of Australians batting above him in the order. He is a bit uncomfortable with the aggressive 'sledging' that has become common-place in club cricket and sometimes wonders why umpires can be bothered listening to the abuse so frequently aimed in their direction. He likes a pint or two after the game and probably finds the club atmosphere better and more accommodating than in his rugby, hockey, or soccer club. He will play cricket far longer than those who play other team games and eventually when he succumbs to golf he will continue to play a bit of cricket, if only of the taverner variety. In Ireland he will have thousands of conversations explaining the laws and attractions of the game and why it is not necessarily boring. He may be confronted, as I was once, with explaining the game and its trappings, to an American tourist in College Park. He found the scene, with the white flannels and umpires coats, against the bright green of the field, quite extraordinary. Then at 1.00 pm about 50 medical students emerged from a lecture in the Moyne Institute on the far side of the ground, wearing their lab coats. My American friend stared across the field and pondered on this for a while. Then he asked, 'Say, what are all those umpires doing over there?' Our average club cricketer may sit on a club committee and be torn between spending £5,000 on a West Indian Pro or a new roof for the clubhouse. He will put on weight from eating egg sandwiches at teatime, drinking the amber nectar after play and eating chips on the way home. He will find it difficult to explain to his girlfriend how he can spend maybe twelve hours on a Saturday indulging in his favourite pastime and its compulsory social duties. She may eventually stoop to making egg sandwiches herself when she discovers that as she cannot beat him, she might as well join him.

Cricket was very much a sexist sport and some would say that it still is. Ladies were not permitted in the bar in Phoenix until about 1967, which is, I suppose, much better than the MCC's belated decision to allow lady members in 1997. However since 1967 there have been two lady Presidents of Phoenix and the club's most famous lady cricketer, Mary Pat Moore, became a successful captain of Ireland and was last seen commentating on Sky Sports on the England Women's series with South Africa in 2000. So the average male club cricketer is likely to find much more female company in his club than was the case in the past. However, the resurgence in the ladies game has strangely had little impact in Northern Ireland. The Irish women were disappointed by their performance in the recent World Cup in New Zealand, but nevertheless they do rank sixth in the world. At the 2001 AGM of the Irish Cricket Union, the Irish Women's Cricket Union dissolved itself and was amalgamated with the men's organisation. This was warmly welcomed by all at the meeting and has to be good for all involved in the administration and playing of the game in Ireland.

Wherever the game is played around the world it attracts enthusiasts, fanatics and statisticians. Ireland has always been full of them. John Hill was a Trinity, Clontarf and international cricketer who played 1st X1 cricket in six different decades. When he left Trinity, in the forties, his first job as an engineer was in planning new housing estates in Belfast after the war. He ensured that the lampposts were all 22 yards apart thus creating numerous ready made pitches for a future generation of enthusiasts. An umpire, from the North West, who shall be nameless, was standing in his first international. In the hotel in Dublin he was rooming with his white-coated colleague. He found sleep difficult the night before play and got out of bed at three in the morning. His colleague, feigning sleep, watched as our hero practised raising his finger to himself, in the mirror. Apparently he dismissed enough batsmen that night to warrant an entry in the Guinness Book of Records. Finally, an apocryphal story about the appeal of cricket statistics. About 25 years ago I was driving along a dusty highway in Indian territory in the state of Arkansas. I noticed a sign on the side of the road advertising the world's best memory man, Chief Big Hit. The sign said, 'Ask the chief any question, if he can't answer you win $500'. I pulled in and went into his tent. He beckoned me to sit cross-legged on the floor and then I asked him my question. 'In the North West Cup final of 1948 who hit the winning runs?' Without blinking an eyelid he replied 'Alec McBrine, for Donemana against Strabane.' Astounded, I left the tent having lost my $10 wager. Recently I was driving along the same road and to my astonishment I found the chief still in business. I decided to renew the acquaintance and waited for my turn in what was quite a long queue. As I entered the tent I held my right hand up in the traditional Indian manner and said 'How'. 'A drive through extra cover', came the answer. ■

Colm Smith retired at the end of 2001, after 43 years on the sports staff of The Independent. He has covered tennis, hockey (men's and ladies), badminton, squash, tennis (12 years at Wimbledon), table tennis, golf and rugby at international level. He was rugby correspondent from 1970 to 1979 covering Willie John McBride's unbeaten Lions in South Africa in 1974 and the Irish Tour of Australia where Ireland became the first national side from the northern hemisphere to win a Test series in the Southern Hemisphere (1979). He was golf correspondent from 1970 to 2001. ■

Four months before he died in the most bizarre of air accidents, Payne Stewart walked out of a public house in Waterville, breathed the sea-fresh air and declared 'the great thing about Ireland is that its always daylight'. Waterville is a charming seaside town in the far reaches of Ireland's southwest coast, lapped or lashed as it is by the great Atlantic Ocean. Situated about the halfway point on one of the most famous and ruggedly beautiful coastal drives on the entire island, the Ring of Kerry begins and ends by the lakes and mountains of incomparable Killarney.

In times past, long before it became a 'must' stop on the now world-renowned southwest Ireland golfing trail through the Kingdom of Kerry, it was a much-loved hideaway for Charlie Chaplin. The silent film comedy genius frequented the village to seek solitude and indulge his favourite pastime of fishing. Golf in Waterville was first mentioned in the Sportsman's Holiday Guide of 1897 as 'a private course consisting of nine holes, pleasantly situated on Innystand. To the north are sand dunes and on the other side bog or moorland. The green is considered a sporting one and the views from it are very fine while the Atlantic breezes that blow across it are invigorating and refreshing. Owing to the course being a private one a charge of one shilling per day is charged to visitors.'

Not a lot changed over the decades. It was not until the early '70s that an Irish American millionaire, John A Mulcahy, sowed the seeds of Waterville as a golfing resort. Mulcahy had his roots in Kerry and commissioned the eminent, now sadly deceased, Irish architect Eddie Hackett to design an 18-hole links of quality. Hackett gave him what he wanted and Waterville is now included in all the reputable golf guides of the world. It has been graced down the years by such notable names as Sam Snead, Art Wall, Julius Boros, Sir Henry Cotton, Ray Floyd, Jack Nicklaus, Arnie Palmer and Tom Watson.

They are stars of other eras. More recently Tiger Woods, Lee Janzen, Mark O'Meara, Nick Faldo, Seve Ballesteros, Ernie Els, Bernhard Langer, John Daly, and of course Payne Stewart are multiple major winners who have visited this charming outpost. You might ask what magnet spirited such

ABOVE ■ 12 July 2000. Tracy Stewart, Tiger Woods and Mark O'Meara at the unveiling of the Payne Stewart statue in Waterville.

world stars to such a remote part of the world. It was 1999 and Stewart, Woods, O'Meara and Co. were between majors. Stewart had just won the US Open for a second time and was on this way to Carnoustie on the far east coast of Scotland on a mission to join the elite band of professionals who have achieved the coveted double of the US and British Opens in the same year. ■

Modern day players have such busy schedules, both on and off the course, it is difficult to fathom why they should take a golfing holiday in the middle of the most important part of any season. Perhaps the answer lies in the greeting the Irish give to visitors. Cead Mile Failte, one hundred thousand welcomes. Perhaps it is the tranquil beauty of the place, the folklore, the fishing, the music and the craic. Most of them had been down that way before and like many others did not need much persuasion to return. The mutual attraction Stewart had for Waterville and its people was emphasised by his acceptance of the invitation he received to become the Honorary Captain of Waterville Golf Club for the year 2000. We now know and bemoan the cruel stroke of fate that denied him that opportunity. His passion for the place was recalled by his widow Tracey in the book on his life: 'Payne loved walking through the small town of Waterville, talking to the shop owners and people in the restaurants. The people of Waterville responded warmly adopting Payne as one of their own. Since the town was too small to have a major, the highest honour they could give Payne was to name him honorary captain of Waterville Golf Club.'

By the way, Payne's reference to Ireland and daylight was the direct result of a typical Irish impromptu party. He had arrived in the pub before sundown and left it after sunrise. The intermission was spent indulging in one of his favourite leisure activities – music and song. He entertained the assembled gathering to his prowess at the harmonica, the piano and vocals. What is more he also listened. He was just one of the crowd. That is the essence of the Emerald Isle.

Watson discovered it many years before. Prompted by his great friend, Sandy Tatum a past president of the United States Golf Association, he first visited Ballybunion in 1981. He was a serious challenger to the throne of Jack Nicklaus and arrived as Masters winner. It was to be a private visit, no flags, no fanfare, no fans. Not likely, my dear Watson. You may as well try to part the waters of the Shannon, like the bible tells us of the River Jordan, as keep a secret between the counties of Clare and Kerry. 'We landed at Shannon and hired a couple of cars. We took the ferry from Killimor in Clare on the north bank of the river, to Tarbert in Kerry on the south bank and Sandy met a young boy and asked him what he was doing. He told him he was going to Ballybunion to watch Tom Watson. We had wanted a quiet visit but now the secret was out. When we arrived at Ballybunion the American flag was flying with the Irish flag and there were about 2,000 people there. It reminded me of my first time watching Bobby Jones play with no gallery ropes. People just came up and looked for autographs and just wanted to walk beside you. It was a special moment, there were many special moments.'

It began a love affair between Watson and Ballybunion that will last as long as the great man from Kansas City can draw breath. He has missed scarcely a year without a visit to what he has described as 'his favourite golf course in the world'. Like Stewart, he too was nominated as the club captain for the year of 2000. He fits like part of the furniture. He plays, strolls about, enjoys a pint and a chat in the bar just like any ordinary member.

Tiger, Mark O'Meara and Stewart were also there to usher out the old century but only Woods and O'Meara of that illustrious threesome were back to welcome the new millennium. The return visit was for a two-day charity Pro-Am organised by JP McManus at Limerick Golf Club where he is a member. JP is one of Ireland's best-known sporting personalities, particularly in horse racing circles and was one of those who befriended Tiger during his travels. Woods, as we know can command a million and perhaps even two to play in a tournament outside his own US PGA Tour but the mere mention by JP of the charity he was running was enough for Tiger to offer his presence.

McManus is a wealthy man and the cynics and sceptics were out in force when it was learned that the world's hottest sporting property would play for free. Foreign pressmen came in search of a story – one British tabloid actually published that Woods was being paid a million by McManus for his presence. They were wrong and had to retract. 'We came for JP and his charity. He is a good man and a good friend,' asserted Woods. For the record, a staggering IR£13 million was raised over the two days which included a gala dinner and a lucrative auction! So ended the final decade of the 20th century. Ten years of progress, of boom time for golf in Ireland, of a new generation of golfers, of the Celtic, not the American, Tiger.

While the game's popularity reached its century climax in the nineties with a proliferation of new courses and a dramatic increase in the numbers playing the game, golf in Ireland had been heading towards such a crescendo since the resumption of activities following World War II. Golfing Union of Ireland statistics reveal that in 1950 there were 213 clubs and around 22,000 affiliated players; in 1990 there was a modest increase in the number of clubs to 272 with an approximate 138,990 members of all categories, men, women, family, society etc. To put the phenomenal effect of the Celtic Tiger in proper perspective the latest available figures (2000) reveal that 394 clubs were registered and almost a quarter of a million people were involved in the game.

The remit for this book covered only the years from 1950 to the end of the century but it would be remiss of me not to refer to those players who provided the platform for the phenomenal growth of the game in Ireland in the immediate post-war years. The war, as we know, robbed many great sportsmen and women of their prime time. Some managed to bridge that particular era and some went on to link the first and second halves of the century.

Fred Daly, for instance, left a legacy: The Claret Jug. To this day his is the only Irish name on the Open Championship roll of honour following his victory at Royal Liverpool in 1947. Son of a blacksmith turned motor mechanic, Fred was born in Portrush, earning his money as a caddy and honing his skills as a player on the famous Dunluce links. But it was as professional at the Balmoral club in Belfast that he made his name and his fame as one of the very best players of his time. He was already 36 years of age when he won the Open Championship at Royal Liverpool in 1947 and, while he will be best remembered for that triumph at Hoylake, it tends to cloud his overall record in the world's premier championship.

In four of the following five years he was never out of the top four, finishing second to Henry Cotton at Muirfield in the year of his defence, third to Bobby Locke at Troon in 1950, fourth to Max Faulkner on his home course at Portrush, the only time the Open has been played outside mainland Britain, and third again to Locke at Royal Lytham in 1952. Fred was also the first Irishman to be selected for the Ryder Cup. He played from 1947 to 1953, finishing on a high note when he partnered Harry Bradshaw to a foursome victory over Walter Burkemo and Cary Middlecoff and a sensational 9 and 7 rout of Ted Kroll over two rounds in the singles. If Daly was the first Irish post-war hero, 'The Brad' closely followed him. Their careers were concurrent; the main difference between them being that Fred won the Open and Harry did not. The political divide also separated them. Daly was a Protestant from north of the border and Bradshaw a Catholic from the south but that never interfered with a lifelong friendship that ended only in death.

Fred was born in Portrush in 1911 and Harry in the hamlet of Killincarrig, a mile or so from the village of Delgany in the County of Wicklow, two years later. The area, incidentally, was also the birthplace for two of Ireland's other Ryder Cup players, Jimmy Martin and John O'Leary. Fred died in 1990 and just a short time after Harry attended his funeral in Belfast, 'The Brad' himself passed away in Dublin a few miles from the famous Portmarnock Golf Club where he had been professional for most of his active life. Both learned the basics from their fathers although Harry was privy to, perhaps, greater advice from Ned Bradshaw, the well-known and much loved professional to whom he became apprenticed at Delgany Golf Club. Siblings Eddie and Jimmy also became professionals. They were raconteurs of renown, rivals in combat, friends and companions away from the course and kings of the domestic scene in Ireland. Many a pint was downed in discussion and dispute about their respective merits and peace would prevail with the compromise that The Brad was sergeant of the south and Fred knight of the north but when forces were joined they made a formidable army.

On the Burma Road, the name given to Wentworth's West Course, they could claim a Ryder Cup result of Ireland 3, America 0. It was 1953. Daly was a seasoned Ryder Cup veteran, Bradshaw a newcomer to the biennial match and captain Cotton decided that they should play together in the first day foursome. They were the only winners in the four 36-hole matches and spared the wrath of their skipper when he confessed to being ashamed of his team and told the assembled press that he had 'kicked them around the dressing room'. The headlines the following day reflected his mood and there was marked improvement but, too little, too late. Daly defeated Kroll 9 and 7 and Bradshaw beat Fred Haas 3 and 2. Britain and Ireland lost by a point (6½-5½) with the Irish supplying three of the home total. Daly was to say later, maybe with mock modesty: 'Harry and I were a good combination. We played a lot of people and seldom lost. In Ireland we never lost.' But that was to be the only time they both played in the Ryder Cup. Daly's disappointment at not being selected for the '55 match prompted his decision to cut back on his travels and stay with the domestic scene. He was 44. But before he left the international scene he teamed once more with Bradshaw in the '55 Canada (World) Cup in Washington where they finished eighth. It is hard to imagine an older couple competing so well in such a prestigious tournament. Their combined ages totalled 86!

Both names should also have appeared on the Claret Jug. Harry was robbed of the '49 Open by an outside agency. The story of the 'ball in the bottle' has been told in various forms, embellished and fictionalised by the storytellers and writers but only a handful of people were there to witness the incident. It was at the fifth hole (422 yards par 4) in the second round at Sandwich and Harry has told the story innumerable times. 'There was a strong breeze and my second shot was a little off line but a reasonably good one. It was not a difficult shot to the green but when I got to the ball it was just in the rough lying in a broken bottle.' In those days, of course, there were no walkie-talkies and no referees flying around in buggies. He could, of course, have waited for an official to come from the clubhouse and posed a unique problem. The rule at the time was 'play the ball as it lies' but no one had ever come across a ball lying in a bottle. In any event Harry decided to have a go with a nine iron, ignoring the danger to self, closed his eyes and smashed at the ball, bottle and all. He dislodged it, moved just a few yards, hit the green in four and two putted for double bogey. In the event it was unlikely he would have been granted relief but the incident did bring about a change of rule.

ABOVE ▨ 8th July 1949. Harry Bradshaw driving from the 10th during the Open championships at Sandwich. He tied with Bobby Locke to go into the first play-off in championship history.

There was an obvious effect on his concentration and he took 77 but it is to his eternal credit that he recovered to shoot 68 in the third round and 70 in the last to equal the Open Championship record of 283. The only man left to deny the Irishman victory was Locke the South African. He needed a par finish of 3,4,4, to tie and force a 36-hole play-off the following day. He bogeyed the short hole, birdied the 17th, parred the 18th and then won the play-off by a handsome 12 shots.

The Brad should have been on the Ryder Cup team that same year and, indeed, in 1951 but because he lived in the South he was considered 'an overseas player' and consequently not eligible for selection. The rule was changed for the '55 match by which time Christy O'Connor was in the process of establishing himself as the Irishman of the future.

So much for the professionals who led the way into the second half of the 20th century but there were others who were leaders in different codes. Ireland has always had a strong amateur tradition and even when the drain of top talent to the professional ranks that became increasingly more prolific from the seventies onwards, the country could hold its own in the best of company. Maybe there was a lack of strength in depth but there have always been players at the top to keep the country at the forefront even when the emerging nations of Europe were growing in strength and the amateur status rules were relaxed to allow for what we now call 'full-time amateurs'.

26 Irishmen men have played for Britain and Ireland in the Walker Cup, half of them in the last 20 years of the last century. Joe Carr, of course, is the name that springs to the forefront of the mind when the amateur game is discussed. And so it should be. JB is a legend in Irish, indeed,

ABOVE ■ Joe Brown (Ireland home international 1933-53 9 times), Clarrie Reddan (Curtis Cup 1938, 48 played 3, won 2, lost 1. Ireland 1935, 36, 38, 39, 47, 48, 49) with Jimmy Bruen (Walker Cup 1938, 49, 51 and Ireland 1937, 38, 49, 50).

international sport and at the age of 79 he can reflect with great pride on a championship-winning career that spanned a remarkable 28 years from 1941. During that time he was four times a finalist, three times a winner in the British Amateur Championship; took part in 11 Walker Cup matches; played for Ireland from 1947 to 1969; was awarded the Association of Golf Writers Trophy, won the Walter Hagen and Bobby Jones awards and achieved the highest honour in the game when he was elected captain of the Royal and Ancient Golf Club of St Andrews.

Throughout his life Joe never lost touch with reality. He was a tough but fair competitor, a hard taskmaster as captain, he recognised effort and talent but, probably, had more respect for the former. The Bobby Jones Award, which he received in 1961 when his career as an international player was still far from over, is the ultimate accolade. 'Presented annually since 1955, the United States Golf Association's top award is given in recognition of distinguished sportsmanship in the game. The award seeks to recognise a person who emulates Jones' spirit, his personal qualities and his attitude toward the game and its players.' Need we say more? ◾

Jimmy Bruen was another of those trailblazers in the years before and after the war. Belfast born and Cork reared, Bruen was a player of exceptional qualities. There was, and probably still is, among those who saw and played with both in their prime, doubt as to who was the better player, Carr or Bruen. Jimmy's record is unequalled in the annals of amateur golf. He was a boy wonder, youth extraordinaire and adult amazing. He won the British Boys at Birkdale in 1936 while still a schoolboy at Presentation College, Cork. He was 16 years and three months and his opponent in the final, one W. Innes from Lanark, had the misfortune to run into the very best of the Irishmen. Bruen won by 11 and 9. He won the Irish Close Championship in 1937 and 1938, the Irish Amateur Open also in 1938 and the same year at St Andrews became the youngest man to play in the Walker Cup. Furthermore, it was the first victory for Britain and Ireland in the history of the event and they had to wait another 33 years to taste another triumph, again at St Andrews. Cecil Ewing, another great and successful exponent of the game from County Sligo, also played on the team. Ten years after his Boys Championship victory Bruen returned to Birkdale to complete a rare double by winning the Amateur Championship beating R.F. Sweeney junior by 4 and 3 in the final.

His game was characterised by the famous 'Bruen Loop', which no less an expert than Henry Cotton described as 'the most extraordinary swing I have ever seen. People asked how could anyone play golf with the clubhead right over the ball at the top of the swing? But I saw immediately when he got to the top, his right elbow came down to his right hip and his hands flashed the clubhead through with such speed that the ball was hit with the biggest carry you

Beamish *A sporting family*

LEFT Cecil Beamish.

Cecil Beamish had three brothers and two sisters; all had distinguished careers in the RAF Cecil Beamish was born in Northern Ireland, became a Wing Commander and played golf for Ireland in the home internationals in 1950, 51, 53 and 56. This was a great era for Irish amateur golf; W.N. O'Sullivan, J.B. Carr, C. Ewing, J.C. Brown, J. Bruen, N.V Drew and Sam McCready were members of Irish sides which won the home internationals in 1950, 1951 (tied with Scotland) and 1955. Cecil Beamish was runner up in 1952 to Norman Drew in the Irish Amateur Open championship and amongst other achievements he won the Club Championship (1970) and Tarleton (1971) at Denham Golf Club and the West Hill Family Foursomes with his eldest son, Michael. John Sheridan BEM, the much respected and, for more than half a century (1946-96) the professional at Denham, remembers Cecil Beamish as a friend and a delightful man: 'He had a repetitive swing with excellent rhythm and a fine extension of the hands. I remember him as a dentist and stationed for some time at RAF Uxbridge. Whilst a member at Denham he won the Denham Bowl two or three times, but perhaps his greatest achievement was in the Amateur Championship of 1958 at St Andrews. In the semi-final against Joe Carr, he was two up with two to play but lost on the 37th hole. Carr went on to win the final against Allan Thirlwell.'

Two of Cecil's brothers, George, an Air Vice Marshall and Charles, an Air Commodore played rugby for Ireland, the RAF and Leicester – they were formidable forwards. George had 25 caps between 1925 and 1933 and captained the Irish side in 1932, when they beat Wales and Scotland; he also went on the Lions tour to Australia and New Zealand in 1930 and won 5 Test caps – one v Australia and four v New Zealand; only the Dunedin Test was won (6 points to 3). Charles Beamish played 12 times for Ireland between 1933 and 1938. The brothers were on the winning Irish side against Wales in 1933. Cecil Beamish's sons Michael and David won the Denham Foursomes (Rudds) in 1990 to add to the family sporting achievements.

have ever seen – up to 300 yards. On the long fifth of 530 yards (at the time) on the championship course at Birkdale I saw him pitch the ball onto the green with two woods. The ball pitched right into the heart of the green and stopped dead. How many of today's big hitters among the tournament professionals could do that? Few indeed.'

Cotton was a great admirer and a great friend. They played a lot of golf together at Penina in Portugal where Cotton lived and Bruen had an apartment. But his career, and indeed his life, was to be cut tragically short. An accidental injury, not related to golf, tore the ligaments at the back of his right hand thus restricting the movement. He continued to play championship golf after the injury – including the Walker Cups of 1949 and 1951, but he was never the same player. Sadly, he died in 1972 just a few days short of his 52nd birthday. Sam McCready, an Ulsterman who played at Sunningdale, followed him to the British Amateur title when the championship came to Portmarnock in 1949, the first time it left Britain. McCready beat the great American Willie Turnesa by 2 and 1 in the final. He was rewarded with a place on the Walker Cup team of '49, a side that included Bruen, Ewing and Carr – a marvellous Irish quartet. ▪

The ladies who flourished just before and just after the war also had a profound influence on the future of the game and its growing popularity. The year of 1946 saw the beginning of the career of the most remarkable and successful Irish player in the entire history of the women's game in this country, indeed, in Europe and perhaps beyond.

Philomena Garvey was 19 years old when the Irish Close was resumed after the war. Having won her earlier matches by huge margins she met her more experienced neighbour Clarrie Reddan

ABOVE ■ 1946 Irish Senior Cup Team photo. Clarrie Reddan (seated with cup) and Philomena Garvey to her left. Also in the photograph are Jan Murdock, Theresa Clarke, Josephine Connolly and Irene Lowry.

(nee Tiernan) in the most extraordinary match ever played in the championship before or since. They both lived, and still do, in the hamlet of Baltray hard by the superb County Louth links at the mouth of the River Boyne. Clarrie had won the championship 10 years earlier and played in the Curtis Cup in 1938 as she was to do again in 1948. The young Phil was playing in her first championship. Hole-by-hole descriptions are normally boring but on this occasion it makes remarkable reading. Phil had completed her previous four rounds without venturing beyond the 13th green but was one down at lunch to Clarrie in the 36-hole final. On the resumption, Mrs Reddan lost the first six holes and seven of the first nine that would surely have put the match beyond recall. But no. The older lady staged an astonishing revival that saw her win six of the seven holes from the 11th through the 17th to leave them all square with the last to play. That was halved but still the drama continued at the first tie hole, a par three. Mrs Reddan missed the

ABOVE ■ Philomena Garvey played Curtis Cup Golf 1948-60 (6 times), Vagliana Trophy 1959-60. For Ireland in home internationals 18 times 1947-69 (missed '55; professional in 64, 65, 66, 67; played 68 and 69). Curtis Cup 11 matches (won 2, lost 8, halved 1). Here she is shown with the Ladies British Amateur Championship trophy which she won in 1957. She was also runner-up 1946, 53, 60, 63 and Irish Ladies winner 1960, 62, 63, 70.

green while her opponent was safely on with her tee shot. Reddan chipped on but Garvey's putt stopped in front of the hole directly in her opponent's line – a stymie. There was no way home. A stymie was akin to a snooker and perfectly, if ridiculously, legal.

Miss Garvey went on to win 15 Irish championships, 14 of them in 18 years from 1946 to 1963. The last did not come until 1970 when she was 43 and a reinstated amateur. She turned professional in 1964 but was well before her time and returned to the amateur ranks in 1968. To emphasise her superiority over all others she was never taken beyond the 16th green in all but two of the 15 finals, the first and the last when she won in tie holes. Her winning margins before the final was reduced from 36 to 18 in 1964 include 14 and 12; 13 and 12; 12 and 10 twice and 10 and 8. She was also five times a finalist in the British Amateur Championship, winning just once in 1957 and played in six Curtis Cup matches. These were the people that set the standards

ABOVE ■ Christy O'Connor, 1959 Dunlop Masters winner with his caddy Frank Day.

for others to follow in the second half of the century. When their successors arrived on the scene they were not found wanting. ▪

The '50s heralded the arrival, albeit belated, of Christy O'Connor. He was 27 years of age before he played in a tournament and that was the 1951 British Open at Royal Portrush, the only time the Open was played outside the mainland. There was an immediate indication of his ability when he finished 19th behind Max Faulkner. He won £19–a small fortune for a young man who had come from a family of 11 children on a small farm in the village of Knocknacarra near the Galway Golf Club in Salthill. The reason for his late entry in the tournament scene was due to an oversight by Bob Wallace his boss, mentor and tutor at Galway Golf Club to whom he was apprenticed. Bob omitted to sign the necessary forms to register him with the Irish Professional Golfers' Association but it didn't hold him back. In only his second year as a tournament professional he won the Irish Dunlop Tournament and Ulster Championship, performances that served only to emphasise what he missed in those lost years. But O'Connor kept on winning. In the 30-year period between 1953 when he won that first Ulster title to 1983 when he captured the last of six PGA Seniors' championships hardly a year passed without a victory at home or abroad. On the European tour he won 24 titles not including the 10 Irish PGA championships, a record he shares with the his great friend The Brad. He also won two World Seniors, played in ten Ryder Cups (including the famous win at Lindrick and the draw at Birkdale) and 15 World Cups.

Yet, there are two vacant spots in the expansive trophy cabinet in his modest, very homely abode in the north Dublin suburb of Clontarf, just a brisk walk from Royal Dublin where he spent the majority of his professional career. There were few chances to win the Irish Open. Under the auspices of the Golfing Union of Ireland, it ceased because of lack of funds after the genial Scot Eric Brown won at Belvoir Park in Belfast in 1953. It was not revived until 1975 and O'Connor did get consolation and cause to celebrate at Woodbrook that summer. He witnessed the dynasty continue when his nephew Christy junior became only the third Irishman to win the national title. Much to the disappointment of the massive home crowds who trooped religiously to the great links at Portmarnock and Royal Dublin for 15 years and subsequently to other classic venues around the country like Mount Juliet, Killarney, Druids Glen and Ballybunion only one other Irishman gave cause to celebrate. Colourful Dubliner and gifted sportsman, John O'Leary won at Portmarnock in 1982.

But back to the Master and the other one that got away: The Open. Several times he was in position but just failed to convert his chance to be champion. There was 1958 at Royal Lytham and St Annes where he led at the halfway stage with 135, the lowest total since Henry Cotton's

132 at Sandwich in 1934. Two rounds were played on the last day and O'Connor and Leopoldo Ruiz from Argentina were behind Peter Thomson and Dave Thomas. 'Himself' recalls that their pace of play was so slow that they had lost two holes on the group in front. In frustration, the Irishman carded 73 to fall three shots behind. He complained to the R & A officials but they suggested he slow down! They did give the concession of allowing Thomson and Thomas a hole and a half start in the final round. Still they caught them and coming to the last, a short par four of 379 yards, O'Connor needed a birdie to win and a par to tie Thomson and Thomas who had finished with 278. Unfortunately, his three wood tee shot caught a bad lie in a bunker and he could only splash out. His putt for par and a place in the play-off stopped on the lip. Frustrated and furious at the slow play which he believes cost him the title, he had to be satisfied with third as the Australian beat the Welshman in the play-off.

He is convinced to this day that it was his best chance of winning the Open. There were others like at St Andrews in '55 when he stood on the tee at the long and treacherous 14th in the last round needing level fours for a 65 which would have pipped Thomson who finished on 282. A difference of opinion with his caddie over the fairway club put doubt in the Master's mind. Aggressive as usual, he wanted the driver but he took the caddy's advice of the three wood and promptly buried in Hell bunker. Extraction took three attempts and he wound up with a quadruple bogey nine. Ten times in 26 Opens he appeared in the top ten and he will be forever remembered as the world's best player of his time never to win a Major. Mind you, he never played in the three American Majors despite several invitations to the Masters at Augusta but Christy was, above all, a home bird and world travel did not really appeal to him. Furthermore it wasn't easy to break into the American club and he was never really at ease when he went there.

Christy set many records in his career including winning the first £1,000 and £2,000 prizes in European golf and in 1970 at Hollinwell in Nottinghamshire, he lifted the world's biggest cheque of the era – £25,000 for winning the John Player Classic. He played with and was respected by all the great players of his era. Like his friend and partner The Brad, he was sought after by stars of stage and sport. Still a sweet swinger at 77, he regularly shoots lower than his age which seems to come easier to him the older he gets. His time was the '50s, the '60s and the '70s and before the first of these decades was out, he had partnered The Brad to the country's first great team championship. They went to Mexico City in 1958 to take on the world in the Canada (later World) Cup and came home with the spoils. Harry also tied for the individual prize but lost to Angel Miguel of Spain in the play-off.

The victory enhanced Ireland's image on the international stage and was an influential factor in the International Golf Association's decision to bring the tournament to Portmarnock in 1960.

One of the anomalies of the time was that the Golfing Union of Ireland and the chairman of the tournament committee (another of Ireland's great players and characters in the amateur game Dr Billy O'Sullivan from Killarney) nominated the Irish team. The world expected the Old Firm, particularly as Harry knew every blade of grass in the place and Christy had won the Dunlop Masters from an elite field there the year before. But, in their wisdom, they chose Norman Drew to partner O'Connor. Drew was one of the best of players both as amateur and professional. He was in fact the first British or Irish player to play in the Walker Cup, the Ryder Cup and the Canada (World) Cup but on this occasion, his selection was a surprise. Ireland finished down the field as two great Americans Sam Snead and Arnold Palmer walked away with the title.

There were many other great achievements in the '50s. Perhaps the decade is a little dulled in the memory of those who were around during that time, but history records that John Glover from Campbell College, Belfast won the British Boys at Royal Lytham and St Annes. John, many times an international, later became the Royal and Ancient Rules Secretary. The following year Kitty McCann from Tullamore won the British Women's Amateur Championship at Broadstone and Max Faulkner won the only British Open to be played in Ireland; Phil Garvey followed her in 1957. Both ladies were selected for the British and Irish Curtis Cup team in 1952 at Muirfield when the Americans were beaten for the first time in the history of the event. In all, Miss Garvey played in six Curtis Cups between 1948 and 1960 and was selected for the 1958 match but caused great controversy when she refused to play. The Ladies Golf Union, the women's equivalent to the R & A, changed the emblem from the badge of the four home unions to the Union Jack without reference to the ILGU. Miss Garvey, being from the Republic, said could not play under the Union Jack and she was fully supported by the captain of the team Daisy Ferguson, from Royal County Down, who also happened to be the President of the ILGU. The Union relayed their disapproval to the LGU but the badge remained and Miss Garvey did not play but logic prevailed when the badge was changed for subsequent matches.

There were many other significant features during that period, like Joe Carr winning his three British Amateur titles and the Bradshaw and O'Connor each winning two Dunlop Masters as well as other events. It is worthy of mention that, although Carr never turned professional, he always had a yen to take them on. The two most notable occasions were at the '59 Dunlop Masters at Portmarnock where he led the field going into the final day with rounds of 68, 69, 69 but O'Connor produced a blistering 66 against Carr's 74 to win the title. In the centenary Open at St Andrews in 1960 he was lying fourth behind Kel Nagle, Roberto di Vicenzo and Arnold Palmer going into the last round. The Irishman began birdie, birdie when a violent storm abandoned play for the day. The tournament finished on the Saturday with Carr shooting 73 to take eighth place behind winner Nagle.

There has never been another decade like it for achievement but Irish players kept winning around the world. There is no doubt that the winning of the Canada (World) Cup by O'Connor and Bradshaw in 1958 and the successful staging of the tournament at Portmarnock in 1960 were two of the most significant events in the latter half of the century. In the year between, Portmarnock also hosted the Dunlop (British) Masters, one of the most prestigious events on the European calendar. It was won by O'Connor but only after Joe Carr, who had always fancied the idea of pitting himself against the pros, led going into the final round. ▪

Ireland was now firmly on the world map of golf. In order to keep it there a major sponsor was required and the tobacco firm of P.J. Carroll and Co. stepped in with the Carrolls International Tournament at Woodbrook in 1963, a follow-on from the Irish Hospitals Tournament which had started a few years earlier. The International ran until 1975. The time had come then to revive the Irish Open and the company did so at the same venue when Christy O'Connor junior won. Under the Carroll banner the championship became one of the best, biggest and most popular events on the European Tour's international schedule. It was more than just a tournament. It was a national festival with crowds of 150,000 turning up through the week.

His fellow professionals used to call the International 'the O'Connor Benefit' as he won it four times including one famous occasion on his home course at Royal Dublin when he finished eagle, birdie, eagle to beat the Scot, Eric Brown who was about to begin his celebrations in the clubhouse. A second tournament, the Gallaher Ulster Open, ran for 7 years during the '60s and early '70s until the economic and political climate in the North, where it had its home, forced its demise. After 30 years of support for golf, Carrolls handed over the title and the sponsorship to Murphys under whose banner it has been held since 1993.

The roll of honour is impressive: Ben Crenshaw, Hubert Green, Seve Ballesteros, Bernhard Langer, Ian Woosnam, José Maria Olazabal and Nick Faldo are all multiple Major Championship winners. The event has visited Portmarnock, Royal Dublin, Killarney, Ballybunion, Mount Juliet and Druids Glen – all top quality courses; thus, with the advent of satellite television exposing Ireland to the world at large as a premier golfing destination. ▪

By the time Phil Garvey announced her retirement in 1970. Mary McKenna was ready to take over the mantle as leader of the next generation. The girl from Donabate wore it well, with pride and distinction and while she did not win as many Irish titles (8), her international career spanned 25 years. She first appeared on the senior scene as a schoolgirl in 1968 and to this day she is respected, not alone for her talent, but as a great and gracious ambassador for the country.

During a spectacular career, Mary played in a record nine Curtis Cups, nine Vagliano Trophy matches against the Continent of Europe, four World Team Championships and represented Ireland in the Home Internationals and European Team Championship between 1968 and 1993. She also served as non-playing captain of the Vagliano and World Championship teams. On the individual front she was eight times Irish champion (three times runner-up), won the British Ladies Stroke Play and went to the semi-final of the US amateur championship.

Mary's proudest moments were winning with Ireland. She had to wait more than a decade to savour outright international success and when it came it was with a rush. By the end of the '70s Maureen Madill from Portstewart had joined the Irish squad and in '79 they spearheaded a famous victory in the European Team championship on home ground at the Hermitage club just outside Dublin. They beat Germany comfortably in the final with President Paddy Hillary joining the celebrations with a few thousand singing the Rivers of Babylon and Hallelujah. The others members of the team were Susan Gorman, Mary Gorry, Claire Nesbitt and Rhona Heggarty. A short time before, Maureen had become the first Irish winner of the British Amateur title since Phil Garvey 22 years earlier and shortly afterwards Mary completed a historic summer by becoming the first Irish player to win the British Stroke Play championship.

If the '70s were a memorable and historic decade for the women it was equally so for the men. Although O'Connor and Carr ruled respective codes through the '50s and '60s there were others who won international honours. Jimmy Martin, Norman Drew and Hugh Boyle all played in the Ryder Cup and World Cup while David Sheahan and Tom Craddock were two of the game's best amateurs. They both completed the Irish Close and Open Double and played in the Walker Cup while Sheahan upstaged an international professional field when he won the Jeyes Professional Tournament at Royal Dublin – the last amateur to win a European tour event. Both Sheahan and Craddock were Walker Cup players and members of the Irish teams that won the European Team Championship in 1965 and 1967. Others were Carr and Vincent Nevin, who played in both, Bill McCrea, Rupert de Lacy Staunton, David Madeley, Peter Flaherty and Tom Egan.

But a new generation was on the crest. O'Connor senior teed off the new decade by winning the game's biggest cheque of the era. He picked up £25,000 by winning the John Player Classic; Paddy Skerritt won the Alcan International Tournament, a secondary event run concurrently with the Alcan Golfer of the Year Championship at Portmarnock, but the majority of the thousands were not interested in Bruce Crampton winning the main event. They carried their home hero shoulder-high around Portmarnock as many of the world's best players were still playing for the big money. The celebrations continued in Paddy's home club, St Annes, further along the Bull Island that also houses the Royal Dublin Club. In those years the only way onto the island was by bridge (a causeway was later built as a second access) so there was no fear of intrusion from the law because the lights of their car could be seen long before they reached the clubs and travelling without lights could mean getting stuck in the soft sand. The singin' and drinkin' went on through the following day. In 1971, Roddy Carr made history by following his father JB on to the British and Irish Walker Cup team. They are the only father and son to have played in the match. Roddy, one of four brothers all of whom were single figure golfers was unbeaten with three and a half points out of four as the home side won at St Andrews for the first time since the time of Jimmy Bruen in 1938.

Four young and highly talented young men who were to have a major impact on the home and international scene launched themselves into the professional arena in the following few years. Christy O'Connor junior, Eamonn Darcy, John O'Leary and Des Smyth carried on the influential status in European golf established by their illustrious predecessors. All four were multiple tournament winners over the next two decades although O'Leary's career was cut short because of injury. But, before his days as a player came to an end he etched his name in the annals of Irish professional golf. JohnnO, Junior and The Darce were a great three-ball both on and off the course. They made history in 1975 when all three played on the Ryder Cup team, the only occasion on which Ireland had three representatives. O'Leary was the fourth, and, so far the last home player to win the Irish Open at Portmarnock in 1982. Philip Walton came closest in 1989 when he lost a play-off to Ian Woosnam.

LEFT ■ 1989 Carrols Irish Open. Philip Walton, the runner up to Ian Woosnam.

Smyth put his name alongside them in 1979 when, after wining the European Matchplay Championship by beating Nick Price with an eagle at the final hole in Fulford, York, he joined the first European Ryder Cup team in the Greenbrier, West Virginia. Des went on to a highly successful career which included the Ryder Cup of 1981 against an American side that was arguably the greatest ever. He also challenged for the British Open in '82 when he birdied the 11th on the final day to be just one shot off the lead, eventually finishing fourth. He was a member of the Irish team that won the Dunhill Cup at St Andrews in '88, won eight European Tour events over four decades when he won the Madeira Island Open at the age of 48 years and

34 days. Junior also made a serious bid for that most coveted of titles at Royal St George's in Sandwich in 1985. In the first round he broke the 51-year course record set by Henry Cotton in 1934 when he won the title. His 65, after which the famous Dunlop 65 golf ball was named, came in the second round. Christy's 64 included seven consecutive birdies from the fourth but his putter became ice-cold in the subsequent rounds. From tee to green he outplayed the winner Sandy Lyle but missed countless birdie putts in the middle of rounds two and three and finally finished in a share of third place two shots behind.

The distinguished career of the Senior O'Connor was still far from finished. In 1976 he won the first of six PGA Seniors Championships and the first of two World Seniors titles while in the same year Darcy became World under 25 champion. These were the years of some of the greatest characters ever to play the European Tour. Men like Jack Newton, Ian Stanley, and Bob Shearer from Australia, Simon Hobday from South Africa, Dale Hayes and Hugh Baiocchi from South Africa, Brian Barnes, Sam Torrance and Ronnie Shade, to mention some, were players with whom the Irish public could identify because they mingled and hung around in the clubhouse for the craic.

It was not the greatest of decades for the unpaid men, although Pat Mulcare stood out above all others. The man from Ballybunion was one of the finest strikers and links player in the game and was honoured by the British and Irish Walker Cup selectors in 1975. His defining moment came in that match on the 18th green of the Old Course at the Home of Golf. He holed a birdie putt to beat one of America's best-ever amateurs Dick Siderowf. He won two of his three matches, losing to the current US Ryder Cup captain, Curtis Strange.

Ronan Rafferty from Warrenpoint, still only 15 years of age, won the British Boys Championship and was part of an historic and successful Irish Youths team in Marianski Lanze in the former Czechoslovakia. It was the first international golf tournament of any kind played behind the Iron Curtain. The rest of the team was Philip Walton, Brendan McDaid, Tom Corridan, Roy Hanna and John Collins. Walton and Rafferty were to play together in the 1981 Walker Cup at Cypress Point in California. In the opening foursomes the two young Irishmen were pitted against America's strongest combination, Jay Siegel and Hal Sutton. Philip and Ronan came from three down to win after Walton had holed a chip for birdie on the 15th and Rafferty repeated the dose at the 16th. The course may be one of the best in the world but the club was certainly not the most hospitable. Entry to the clubhouse was permitted only with jacket and tie, even for the teams, which meant changing for lunch before the singles. As it happened a local resident ran a barbeque just outside the club and invited teams, officials and spectators to take part – free, gratis and for nothing. Walton, incidentally, was the first Irish golfer to join an American University and helped Oklahoma State to win the NCAA Championship. Ronan turned professional in '81 and Philip in '83. ■

The '80s were, without doubt, the most successful decade in the entire history of Irish golf. Space would not permit a listing of the worldwide victories achieved by players in all codes. The team triumphs were unprecedented. On the same June Sunday, and almost at the same time, the Irish ladies and men's teams became Champions of Europe – again. The women won at the Waterloo Club in Belgium and the men at Chantilly in France. By then Claire Dowling (nee Hourihane) had arrived on the international stage which she was to dominate for nearly a decade with five Irish Close titles. Mary McKenna and Maureen Madill were the sole survivors from the 1979 success and Claire Hourihane, Eavan Higgins and the Wickham sisters Phil and Carol from Laytown and Bettystown joined them. King Leopold of Belgium and the Irish Ambassador Mary Tinney were there to witness a famous victory over the Auld Enemy. A few hours drive away on the outskirts of Paris, there were more celebrations as Ireland won the men's equivalent, beating Spain in the final. Walton had delayed his decision to turn professional until after the Europeans, an invaluable asset for Ireland as the Dubliner won 10 of his 12 matches between 1981 and 1983.

Ireland also won the Home International Championship that same year and was to repeat the double in 1987 winning the European at Murhof in Austria and the Triple Crown on home territory at Lahinch. Garth McGimpsey is the only player to have taken part in all four triumphs, while Arthur Pierse played in three. John Carr, Mick Morris, Tom Cleary, Neil Anderson and Padraig Hogan achieved the double. Eoghan O'Connell was on the European team in 1987 and went on to earn an invaluable halved match against Phil Mickelson in the historic first victory by Britain and Ireland on American soil in the 1989 Walker Cup at Peachtree. He was also on the GB&I team that won the Eisenhower Trophy for the World Team Championship in 1988.

One of the greatest of all Irish triumphs occurred in that same year. Eamonn Darcy, Des Smyth and Ronan Rafferty took on the world in the Alfred Dunhill Cup at St Andrews and won. It was a sensational victory full of drama and incident. In the semi-final, the match between Ireland and England depended on the final singles. Smyth was one up on Nick Faldo playing the final hole in the gathering gloom of the Haar that regularly sweeps across the course from St Andrews Bay. The pair had teed off the 18th and Smyth had played his second shot to the back of the green, a measured 54 feet from the hole while Faldo declined to play his pitch from 86 yards because he could not see the flag.

Back they came the following morning when the Englishman left his second five feet from the hole. Smyth putted down dead, Faldo missed, Smyth holed and Ireland walked into the final amid the cheers from the unruly students of St Andrews University who had draped banners uncomplimentary to Faldo from the Halls of Residence, for which they later had to apologise. Smyth was again the man of the moment in the final. Rafferty was beating David Graham handsomely and Greg Norman was on his way to a record score against Darcy. Smyth was two behind Rodger Davis on the 16th. He birdied and stood on the treacherous 17th tee and lashed one across the Old Course Hotel to the middle of the fairway. The Australian sliced out of bounds and made six to Smyth's four. To finish with a flourish the ever-popular Smyth holed for birdie and danced around the hallowed ground. His pride and delight were embodied in his exclamation 'imagine little ol' Ireland beating the mighty United States (to win the group that put them in the semi-final) and the rest of the world'.

The team came home to a civic reception and two years later the team was feted for a second time. David Feherty and Philip Walton joined Rafferty in 1990 and this time it was Feherty who was in the hot spot. England and Ireland finished level with a point and a half each leaving Feherty to go to sudden death with Howard Clarke. The match ended on the second extra hole, the infamous 17th, where Feherty hit 'the best three iron of my career' to 20 feet from the pin. Par was perfect for another victory.

On an individual front the '80s began with Maureen Madill winning the British Amateur Stroke Play and in 1982 John O'Leary became only the fourth, and so far, last Irish player to win the Irish Open. The greatest individual double ever achieved by Irish players was in 1985 when McGimpsey and Lillian Behan each won the British Amateur Open Championship. Lillian was gifted player who burst on the scene in the early '80s. Born and bred in the Curragh, the kernel of the Irish Bloodstock industry, her real sporting love is horses and she still works as a groom. In 1986 she joined Mary McKenna and Claire Hourihane on the first British and Irish team to win any international match, amateur or professional, on American soil when they won the Curtis Cup at Prairie Dunes in Kansas. She later turned professional with little reward but returned to the amateur game to win the Irish Close Championship in 1998.

Maureen Madill also turned professional with some success but her forte nowadays is as a highly respected teacher and is currently the official coach to the Ladies Golf Union having charge of all British and Irish teams. Ita Butler, a Curtis Cup player 1966 and a former Irish champion, had the distinction of captaining the Irish ladies team to victory in the Home Internationals at Whittington Barracks in 1986. Her greatest moment of all came by the Lakes of Killarney in 1996 when she captained the British and Irish Curtis Cup team (without an Irish player) to victory over the United States. Eileen Rose Power (nee McDaid), who had played in the previous match, was a non-travelling reserve but the talented Irish champion from Skibberreen in West Cork, did play on the 1994 team.

By the end of the decade Ronan Rafferty had climbed to the top of the European ladder, taking the number one position with victory in the Volvo Masters at Valderrama in 1989. He and Christy played on the Ryder Cup team at the Belfry and while both won their singles, they never gelled as a foursome partnership. The Golfing Union of Ireland's youth policy was by then firmly in place and when members of the previous generation were in the autumn of their careers, there were others to replace them. The Irishmen of the '90s were Darren Clarke, Paul McGinley and Padraig Harrington.

Clarke never played in the Walker Cup because he gave up a cast iron spot on the 1991 team to turn professional. He has been highly successful in that code and came closer than anyone since Christy O'Connor senior to winning The Open. He was in the last group on the final day, just

ABOVE ▧ 1st November 1998. Daren Clarke after winning the Volvo Masters at Montecastillo Golf Club in Jerez, Spain.

one shot behind Jesper Parnevik, but a sudden shank with a three iron onto the beach from the second tee at Troon dented his confidence. He soldiered on to finish second with Parnevik three behind Justin Leonard.

McGinley and Harrington waited for the Walker Cup in Portmarnock, the first time the match was played outside mainland Britain. McGinley had just completed his term at San Diego University and Harrington was still studying accountancy in Dublin. They had both lived and been to the same school in the Dublin suburb of Rathfarnham and also played for the same Gaelic Football club. Both were rookies while Garth McGimpsey, the third Irishman, was playing in his third match against the Americans. The United States team included Phil Mickelson, Bob May, and a 19-year-old David Duval. The Americans won all four of the opening series of foursomes, which put the home team at a huge disadvantage. They rallied to share the remaining 24 points but it was not enough.

ABOVE ■ 8th October 1994. Paul McGinley drives his tee shot of the 18th against Tomohiro Maruyama of Japan at the Alfred Dunhill Cup at St Andrews, Scotland.

Harrington went on to play in two more matches and in 1995 at Royal Porthcawl he achieved his ambition – to play on a winning side. His hugely successful partnership with Jody Fanagan playing for Leinster and Ireland struck again when the two Dubliners won their two foursomes matches, including beating Tiger Woods and J Harris on the last day. Fanagan scored the winning point by beating Jim Courville in the singles on a dreadful final day but the torrential rain didn't dampen the celebrations. Harrington delayed his plans to become a professional to be on, he hoped, a winning Walker Cup side. He won three out of his four matches losing only his singles on the last day when the Walker Cup had already been won. Jody Fanagan won all three of his Walker Cup matches. Remarkably, Fanagan's sister Suzanne was undefeated in her Curtis Cup matches of 2000.

ABOVE ▧ 1995 Royal Porthcawl. Jody Fanagan and Padraig Harrington.

FANAGAN FAMILY

Jody Fanagan comes from a sporting dynasty that dates back to the '30s. His maternal grandfather, Paul Murray played centre, out-half and scrum-half during his 19 rugby internationals (1927-33), he went on the 1930 Lions tour to Australia and New Zealand, played in four tests and also won the South of Ireland Amateur Championship at Lahinch in 1940. His daughter Oonagh was a hockey international and his son John played rugby and Davis Cup tennis for Ireland. He was a member of the Irish Universities side who defeated the South Africans in 1965. Another daughter Rhona, a single figure golfer, married Joe Fanagan who captained St Mary RFC to victory in the Leinster Senior Cup in 1958 and was also chairman of the international selectors.

Jody Fanagan followed in his grandfather's footsteps to win the South of Ireland Amateur Golf Championship at Lahinch in 1985. He was a long-time Irish international golfer (1989-97). He won all three of his Walker Cup matches in 1995 His sister, Suzanne O'Brien was an Irish Close champion, she played Curtis Cup, the World Team Championship (Espirito Santo Cup) and Vagliano Trophy for Britain and Ireland. She was unbeaten in her Curtis Cup matches and in the 2000 Curtis Cup match at Ganton, Yorkshire, she won three and a half points out of four in the home side's 8-10 defeat; as befits a family who have an undertaking business they 'buried' the Americans – a remarkable family record.

Interestingly, Claire Dowling (nee Hourihane) was the non-playing captain and Maureen Madill the coach. Suzanne O'Brien turned professional in 2000 and won her card for the Ladies European tour in 2002.

I have, so far, made little mention of the Ryder Cup but Ireland's contribution deserves special attention. The biennial match was losing its appeal, particularly among Americans, and it might have disappeared completely from the calendar had not the suggestion by Jack Nicklaus been taken on board to broaden the selection net to involve European players. The change to a European side in 1979 plus the inspired appointment of Tony Jacklin as captain in 1983 revitalised the match and from the mid '80s it has become one of the greatest sporting events in the world. That famous first victory over the Americans at The Belfry in 1985 did not include an Irishman but from then to the end of the century the contribution has been stunning and vital to the European cause.

Eamonn Darcy's putt on the 18th green at Muirfield Village in Dublin, Ohio to ensure the first ever victory on America soil; Christy O'Connor's incomparable two iron to the 18th at The

Belfry in 1989 to secure a draw and the retention of the Cup for Europe; Philip Walton's knee-knocking last hole victory over Jay Haas to regain the Trophy at Oak Hill in '95 and Darren Clarke's victorious partnership with Colin Montgomerie in another heart-stopping encounter at Valderrama in '97 were dramas that could never have been scripted. We must not forget David Feherty's victory over Payne Stewart on the final day to help force a last hole, last match, last putt decision in the infamous 'War on the Shore' at Kiawah Island in '91 nor Padraig Harrington's debut victory over Mark O'Meara during an incredible American comeback at Brookline.

ABOVE ▨ Eamonn Darcy's delight at holing his vital putt.

People will remember Darcy for That Putt and so they should but the shot that made it possible was an immaculate seven iron to a foot for a birdie three on the 17th to level his match with Ben Crenshaw. I remember standing by the 18th green when Darcy was left with a five-footer fraught with danger coming down the hill of a glass-like green. Captain Jack Nicklaus was standing with some of his team and whispered to them that Darcy was in three-putt area. He knew because he designed the course. I asked The Darce sometime afterwards what went through his mind standing over the ball. He said: 'I had only one thought. Don't bloody miss'. ■

ABOVE ■ 24th September 1989. Christy O'Connor Junior's victory ensures the retention of the Ryder Cup for Europe.

Who will ever forget O'Connor's reaction to his victory over Fred Couples as he held his hands high towards the heavens in thanksgiving for the vindication of his selection. He was 41 and it was 14 years since he had last played. The great irony was that Jacklin had declined to pick him four years earlier when he was only a few pounds short of automatic selection. This time he was further away. The captain was criticised for selecting him (and Jose Maria Canizares who was 42 and also won) and some British papers were pretty cruel with their criticism on the Sunday morning. Seve Ballesteros, being the great team man and motivator, said to Christy at breakfast: 'Don't worry, you are a great player and you will win today'. He did. And then went on to an even more remarkable second career in the senior ranks. He shocked the seasoned senior citizens of the US Tour with a sensational season in 1998 with two victories. On this side of the Atlantic he won the British Open Seniors at Royal Portrush in '99 and retained the title at Royal County Down the following year. He is, without doubt, one of the great Irish professionals.

Similarly, Philip Walton was shattered when his trial was all over. He was three up with three to play but Haas holed a near impossible bunker shot at the 16th, Walton missed a three footer on the 17th, but as the nerves were stretched to the limit the American cracked with a drive into the trees. Players, wives and officials from both sides were swarming all over the fairway but the man from Malahide held firm – he still doesn't know how – and secured the half for victory. 'I had no feel in my hands or legs coming down the last hole,' said Walton.

Ireland has hosted every major international event possible except the Ryder Cup. In the year 2000 there were three men's European Tour events, the Irish Open Seniors, the British Seniors, the women's Irish Open professional championship and the women's professional World Cup. We now look forward to the Ryder Cup at the K Club in the County Kildare in 2005. And, who knows, the first Irish captain? That's not bad for a little island. But such things don't just happen; they have to be made to happen. It requires communal effort – and money, lots of money. The Government, through Bord Failte (Tourist Board) has spared no effort in promoting Ireland as one of the great golfing destinations. Millions of pounds has been fed into the effort by the Bord and the private sector and by the time the match is played, the European Tour will have extracted upwards of £20 million from the country through tournament prize money and annual payments for the right of the Irish Tourist Board to promote the country at a number of European Tour events over an 8-year period.

Ireland certainly has the resources, the courses, perhaps not the climate but certainly the commitment to make visitors welcome. The proliferation of new golf courses through the '90s mostly of the proprietary kind, hugely enhanced the variety of courses on offer. There are some 150 links courses in the world and 39 of them – 40 if one includes Greg Norman's current creation at Doonbeg on the Clare coast just south of Lahinch – are in Ireland. The South West courses like Ballybunion, Lahinch, Tralee, Killarney and Waterville are famous throughout the world, as are Portmarnock and Royal County Down on the east coast and Royal Portrush on the north.

There are also excellent commercial concerns like Mount Juliet, a wonderfully tranquil estate with a quiet elegance in the county of Kilkenny where the World Golf Championship Amex tournament will be held in 2002, and a personal favourite, the charming Druids Glen in County Wicklow and the luxurious K Club in Kildare, venue for the 2005 Ryder Cup, which have all hosted major events in recent years. But Ireland has a plethora of lesser-known gems around the entire coastline. Royal Dublin, The Island and County Louth at Baltray are links of the highest quality on the east coast north of Dublin; Portstewart, Port Salon, Ballyliffin on the north coast; Murvagh, Rosses Point, Enniscrone, Westport and Connemara along the west and Rosslare and the European club in the south east, to mention a few.

When you're in Donegal find your way to Kincasslagh, stop at Igy's pub and ask the way to Cruit (pronounced Critch) Island. Travel as far as you can and there lies a charming nine-holer in a corner of heaven on earth. But, no matter where you go, you are sure of good golf and a grand welcome. That, as I have said, is the essence of Ireland. ■

Dr Cyril White trained at Loughborough College in England before starting a teaching career at St Columba's in Dublin and becoming Athletic Coach to Trinity. Malcolm Argyle, the Warden of St Columba's advised him to move into the academic world. A degree in sociology and a career that included the positions of Senior Lecturer in Sociology at University College, Dublin and Academic Professor and Dean of the American College in Dublin, followed. His special interest has been socio-economic change in Ireland and a comparative study with Israel and Finland of Ireland's recent economic success. He has maintained his passion for athletics and writes about the influence of the universities and the 'focused perseverance of the athletes'. ∎

I rish athletics has had a somewhat chequered history mixed with its great athletes and outstanding personalities and its share of disappointments and unfortunate divisions; this chapter looks at a history of athletics in Ireland and selects the five great athletes of the period 1950-2000.

The period pre-1950 provides an important insight into the modern era. A strong university athletics tradition has been the foundation of Irish athletics. The first athletics meeting held was when, on Saturday, 28th February 1857, the Trinity College Dublin (rugby) Football Club held what was termed, 'The Dublin University Football Club Foot Races' at College Park. This meeting, hereinafter called 'The College Races', was the third oldest athletics meeting in the world, preceded only by the meeting organised by The Royal Military Academy at Woolwich, London in 1842 and at Exeter College, Oxford in 1850. Professor Trevor West, in his book

The Bold Collegians wrote: 'The difficulty of arranging a major athletics meeting in College Park, which at that time had no pavilion and no spectator accommodation to cope with athletes and spectators (sometimes numbering 20,000) who flooded in to view the sports, was overwhelming. There were problems with distributing tickets (a membership scheme had to be devised), handicapping the races, communicating the results (a telegraph board was erected) and with keeping the spectators away from the track. There was constant bickering about prizes, which were handsome indeed, but the music of a couple of military bands helped to soothe the nerves of exhausted competitors, harassed judges and irritated spectators.'

University athletes made their contributions in many ways to sport. H.W.D. Dunlop, for instance, was an outstanding athlete whilst at Trinity, who wished to develop athletics and other sports outside the universities for young men, both graduates and others. He was the founder of the Irish Champion Athletics Club in 1872 and this Club organised the first All Ireland Athletics Championship, held in College Park in July 1873. But, perhaps Dunlop's most lasting achievement was the creation in 1872 of Lansdowne Road Rugby Ground, now the oldest international rugby ground in the world. After he created the Lansdowne Road venue he built a cinder track, a cricket pitch, a croquet green, three football pitches and facilities for archery and tennis, in fact a multi-sports centre with the emphasis being on athletics. The tennis courts were so well regarded that the first Irish Tennis Championships were played at Lansdowne Road and on 5 June 1876, the world's first international athletics match, between Ireland and England, took place at Lansdowne Road on the track that Henry Dunlop had constructed four years earlier.

University athletics were still the basis for the sport, both in interest and as the nursery for champion athletes of the future. The success of the College Races had not gone unnoticed at the other universities in Ireland. Students at Queen's College, Cork invited their fellow students at Queen's College, Belfast, Queen's College, Galway, and Trinity College, Dublin to join them in an intervarsity athletics meeting on 13 May 1873 on a grass track laid down at Cork County Cricket Club at the Mardyke. All agreed except Trinity College which stated that it would interfere with the arrangements for the Irish Champion Athletics Club's All Ireland Championships to be held in College Park. Thus it was that in 1873, the first Irish universities athletics championships took place without the participation of Trinity. This initiative from Queen's College, Cork brought into being not only Ireland's first intervarsity athletics meeting but also the world's first national intervarsity athletics meeting and championships. Oxford and Cambridge universities had their first athletics meeting nine years earlier in 1864 but the Oxbridge meeting was organised as a dual meeting, not as a national university meeting and championships. It remains a dual meeting to this day. The Queen's College Cork students therefore established the world's first national university track and field championships. These Irish universities athletics championships continue to the present. ■

The late 19th and early 20th centuries provided an unprecedented expansion in the athletics scene, albeit largely outside the universities, with the formation of clubs and other bodies around the country. The Civil Service Athletics Club, founded in 1867, remains Ireland's oldest athletics club. Irish university championships continued throughout this period on a somewhat haphazard basis, with the exception of the College Races and Queen's College Cork's annual sports competition, but university athletes and graduates were more inclined to join clubs with their better facilities or even form clubs of their own. There was a very strong relationship between athletes and rugby players as most top class athletes were also outstanding rugby players. Many represented their country at both sports with the Bulger brothers, Daniel, Michael and Lawrence being outstanding examples. Michael and Larry were rugby internationals with Trinity College football club and Lansdowne rugby club and also Irish athletics champions and officials, whilst Daniel played rugby for both Trinity and Lansdowne and was a multiple Irish athletics champion as well as a five-times British AAA champion, concluding his sporting career in 1892 by winning the AAA long jump championship and 120 yards hurdles championship at Stamford Bridge, London. A month later, back in Dublin, Dan Bulger equalled the world record for the 120 yards hurdles in his final competition before retiring and devoting himself to the sport's administration, becoming Vice-President of the Irish Amateur Athletics Association.

Larry continued to sprint competitively, winning the Irish 220 yards championship and going on to play international rugby for Ireland and the British and Irish touring team in South Africa in 1896, playing in all four Tests. The tourists won three of those Tests and Larry Bulger set a record by scoring twenty tries on that tour. His brother Michael had been a founder member of London Irish rugby club in 1898 and acted as medical officer to the club for many years. His greatest sporting involvement however was at the London Olympic Games of 1908 where he was senior medical officer for the marathon from Windsor Castle to White City. Together with the other SMO, Dr Arthur Conan Doyle, they assisted the Italian runner, Dorando Pietri, at the conclusion of the race, thereby contributing to Pietri's disqualification after crossing the finishing line in first position. Photographs of the finish clearly show Dr Bulger and Dr Conan Doyle giving medical and other assistance to Dorando Pietri and controversy still continues today over the part played by the medical officers at the conclusion of this 1908 Olympic Marathon in London. Other prominent athletes in this early period included Edward Walsh (high jump and 120 yards hurdles), Patrick Kelly (high jump), John Lane (set a world record in 1874 of 23 feet one and a half inches in the long jump), A.C. Courtney in 1873 held the world record for 1000 yards in 2 minutes 23.6 seconds, Charles Wadsworth (shot putt), and John Daly (hammer, shot, 120 yards and hop, step and jump).

The 1920s and 30s provided the universities with their share of national and international champions such as Sean Lavin, Eamon Fitzgerald, P.C. Moore, Len Horan and the Olympic champions Pat O'Callaghan (1928 and 1932 hammer) and Bob Tisdall (1932 400 yards hurdles); but in November 1934 came the greatest upheaval and tragedy with the suspension of the NACAI (National Athletics and Cycling Association of Ireland) from all international athletic competitions. The whole situation resulted from IAAF introducing a new boundary rule in the definition of membership, namely: 'the jurisdiction of members of the International Amateur Athletics Federation is limited by the political boundaries of the country or nation they represent.' Ireland, as the Irish Free State, could thereby include only 26 counties and not the 32 counties as previously. It led to the formation of the Amateur Athletics Union Eire (AAUE) and its membership of the IAAF in March 1938 with the Northern Ireland Amateur Athletics Association (NIAAA) as a regional authority and part of the British Amateur Athletics Board (BAAB). Thus began the disastrous division in Irish athletics between those who could compete internationally and those (the majority) who could not and the resulting decline in standards and performances from then on.

The intervarsity championships restarted after the Second World War but the split in Irish athletics between the NACAI and the AAUE had deepened and become more acrimonious. By the Olympic year of 1948 the relationship between the main athletics bodies had grown even worse. In consequence NACAI athletes were not permitted to compete or even march in the Opening Ceremony. AAUE athletes were able to take part but had to march at the back of the Irish Olympic team at that Ceremony and in the final official report, required by the International Olympic Committee, the Irish athletes and team officials who took part in the Games with some distinction, were not even mentioned. Such pettiness was absurd and deeply distasteful and damaging to the country's international sporting standard and good name. However, the 1948 London Olympics had two immediate, positive benefits. They opened the door to American university athletics through American sports scholarship schemes. Two competitors at the London Games were offered scholarships to Villanova University, near Philadelphia, namely Jim Reardon and Cummin Clancy, both of Donore Harriers. Reardon was a 400 metres finalist and the fastest European 400 metres runner at the Games. Clancy won the British AAA discus championship two weeks before the Games. One year later John Joe Barry, perhaps Ireland's greatest middle-distance runner up to that time, joined Reardon and Clancy at Villanova and thus established a long line of Irish athletes who were to go to the USA on sports scholarships. They also led to the reorganisation of the Irish Olympic Committee under a new

President, Lord Killanin. As President he not only restored Ireland's good name and standing at Olympic level, but also went on to become President of the International Olympic Committee, leading the Olympic movement through many revolutionary changes from 1972 to 1980.

Back in Ireland, university athletics recommenced in 1946, with the first post-war meeting taking place at University College Galway's grounds. This first competition was won by University College Dublin and they now became the dominant force in university athletics, partly due to the absence from the competitions of Trinity College and Queen's Belfast from 1938 to 1961. In the organisational arena senior officials met and in 1961 finally managed to heal the divisions that had been created in the late '30s and university athletics was able to revert to its full intervarsity status. The first competition between Trinity and UCD for over 20 years was held at College Park in June 1961. A memorable contest ended with Trinity beating their long time rivals by a decisive margin and both became dominant in their respective associations, Trinity in the AAUE and UCD in the NACAI. This meeting proved to be the breakthrough that had long been required and, when Queen's Belfast rejoined the family, full intervarsity athletics competition was able to resume.

But greater and unforeseen changes were on their way in the 1960s and '70s with the first change being the introduction of women's athletics into the university championships. Trevor West in his book The Bold Collegians writes: 'The development of women's athletics south of the border in the postwar period forms an eccentric codicil to the convoluted legacy left by their male counterparts. Little competition had been arranged for women athletes before the Second World War, although there had been an occasional event in the College Races; but in 1948 activity on this front received a stimulus from the achievement of the Dutch athlete, Fanny Blankers-Koen, in winning four gold medals in the sprint events at the London Olympics. Mrs Blankers-Koen then ran in a meeting at Lansdowne Road, but the emergence of women's athletics in the south of Ireland was nipped smartly in the bud by the Catholic archbishop of Dublin. Dr John Charles McQuaid was a conservative churchman who rarely missed the opportunity offered by the penitential season of Lent of warning his flock against the dangers of teenage dancing or attendance at Trinity College. Taking a lead in his Lenten pastoral of 1950 from Pope Pius XI, he expressed grave disapproval of the practice of "permitting young women to compete in cycling and athletics in mixed public sports", and quoting papal regulations to be observed by women athletes, he emphasized that it was "extremely unbecoming for them to display themselves before the public gaze".'

Northerners, naturally looked on things rather differently and in that very year, Ulster women formed the Northern Ireland Women's Amateur Athletic Association; but south of the border, women's athletic competition was obliterated for the next ten years by a stroke of the archiepiscopal pen. Colin Shillington, an Ulsterman and holder of the college record at 880 yards, was the 1960 Trinity athletics captain. He invited Maeve Kyle (a Trinity graduate and then the foremost Ulster athlete) to bring a team of women from Ballymena Athletic Club to run in the College Races against opposition to be provided by members of the Ladies' Hockey and Tennis Clubs in the 100 yards and 4 x 100 yard relay. This innovation, for innovation it was in the Republic of the day, was a success, so much so that the women athletes were presented to President de Valera who was attending the races and at his own request. Thus the ice was broken and organizers of Dublin athletics gingerly included a women's race in their subsequent meetings. But the aura of prohibition did not fade overnight, and it was 1965 before a women's section of Dublin University Harriers and Athletic Club was formally resuscitated.

From 1966, women's intervarsity athletics now made its appearance with UCD ladies being prominent in the championships from that time on, but challenged by strong competition from Trinity, Queen's Belfast, the University of Ulster and more recently, the University of Limerick. But women in university athletics go back well before 1966. Trinity's Maeve Kyle was the first women's athletics champion in university and national athletics, and was Ireland's first women's athletics competitor in the 1956 Melbourne Olympics. She was also an international hockey player and played a major role in the establishment of women's athletics competition at local, university and national levels. Her contribution over nearly half a century has been vast and she still continues as coach, administrator, club member and athletics official right up to the present day. She lives in Northern Ireland with husband Sean, also an active and outstanding coach and international athletics official, and they continue to provide channels of communication, athletes and officials from the NIAAA and their opposite numbers in the rest of Ireland. ▪

Whilst the new decade of the '60s opened quietly with the Rome Olympics the changes made throughout the decade were to affect the whole sporting arena in Ireland. Perhaps the most significant change, from a national athletics perspective, was the partial healing in 1967 of the split between the NACAI and the AAUE with the establishment of Bord Luthcleas na hEireann, known as BLE (Irish Athletics Board) out of an amalgamation of those bodies. Despite breakaway action by some of the NACAI the vast majority of Irish athletes were now eligible to compete internationally. This situation further improved in 1999 when a new athletics body called The Athletics Association of Ireland was formed out of the NACAI, the BLE and the NIAAA. This finally succeeded in reuniting athletics in Ireland, a position last applicable before 1934.

The last 30 years has also seen the introduction of perhaps the greatest influence sport has had to deal with, namely the televising of events on a mass basis, particularly at national and international levels. Television has influenced the popularity of a number of traditional sports in Ireland to an extraordinary degree, association football and Gaelic football being prime examples. Other minority sports such as snooker have grown from relative obscurity to national obsession. Some traditional sports such as athletics have declined as a consequence of television's intrusion. Television has popularised sport and created a new sporting hierarchy. This in turn has brought into sport unheard of amounts of money which has turned popular recreation into important business and leisure industries, a situation far removed from the 1960s. With the introduction of professionalism into athletics in the late 1980s national athletics changed irrevocably, some would say not for the better. Only university athletics remains relatively unchanged and comparable to traditional athletics of the past. So the 1960s, in hindsight, served to bring to an end the second era in Irish athletics.

The great influx of students into universities and other third level education from this time, an increase from less than 20,000 in 1961 to more than 120,000 in 2001, did not halt the relative decline in the standards and popularity of athletics. Athletics, both in the universities and clubs, now had to compete with other sports as never before. The increase in pressure on standards of entry and achievement in all courses and degrees put restrictions on the time formerly available, while the time demands of modern training also cut into the limited time available. All these added restrictions from a sporting perspective go some way to explaining the relative decline in athletics at university level, offset to some extent by improvements in diet and nutrition. Surprisingly, increased numbers, while not improving national athletics standards and performances to the level expected, has in fact improved vastly the provision of sporting and athletics facilities. Universities generally have first class, modern facilities with Trinity College having access to the finest athletics stadium in the country at the Morton Stadium in Santry as well as College Park where it all began back in 1857.

There is increased competition internationally against the British, European and American Universities both at home and abroad and these developments serve to sustain a high level of interest if not overall standards in university athletics and the ongoing flow to the athletics clubs. The introduction of sports scholarships has certainly raised the standard at individual level, albeit not to the same extent as in the USA. In the US the sports scholarship athlete is the norm. In Ireland he or she is the exception. However, the reorganisation of the intervarsity championships, the superceding of outdated modus operandi and the formation of the new Irish Universities Athletics Association (IUAA) in October 1990, with the redoubtable Dr Cyril White as its first President, has brought together all the parties in encouraging mode and thereby begun, in this third millennium, what it is hoped will prove to be an exciting new era in Irish athletics.

It is always invidious to pick out individuals in any review, such as this chapter on athletics, but if one were to pick out five Irish athletics champions that epitomise the remarkable achievements of Irish athletes in the last half century then the names of Ron Delany, Eamonn Coghlan, Mary Peters, Sonia O'Sullivan and Catherina McKiernan, would surely predominate. Of these only two developed their potential in Ireland. The other three, Delany, Coghlan and O'Sullivan were, as senior athletes, the product of the American University Athletics Scholarships system as outlined earlier. Since the 1950s a constant stream of Irish schools athletics champions and other young athletes have made their way to American Universities to further their athletic careers and education. Irish athletes who achieved success through US sports scholarships were Jim Reardon (400 metres); Cummin Clancy (discus); John Joe Barry (perhaps Ireland's greatest middle distance runner); John Treacy from Providence College, Rhode Island, who won two World Cross-Country Championships in 1978 and 1979 and a silver medal in the 1984 Los Angeles Olympics; Marcus O'Sullivan and Frank O'Mara, both indoor World Champions. It is these athletes and others such as Thelma Hopkins who would compete for recognition as Ireland's five greatest athletes.

'... with 300 metres remaining he was trapped on the inside edge of the track, back in 10th place. A gap opened and the Irishman flew through, picking off the men in front amidst tumultuous reaction. RON DELANY was a clear winner, running the last 100 metres in 12.5 seconds, to finish well ahead of Klaus Richtzenhain of Germany, the favourite, John Landy of Australia, and the rest of the pack...'

And so it was, that in the Melbourne 1956 Olympics, Ron Delany won only the second Irish gold medal on the track in the history of the Games (Bob Tisdall won gold in the 400 metres hurdles in Los Angeles in 1932). It was a classic final, involving six of the ten runners who had broken the four minute mile barrier; the excitement, with one lap to go and the field tightly bunched, was such that an excited official forgot to ring the bell to signify the beginning of the last lap!

Ron Delany is recognised as the best track athlete produced by Ireland, and perhaps its most outstanding sportsman of the 20th century. Delany came from a sporting family with a brother Joe, who was, in the view of some knowledgeable people, even more talented than his brother Ron. Joe Delany was a few years older than Ron and, as a schoolboy athlete, far more successful than his brother. The essential difference however, was not a matter of athletic talent alone, but of focused perseverance, a significant factor in not only Ron Delany's

ABOVE ■ 1956 Melbourne Olympics. Ronnie Delany wins the 1500 metres creating one of the biggest surprises in the history of the Olympics.

success, but also of all the other Irish Olympic or world champions or medal winners. Joe Delany, after a successful year or two in senior ranks in Irish athletics, emigrated to Canada and retired from the sport. His potential as a sprinter and long jumper was never developed or realised, but he did provide the 'big brother' example for the younger Ron. As a schoolboy, Ron Delany was also a schools champion but only in his last two years at school concluding his schoolboy athletic career in 1953 by winning the Irish Schools Senior 880 yards championship in the very modest time of 2 minutes 7.4 seconds.

During his school days, Ron Delany was fortunate in having as his athletics coach Jack Sweeney, a mathematics teacher, at his school. Sweeney encouraged Delany to continue his running career after schooldays, but suggested that he concentrate on the half mile as his racing distance. This advice was the first step in Ron Delany's subsequent athletic career and Olympic success. In 1954, Delany first won the Irish Senior 880 yards championship, broke the Irish record for this distance in College Park, and competed in the European Athletics Championships in Berne, Switzerland. It was at these European Championships that Delany reached the final of the 800 metres, breaking the Irish record en route and as a result, received the offer of an athletics scholarship to Villanova University, located just outside Philadelphia in the US. Delany registered as a student there in the autumn of 1954 and came under the guidance of 'Jumbo' Elliott, the University athletics coach.

At Villanova, Delany competed in cross-country (run over the golf course), indoor and outdoor track meetings. His outdoor and indoor races were at 440 and 880 yards. During the summer vacation of 1955, Delany returned home and competed in a number of athletics meetings sponsored by Clonliffe Harriers. At the last meeting before his return to Villanova the energetic and far-seeing secretary of Clonliffe, Billy Morton, persuaded a very reluctant Delany to run his first ever mile race. He completed the four laps of the famous grass track of College Park in 4 minutes 5.8 seconds for a new Irish record and one of the fastest mile times of that year. On returning to Villanova, coach Elliott told Delany that his athletic future was as a miler and set out a training and racing programme to this effect. Indoor racing was the first phase of this racing programme, with outdoor competition following, all in various parts of America. Of course, Delany did not neglect his 880 yard or even his 440 yard racing, as he was not yet a miler but had the ultimate view of competing in the Olympic 1500 metres championship in Melbourne, Australia in December 1956. But on 1st June 1956, after an outstanding indoor and outdoor season, Ron Delany became Ireland's first four-minute miler when he ran 3 minutes 59 seconds for the distance in Compton, California.

After summer again at home in Dublin, and without too much success due to an injury sustained in a race in Paris, Delany elected to return to Villanova to prepare for the Melbourne Olympic Games to be held in December. 'Jumbo' Elliott now prepared him with a 10 to 12 week programme of training over the terrain of the golf course, intermixed with speed endurance work on the track over shorter distances than the mile or 1500 metres. This, together with other strengthening and stretching work proved to be an excellent preparation for the Olympic 1500 metres. Back in Dublin, the Olympic Council of Ireland was in two minds as to whether they would send Ron Delany to Melbourne. By one vote, Delany was selected and shortly afterwards joined the Irish Olympic team as it prepared in Berkeley, California, before its final journey across the Pacific to Melbourne where, on 1st December 1956, Ronald M. Delany of Crusaders Athletic Club, Dublin and Villanova University, became the Olympic 1500 metres champion.

Ron Delany returned to Ireland that December to a 'Hero's Welcome' and a Civic Reception at the Mansion House, Dublin, reminiscent of Tisdall and O'Callaghan's victorious return from Los Angeles in 1932. Delany went on to have an outstandingly successful indoor running career in America with 34 consecutive victories and the world indoor mile record. He was never beaten indoors at the mile. Nevertheless his greatest success was to be his Olympic victory at the

Melbourne Olympic Games. While many of his races in America outdoors were of an outstanding quality, his half mile and mile victories in the American Universities Championships in California in 1958 – both within 50 minutes of each other – were equal to the best in the world. But his greatest running all occurred outside Ireland, except for one most notable race. This was to be the world record mile which took place at Santry Stadium, Dublin (now re-named The Morton Stadium) in August 1958. That evening the indefatigable Billy Morton managed to gather together some of the greatest milers in the world for a mile race at another Clonliffe Harriers sponsored meeting at their new stadium in the north Dublin suburb of Santry. Thanks to Delany's Olympic success, athletics in Ireland had once again become a highly popular sport with many young athletes all over the country wishing to emulate Delany.

This was the basis on which Billy Morton had raised the money to build an international track and small stadium in Santry. The stadium and track was opened in May 1958 and in August, Morton had arranged a mile race that was to become perhaps the greatest mile race in athletics history with Herb Elliott of Australia breaking the world record by nearly three seconds; the second finisher, Merv Lincoln also breaking the previous world record and the first five finishers all running inside four minutes. Delany ran a fine race that evening, but it was to be Elliot's greatest race over this classic distance. Delany was third but it was his running that evening and his reputation that made Elliot's outstanding time possible in the same way that Ron Delany's Olympic victory helped make The Morton Stadium the Irish athletics Mecca. Delany finally retired to Dublin in the early 1960s and continues to live there making a positive and visible contribution to Irish athletics and Irish sport right up to the present day. ▪

One of the young athletes who sought to emulate Ron Delany and his sporting achievements was a young Dublin boy named Eamonn Coghlan. Eamonn's father, Billy Coghlan was deeply involved in athletics at youth level, and Billy was to become the President of the youth section of Irish Athletics and subsequently was to become President of the BLE–the Irish National Athletics Board. Like Delany, Coghlan came from a sporting background and had been a fine, though not outstanding schoolboy athlete, winning an athletics title as did Delany seventeen years earlier. On the strength of his schoolboy success, and thanks to Delany's influence, Eamonn Coghlan was offered an athletics scholarship to Villanova by Delany's former coach Jumbo Elliott. Also, like Delany, Coghlan was to become an indoor champion breaking the world indoor mile record with a time of 3 minutes 49.78 seconds in February 1983, but as a member of the New York Athletic Club, not while a student at Villanova.

While at Villanova, Coghlan had been an outstanding miler and was selected to compete for Ireland in the 1500 metres at the Montreal Olympic Games of 1976. At these games, Coghlan had hoped to win a medal and if lucky, even an Olympic championship itself. But luck was not on his side that afternoon in Montreal. After leading until 150 metres from the finish, he was passed by John Walker of New Zealand, Ivo van Damme of Belgium and, just on the finishing line, by Paul-Heinz Wellmann of Germany, thereby putting Coghlan in the unrecoverable position of fourth place in an Olympic final. So close were the first four finishers that the winner, Walker, was only 0.34 second (less than two metres), and bronze medallist Wellmann just 0.18 second (about 3 inches) ahead of Coghlan over the 1500 metres.

Sadly, this traumatic athletic experience was to be repeated yet again four years later at the Moscow Olympics in 1980. By this time, Coghlan had moved up to 5000 metres where he reached the Moscow Olympic final with an outstanding chance of an Olympic medal and even an Olympic win. Unfortunately, this was not to be his destiny; in a race that he could have won, Coghlan lost the Bronze medal this time by only 0.8 seconds, inches away from an Olympic medal. This must make Eamonn Coghlan the most celebrated Olympic athlete of all time not to win an Olympic medal. But as was mentioned at the start of this section, Eamonn Coghlan had focused perseverance and after two Olympic traumatic experiences, he was to bounce back just three years later to become the first world 5000 metres champion in the Olympic stadium

LEFT ■ July 1979. Eamonn Coghlan throws his arms up after winning the 5000 metres event at an athletics meeting at Crystal Palace.

in Helsinki, Finland. Coghlan's victory in this race was so dominant that he and many others thought that the Los Angeles Olympics in the following year would be for him, third time lucky. But it was not to be as he sustained a lingering injury and thereby missed competing in those games. John Treacy, his team-mate from Ireland in the 1980 5000 metres final, was a competitor at Los Angeles and won the silver medal in the classic event of all Olympic games – the Marathon. This event finished in the same Olympic Stadium in Los Angeles where Tisdall and O'Callaghan had won their Olympic titles in 1932.

Before he retired from both Olympic and International competition, Coghlan was to achieve many outstanding successes. He won the European Indoor 1500 metres in Vienna, the silver medal in the European Outdoor 1500 metres in Prague and on seven occasions, won the prestigious Wanamaker Indoor Mile in Madison Square Gardens, New York. After he had retired from international competition he continued to compete in Veterans (or as it is also called, Masters) races and has achieved the unique position of being the one and only person over forty years of age to have run a mile in competition in less than four minutes, a remarkable sporting achievement. Eamonn continues to be involved in sport and lives, like Ron Delany, in Dublin. ▨

Sonia O'Sullivan's silver medal at the Sydney Olympic games in September 2000 is the latest in a long line of Olympic medals won by Irish athletes but the first Olympic medal to be won by an Irish woman. This makes O'Sullivan the first of what it is hoped will be a succession of successful Irish international and Olympic women competitors. At present, Irish women athletes are developing their athletic abilities at an unprecedented rate. This is due in very large measure to the long-term success of Sonia O'Sullivan who, for most of the last decade, has been winning international and world championships both on the track and at cross-country. She has won races on all types of surfaces, track, country and road and in October 2000, ran and won her first ever marathon.

From the time Sonia was a school girl in her native Cobh, Co Cork, she has shown extraordinary running ability and as a 17 year-old won both the Irish Women's Senior Cross-Country Championship and Irish Women's Junior Cross-Country Championship in the same year, 1987. Her first track race was at the Cork City Sports where as a teenager she ran a fine race beating many well-established senior Irish women athletes. From that time on Sonia has developed into one of the greatest women athletes in history. Her double world cross-country championship wins at Marrakech, in 1998 only one day apart is unique. Her world 5000 metres championship in Gothenburg, Sweden in 1995 and her world student games 1500 metres championship in Sheffield in 1991, forever secured her place in international athletics history.

ABOVE ▪ 25 September 2000 Sydney Olympics. Sonia O'Sullivan with her silver medal for the Womens 5000 metres.

Sadly, like all great athletes, she has had a number of relative failures that unfortunately are always remembered. Her fourth place in the Barcelona Olympic games in 1992 over 1500 metres reminds us of the similar experience that beset Eamonn Coghlan in Montreal in 1976. A more difficult Olympic experience was to be her fate in Atlanta in 1996, when most unexpectedly, she failed to finish in the 5000 metres final. She was expected to win, yet failed to qualify for the final of the 1500 metres in these same games. But in the true fashion of the great athlete she undoubtedly is, she bounced back with two great European Championship successes in both the 5000 metres and 10000 metres in Budapest in 1998. Finally, her Olympic silver medal in the women's 5000 metres in Sydney in 2000 and her first marathon run and win in the Dublin City Marathon in late 2000 clearly shows that she is still one of the great women athletes of the present time.

O'Sullivan, like Delany, Coghlan and many other Irish athletes won sports scholarships to Villanova University and there came under the coaching of Jumbo Elliott's successors. The American university system of professional coaching and high level, continuous competition either makes or breaks an athlete. Sonia was successful in this most competitive of athletic environments. It was at Villanova that she learned to compete effectively and this gave her competitive experience that she would not have got elsewhere, certainly not in Ireland. This is where the American athletes score over others; it is not facilities or even coaching and training that makes the difference, but in competitions that American athletes learn to participate so effectively. Their coaches are not technically ahead of others and can even be inferior to their European counterparts in some cases, but the one thing all American sports coaches know is how to prepare their sportsmen and sportswomen for competition at all levels. It is this acquired ability and the related discipline in training and preparation that characterises American coaching. These are the significant things Sonia, Ron Delany, Eamonn Coghlan and others learned while students at Villanova.

Despite occasional and unexpected defeats, Sonia O'Sullivan continues to have a highly successful athletic career particularly on the Grand Prix Circuit around the world. She now makes London her home and base but returns to Ireland on a number of occasions to run or visit her family and friends. Her final Olympic aspiration and appearance as a competitor will

LEFT ▧ 12th August 1995. Sonia O'Sullivan goes past Fernanda Ribeiro of Portugal on her way to victory in the womens 5000 metre final at the 1995 IAAF World Athletics Championships at the Ullevi Stadium in Gothenburg, Sweden.

be perhaps the Olympic marathon in Athens in 2004. If she is in luck and injury free, she could well win this classic event to be run and decided over the original marathon course. ▪

f one athlete demonstrated focused perseverance over a period of fifteen years of competition, it is Mary Peters. She started as a big strong schoolgirl who put the shot and took part in the high jump but reached the pinnacle of her athletics career by winning the Olympic Pentathlon championship with a world record performance in Munich, Germany in 1972. Mary Peters has clearly demonstrated that champions, even Olympic champions, are made not born. This is not to say that any one can be developed into a champion athlete – one needs the basic talent and other necessary attributes to start with, but it is to say that all champions have to develop their winning abilities over many years of training and competition. It is this requirement of focused perseverance over many years that makes the essential difference between those who succeed as athletes and those with even great natural talent who do not. Mary Peters is an excellent example of a champion athlete who, in the most unlikely athletic environment of Northern Ireland, became an Olympic champion and world record holder and at the advanced age for an athlete of 33 years. But Mary, like Eamonn Coghlan and Sonia O'Sullivan had also tasted the very bitter experience of being fourth in an Olympic final, in the pentathlon at Tokyo in 1964.

In the following Olympics, held in Mexico City in 1968, Mary Peters was only placed ninth in this most demanding athletic event. This looked like the end of her Olympic aspirations since by the time the Munich Olympics came around in 1972, she would be a mature 33 year-old athlete, an age where one was considered well past one's best athletic years. Yet at 33 years of age, she managed to achieve personal bests in three of the five events of the pentathlon, the 100 metre hurdles, the high jump and the 200 metres. The long jump and 200 metres were Mary's weakest events, particularly the 200 metres, yet it was her time in the 200 metres, the last event of the pentathlon and her weakest event up to this time, that won her the Olympic championship and the World record. Interestingly, if Mary Peters had run just 1/10th (0.01) of a second slower, she would have lost the Olympic championship and world record.

Mary's opponents that day included the world record holder, Burglinde Pollack of East Germany and Heide Rosendahl of West Germany, the world record holder in the long jump, who two days before had won the Olympic long jump in front of her home crowd. The remainder of the finalists were also of the highest calibre, presenting the greatest gathering of pentathlon athletes

RIGHT ▪ Dame Mary Peters DBE and Mary Peters the athelete.

ever assembled at that time. Rosendahl, who finished second, also broke the world record and third placed Pollack was the current world record holder up to this Olympic competition. This was the ultimate measure of her Olympic achievement. Peters would continue in top class competition, winning the Commonwealth games title in 1974, but her greatest achievement was her Olympic win in Munich in the Summer of 1972.

While a pupil at Portadown College, Mary was introduced to athletics by Kenny McLelland the PE teacher at the school. As Mary progressed, she became Northern Ireland High Jump and Shot Putt champion, then Irish champion and British champion. At this point Mary worked hard to develop her hurdling technique and became an Irish international athlete in this event along with her high jumping and shot putting. It was now a natural progression to the pentathlon as her major international event. As Mary had been born in Liverpool, but came to live in

Gold at the 1972 Munich Games

Mary Peters' pentathlon win of the gold medal in the Munich Games (1972) at the age of 33 earned her the title 'the greatest woman athlete in the world'. Her victory was not achieved easily. She had outstanding rivals in Heidi Rosendahl (West Germany), Burglinde Pollack (East Germany), Christine Bodner (East Germany) and Valentino Tikhomirova (Russia) and a number of incidents caused irritation and potential loss of concentration. To start with, Mary Peters' official car to the stadium failed to turn up, she was placed in what appeared to be the slowest heat of the 100 metres hurdles, her running shoes were unacceptable to the German officials, she was delayed with her warm up programme, she couldn't find her coach Buster McShane at a vital time, she was besieged by autograph hunters and the Russian girl had adopted distracting tactics! However after day one she had achieved personal bests in the 100 metres hurdles (13.3 secs), shot putt (53ft 1¾ins, best in pentathlon) and high jump (5ft 11½ins) to lead the field, but Pollack in second place and Rosendahl in fifth place with her two best events to come still posed a real threat. Mary Peters' only thought was 'it's got to be the gold'. Nothing else by this time was worth thinking about and encouraged by Buster McShane: 'It's all right P, we can do it'. Rosendahl won both the long jump and 200 metres but Mary Peters with a very gutsy performance in the 200 metres in which she managed to record her best time, held on to win the gold with 4801 points from Rosendahl 4791 points and Pollack 4768 points.

TOP LEFT ■ Pre-Munich determination and focused perseverance in the hurdles.

TOP RIGHT ■ A career best performance in the high jump at the end of the first day puts the gold medal in sight. **ABOVE** ■ Rosendahl is in front and out of the picture, but Pollack is in close proximity in the last event of the pentathlon.

Northern Ireland when she was four, she was eligible to compete for Britain in the Olympic games and she decided to do so for the 1964 Tokyo Olympics and subsequently in Mexico City in 1968 and Munich in 1972. Her brother John had been a fine high jumper so, like Ron Delany, she had an older sibling to emulate and encourage her at an early age. But then, while many other younger sisters or brothers have been encouraged they do not make Olympic champions; it must be something much more significant. Mary Peters illustrated the highly significant characteristic of focused perseverance over many years, even in a far from perfect athletic environment where the weather, facilities and opportunities for high-class competition were limited (in her autobiography she recalls she and her father building what was to be the first Irish concrete shot putt circle outside their back yard at home in Portadown!). Despite those limitations Mary Peters had to pursue a level of development and reach a standard at home that would enable her to go out into the wider athletics world where the competition necessary for athletic development was available. It was this ability that made Mary Peters the great Olympic champion that she became. Today, Dame Mary Peters brings her leadership characteristics to the administration of athletics both in Ireland and Britain. ▪

Catherina McKiernan first came to prominence as an 18 year-old schoolgirl when she won the Irish Schools cross-country championships. This was her entry into national athletics. Prior to this, Catherina had enjoyed playing camogie (womens hurling) and football and as a 16 year-old had won a duathlon which consisted of a 12-mile bicycle race followed by a 3-mile foot race, 15 miles in all. One of her teachers, Joe Doonan had encouraged her in her sporting activities and now started to coach her as a cross-country runner. Catherina had a tall and very slim physique, the ideal build for an endurance athlete and on this basis, she and her coach built her running career. Within twelve months of her schools championship success she had developed her running standard up to national senior level and finished third in the Irish Senior Cross-Country championships. By this time she had left school and had started work with the Cavan County Council.

Her coaching partnership with Doonan continued and in 1990 she won her first National Senior Cross-Country championship in Limerick. Catherina was to retain her Irish championship at cross-country for the next two years but also tried her hand as a track athlete at 3000 metres, 5000 metres and 10000 metres. However, by 1992, she had attained international level in cross-country and was selected to compete for Ireland in the World Cross-Country championships held at Boston, in March 1992. In this race Catherina McKiernan clearly demonstrated that she had become a world-class cross-country runner when, against the best women athletes in the world, she won the silver medal, being beaten for first place only in the final 100 yards. The young Cavan woman had clearly shown that, even in a cross-country area with little tradition of cross-country running for men and very little, if any, tradition of women's cross-country or track athletics, an athlete with focused perseverance based upon good planning and detailed preparation could go right to the top in world-class competition. Like Mary Peters, Catherina had turned an unfavourable athletics environment into a supportive and beneficial base for the development of a world-class athlete, and a world-class athlete she continued to be for the next three years, winning the European Cross-Country championship in 1994.

In 1993 at Amorebriel, Portugal, in 1994 at Budapest and finally in 1995 at Durham, England, Catherina was again to win the silver medal in the world championship. Four runner-up medals in the world championships were an outstanding athletic achievement, but sadly, she was never able to go that little bit further and win the World Cross-Country championship. But in 1997 she had found her true racing distance, the most demanding endurance race of all: the Marathon. This classic race is run over a distance of 26 miles 385 yards. Her coach Joe Doonan had kept detailed records of all her training and as part of her development, had Catherina regularly tested at the Human Performance Laboratory in Trinity College, Dublin. Treadmill and other tests had provided information on a variety of physiological parameters such as heart rates, CO_2 uptake and blood lactate. These were all used as a guide to training, development and specific conditioning. It was at the Human Performance Laboratory at Trinity that it was first noticed that Catherina's physiological condition was most conducive to marathon running and it was here that her potential as a marathon runner was first identified.

Catherina and her coach now planned her entry into marathon racing. The event chosen was the Berlin marathon to be run on Sunday 28th September 1997. Doonan prepared an intensive 14-week training programme for Catherina's first marathon. The Berlin marathon was no easy run where one could try out the distance, but one of the most public and biggest races of its kind with the world's best and most experienced runners taking part. It would be a baptism of fire for any beginner at marathon racing. It also offered very considerable financial rewards to the winner and leading finishers. Doonan's build up programme over 14 weeks consisted of long runs and specific pace work. Catherina was running over 100 miles per week and, in addition, on Sundays she ran for 2½ hours non-stop with a group of 10 male athletes. Doonan had also drawn up plans for the race itself including projected split times over the first 20 miles.

In his meticulous way, he was preparing McKiernan so her outstanding endurance talents would be utilised to the full. This was considered essential on her debut as a marathon runner in a world-class field. By the time Catherina reached Berlin in late September, she was very well prepared and she had reason to believe that she would run a fast time – an essential psychological advantage. The course was relatively flat and the mild weather ideal for endurance running. So

ABOVE ▨ 1st November 1998 Catherina McKiernan comes in to win the Amsterdam Marathon.

it proved, for running an average of 5 minutes 45 seconds per mile, she reached the halfway mark in 1 hour 14 minutes 42 seconds and then went on to run the second half of the race in the faster time of 1 hour 11 minutes and 2 seconds. Her final 10000 metres was run in an astounding 32 minutes 52 seconds. This kind of pace in the closing stages of a marathon left all the others floundering in Catherina's wake. She won by more than a minute in 2 hours, 23 minutes and 44 seconds – the fastest time ever for a first marathon by a woman and the eleventh fastest women's marathon of all time. To appreciate the merit of McKiernan's time, it only needs to be noted that her time in Berlin was better than any Olympic winning time for men, up to Emil Zatopek's win in the 1952 Olympic marathon, which was then the world's best time for the distance. Catherina's Berlin time was faster than the second man in Zatopek's Olympic win by nearly two minutes. McKiernan had now found her best event and she was to go on and win two more top class marathons in London in April 1998 and the one after in Amsterdam in September 1998 with an even faster time than in Berlin, 2 hours 22 minutes 24 seconds. This final time incidentally was a faster time than Zatopek ever ran in the marathon!

The Sydney Olympic marathon of 2000 was now the target, with high expectations of at least an Olympic medal and even an Olympic win. But, like Eamonn Coghlan in 1984, a persistent back injury put an end to Catherina's Olympic hopes and even her running career, as the 1999 and 2000 seasons demonstrated. For some reason, her back injury did not respond to all the medical attention that she received. However, she has started racing again in the early part of the 2001 season and after her marriage in late 2000 we all look forward to a return to her best running in the 21st century. ▪

Micheal Johnston was born in Dublin in 1935. He rowed for Christ's College, Cambridge and was Hon Secretary and Captain of the College Boat Club. He coached many of the Dublin clubs at various times, notably Trinity College, Dublin, Garda Siochana Boat Club, UCD, Neptune RC and much later DULBC. He was Hon Secretary and President of the Irish Amateur Rowing Union and briefly Chairman of the Dublin Metropolitan Regatta Council. He was a FISA (International Rowing Federation) International Umpire from 1969 to 2000 and is a Steward of Henley Royal Regatta. He is President of DULBC and of the Bluecoat Club, an Honorary Vice-President of Commercial Rowing Club and is the Secretary of the Dublin Sculling Ladder. He wrote: The Big Pot: The Story of the Irish Senior Rowing Championship 1912-1991. His career was in broadcasting, radio and television with RTE in Dublin and he wrote on rowing in Dublin's Evening Press. ∎

The year 1950 was something of a landmark for Irish rowing: three Irish crews made finals day at Henley. Trinity was in the final of the Ladies' Plate for college eights, losing that final by the tiny margin of one-third of a length to New College, Oxford. UCD was in the semi-final of the Thames Cup, in those days the playground of American 110lb. crews, the forerunners of the lightweight crews of today; they lost to the overall winners Kent School by two lengths. Perhaps most remarkably of all, a young Dutchman named Rob van Mesdag, sculling for Trinity College, beat the Dutch national champion in a tremendous semi-final, and went on to contest the final of the Diamond Sculls, the individual zenith of Henley Royal

Regatta. Henley is not of course part of Irish rowing, but since 1870 it was the one international yardstick against which Irish rowing could be measured. In 1948 there had been another important first when Ireland competed in the Olympic Regatta for the first time. That year FISA, the International Rowing Federation, held its Congress in Henley, and the Irish Amateur Rowing Union, founded in 1899, was elected a member of FISA, representing all Ireland. An Irish eight took part in the Olympic Regatta held on a modified Henley course adapted for three-boat racing over 2000 metres. Ireland had two races, a heat and a repêchage – that word had never been heard of till then – and was last in both. But those pioneers had ushered in a new international era for Irish rowing, which would make its impact over the next half century.

Domestically, 1950 was the middle of a long period of university domination on the rivers of Ireland. The Irish Senior Championships for men's eights had been started in 1912, and in its early days it had been the domain of some of the Grand Old Clubs of Irish rowing: City of

LEFT ■ 1948 Henley: The Irish Olympic eight at the slip.
RIGHT ■ 1950 Shooting O'Connell Bridge in Dublin: the Gannon Cup; the only time Trinity and UCD deadheated for the Cup.

Derry, Bann Rowing Club from Coleraine, Belfast Boat Club and Drogheda from the northern half of the country, a relatively new Neptune from the capital which replaced a much older Neptune that had become defunct; Athlunkard, Limerick, and Clonmel from the south – though extraordinarily never to this day a crew from Cork. There was a remarkable club named Emmett's from Galway, which won in 1929 and 1931 made up of Corrib watermen from the tiny Irish-speaking village of Menlo and just occasionally, in those early days, the students of Trinity College or Dublin University Boat Club, who had had a crucial and creative role in Irish rowing stretching back to the 1830s.

But in 1932 things changed radically: Trinity won the Senior Championship and from that date right up to 1950 (with just one exception) and for another dozen years beyond that the Irish Senior Championship became the preserve of the university clubs; Trinity first of all, but then UCD and Queen's University, Belfast joining in the act. By the 1960s clubs and regatta committees were desperately trying to invent events from which the universities could be excluded so that club rowing could start winning races again. The Championship programme was enlarged in 1934 with the inauguration of a men's Junior Eights Championship, and again in 1945 with a new men's Maiden Eights championship, and these did help to spread Championships around the country, although quite quickly the universities were picking at least their fair share of these new titles too. ▪

n 1950 I knew nothing at all about Irish rowing, or indeed about the sport at all. I vaguely knew my father had rowed himself when he was at college and I'm sure I had listened to the Oxford and Cambridge Boat Race on the radio. Four years later I went to study at my father's old college in Cambridge and I was hooked. I didn't come across Irish rowing for another three years. When preparing for Reading Head of the River I asked the crew from Trinity College, Dublin, my home town, if they would like to practice some starts with us. They were a formidable sight in their black and white striped vests, and they left us for dead in those practice starts – they took a length from us in a ten-stroke start, not good for our morale and they finished way ahead of us in the race. That evening we met them again after the prize-giving; I remember vividly one of them careering skilfully down the banisters of the staircase in the foyer of the Caversham Bridge Hotel and I remember that evening their considerable repertoire of song. We met them again a week later at the London Head of the River, where I also met members of another Irish club competing there for the first time, the Garda Siochana Boat Club. We performed somewhat better in London, but we still finished some fifteen places behind the two Irish crews who both made it into the top division, 21st and 25th, with just a second between them, while we were another 12 seconds behind them in 37th place. The Garda captain Jim Maguire asked me to coach his crew for the interprovincial race run in those days slightly out of the Regatta season and sponsored by the Evening Press, when I was home on holidays. I was delighted to do this and bullied them non-stop up and down the river at Islandbridge for about a week before their race – and they won!

It was that year I think that I turned up with an English friend of mine at Fermoy 'At Home', where we had seen signs of impending boat racing. We asked if we could take part, and we were heartily welcomed. We were a little embarrassed to be announced over the tannoy as Cambridge University but we joined in the spirit of the affair and enjoyed ourselves thoroughly. And although there were only two of us we raced in pair, four and eight for anyone who would have us. We enjoyed several pints in the Corporals' Mess at the local barracks, and then were invited to join in the judging of the Beauty Queen at the Regatta Hop. It was a long serious process but it had finally to be hurried and my very proper English friend Peter Dixon felt that justice was not done at the end of all. He found and had a dance with the beauty he felt had been robbed and when he swept her into a second dance as the music struck up again she froze in his arms. It was all over; he mused sadly afterwards, perhaps back in the Corporals' Mess: 'how could I have known they were playing Soldiers Awake?'

I had one further year to do at college, and there were two further connections with Irish rowing. My sister told me to look out for Henry Clark, a great rower at Trinity, who was back for a year from the colonies. As I was walking across the road from my college with a great box of books and cups and saucers towards my new flat above a Cypriot restaurant, I saw a large man coming out of the door of the Colonial Services Club. He had on him a Trinity graduates tie and a Leander blazer and I said: 'You must be Henry Clark, will you coach my Fairbairn eight for me?' He agreed, and we've been good friends since. He first introduced me to the lore of Irish rowing. I sent my second eight back to Dublin to row at Trinity Regatta that year where they won the Chapelizod Challenge Trophy. Our first eight went to Henley where we drew Trinity in the first round of the Ladies' Plate.

In those days Cambridge colleges arrogantly looked on Trinity as a 'lucky draw' – a situation which has radically changed since then. By coincidence we were both being coached by Pat Bradley who brought the two crews down to his turkey farm in the country on the Sunday before our race. The two captains had simultaneously congratulated him at the draw on being the first coach to be certain of having a crew in the second round. The race is etched on my mind: they led us early in the race, not by much, but definitely a lead. As we approached halfway I found myself repeating myself as I took each stroke: 'If we don't win this race... I can never go home. If we don't win this race... I can never go home.' I've no idea what my British crew-mates were thinking, but somewhere just after a mile we were level again, and we squeezed past for a narrow victory. When I did come home a few years later I soon forged a connection with Irish rowing which continued from then until now, first as a coach, then as an administrator, reporter, umpire and then out the other end as an alickadoo, archivist and a sort of *éminence grise*. ◼

In the 1930s and '40s the international yardsticks of Henley and indeed the London Head of the River showed the best of Irish rowing – the best colleges, to be pretty competitive with the equivalent comparable crews in England, but to be well behind the English international standards. The Grand Challenge Cup at Henley and the Diamonds – saving Rob van Mesdag's presence – the international-class events, would be beyond Ireland's grasp, but Irish crews were reasonably competitive at the next level, the Ladies' Plate and Thames Cup level for college and club crews. But as the '50s progressed and with the colleges generally unchallenged at home, this situation was deteriorating. After the high of 1950, Henley results got worse by the year, sometimes admittedly with unlucky draws, but crews were definitely becoming less competitive. The 1958 race was probably between the two worst crews in the Ladies' Plate and the loser came home to win the Irish championship.

In Ireland, coaches and captains were aware that something was wrong; they were looking at what was happening abroad, and they were beginning to react. Queen's University, Belfast in their golden period in the '50s and '60s were beginning to use the new growing understanding about fitness training. Peter Spillane, coaching UCD in one of their most successful periods,

ABOVE ▧ 1960 Trinity Regatta. Trinity VII beat the Garda by two and a half lengths. In the Final the Trinity VIII beat UCD by one and a half lengths.

BELOW ▧ 1960 Ladies' Plate – 2nd round (Henley). Dublin University Boat Club beat St Edmund Hall. Norman Gillett (cox), Frank Tisdall, Peter Martin, Bill Keatinge, Simon Newman, Mike Duncan, Dick Longfield, Mark Goodbody, Peter Reynolds.

wasn't afraid to use new equipment like the spade blade. Simon Newman, captaining Trinity unusually for a second year with Pat Bradley still his guru, was prepared to look at modern boat design and new styles of rowing like the American Conibear style. In England, style was becoming a dirty word as coaches started looking to achieve solid boat-moving technique, which preferably could be learnt quickly by big men with potential, if no rowing background.

The Garda Siochana Boat Club came on the Irish rowing scene in 1954-55. They made an immediate impact on the rowing scene, and everyone knew they had enormous potential. They won almost at will, junior and maiden championships from the start, sometimes notoriously like the seven-man crew that won the Maiden Eights at Blessington in 1960. Damian O'Leary, stroke of the crew developed a carbuncle on his back and had to go to hospital. They tied up the four seat in the boat, put Billy Dunphy up to stroke and won the championship by a third of a length from Queen's. Garda won senior races too, but the Senior Championship eluded them again and again.

It was Gerry McDonagh, Captain of the Garda Boat Club in the 1960s who went out searching for coaches to help Garda over this barrier, now clearly a psychological barrier as much as anything else. He approached people first who had experience abroad and were not tied to clubs at home: Bill Windham and Bill Masser – two former Cambridge Blues and British internationals; Rynne Stuart, a former Oxford Blue; myself, Jonathan Virden, an Oxford Trial Cap working at Guinness; Peter Martin and Derry McCaffrey, a couple of former Trinity oarsmen not coaching for the College; former UCG and London Rowing Club oarsman, Ivor Kenny and Henley people like Henry Clark and Ben Moore. This group met regularly to plan the campaign, and coached the club's various crews for periods of two or three weeks at a time. They set two targets: to win the Senior Championship for the first time and to win at Henley. 'The first since '03' became their watchword, recalling the last Irish win at Henley when Trinity won the Thames Cup. This new set-up immediately transformed the club although the targets would not be achieved for a few years. But the club started winning like never before at Maiden, Junior – and Senior levels.

But curiously it was not Garda, but the Old Collegians who broke the University stranglehold on the Senior Championship. Peter Spillane had coached some fine UCD crews from 1959 to 1961 winning the Senior Championship twice. He then went on to break a long-established tradition in Irish rowing. He decided to concentrate on the four instead of the eight and to seek better results from Henley. Most of the crew were graduates, but the move was not too popular with the College club. In 1963 a four made the semi-finals of the Wyfold Cup at Henley, Ireland's best Henley result since 1950 and the following year they were selected for the European Championships in Amsterdam – Ireland's second venture on to the world rowing scene.

There were no spectacular results from them, but the path was being laid. In both 1963 and 1964 the Old Collegians took on four other available senior oarsmen from Trinity, from UCD or wherever and they won two Senior Championships back to back. In the final in 1964 at Coleraine they were between two Garda crews and beat them both. This gave warning of what was to come, but it was Old Collegians who brought to an end 27 consecutive years of university domination of the Senior Championship.

Another new practice came from the Old Collegians success; the idea that three or four years of college life constituted a full rowing career, maiden, junior, senior, was finally hit on the head. Des McCann won six Senior Championships, two with College, two with OC, then a third one with College and a final one with Neptune. Suddenly a normal university rowing career of three or four years was turned into a mere apprenticeship for senior rowing – which is what it is today. In the early '60s we see the start of a much longer rowing life for the top competitors.

Garda, with their coaching team of outsiders, continued their policy, racking up junior and maiden championships and gradually getting closer to that elusive first senior title: third (with their junior eight) in 1963; second and third in 1964 and then finally they were through the barrier and took the title and were runners-up in 1965 with their junior eight actually beating their own senior eight to claim the first one. Their results at regattas throughout the country were awesome, and their strength could be well demonstrated by their results in the Dublin Head of the River, where between 1965 and 1969 they generally had three crews in the top six placings, indeed on one occasion, three in the top four. It also of course illustrated how narrow the spectrum of Irish rowing was, like a concertina that was closed, how small was the spread between maiden and senior standards. The coming of Garda was the start of the opening out of that concertina, the start of the stretching out of the standard from the bottom to the top of Irish rowing. ▨

At that time the eight was still the cornerstone of Irish rowing. This dated quite clearly back to 1870, when Trinity was the first Irish club to race at Henley; there were no eights rowing in Ireland before that. Soon the situation had totally changed and clubs considered they had no crews if they had no eight. This was not particularly healthy for a small country with many small clubs – a rough rule of thumb used to be that there was a rowing club in Ireland for each week of the year, about 52 clubs across the whole island. The focus on eights favoured the larger clubs like the universities and Garda as we have seen. But abroad there were many new ideas – ideas about fitness, about boats and equipment, about training methods and about all-year rowing (traditionally in parts of Ireland the rowing year started around St Patrick's weekend in March when the provincial rugby cup campaigns were over).

In West Germany Dr Karl Adam had revolutionary ideas about composite squads, about objective selection methods, about sculling as an essential component of training for rowing. He specified what training was required but that his oarsmen could train in sculling boats over the winter with their own clubs, only coming together occasionally in Ratzeburg for full squad training. At the 1968 Mexico City Olympics his crew with a substitute on board won the eights title ending a period of domination by the USA which had won nine of the ten Olympic titles between 1920 and 1964.

In Ireland sculling had always been active, but mostly it was pretty casual and the Eblana Cup at Dublin Metropolitan Regatta, recognised informally as the Irish title, was rarely contested by more than a couple of scullers who had probably done a little sculling when they had been at school. The Garda coaching team evolved a plan to improve sculling in Ireland: the Dublin Sculling Ladder. It was intended to benefit rowing, to improve individual watermanship, to give a competitive edge to the winter months of training and to act as an objective aid to selection – any full-blooded scullers produced would be a bonus.

The result of this initiative was Sean Drea. He sculled in the time trial for the first ladder in October 1966 and finished 13th; he was sufficiently unknown then that his name appears as Drey on the first official results. Sean Drea really launched Irish top-level sculling and he took Ireland's international participation off its shaky launching pad into full flight.

International participation had been thought about, talked about in Ireland in the '20s and '30s, and finally came to bud, if not fruition, with the Irish eight selected for the 1948 Olympics. That participation sparked off new ambitions, and the Dublin Metropolitan Regatta Council particularly started thinking about a modern international course for Ireland. The 'Metro' had been held since 1869, first at Ringsend in the heart of tidal Dublin, then out at Islandbridge. The flotsam of a busy port, the vagaries of the weather and a patently unfair tidal course resulted in a change from Ringsend to Islandbridge but its narrow, two-boat, twisty course no longer seemed attractive once international rowing had been tasted.

In 1959, the Metro moved to Blessington where except for one year it has been ever since. Blessington with six lanes, no tidal variations and still water seemed like the prototype for future development. Perhaps in the early days the wind and waves that can be seen on all such courses had not yet been imprinted on the minds of the enthusiastic pioneers who developed the new course. It was the 90th anniversary of the Metro and in keeping with the international aspirations of the move, Frankfurt Germania, from West Germany, raced in senior eights and fours. The following year there was the Irish Rowing Championship Regatta, incorporating the three eights Championships, senior, junior and maiden and an Olympic trial in coxed fours. The following day was the Metro itself, with another German entry Rhenania Koblenz and the regatta's first truly memorable bad weather. No Olympic crew was selected for Rome which generated its own disappointments but the intentions were clear – Ireland was looking for an international dimension to its rowing.

In 1969, the centenary of the Metro, it all came together: the West German national squad sent crews and three special centenary trophies were commissioned from the young Irish sculptor John Behan. The trophies were won outright by the Deutscherruderverein in eight, by the Garda Siochana Boat Club in four and by Sean Drea of Neptune in single sculls. Drea was selected that year to race in Ireland's third international championship entry at the European Championships in Klagenfurt, Austria. Like his predecessors he was last in his heat, last in his repêchage, but that painful learning experience was now passed and over the next few years Drea, with superb self-motivation, dragged himself into international prominence and perhaps it could be said that he dragged a somewhat ill-prepared Irish Amateur Rowing Union with him into the world of modern international rowing. Sean went where he had to go: to London first where Rob van Mesdag encouraged him and then to the USA to find the coaching environment he needed. He was a finalist in the Diamond Sculls at Henley in 1972 and won at all the great venues of the north America and Europe. He won the Diamonds three times in a row and he squeezed himself up the world ratings. 12th in St Catherine's (1970), seventh in the 1972 Munich Olympics, sixth in Moscow (1973). He should have won the world championships the following year in Lucerne, but was struck down with a kidney illness and had to withdraw. He was silver medallist in Nottingham in 1975, Ireland's first medal in international rowing and there were great expectations for Montreal – he ended fourth with Eamonn Coghlan, the top placing for the whole Irish Olympic team. But it didn't end there because Sean, working abroad, was an inspiration to the top clubs at home.

Trinity had reached a Henley final again in 1968 (the Visitors' Cup for college coxless fours), helped somewhat it should be said, by exceptional weather conditions, but as the '70s dawned, Henley was a major target for the top clubs. Top coaches were brought on board as consultants and advisers by the leading clubs and the Union itself; Geoffrey Page for UCD, Lew Barry for Garda, Jim Railton for the Union. UCD was the first to make the big breakthrough, as Geoffrey Page resolutely sacked a UCD senior eight and promoted a bunch of large athletic juniors in their place. This crew was christened 'The Animals' by the lively women who were rowing for Commercial Rowing Club and they would be remarkably successful. The Animals won three Senior Championships in a row and the Ladies' Plate at Henley in 1974, the year Sean Drea won his first Diamond Sculls; they were finalists too in the Britannia Cup for coxed fours.

The next year Garda won the Thames Cup for club eights. Queen's were finalists in the Ladies' Plate in 1976 and in 1977 Garda won the Prince Philip Cup for international coxed fours and Trinity won the Ladies' Plate for the second time (The first time had been in 1875; in the 1870s Irish crews had won five times at Henley, and had been in seven other finals). In the 1970s there were eight wins (five of them international class), and two other finals. The 1970s represented a remarkable decade for Irish rowing, comparable in achievement to the 1870s. The years between had seen little of note in international achievement. An exception being Trinity's 1903 win in the Thames cup at Henley. ■

ABOVE ■ 1971 The UCD senior eight – 'The Animals' at Islandbridge.

Despite the club results at Henley the very amateur IARU was struggling to take part at international level and in spite of a lack of funds and organisation, was making progress. Sean Drea, based in Philadelphia, was the spearhead achieving fourth place in the Montreal Olympics and second place in Nottingham and his commendable results were being matched at home by Garda and National Squad crews. Garda scored three successive seventh places in coxed fours in world championships and Olympics between 1975 and 1977. A coxed pair from Belfast was eighth in 1977 and in Karapiro, New Zealand the following year two Irish pairs, one coxless, one coxed, made the grand finals of the World Championships, finishing fifth and sixth overall.

ABOVE ▓ Henley 1977 Garda beat Harvard in the Grand Challenge Cup

The IARU continued to struggle, but the situation was starting to improve with the first signs of government financial support and aid from the Olympic Council of Ireland and with sponsorship and fund-raising at many levels providing additional finances. The Olympic Regatta at Moscow in 1980 was to be the culmination of this first stage of real Irish participation in international rowing and everything was proceeding excellently until President Carter's announcement of the boycott of the Moscow Olympics because of the war in Afghanistan. He also asked all western countries to join in this boycott, and the Irish government asked the Olympic Council of Ireland to join them. I was President of the IARU that year and went to the Olympic meeting called to consider the government's recommendation. The Boxing Federation's representatives, mostly army officers, proposed that we comply with the government's recommendation. I spoke second on behalf of rowing and I acknowledged immediately the position in which the government found itself. On the other hand I argued that our first responsibility was to our athletes who had been training for four years towards the Olympics, many of whom would not have the possibility of competing again in the 1984 Olympics. I recommended that we should respectfully reject the government's advice, and confirm that we would go to the Moscow Olympics. I further suggested that the OCI should take a leading part at the Olympics in promoting a West European protest against the war in Afghanistan. The decision to go to Moscow was massively endorsed by the delegates at that Olympic Council of Ireland meeting. The downside was that all government funding towards Olympic preparations by the OCI and the sports federations ceased from that date.

The aim for Moscow was to win medals and right up to the final preparatory regatta in Lucerne this goal seemed achievable. This was the only occasion on which the Moscow participants and the boycotters were all present and the top Irish crew, Denis Rice and Christy O'Brien with Liam Williams in a coxed pair, won two silver medals. Ahead of them were the reigning Olympic champions and behind them the World Championship silver and bronze medallists. Those two results remain to this day the best results achieved by an Irish-based, open-class crew. But there was disappointment to come in Moscow when one member of the crew was sick for the heat of their event and the other for the repêchage. There is no such thing as certainty in sport; two fine seventh places were scored by other elements of the Irish team in men's coxless pair and women's single scull, but they would have looked so much better behind silver or bronze medals.

While this was taking place at senior level there were other developments taking place. School rowing was developing into the international junior rowing class. A schools eights championship had been introduced in 1960. In its early years it was much contested amongst the northern schools, but ten years later when a fours championship was added, the Galway schools were breaking the northern monopoly. Four years later when a sculling championship was instituted, club juniors were making their mark. In 1973 the first junior crews were sent to the FISA Junior Championships, the forerunners of the World Junior Championships.

Another serious growth area was women's rowing. It is difficult to date precisely the start of women's rowing; it probably dates back into the 19th century. From the mid-1920s to the mid-1930s there was a period of quite serious women's rowing, with crews from Newry, Dublin and Galway vying for the top honours at the Dublin Metropolitan and other regattas. Women's rowing was not included in regatta programmes again until much later. It was not until 1970 that women's rowing was back on the Metro schedule; the regatta was well established at Blessington by that time, but if I recall correctly the winning crew from Commercial Rowing Club declined to accept the powder compacts that were offered as prizes that day. Since then their prizes have been the same as the men's prizes and an important statement had been made – and heard. The 1970 crew substantially made up the first women's crew which went to the World Championships in 1975. The first national championships for women were offered in 1976 for single sculls and coxed fours and the singles title that year was won by Frances Cryan a young schoolgirl from Carrick-on-Shannon; she won that title 11 times consecutively and was the sculler who finished seventh in the Moscow Olympics in 1980.

ABOVE ■ 1995 Inniscarra: Ireland's junior women's team at the Home International.

There were other important changes: the so-called commercial clubs were winning against the institutional clubs such the universities and the Garda. Neptune won the Senior Championship in 1970 for the first time since 1934, but with a real 'mixum gatherum' crew carefully gathered together by Gerry Buckley with oarsmen from the colleges and Garda who weren't currently in crews; Gerry, a vet, lost his own place in the crew after being kicked by a horse and this let in Jim Muldoon, later an outstanding Garda international, who had been sculling that year. In 1978 the first composite crew won the Championship: Commercial/Garda/Lady Elizabeth, showing another way for small clubs to approach serious senior competition. Curiously enough, since that win, only two more composites have succeeded in winning the men's senior eights championship, belying fears that clubs would be wiped out by the introduction of composites.

The number of national championships has burgeoned from that single Senior Championship for men's eights established in 1912 to championships for seniors, intermediates (formerly junior), novices (formerly maiden) and juniors (formerly schools, or schoolboy/youth); for men and women and for a range of boats, eight, four and pair in sweep rowing and quadruple, double and single sculls. There are currently 39 events on the championship programme. For the universities there were special events, notably the Wylie Cup which started in the 1920s as a race in coxed four between Trinity and UCD and has developed first into a team event for three levels of eight: senior, junior and maiden and eventually into the University Championship Regatta, generally held in the Forest Park at Castlewellan, Co Down. Another new class to be developed was lightweight rowing (for men of around 70 kilos or 11 stone, and women of around 57 kilos) and it was to become very significant, particularly for Irish international participation in the 1980s and 1990s. Prior to that, the international focus had been on open-class, sometimes known as heavyweight rowing, at international level. The aspirant lightweights had a lonely track to gain recognition and selection. Tony Corcoran and John Armstrong were the pathfinders in the '70s and early '80s, but since then men's lightweight have formed the central core of Ireland's top international teams. Gradually they have pushed Ireland up the international ladder.

In the 25 years since Sean Drea's world championship silver medal, 36 individuals have rowed in grand finals and there have been one gold, five silver and five bronze medal crews. Niall O'Toole in Vienna in 1991 won the first and to date, the only gold medal in men's lightweight single sculls and he won silver in 1994. Neville Maxwell and Tony O'Connor together won two silvers and two bronzes in men's lightweight pairs. Two lightweight quads won bronze, and Sam Lynch and Sinead Jennings closed the century out in the year 2000 with silver and bronze medals in the men's and women's lightweight sculls. ■

International rowing has now developed an interesting ladder of opportunity for all the clubs in Ireland with the Home Internationals, the annual quadrangular match between England, Ireland, Scotland and Wales as the bottom rung. This event arose quite curiously from an accidental happening at the Commonwealth Regatta on Lake Padarn in Wales in 1958, where England, Scotland, Wales and Northern Ireland came together in a repêchage. Someone said, 'why not?' And the first three Home Internationals were held on the Serpentine in Hyde Park over a sprint course sponsored by the News of the World. These events concluded with a relay race, which was rather an oddity in rowing. After a brief gap the event was revived in 1966, and it has run since then, gradually increasing in size. It now involves four matches for senior men and women and junior men and women in a wide range of boats – a very large logistical challenge each year with the venue rotating around the four countries and even to Ghent in Belgium on one occasion. Many wise old heads nod and dismiss this event as of no importance, but Ireland for one has done well out of it, giving many oarsmen and women and their clubs their first taste of representative rowing. World champions Steve Redgrave, Peter Haining and Niall O'Toole all cut their international teeth in the Home International.

Up the ladder from the Home International there have in recent years been two further steps: for seniors the Nations Cup, formerly the Match des Seniors, an unofficial under-23 European Championship, and for juniors the Coupe de la Jeunesse, the equivalent at junior level. Ireland has competed in the Nations Cup since 1987 on a slightly intermittent basis and in the Coupe regularly since 1993, hosting it very successfully at Inniscarra in 1999. At the top of the international pile are the World Championships, senior and junior and at the apex, the Olympic Regatta every fourth year, its rowing status rarified by the fact that not all of the FISA rowing categories are included on the Olympic programme. When lightweight rowing was accepted by the IOC, the Olympic governing body rationed the number of individuals and events that they would accommodate on the Olympic Regatta programme. Only two lightweight events for men and one for women were admitted and to accommodate them, several open-class events had to be dropped from the Olympics. Qualifying for the Olympics became a new reality, a new obstacle to overcome and the new non-Olympic events lost status, while the Olympic events became even more intensely competitive.

The last 20 years of the 20th century saw many changes in Irish rowing, many arising from the new interest in international rowing. The university dominance of senior rowing came to an end, as the university model of rowing, three or four years, maiden, junior, senior, ceased to be an adequate one for modern top-class rowing; university rowing became more like an apprenticeship as many of the top senior participants in the sport continued rowing seriously, well into their 30s. The rowing year dramatically changed: the old Limerick pattern of rugby for the winter, followed by rowing when you had been knocked out of the Munster Cup no longer would do. Rowing became an all-year sport, with clubs starting their training programmes in September, and the top performers continuing through to international competition at the end of August. Many of the grand old clubs found the going tough, but others like Neptune and Commercial found the new situation to their liking, but in quite different ways. Neptune became a honey-pot club, attracting fine oarsmen into their club from the universities and from around the country, grafting them onto their own strong junior and novice programmes. Their record in men's senior eights from 1980 to 1999 was amazing: 13 senior eights championships in 20 years and from 1976 to 1999 never worse than third. Commercial went about it differently: their specialities were women's rowing which they pioneered into the big time and small boats; they also had a strong junior programme. These two clubs took off during the last 20 years and from being enthusiastic followers of the universities for the first 80 years of the 20th century they both shot from nowhere to the head of the championship winners table in the final 20 years. At the end of the year 2000 Neptune headed that list with 116 wins, ahead of Commercial with 90 and new clubs like Skibbereen and Offaly are pushing their way past the universities which so long dominated that list.

ABOVE ■ Henley 1986. Neptune beat Garda in the semi-final of the Ladies' Plate.

So where from here? There are enormous changes in the pipeline. The old administration on the kitchen table has given way to an organisation with a paid administrator and most recently a chief executive – and that is certainly about time. There are offices in the House of Sport. The annual expenditure of the Irish Amateur Rowing Union in 1950 was £240 15 shillings according to the financial report for that year; in 2000 it was £464,671, much of it concerning and arising from the growth of involvement in international rowing. Our top performers now are full-time athletes, benefiting from the government carding scheme which provides them with funds to allow them train and work full-time at the sport. They will not become rich like footballers or pop stars, but they can work at their sport full-time.

This transition will cause some problems for a few years; is it fair, it is asked, that the carded athletes compete for championships against the top club amateurs? It is not an easy question to answer, or problem to resolve. But obviously there must be an interface to allow people to pass from one category to another and I would think the National Championships are a good place for that to happen. Clubs must reassess their targets, and perhaps make intermediate supremacy the level at which they should normally aspire and accept that the senior level is where the very best must fight it out, the chosen carded athletes proving their merit, the ambitious amateurs staking their claim to join that elite.

Personally while I admire greatly the work and effort of everyone, oarsmen and women, coaches, administrators and supporters in the modern game I am happy enough to have been one of the old Corinthian contributors to the sport in an earlier time. Those who know me now may be surprised to hear that I was a lightweight oarsmen before lightweight rowing was invented. I enjoyed my rowing, and the camaraderie that went with it; I enjoyed the challenge of coaching at various levels; I enjoyed the administration, even when the structures were inadequate for the job in hand. I became involved in umpiring quite early on, helped to set up our own structures for this and enjoyed quite a long international umpiring career, which took me to two Olympics and many world championships. I always said that as far as rowing was concerned the best seat in the house was the umpire's launch, whether that's an Olympic final, at Henley Royal Regatta, at our own national championships, or on the start at Trinity, Castlewellan or Commercial.

It is an extraordinary sport, one of the classic sports and perhaps so far the one least corrupted by money, commercialism or drugs. Being a minority sport has some advantages. Long may it continue that way. In 2001, to usher in the new century and the new millennium, Ireland won three gold medals in the World Championships in Lucerne: Sam Lynch won the men's lightweight single sculls; Sinead Jennings the women's lightweight single sculls, the first women's title for Ireland; and Gearoid Towey and Tony O'Connor the men's lightweight pairs, Ireland's first title in sweep rowing. A new era is under way. ▦

ABOVE ▦ 1997 Garda v Defence Forces. Islandbridge 1997.

ABOVE ■ 26th August 2001 Gearold Towey and Tony O'Connor on their way to winning gold in the final of the men's lightweight pairs race at the FISA World Rowing Championships at Lucerne, Switzerland.

BELOW ■ 25th August 2001 Sam Lynch on his way to winning gold in the men's lightweight single sculls race at the FISA World Rowing Championships at Lucerne, Switzerland.

Irish boxing has a proud history. Between the turn of the century and 1950, Ireland had a number of world champions and boxers who fought and lost a championship. For instance in the heavyweight division in 1899 in New York, Tom Sharkey lost on points to James J. Jefferies. In 1908, Jem Roche, fighting in Dublin at the Theatre Royal, was knocked out by Tommy Burns in the first round in 88 seconds. Records show this fight to be the first world championship title bout to be fought in Ireland. In the light-heavyweight division, George Gardiner knocked out Jack Boot in the 12th round at Fort Erie in 1903 before losing on points in the 20th round in San Francisco later in the year to Bob Fitzsimmons.

In the middleweight, Jack Dempsey was world undisputed champion between 1886 and 1891. In 1891 he lost in New Orleans by a knockout to Bob Fitzsimmons of England. In 1913 Jimmy Gardiner lost in Boston by a knockout in the third round to Frank Klaus. In the welterweight division in 1895 Jack Dempsey lost to Tommy Ryan in New York by a knockout in the third round, but in 1908 Jimmy Gardiner was the champion. In 1914 Tommy McCormick held the title with wins over Waldemar Holberg (Denmark) and Johnny Summers (England), but lost it in 1934 to Barney Ross on a points defeat over 15 rounds.

In the lightweight division, Jack McAuliffe, one of Ireland's greatest fighters, retired with an unbeaten record of 31 wins, 5 draws and one no decision. He reigned as champion in both the bare knuckled and gloved eras. He was first world champion in 1886 and retired in 1897. He fought a draw with Jem Carney of England over 74 rounds in Revere in 1887, and defeated Jimmy Carroll of England in 1890 in San Francisco by a knockout in the 47th round. In 1928, Jimmy McLarnin, lost to Sammy Mandell in New York on points. At featherweight, Jack Shelly on his professional debut, in 1892 in New Orleans, lost by a knockout in the eighth round to George Dixon.

My introduction to Irish Boxing came through the Trinity gym in 1957. Although I remember in prep school days at Mostyn House towards the end of the Second World War, watching Rinty Monaghan sparring. Monaghan came from Northern Ireland and held the World Flyweight Championship in October 1947 when he won the National Boxing Association Championship from Dado Marino of Hawaii and in March 1948 in Belfast, he knocked out Jackie Paterson of Scotland in the seventh round to become the undisputed world champion. He was still the champion in September1949 having fought a 15-round draw with Terry Allen of England.

Trinity boxing was at a peak in the 1950s. Frankie Kerr, a Dublin tailor, was the trainer; he created a very special atmosphere in the rather dilapidated gym at the far end of Trinity. He won six Irish National titles – in 1932 at flyweight and in 1933, 34, 35, 36 and 38 at bantamweight. David Millar, a prominent Trinity boxer of the 1950s writes: 'Styled the Dublin University Boxing and Gymnastic Club to differentiate it from the initials assumed by the Dublin University Boat Club, the DUB&GC prided itself in being one of the university's senior athletic powers, producing a number of national champions and international competitors. From the end of World War II, Trinity's pugilistic ranks were fuelled by many who had seen active service, as a result of which their third level education had been delayed – one of whom was Sir David Orr, MC, later chairman of Unilever. The "tradition", whether real or imagined, of rating Dublin University as the strongest third choice after Oxford and Cambridge was a well-established myth on the other side of the water, so it was no accident that the sporting excellence of the college was well maintained throughout the 1950s.

'No biography exists of Frank Kerr, Trinity's legendary coach and trainer from 1947, but some valuable notes were gathered by Tim Harward, at one time a dedicated secretary to the Club. Frank was born in Belfast in 1916 and was brought up mainly abroad, particularly in India, as a Royal Ulster Rifles officer's son. Ulster flyweight champion at 15 and Irish flyweight champion from 1932 to 1937, he retired the following year, the veteran of 300 bouts in which he was never knocked out. A lifelong friendship with Sergeant Jim ("Lugs") Brannigan, one of Ireland's most famous boxing referees, ensured that "Trinity" continued to play its part in the world outside and I certainly remember being told to "blacken your face–you're on next" as the phrase was, as there was a car going up to Longford on Sunday when DUB&GC would be top of the bill that evening; and there was another memorable occasion when we boxed against the junior prison at Mountjoy.

'Frank was also a guide, philosopher and friend out of the ring to many who passed through the Club. And as a Second he was in a class of his own. You couldn't honestly say that he could raise the dead – but he could quietly talk one into winning a fight and that's not a gift given to many. He was made a Knight of the Campanile, the only Honorary Knight of his day. He died in 1968 but his expertise lives on in his son, Brian, the highly successful manager of Ireland's under-16 and under-18 soccer teams. Doug Baxter (a distinguished Trinity international boxer and Oxford Blue) recalls in the Hilary 1999 journal of the Knights that in the 1950s, DUB&GC was one of the college's most successful sports clubs, winning the Harry Preston Cup for the British and Irish Universities' and Hospitals' (later UAU) Championship every year from 1952 to 1960. Several boxers, including Bill Chinn, Bill Gregory, Co Welsh, Doug himself, and, later, Ronnie Taylor at heavy and Dermot Sherlock at fly, were capped. Indeed in 1956, the college produced no less than six internationals.

'Frank's mantle was taken over by the 1956 Olympic silver medallist Fred Tiedt. The club had played a part in his training before he joined the professional ranks and he, too, was made an Honorary Knight and was also conferred with an honorary MA, before his untimely death in 1999. All good things come to an end, but before the magic days of the Christle brothers which saw the revival of the university's fortunes in the ring and a return to the good old days, several members of DUB&GC won Oxford Blues–most notably Dan Hearn, one of the very few Trinity men to play rugby for England and John Coker, also a Trinity rugby player, the heavyweight in the winning 1966 Oxford team.'

Despite the appointment of Fred Tiedt in the early 1960s, interest in boxing at Trinity declined until the arrival of the Christle brothers in 1976. Fred Tiedt won the welterweight silver medal at the Olympic Games held in Melbourne in 1956, or more accurately, was robbed of the gold medal. Nat Fleischer, the editor of The Ring magazine, said 'It was the most disgraceful decision that he had ever witnessed'. The Australian crowd booed the decision and sat during the victor's national anthem. Nicolae Linca, the winner of the welterweight gold medal, came from the poor village of Feisa in Romania. He is the only Romanian boxer to have won a gold medal. Paul Howard, chief sportswriter of The Sunday Tribune, visited Linca in the year 2000. He found a forgotten figure suffering from Parkinson's and arteriosclerosis, wasting away and unnoticed in his beloved Romania. He is nursed by his wife Marie Elina but they are barely able to pay for the medication he needs.

Three other Irish boxers won bronze medals in the Melbourne Olympics. Tony Byrne, whose trip to Australia was said to have been subsidized by publicans in his native Drogheda putting a penny a pint on the price of a pint, reached the semi-finals in the lightweight division. 'Socks' as he was nicknamed, had quit boxing after being dropped from the squad for the 1952 Olympics in Helsinki, but he was persuaded back into the ring and captained the boxing team in Melbourne. His reward came when he beat the American Louis Molina to guarantee himself a medal and was eventually halted in the semi-final by German fighter Harry Kurschat.

Johnny Caldwell, the flyweight from Belfast, was controversially included in the team, despite losing to Chris Rafter in what many presumed to be an Olympic trial. But he brought home a bronze after beating the Australian Werner Batchelor in the quarter-final. Freddie Gilroy, his local rival from Belfast's Ardoyne, sensationally knocked out the European champion Boris Stepanov in his first fight, then beat the Italian Mario Sitri, before losing in the semi-finals to Willi Behrendt of East Germany, again by a highly dubious judging decision. Fred Tiedt turned professional shortly after the Melbourne Olympics. He failed to make an impact as a professional and became a maintenance supervisor for Smurfit the paper manufacturers. He also became a boxing coach and referee. He died in 1999, a much respected member of the Irish boxing community. Fred was the official Trinity trainer from the 1960s to 1991 when he retired. In 1992 he was awarded an honorary doctorate by the University. The Christle brothers remember the huge funeral and genuine grief expressed by the congregation, drawn from all sectors of society, which bore witness to the love and affection in which Fred Tiedt was held. ∎

Boxing, should it be banned? The life-threatening injury to Paul Ingle in a featherweight world title clash in Sheffield, England on 16th December 2000 with Mbulelo Botile of South Africa brings up the question once again of the credibility of boxing. Ingle's blood clot on his brain added to the boxing list of recent tragedies. Amongst those who have lost their lives or battled to recover from horrific injuries are Spencer Oliver, James Murray, Gerald McClellan, Bradley Stone, Michael Watson, Rod Douglas, Steve Watt and Johnny Owen. Simon Block, general secretary of the British Boxing Board of Control, answering the demand that boxing should be banned said, 'there are more dangerous sports (e.g. five top riders died in 2000 in three-day eventing), boxing is a dangerous sport... we endeavour to lay down rules to minimise the risks... as well as the dangers there are the positive sides such as developing discipline and character'. Many regard boxing as a noble art; a test of one man's courage against another. Many, though, regard it as morally indefensible; any sport whose object is to incur maximum damage on another human being cannot be condoned. No man, however, has to box; medical precautions are in place and so the arguments go on. A further look at boxing in Ireland gives an interesting insight.

In the years after 1950, Ireland continued to enjoy success in the professional boxing world. Steve Collins (in the early 1990s) held the WBO version of the super-middleweight division; Eamonn Loughran in the mid '90s held the WBO welterweight title; Barry McGuigan in the mid '80s held the WBA featherweight title; Johnny Caldwell held the EBU bantamweight title in the early '60s. Wayne McCullough took the WBC bantamweight title in the mid '90s and Dave McAuley held the IBF flyweight title in late '80s and early '90s. Six world champions: a magnificent achievement for a small country and the following competed in, but lost world championship fights. Steve Collins (at middleweight), Eamonn Loughran (welterweight), Barry McGuigan (featherweight), John Lowey and Wayne McCullough (super-bantamweight), Freddy Gilroy and Johnny Caldwell (bantamwieght), Dave McAuley (flyweight).

On the amateur front at the Olympics, Ireland has had considerable success, but at the recent Games Atlanta (1996) and Sydney (2000) failed to win a medal. At Helsinki, in 1952, John McNally won the silver medal at bantamweight – Ireland's first Olympic boxing medal; whilst at Melbourne in 1956, four medals were won. In 1980 at Moscow Hugh Russell won a bronze medal at bantamweight, losing in the final to a very good Cuban Joel Casamayor; Michael Carruth, however, won Ireland's first ever gold medal at welterweight. I remember, travelling round the west of Ireland at the time of the Olympics with a friend, and that every time we stopped we saw Wayne McCullough's and Michael Carruth's fights on the TV, and very good they were too.

In the years since 1950 there have been many characters associated with Irish boxing – the boxers, both amateur and professional, promoters, administrators, newspaper correspondents. Some have already been mentioned and some will not get the mention they deserve but there follows an appreciation of some of the personalities associated with Irish boxing in this period. These include a British heavyweight champion, an influential figure in boxing , two great world champions and the boxing brothers with multi-talents. In the heavyweight division, only Danny MacAlinden held titles of renown. A successful heavyweight, he was born in Newry, Northern Ireland on 1st June 1947. He had a professional career of 45 contests, winning 31, drawing two and losing 12. He was the British and Commonwealth champion between 1972 and 1975 winning the title by a second round knockout of Jack Bodell. He lost the title in January 1975 in London to Bunny Johnson by a ninth round knockout and later in the year in an attempt to regain the title, lost at the Wembley Stadium to Richard Dunn by a second round knockout.

Barney Eastwood has been a most influential figure in the world of sport and business. He was born in Cookstown, Co Tyrone, some years after the First World War. His major interests included property development, bookmaking (he built up a chain of 50 betting shops), dogs and horse racing and the stock market, but it is in boxing that he made his major contribution to Irish life. It was to Eastwood's gym in Belfast that Barry McGuigan and Hugh Russell came to learn the skills of professional boxing. At first Eddie Shaw was the coach. He was followed by such top class coaches as Bernardo Checa, Paul McCullagh and John Breen. They produced a number of world champions including McGuigan, Cristano Espana, Paul Hodkinson, Victor Cordoba and Dave 'Boy' McAuley.

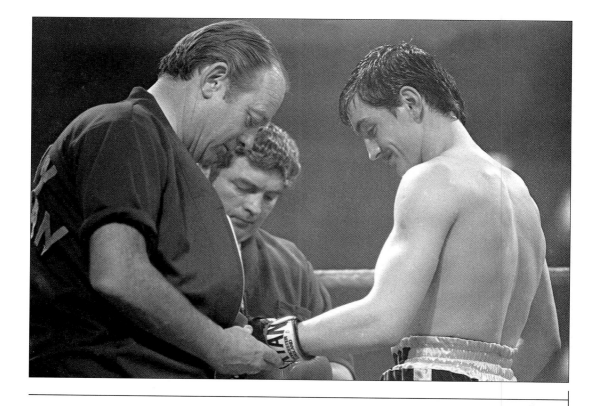

ABOVE ▦ 26th May 1983. Barry McGuigan with Barney Eastwood.

A former Gaelic footballer, Eastwood's first involvement as a promoter was in the late '50s and early '60s; John Caldwell and Freddie Gilroy filled the Belfast stadiums. He promoted fights at the Ulster Hall and in Larne. Peter Sharpe, the Turkington brothers, Jimmy McCann, Sean McCafferty and the McCormack brothers came under his influence. He continued his interest in Irish boxing in the '70s but it was his association with Barry McGuigan that won both manager and boxer fame. Sadly the relationship was to end in acrimony with McGuigan's points defeat over 15 rounds by Steve Cruz in the desert heat of Las Vegas on 23rd June 1986.

Barry McGuigan and Steve Collins, born either side if the Irish border, can claim to be the best boxers produced in recent Irish boxing history. Barry McGuigan was born in Clones, Northern Ireland on 28th February 1961. He was Irish national senior bantamweight champion and commonwealth gold medalist at 17. He became a professional in 1981 and won the WBA featherweight title in a points decision over 15 rounds. He defeated the great Panamanian Eusebio Pedroza before a 27,000 crowd at Queens Park Rangers' Loftus Road ground. He

ABOVE ▪ 10th June 1985. Barry McGuigan returns home to Clones, Co Monaghan after defeating Eusebio Pedroza of Panama on points in 15 rounds to win the WBA World Featherweight championship.

successfully defended his title in Belfast against Bernard Taylor and in Dublin against Danilo Cabrera but suffered a shock defeat to Steve Cruz in 1986. McGuigan retired after this fight, split with Eastwood and in April 1988, he launched a comeback as a junior lightweight under Frank Warren. He had three victories but after being beaten in May 1989 by a cut eye to Jim McDonnell he retired with a record of 32 wins and 3 losses and is now the highly respected boxing analyst for Sky TV.

Steve Collins was born in Dublin in July 1964. He came from a boxing family; his uncle Jack O'Rourke won four national senior titles, at middleweight in 1963 and at heavyweight in 1965, 66 and 71. Collins won the national middleweight title in 1986; he was undefeated in five internationals. He turned professional in October 1986 and in a remarkable 11-year career retired as holder of the WBO super-middleweight title. He had 39 fights, winning 36 of them and losing the other three. He is the only Irishman to win world crowns at two different weights, won more world championship bouts than any Irishman and is the only Dubliner to win a world professional fight. He spent four and a half years fighting out of Boston as middleweight. During this period he won the Irish and United States middleweight titles, but lost World WBA title attempts to the great Jamaican champion, Mike McCallum and controversially to Reggie Johnson (USA). Also a European title challenge was lost in a hotly disputed decision to Sumbu Kalambay. All these were points decisions over 12 rounds. His defeats by Johnson and Kalambay came after his return to Dublin in 1991 but these were followed by two World titles and 15 fights, nine of which were World title fights. He remained undefeated during this period. ▪

The Christle brothers are the most outstanding boxers produced by Trinity, but not only were they boxers but also highly successful in their chosen professions. It was a wet Monday in early November 2000 when I arrived late at Mel Christle's Law Chambers in Chancery Place, Dublin. Ryanair from Luton had been delayed by heavy rain. Mel began: 'Joe, Terry and myself entered Trinity in 1976. Joe did a theoretical physics degree – I think he got a second-class Honours. Terry studied medicine, so he spent a little while longer than the normal four years in Trinity. I did law. The last year, 1980, I was in the King's Inns, Dublin; that year

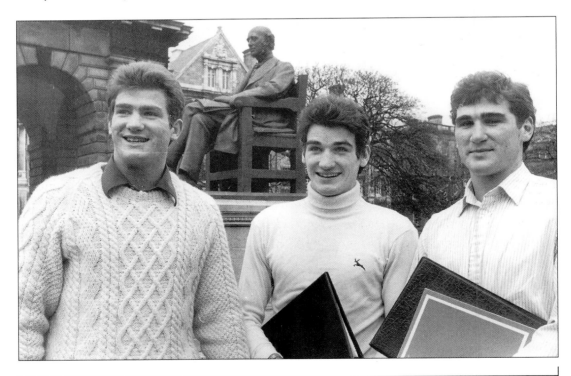

ABOVE ▪ Christle brothers at Trinity – The Academic Boxing Champions – Mel, Terry and Joe.

was spent taking the qualification of a barrister. During those four years we were members of the Trinity Boxing Club. It wasn't the strongest sporting club on the campus however, we were joined by Michael Telford who later founded the John Scotus School in Dublin. The four of us formed part of a boxing team which won four titles in the British and Irish University Championships at Bath. We all won inside the distance: Joe, Terry and myself won our semi-finals and finals in the first round and Michael won his fights in the second round. Trinity won the title as the best and most successful university but I think it was a Mr James who was not so happy; David James was coach of the British Olympic boxing team and had coached Chris Finnegan to victory in Mexico in 1968. A vote was taken and we were banned from participating in university matches – the four of us were too good! Anyway the gentleman I beat in the final used to write to me every year and said that the final was one of the proudest occasions of his life.

'Our boxing careers progressed. Terry and I entered the Irish senior university championships in 1976. Joe was only 16 and although he was at university, he was too young to enter the senior championships. We then went on to fight in the Irish senior championships: Terry won the middleweight title in 1978, 79 and 80, I won the light-heavyweight title in 1977 and the super-heavyweight in 1980, whilst Joe won the heavyweight in 1979 and 1980. Thus all three of us held titles in 1980 – that was the first year that super-heavyweight titles were held at amateur level. You had to be over 15 stone, or perhaps it was 15.2 or 15.5 – anyway I had to have an extra large breakfast to make the weight. Also in 1980, Terry won the French middleweight amateur championship.

'I was born in France – my mother is French; we used to spend our summers there and so we have a strong affection to France and we all speak the language. Terry boxed for a prolific club, Ring de Montreuil which is on the outskirts of Paris; he won the Paris championships and, finally, won the French championships in Agen at middleweight – the week after winning the Irish title. He also boxed for France against an American selection on the anniversary of former French world middleweight champion, Marcel Cerdan's death and, of course, his fight being at middleweight was the highlight of the programme; he beat his American opponent.

'Terry was very good; he was naturally gifted as a fighter because he had an uncanny power for such a slim individual. He was tall and rangy for his weight and basically, when he hit someone flush it was described as a "linger on" effect. His opponent would appear to be normal and have no ill effects for about five to ten seconds after the punch landing and then it would paralyse his nervous system – it was amazing. Internationals in the National Stadium were sell-outs and tickets were only available through the black market. The Irish fans got to know Terry's style so much that they used to start shouting a warning when they saw the punch land as they knew

ABOVE ▓ Filming the Raging Bull – This was the film about Jake LaMotta, who defeated the Frenchman Marcel Cerdan for the undisputed World Middleweight title in 1949 in Detroit, USA. Marcel Cerdan died in a plane crash in the Azores on 27th October, 1949 while on his way to America for a return fight with Jake LaMotta. LaMotta was to lose the Middleweight title to Sugar Ray Robinson in February 1951. In the foreground is Fred Tiedt, to the left is Cathy Moriarty who played Vicki LaMotta (right) in the film, and to the rear are the Christle brothers.

the end of the bout was imminent. The opponent would still continue for five or ten seconds until, suddenly, his legs would give way. They would say 'Oooogh' and some seconds later, the legs would give way. It was a form of paralysis – he just had an uncanny knack of having this phenomenal punch.

'None of us were considered for the Moscow Olympics because of an unfortunate dust-up between ourselves and the Irish boxing authorities. It was petty. However, in retrospect, I am sure the new powers-that-be would accept that what we were doing was right. For one year prior to the Olympics, every weekend we flew to London to spar with professionals in the Thomas A'Beckett Gym in London on the Old Kent Road – the gym has gone now and in fact is a pub. We used to travel over to be under the supervision and tutelage of Bobby Neill who was a very good featherweight; he was British featherweight champion and also a great trainer of the likes of Alan Minter and Alan Rudkin. Bobby Neill trained Maurice Hope for a little while, also Joe Tetteh, but at that time he took us under his wing. It was an unusual relationship we had with him because there was nothing ever signed. We never signed any contracts with Bobby, nor did he ask us but he agreed to look after us. We used to fly over on a Friday, train that evening, train Saturday and Sunday – sparring on all three days and returning to Dublin Sunday evening where we continued our training until the following Friday. It came to a head when the IABA insisted that we attend training sessions in Drogheda prior to the Olympics. We refused to do so and they said basically that if we didn't attend we wouldn't be considered for selection. We had a chat with our father who was 100% behind us and decided that to go training in Drogheda where there was no professional coaching would clearly be a backward step.

'In 1992 for the Barcelona Olympics the Irish Amateur Boxing Association saw the logic in Wayne McCullough returning from East Germany and getting proper sparring in Belfast prior going to the Olympics. Had they had the same wisdom back in 1980 I am sure, in fact I am

ABOVE ■ The Christle brothers training in England at the Thomas A'Beckett Gym in London. George Francis (Trainer), Lotte Mwale, Mel Christle, Terry Christle, Bobby Neill.

convinced, that Terry would have certainly done something at middleweight – he would have been mentally as well as physically prepared for the Moscow Olympics. You have got to remember that we never went in half-cocked for anything, whether it be academic or of the sporting variety. In fact Terry visited Moscow in 1979 and was able to tell us about facilities at the hotel where we would have stayed, what gym we would be training at, the amount of time that it would take to get from hotel to gym, from hotel to stadium and so forth. He had made all the preparations so that it wouldn't come as a culture shock were it to happen that he, Joe or myself – two or all three of us – were to be selected for the Olympics. Thorough preparation was the order of the day and that is why we went to England. But in 1980, with a different mentality, the IABA said rules were rules and we had to appear up at Drogheda at this training camp. We refused so that was the end of the Olympics but, as our father explained to us: "Listen, if you want to go to Moscow, you can always buy a ticket – it is not a question of having to be in a boxing team to see Russia or any other part of the world", and that is the way we accepted it.

'The obvious thing to do now was to turn professional. However, we felt and our father supported us, that boxing should not take precedent or trespass on our chosen careers as barrister, accountant and medical practitioner, respectively. Joe and Terry went off to America – Joe to study accountancy. He joined up with the Gerry Cooney camp. Cooney was knocking on the world heavyweight ratings and Joe had a fantastic time; three years with Gerry Cooney and in particular his trainer Victor Valle and his stablemate Billy Costello. Costello was world light-welterweight professional champion and is immortalised in the literary boxing classic Black Lights by Pulitzer prize-winning author, Thomas Hauser. Joe was based in New York with Gerry Cooney and then, of course, Cooney used to train a lot in Palm Springs, California. They would be flying from the east to west coast and as Joe says he calls them his "lost" years because he seemed to have had more of a good time than a productive time.

'Terry was based at Waltham General Hospital, Boston. In his professional boxing career he was under the guidance of Goody Petronelli who was Marvin Hagler's trainer/coach in Brockton, Massachusetts. Terry used to train with Hagler and Hagler's half-brother, Robbie Sims (who knocked out Roberto Duran) who was a leading contender at the same time as Hagler was champion; he was a very good fighter in his own right. So, Terry spent his time there and in fact had 18 professional fights under Goody Petronelli's tutelage, winning 17. Considering that he was doing exams during this three-year period on a quarterly basis – every three months, it wasn't a bad record. In fact, his only loss was in his last fight, a split decision to Dave Tiberi who in his next fight lost a disputed points decision to James Toney for the IBF world middleweight title. That decision was the subject of a Senate investigation into corruption on the basis that Tiberi should have got the decision over Toney.

Terry never fought again, not through any lack of interest, but because of an offer from The Cottage Hospital, Santa Barbara, which was Ronald Reagan's hospital. This meant having to split from Goody Petronelli, which he did in late 1987. Terry pulled up stakes and moved from Massachussett to California but not before being involved in a famous debate on a popular TV show on ABC television called 'Sixty Minutes', a nationwide broadcast in which he teamed up with Sugar Ray Leonard to argue in favour of boxing against the American Medical Association. At the end of the programme it was adjudged to be a points decision in favour of Sugar Ray and Terry in the arguments for boxing.'

In the May 2000 edition of Medicine Weekly, journalist Darren Boyle wrote: 'Terence or to correctly identify him Dr Terence J. Christle MD General Surgeon at the Holy Family Hospital in Methven and Lawrence General Hospital lives just outside Boston, USA and he spoke to me: "In our training the main emphasis in our boxing was learning how to defend yourself. We spent hours practising the various defence mechanisms. That is what boxing is to me. The one main thing that boxing has going for it is that it is a very individualistic sport. No matter what anybody says, it is the rawest type of challenge between two guys – or now even between two women. Boxing was always very personal for me. When I stepped in the ring the other guy would be my enemy. I never really liked my opponent. Whatever defensive moves I worked on I would use them against my opponent. It is a very tactical sport – very similar to a mini military campaign. From my standpoint boxing gave me a tremendous amount of discipline. There is no way you can smoke cigarettes and box at the same time. I never had an unhealthy lifestyle, because you would lose your next match. When you are fit you do better academically. It can keep your head clear as well."

'The chance of fighting in an Olympic finals was a real possibility for Terence. In 1980 as he was rapidly rising up the ranks he secured the amateur middleweight championships in Ireland and France. Fighting as an amateur, the French middleweight championship was one of Terence's most impressive fights. "Before the final round my brothers told me that as far as they were concerned I had lost the fight so I had to knock him out. It occurred to me that my mistake was that I was allowing that guy to take advantage. But I outwitted him in the final round and knocked him out. It was an excellent fight and a particularly enjoyable win because it was in France. The French didn't like it because I brought home the French title," he added. Before the semi-final of the French Championships, Terence was due to sit a physiology exam at Trinity but other arrangements had to be made to travel out to France. "The professor allowed me to sit the exact same paper when I came back as long as I didn't talk to any of my classmates. I think Trinity were proud of the fact that we were involved in sports. That is the main reason I chose Trinity ahead of UCD. Trinity's boxing trainer was far better."

'After turning professional, Terence won 17 of his 18 fights, only losing his final fight on points. He fought out of Marvellous Marvin Hagler's camp and once was on the undercard of the Hagler-Sugar Ray Leonard bout. He also fought in Madison Square Garden. At the beginning of one fight, ringside announcer Jimmy Lennon Jnr wound himself up into a frenzy when he discovered Terence was a doctor. In true showbiz style he declared "...and from Dublin Ireland we have the fighting physician Terry Christle."

'But despite his impressive record. Terence never managed to get a chance of a world title. "When I arrived in the US my intention was to carry on boxing as long as I wanted to. I was making a good living, but I retired in 1988, several months after the Hagler-Leonard fight. Part of the decision was because I was 29. There was one younger fighter being groomed for a shot at the middleweight championship – so it could take three years for my chance. I was looking at

LEFT ▪ Dr Terry Christle: 'The Fighting Physician'.

weighing up all my options and I still had to do my residency training which takes about six years. I would be approaching 40 before completing residency – and I simply didn't want to do that.'"

Mel Christle continues: 'Joe had about seven or eight professional fights as a heavyweight; he won four fights and lost three by decision. I only had two fights. One immediately prior to being called to the Bar and one six months later. My pro debut was in Lewisham against another Irish fighter who was in the top ten of British heavyweights. His name was Martin Nee. I stopped him in the fifth round. Then I was called to the Bar and my second fight was an unplanned bout against a fellow called Steve Gee from Manchester – it was the first and only pro tournament ever held in Killarney, Co Kerry. The only reason I found myself against Steve Gee was because he was supposed to fight Joe, who came down with a 48-hour virus. It was a case of "the show must go on". The fight was a complete sell-out but, having done no training I fought and I lost –i t was stopped in the eighth and final round. I was ahead by a round going into the last round on the Judge's card but it was a cut eye and it didn't surprise me that I was stopped because I was so exhausted and couldn't get out of the way. He deserved to win as far as I was concerned. My abiding memory of the fight is, having been out of the ring for six months, how ring rusty I was. The next day I was so stiff and sore that I had to walk backwards down the stairs – I couldn't take any pressure at all on my thighs. It was just agony.

'Approximately two years later, in 1983, having consulted with Terry from the medical side, I thought it would be a good thing to set up a professional controlling body here in Ireland: The Boxing Union of Ireland. We were given European recognition by the European Boxing Union in 1983 or 1984. Ray Clarke was the Secretary of the British Boxing Board of Control at this time. I have always had a very good relationship with the British Boxing Board of Control, it was not only in relation to Irish professional boxers fighting in England and vice versa, but Irish fighters boxing in Belfast and also British licensees based in Belfast fighting down here. We have a very good working relationship which has continued through with John Morris and currently with Simon Block and Robert Smith. Robert Smith, in fact, was a very good professional himself and is now second in command at the British Boxing Board of Control. His father Andy used to train Joe Bugner. You know, I find it very refreshing to deal with someone who knows the game both inside and outside the ropes. Robert Smith thinks not only from a professional administrator's point of view, but he thinks from a professional fighter's point of view which I believe is invaluable to any professional controlling body.

'From the medical perspective I think I should mention also that we were the first association to insist on MRI scans for our fighters before giving professional licences. Two years later the British Boxing Board of Control saw fit to bring in similar protection for their licensees. We are particularly proud of the fact that on our Board we have the eminent consultant neurosurgeon in Ireland, Professor Jack Phillips. His professional advice is of invaluable assistance to our Association and he is also a fan of the sport. It is nice to have not only medical experts advising you, but medical experts who have no ethical difficulties with the sport of boxing whether it be amateur or professional.

'Professional boxing promotions in Ireland are like "hens' teeth". In the Republic, you are fortunate if there are two or three professional promotions in any one year. However, we have had some very successful world professional promotions, such as for example the world featherweight title fight in Dublin between Barry McGuigan and Danilo Cabrera. This was a huge success and one which after a few shaky moments Barry McGuigan successfully came through and stopped his opponent in the 13th round.

'We have also had another world featherweight title fight, this time involving Paul Hodgkinson, the Liverpudlian who was based in Belfast because he was managed by B.J. Eastwood. He defended his WBC featherweight crown against Gregorio Vargas in the National Stadium in

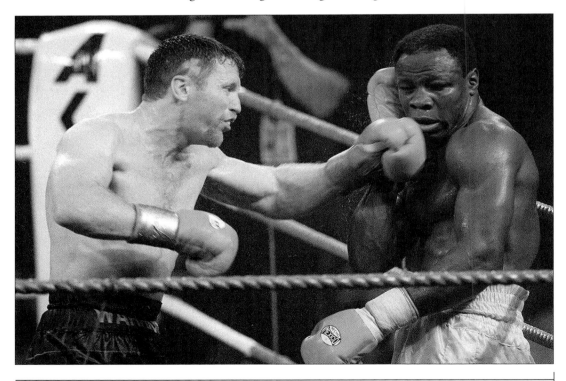

ABOVE ■ 18th March 1995 Steve Collins lands a left on Chris Eubank's chin when Collins defeated Eubank to win the WBO World Super-middleweight title in Millstreet, Co Cork.

Dublin which was televised live on ITV. At the end of the day he was stopped in the seventh round. We have also had a number of fights involving Steve Collins and world title defences in Dublin. However, his most famous fight, I suppose, involved Chris Eubank and the world title fight in which he won the title. This fight was held on St Patrick's night 1995 in Millstreet, County Cork. It was probably one of the greatest sporting spectacles ever seen in Ireland and certainly deemed to be so by the Sky TV crew that covered the event. Then there was the return match, which drew a crowd in excess of 18,000 to the GAA stadium in Cork City in an open-air contest the following summer. This was a huge success in which, after a bitterly fought contest, Steve Collins came out on top once again. Besides that we have had the likes of the Lennox Lewis fight here on Irish Derby Day at the Point Depot, Dublin.

'We have also had Wayne McCullough defend his bantamweight title in the Point Depot Arena, Dublin against Jose Luis Bueno – a fight in which he was very lucky to escape with his title intact because he took a ferocious drubbing over twelve rounds. I think home advantage basically won the fight for him at the end of a very close contest. So, all in all, in recent times we have had a lot of world title action in the Republic. This has been of great benefit to Irish professional fighters both north and south of the border and they have been given exposure before fans down in the Republic of Ireland. There has always been a strong boxing history in Belfast. As a result, one has at least seven or eight tournaments a year in Belfast City, whether they be in the Ulster Hall or – for the bigger tournaments – in the King's Hall on the outskirts of Belfast City. It seems to me that Belfast is the centre of professional boxing as far as Ireland is concerned and will continue to be so.

'On the amateur front, the Irish Amateur Boxing Association is not the force that it used to be although with plans currently in place for, shall we say, a higher level of coaching among amateur clubs, fortunes will change. For example, one of the high watermarks of amateur boxing was the 1992 Barcelona Olympics, with two medals, one gold and one silver won by Michael Carruth and Wayne McCullough respectively. However, in Atlanta and, indeed, more recently in Sydney, the fortunes of Irish boxers have not been anything to write home about. However, with government funding, that should change. We now have a Cuban coach, Nicholas Cruz, who should be in a position to bring home the medals from Athens. He has been given the finance to coach at club level throughout Ireland and seek out, shall we say, the raw talent and hopefully develop that talent in the National Stadium in Dublin, the Amateur Boxing Association's headquarters. We will have to see whether that will produce results but I hope it will in the future.

'I am delighted to say that, again, from the family point of view, my brother Joe was recently appointed a trustee of the Irish Amateur Boxing Association which he accepted as an honour and privilege. Old divisions, therefore, between professional and amateur boxing would not appear to be there any more in that the Irish Amateur Boxing Association has seen fit to avail of Joe's expertise in legal matters and matters pertaining to The Board of Trustees.

'At the Sydney Olympics, for the first time in Irish boxing history, Ireland had only one representative; this was Michael Roche from Cork, who fought as a light-middleweight He lost his opening bout to a Turk. Dermot Sherlock formerly of Trinity College, in his capacity as Secretary of the Olympic Council of Ireland to give him his official title, was the "Chef de mission" of the overall Irish team in all sports at Sydney. That at least was a Trinity connection and he seems to have performed his duties admirably. But one thinks of only one entrant in boxing and considers the fact that in Melbourne, the last time the Olympics were in Australia, there were no fewer than six Irish competitors in the boxing end of the Olympics. Also they won no fewer than four medals – I think it was one silver, three bronze. You know, the quality has obviously gone down since those heady days. That said, it may come up again. There are factors such as the new scoring system which has thrown amateur boxing out of sync.

ABOVE ■ 30th March 1996 Wayne McCullough retains his title against Jose Luis Bueno of Mexico.

It is a different sport now because of the points scoring system, which is computerised and with five judges scoring a bout on the amount of hits –a hit only scores where three judges press a button at the same time. It seems to me that boxing has gone into the pinball machine variety of sport rather than the science that it once was. Body punching, which is an art form, does not count for any points in amateur boxing which, to me, is a disgrace because it rules out what was heretofore a major part of a boxer's arsenal and will continue to be a major part of a professional fighter's arsenal. If amateur boxing continues to be emasculated the way it is at present, the gulf between amateur and professional boxing will widen. One will see professional prospects turning professional at a much earlier age rather than hanging on to fight for titles in the amateur code when the scoring system is so arbitrary and hard to define.

'In relation to Trinity College one should also mention that Dessie FitzGerald, the Irish front row who won titles under Fred Tiedt's tutelage in the early 1980s. The interesting fact about the Trinity Boxing Club is that at any time it was 70% medical students who frequented the training sessions as opposed to any other academic discipline in Trinity. This seems to be at odds with the attitude that the profession takes in its official stance vis-à-vis boxing. Another gentleman who won titles with Trinity College was a Dr Patrick Troy who is now based in the midlands of Ireland treating AIDS sufferers and drug abusers and has gained quite a reputation for his work in that area.' ▪

To me Irish boxing is epitomized by the examples set by the likes in the amateur scene of the Trinity boxers of the 1950s, Fred Tiedt's acceptance of the silver medal at Melbourne, the Christle brothers as both amateurs and professionals and the pride created by the successes of Wayne McCullough and Michael Carruth in the 1992 Barcelona Olympics. I find it something special to accept a heavyweight fight as Mel Christle did as a replacement for a brother and despite not being match-fit, to put on an excellent fight, which he was unlucky to lose on a cut eye decision. Even more praiseworthy is that the brothers have reached the pinnacle in their chosen careers as Senior Counsel, Junior Counsel and General Consultant Surgeon respectively. In the professional scene the standards, sportsmanship and integrity set by the likes of Barry McGuigan, Steve Collins, Dave 'Boy' McAuley, Johnny Caldwell, Wayne McCullough, Eamon Loughran and Danny McAlinden to mention just a few. Boxing in Ireland is indeed a 'noble art' and justification for its continuation can be made.

To conclude, Medicine Weekly, the voice of Irish Medicine said in May 1999: '"Boxing is a very traditional sport in Ireland", believes Consultant Neurosurgeon and Adviser to the Boxing Union of Ireland (BUI) Professor Jack Phillips, "At an amateur level I have never seen an amateur boxer admitted into a neurosurgical unit in the 19 years I have been in Dublin. The boxing clubs here are very well supervised."

'Professor Phillips argues that Ireland is one of the safest places in the world to fight. "We have in place the professional structures to care for any professional boxer who suffers a serious brain injury. Whenever the BUI have an application to fight in the Irish jurisdiction the fighter is sent to me for an assessment. The neurosurgical assessment consists of a brain scan and the patient has an MRI scan. If this detects any anatomical abnormality it is very seriously scrutinised and often he is denied the opportunity to box in Ireland. If the MRI scan detects any pathological changes he is also denied the opportunity to box."

'Journeymen boxers are at most threat from damage. They are willing to take more punishment because they are fighting for their livelihood. According to Professor Phillips it is the repeated concussion that is the main problem. "A doctor fighting occasionally is not at risk. No doctor is going to subject himself to repeated episodes of concussion in a sport. It is like being a jockey or a person who skis down mountains and falls—you take your chances. If you receive a number of head injuries and are concussed you should stop boxing. If this is the case it is clearly evident that you do not have the talent or the build to succeed in the sport. Repeated concussion is undesirable because it does have an effect, even at a microscopic level."

"Boxing is a tremendous method of relieving stress and getting rid of frustration", opines Dr Mick Molloy, Secretary of the Irish Sports Medical Association and Senior Registrar in A&E at St Vincent's. "There are some people who just train without ever stepping into the ring. It provides an excellent form of exercise. Amateur boxing is entirely safe. Fights consist of five rounds of two minutes and the fighters are well protected. It is a completely different sport to the professional game. Scoring does not depend on knocking the opponent out, rather landing clean punches. Power does not count." He adds: "An old fashioned centre-half in soccer is at more risk because he is constantly heading the ball."

"I used to play rugby and only took up boxing at College," revealed Dr Emmet Andrews, Surgical Registrar at Waterford Regional Hospital. "I fought at light-welterweight, but before that I played rugby. With rugby you could be playing against someone far heavier—particularly when you are around ten stone. With boxing, your opponent is always within half a stone. The people fighting are equals."

'Dr Andrews fought in four consecutive British and Irish University Championships, winning three of them. "The sport is excellent for self-confidence. Once the call 'seconds out' is made and if you quell your fear and remain standing, you are able for anything in the future. No other amateur sport requires such total commitment from the participants. It also makes you respect your opponent and there is very little foul play."'

The Irish love racing. The roar when Arkle jumped the last fence in the Gold Cup at Cheltenham competing with Mill House for the lead, reverberated around the Cotswolds. The subsequent victory was only an excuse for the bars, restaurants and hotels to be filled with celebrating Irishmen. Indeed, win or lose, Cheltenham, Epsom, Listowel or Galway, the scene is still the same. The Irish are there for the craic but underneath is the intent to do well. Ireland has a proud history in racing. The two chapters on racing have evolved naturally. They talk about those who love Irish racing; some have achieved international fame; others have gained their pleasure through being part of the racing scene, but in all there emerges a deep respect for racing.

Two Trinity friends, Peter McKeever and Brian Smith, both of whom have had a life's passion for all things to do with horses kindled my interest in Irish racing in my student days. Peter McKeever had a long association with the Curragh Bloodstock Agency, one of Ireland's leading bloodstock agencies. On a visit to Co Kildare in August 2000 Peter told me that he was born in Co Meath; his parents Jack and Beatrice McKeever were farmers and keen on racing and hunting. On Jack's death at the age of 27, Peter moved with his mother to Glebelands, Ratoath, Co Meath. Soon his mother became ill and Peter lived for a while with his grandmother and Uncle Tom. The uncle was a leading National Hunt trainer and trained the first and second in the Irish Grand National of 1937. The winner Rathfriland was owned by a neighbour, John Margate. It was natural with this environment that Peter should become a sports enthusiast, but racing was his premier interest. After attending Drogheda Grammar School, he went on to Trinity College, Dublin. Friendships made here were to stand him in good stead, particularly later, when travelling abroad for the Curragh Bloodstock Agency.

ABOVE ■ 11th March 1965. Arkle ridden by Pat Taaffe and Mill House ridden by G.W. Robinson take the second fence during the 1965 Cheltenham Gold Cup.

After a time at the home stud in Ratoath, the family had a successful stallion in Ossian II. Aubrey Brabazon, Peter's uncle, offered him the opportunity to be an assistant trainer to his father, Cecil, at Rangers Lodge, The Curragh. Peter spoke of his uncle with great pride, 'He was probably one of the most stylish flat cum National Hunt jockeys of any era, he had many triumphs with the great trainer Vincent O'Brien and apart from that he was a delightful man; he was a great conversationalist and loved telling a story over a pint.'

After two years with Cecil Brabazon, Captain Paddy Harbord, who, together with Aubrey Brabazon founded the Curragh Bloodstock Agency in 1948, offered him a job. Thus began a 40-year association with the Curragh Bloodstock Agency who at the time were, along with the British Bloodstock Agency (formed 1911), the only established bloodstock agencies. They concentrated on every aspect of the industry, buying and selling thoroughbred horses, syndicating stallions, insuring bloodstock, shipping them and attending most of the major sales in the world in order to try and build up clientele. ■

The CBA were the real pioneers of bloodstock airfreight and have remained so ever since. Peter's initial years were spent mainly, with the help of Miss Ann Hunter, putting together charter flights to cater for mares visiting stallions between Ireland, England and France. Peter said, 'This entailed what would nowadays be called consolidation in the airfreight industry; doing our best to fill each leg of the aircraft on a particular flight. This was the major business that I was involved with on a day-to-day basis and it gave an opportunity of the very highest class mares and stallions in England and France visiting each other.'

In 1965 Peter joined the Board of the CBA and in September 1967 on the sudden death of Paddy Harbord he was appointed Managing Director. Liam Spring took over the airfreight department and Peter became involved with the overall running of the company. This gave the opportunity to travel to South Africa, South America, Australia, New Zealand, the USA and all over Europe. The first yearling bought after Paddy Harbord's death was Right Tack. He cost 3100 guineas at the Doncaster Sales and was the first horse to win the English and Irish Guineas in the same season. This began an involvement with many other Stakes and Classic winners and a number of well-known owners, including J.R. Brown the owner of Right Tack. Another yearling bought at Goffs for Jim Brown was Furry Glen; he was sold at a profit, but went on like Right Tack to win the Irish 2000 Guineas. Royal Prerogative was bought for Brooke Holliday. He was a lovely bay horse and he became champion sire of South Africa for many seasons. Peter said, 'I particularly remembered the deal because between the time of purchase and the closing of the sale, the rate of exchange of the pound sterling against the South African rand dropped dramatically and we only got 3% commission instead of our usual 5%. I rang Brooke Holliday to ask if he would make up the difference and he said, "Bad luck, old boy, the coin has fallen my way this time". It taught me a financial lesson forever.

'Nowadays stud fees have risen to astronomical heights but they do tend to go up and down over the years and in the process cause over-production of bad animals. Anyone who has drawn a graph since commercial breeding began will find that the population of mares usually increases over a 5-6 years span and then over-production leads to an elimination of the worst and so the cycle starts all over again. To name the most famous sires and dams would be difficult but it is fairly well accepted that the stallion end was initially carried from The Byerley Turk, The Darley Arabian and The Godolphin. There are many famous stud farms in the British Isles, the USA, Europe and indeed, worldwide but to try and place them in order of merit would only be to express a probably incorrect opinion.

'Of those that influenced the industry in Ireland, one would have to mention John Magnier and the Coolmore Stud, Robert Sangster, Captain Tim Rogers, the Aga Khan's studs, Kilcard stud

ABOVE ■ Right Tack ridden by Geoff Lewis wins the 2000 Guineas at Newmarket 1969 with Towerwalk (M. Thomas) and Welsh Pageant (A. Barclay) second and third. Right Tack, with other big winners such as Red Rum sold at Doncaster, have sale yards named after them.

and the Irish National stud. The first manager that I personally knew of the Aga Khan's stud farms was Major Cyril Hall; he was previously employed at the Irish National Stud. The two great stallions there were Tulyar and Royal Charger, which was probably the most successful commercial stallion in the British Isles in his time. Major Hall then eventually took over as manager of the Aga Khan's stud and lived at Turf Lodge at The Curragh. My wife Biz and I have particularly fond memories of the Cheltenham National Hunt festival where we used to stay either at the Reedsdale Arms, Moreton-in-the-Marsh or with Sir John Guise at Royal Ascot where the Turf Club was our temporary home.

'Just two brief memories of great races, the first was that between Grundy and Busino in the King George VI Stakes at Ascot which I have always said was the best battle I have seen on a racecourse. The other was the win of Dawn Run in the Gold Cup at Cheltenham in 1986. Dawn

Run was trained by Paddy Mullins at Goresbridge, Co Kilkenny; she looked beaten at the last, only for Jonjo O'Neill, her jockey to rally her up the hill and win virtually on the line from Wayward Lad, the English champion horse of the time. All Ireland had willed Dawn Run and Jonjo O'Neill on and Ireland was not disappointed.'

Peter McKeever continues: 'I would like to think that the CBA were always regarded as being of the highest integrity with the leading sales companies such as Goffs, Tattersalls and Fasig Tipton. Goffs was built just outside Kill, near Naas, after a rather divisive meeting of the Irish Thoroughbred Breeders Association in Merrion Square, Dublin. Lord Harrington, the Chairman of the Association said: "Stop this arguing and I propose we build at Kill". Goffs is generally regarded as the best auction amphitheatre in Europe. It is a 40-acre site with stabling for 25 horses and offices and a PR reception area. It has also been used for concerts and the Irish Masters Snooker tournament.

LEFT ■ Goffs saleyard.

Peter McKeever fought cancer and lived with the aid of an oxygen machine for many years. He remained a highly respected figure in the world of Irish racing and was a longtime member of the Irish Turf Club. Later in the year I was to visit his son Johnny at Newmarket; he has followed in his father's footsteps and become a bloodstock agent. Sadly on 1st March, 2001, I had a telephone call from Johnny telling me that his father had died the previous Thursday. A large congregation, many associated with racing attended the funeral service at St David's Church, Naas. ▪

Ireland has been lucky to have many outstanding jockeys. Each era has seen a large number of the world's leading jockeys born and often based in Ireland. It would be impossible to name them all. Aubrey Brabazon, Peter McKeever's uncle, was at his peak in the late 1940s and early 1950s. In the words of Vincent O'Brien, 'Aubrey was a wonderful person, kind intelligent and always honourable... He was interested in everything about racing... Over the years I have seen many riders but in my opinion, very few finer or more stylish horseman than Aubrey. He was a top class jockey on the flat and equally accomplished over jumps – a rare talent that he shared with his great friend and contemporary, Martin Molony. Aubrey had a real understanding of horses and was always able to get the best out of them on the day. He inspired great confidence and when it came to riding a finish he had no peer. I was always confident that if Aubrey was in contention over the last we were as good as home and I knew that he would always be kind to his horse.

'Aubrey rode Cottage Rake for me to win three Cheltenham Gold Cups carrying twelve stone each time and it is extraordinary to remember that more than three stone plus of this was dead weight. One of my favourite possessions is a photograph of him jumping the last fence of the 1950 Gold Cup at Cheltenham with a broad smile on his face. He rode Hatton's Grace brilliantly to win the Champion Hurdle on two occasions and in 1948 achieved a remarkable double with Cottage Rake in the Gold Cup and Masaka in the Irish Oaks. He topped this in 1950 with a unique treble – a Cheltenham Gold Cup (Cottage Rake), a Champion Hurdle (Hatton's Grace) and an Irish Two Thousand Guineas (Mighty Ocean).'

Brabazon rode his first winner Queen Christina at Phoenix Park over a five-furlong flat race in 1935. In the early days he rode mainly for his father, Cecil Brabazon. In 1944 he rode Vincent O'Brien's first win over hurdles, Wren Boy, at Limerick and a few months later he rode Panay at Thurles to record O'Brien's first win over fences. By 1960, when he retired, Aubrey Brabazon had ridden over 450 winners. In the meanwhile he had ridden regularly for his father, Vincent O'Brien, Capt D. Rogers and many of Ireland's top trainers.

The Molony brothers, Martin and Tim, were outstanding horsemen both on the flat and over jumps. Martin succeeded Aubrey Brabazon as undisputed Irish Jockeys Champion in 1947 and held the title until 1951, the year in which he had his career ended, falling on the 4-6 favourite Bursary at Thurles. 1950 was Martin Molony's golden season; he had 119 winners (some sources say 116 winners) out of 380 rides – a quite remarkable percentage. In the same year Tim Molony was the leading jockey in Britain. The brothers were born in the west of Ireland where their father trained horses. In 1939 (aged 13) Martin was sent to be an apprentice with Martin Hartigan's stables at Ogborne in Swindon. He returned to Ireland during the war, together with the other Irish apprentices and was apprenticed to Ginger Wellesley at The Curragh. Shortly he was to move to Capt Harty's stables; Cyril Harty had been on a pre-war Irish army jumping team. Martin won his first race on 19th March 1942 at Rathkeale. He would go on to ride in Ireland, France, the USA and Britain. Perhaps his greatest triumphs were to win on Silver Fame at Sandown (1950) and at the Cheltenham Gold Cup (1951). Vincent O'Brien described Martin Molony as 'one of the very best ever steeplechase jockeys'. He was not just a National Hunt jockey but an all-rounder. He rode long and this gave him the power to get the best out of horses in close finishes. His services were also in demand for the flat race classics. In 1950 he came third in the English Oaks on Stella Polaris. He was part of a 'golden era of Irish jockeys' which included Tommy Burns, Joe Canty, Martin Quirke and the English born Morny Wing. After his life-threatening fall at Thurles in 1951 Martin moved back to the family farm at Rathmore, Co Limerick where he trained horses. His brother Tim continued to ride mainly in Britain and was the champion National Hunt jockey for the fourth successive year in the 1951/52 season. Tim had a number of notable successes in this period including the Cheltenham Gold Cup on Knock Hard (1953) and the Champion Hurdle on Hatton's Grace (1951) and Sir Ken (1952, 53 and 54).

The next generation of Irish jockeys included the fair share of greats such as Bobby Beasley, and perhaps outstanding amongst them were Pat Taaffe, Toss Taaffe, Pat Eddery and Willie Robinson. Pat Taaffe won on Arkle in the Gold Cup three times (1964, 65 and 66, the Hennessy Gold Cup twice (1964 and 65) and the Whitbread Gold Cup (1965). He also won on Arkle in the Irish Grand National at Fairyhouse in 1964. This perhaps was Ireland's greatest combination of horse and rider in its history of racing. Pat Taaffe was a professional jockey between the years 1950 and 1970, although he had ridden as an amateur winning his first race on Merry Coon in a point-to-point at Bray in 1946. He came from a hunting and racing family and although six feet tall, it was always predicable that Pat Taaffe would become a jockey. His career was dotted with unbelievable triumphs, but it was his association with Arkle that was to bring particular fame and his confrontations with Mill House ridden by his great friend Willie Robinson. Mill House before going to England to be trained by Fulke Walwyn was in Pat's father's stables. Pat Taaffe wrote to Willie Robinson, who rode for Fulke Walwyn saying: 'You have now got the best chaser in Ireland or England'. Mill House duly won the Cheltenham Gold Cup in 1963. In the same year at Newbury in the Hennessy Cognac Gold Cup, Mill House and Arkle clashed for the first time. They were neck and neck going into the last fence but Arkle sprawled on landing and Mill House and Willie Robinson won the day. It was their one and only win over Arkle and next year Arkle and Pat Taaffe gained their revenge. They gave a 'tremendous exhibition of jumping and horsemanship'. Mill House was in front as they raced towards the last fence but Arkle

ABOVE ■ Alec Head and Cyril Hall – masters in their field.

produced an electrifying turn of speed and sprinted up the hill to the winning post – a burst of speed which distinguished him from Mill House and made Arkle unique.

Arkle continued his successful way until 1966 on St Stephen's Day competing in the King George VI Chase at Kempton, which he had won the previous year, he cracked a pedal bone and his racing days were over. Pat says of Arkle: 'He was like a human being. He knew exactly what was expected of him and he did it. And how he enjoyed the big days and the crowd! He was a grand quiet horse at home. You need have no fear of putting children on his back – he would just walk round with them.' Pat Taaffe's own career as a jockey ended in 1970, the year in which he won the Aintree Grand National on Gay Trip, a horse he had bought for Fred Rimell. Pat had got the ride because the stable jockey, Terry Biddlecombe, was injured. Pat won the English Grand National twice and the Irish Grand National six times. Pat, however, continued his interest in racing by becoming a trainer. In 1974 Captain Christy ridden by Bobby Beasley and trained by Pat Taaffe won the Cheltenham Gold Cup. Perhaps his greatest pleasure has been his son Tom's victory on Brittany Boy in the Irish Grand National of 1987 and this together with Pat's brother, Toss Taaffe's victory in 1960 completed a remarkable family achievement in the history of the Irish Grand National. ▪

I t was Wednesday, 8th November 2000 that I met Susan (nee Hall) and Willie Robinson in Peter McKeever's home in Co Kildare. I knew them both from the past. Soon we were all chatting. Susan recalled that her father Major Hall moved from England in 1947 to manage the Irish National Stud. 'Royal Charger was one of the stallions and then my father bought Tulyar from the Aga Khan…' In the early 1950s the family moved to manage the Aga Khan's stud farms. My father took over from Nesbitt Waddington who was the Aga Khan's manager for over 20 years. We lived on The Curragh at Turf Lodge and looked after the five studs: Ballymany, Gilltown, Sallymount, Sheshoon and Ayrefield. Each stud had a manager, but my father was the overall manager. Sadly Prince Ali died in a car crash in Paris – as well as being father's boss he was also a great friend. The present Aga Khan then took over. Towards the end of the 1960s the racing business in Ireland was having some problems and the Aga Khan began to cut back. Our three best-known stallions were Saint Crespin III, Charlottesville and Silver Shark and we bred a number of outstanding horses.' (See Statistics).

Willie Robinson has had an outstanding career in racing. He was born in 1934. He began riding at an early age and was always destined to be a jockey – apart from a natural talent he could maintain a weight of around nine stone with some comfort – he still looks a fit man. He rode his first winner as an amateur at Navan in 1955. In 1956 Willie Robinson became a professional towards the end of an era of tough jockeys and horsemen. They were all very competitive. Pay

ABOVE ■ Anzio ridden by G.W. Robinson being led in by Lady Ainsworth after winning the Champion Hurdle 1962 at Cheltenham.

was a little better than in the days of Martin Molony when the rate was three guineas for a flat race and five guineas for a race over fences with a bonus for a win of two guineas. Willie felt he was better looked after than most, but there were some good owners and some not so good. By the time Willie won the Gold Cup in 1963, jockeys were normally paid about 10% of the winner's prize. In the case of the Gold Cup in 1963 this was £20,000 for the winning owner. For a win in a Bumper by 1963 a jockey might earn between 150 and 2000 sovereigns. But life was tough – a jockey was expected to do what he was told and there was always the danger of a serious fall. By 1961 he had begun riding in England and he was retained as leading jockey by a number of well-known British trainers including John Corbett (who trained in Northern Ireland), Dan Moore, John Wood and Fulke Walwyn.

Willie Robinson had a number of distinguished wins. He won the Ulster National for the Queen Mother on Laffy at Downpatrick in 1962; this was the most important event in Northern Ireland racing. The Irish Racing Journal reported the event: 'The man behind the Queen Mother's visit was Major William Brownlow, chairman of the Downpatrick Race Club. "We were having a Committee meeting one evening and a member suggested that since the Queen Mother was coming to Ulster, she might like to run a horse here," Bill recalled. "I was given the task of organising it as I was a friend of her trainer Peter Cazalet. I rang up Peter and asked him to send over a horse for the Ulster National. He told me: 'You're on', and Laffy was duly despatched.

ABOVE ■ Mill House ridden by Willie Robinson – Gold Cup winner Cheltenham 1963.

"We had to reach agreement with the Turf Club to put the date of the meeting back a fortnight but this was no problem and Laffy arrived and was stabled with John Corbett at Tyrelia. The Queen Mother stayed with the then Governor of Northern Ireland, Lord Wakehurst at Hillsborough Castle and travelled up to Downpatrick to be greeted by an enormous crowd. After Laffy had won the race she was mobbed by fans and she told me that shortly after jockey Willie Robinson had dismounted, she was startled to see a little man appear from under Laffy's belt. It was almost as though he had come out of the horse! The Queen Mother was somewhat taken aback but then smiled readily when he thrust out his hand and said: 'I've come all the way from Dublin just to see what you look like!'.

LEFT ▨ Team Spirit, winner of the 1964 Grand National, ridden to hunt back at home in Ireland by Susan Robinson in Autumn 1964.

ABOVE ■ King's Company trained by Willie Robinson, ridden by F. Head, being unsaddled after winning the 1971 Irish 2000 Guineas.

"The race itself was memorable in many ways and at the finish not everyone – including the Queen Mother – was clear whether or not Laffy had won. This was because the leader ran out at one stage in the race and then rejoined the field at the front of affairs. This prompted course commentator Micheal O'Hehir – whose broadcast was also going out on radio – to make the immortal statement: 'The horse in the lead isn't winning the race. The horse that's second is in the lead'." 'Then to cap matters Willie Robinson was still suffering from the after effects of concussion following a fall in the previous race. Still it all ended in fairytale fashion and the Queen Mother never forgot O'Hehir's commentary. In fact years later she recalled it to him when he was a guest in her box at Cheltenham.'

Other big wins were The Cheltenham Gold Cup on Mill House (1963) and Kirriemuir (1965), the King George VI Chase at Kempton on Mill House (1963), the Hennessy Cognac Gold Cup at Newbury on Mandarin (1961), Mill House (1963) and Man of the West (1968). In 1964 he won the Grand National on Team Spirit and on Paddy's Point came second in the English and Irish Derby; thus showing the versatility of the jockeys of the previous decade such as Martin Molony and Aubrey Brabazon. In 1970, after a horrifying fall at Uttoxeter, Willie Robinson started training. He bought Stepaside and its 40 stables from Micky Roberts and dealt mainly with yearlings. Lady Fitzwilliam used the stables, but for the most part Willie took horses as the owners came to seek his expertise. One of his horses, King's Company, won the Irish Guineas and he had eight second places with Peter McKeever's Gun Running. Nowadays Willie Robinson has a small establishment in Calverstown where his main interest is brood mares. Irish racing can be proud of the likes of Willie and Susan Robinson. ■

Brian Smith, the second of my Trinity colleagues to rouse my interest in Irish racing has fulfilled his life-ambition to own racing horses. I was interested in finding out how Brian became an owner. I remembered owning a rather unsuccessful Trotter with Ross Smith, Bruce Robertson and A.N. Other when I was teaching in Auckland, New Zealand. Despite being unsuccessful, our Trotter gave great pleasure. I talked to Brian in London and Dublin in the autumn of 2000; Brian was educated at Castle Park, Dalkey, Co Dublin and Stowe (England) before going to Trinity to study law. He then went into the family business before selling it in 1991 to Northern Foods. He is a keen sportsman but it is racing that is his main interest. 'It is since the Second World War that Ireland has become a real force in the world of horse racing. National hunt or jump racing is much more popular than the flat in Ireland and this is shown by attendance figures at various meetings; I follow both of them avidly.'

Brian went on to talk about Vincent O'Brien and his remarkable successes over both the jumps and the flat. He spoke enthusiastically about Vincent O'Brien's jockeys and, in particular, Aubrey Brabazon, Pat Eddery and Lester Piggott. 'You know Ireland has always had exceptionally talented jockeys. In regard to the flat I think of the above, but of course Lester Piggott was English, and also C. Roche, T.P. Burns, J. Eddery (Pat's father), M.J. Kinane who rides for A.P. O'Brien and J.R. Murtagh.

'In National Hunt the best jockeys have been Pat Taaffe, who was an outstanding horseman particularly around Aintree and Willie Robinson, another remarkable jockey who rode Mill House and was unlucky enough to race at the same time as Arkle. I met Willie a week ago and he seemed in great form, though he did have very bad injuries which affected the length of his career. Charlie Swan is another great jockey. There are many others I could mention. Aidan O'Brien has succeeded Vincent O'Brien as Ireland's premier trainer. He is not a relative of "The Master" and is only in his early thirties, but already has had phenomenal success. You know it is the personality of the horses which draws the crowds to the big races. I think of the likes of

Cottage Rake, Hatton's Grace, L'Escargot, Arkle, of course, and Dawn Run who had the distinction of winning both the Champion Hurdle (1984) and the Gold Cup (1986). It is the hope of acquiring a horse such as those mentioned that draws one to become an owner.

'To talk further about Irish racing, the atmosphere at Irish festival meetings such as Punchestown, Fairyhouse, Listowel and Galway is first class and compares most favourably with Liverpool and Cheltenham, the latter of which has become too much of a rugby scrum. Alcohol, cheerfulness, close finishers and great horses draw large crowds to the meetings mentioned above. 'In September 1998 I attended Listowel. My horse Sheam Town won at the festival. Like many Irish festivals these days it lasts just under a week and I am told takes roughly a year off the life of anyone who stays the course. That year 70,000 people attended the meeting and wagered about IR£6.3 million. Listowel is a small town in Co Kerry in the West of Ireland. The festival is a week of total mayhem. Apart from the racecourse which dates back to 1858, there are 57 pubs, 15 of them situated around Gypsy Kathleen's mystic caravan in the market square. I hate to think how much drink is consumed during the festival. The racing is a bit variable but winning colours were represented by the Aga Khan, Hamdan al-Maktoum and J.P. McManus. Unfortunately there is only one local trainer, who goes by the name of Tommy Cooper, and horses and spectators come from all over Ireland. The evenings entertainment features music and the week commences with the barmen and barmaids' race and concludes with a churn rolling contest. After the racing was over Kerry played Galway in the All-Ireland Gaelic football final. Gaelic football is a religion in Kerry – racing merely an annual party. Brendan Daly has been Secretary of the Race Club since 1951; he is very proud of the festival, but how could it fail with 57 pubs and 83 bookmakers trading on the Tuesday? More recently still, I have been in Galway for an October meeting. There were sixty-two thousand people there on the two days that I was present. I had a runner which was second, second time out – the name of the horse is Houdunnit. It ran extremely promisingly and is a horse to look out for in the future.

'I have owned a number of horses, either in partnership or on my own. Basically most potential owners are in the same boat in so far as they have to educate their children before getting involved to purchase racehorses. It was not therefore until 1988 that yours truly was in a financial position to purchase my first racehorse, a horse called Altmabrocky. It has a record unfortunately of 11 seconds but has won two races. Probably the best horse I have is Sheam Town, which I owned in partnership with Arthur Craigie. It has won four times and finished in the first four in its other races but it has been unable to run recently as it has been injured. Maspolama is a full sister to Sheam Town, both of whom were sired by Camden Town and Jessica Harrington, the trainer, thinks a lot of Maspolama. John Fowler, Jessica Harrington's brother-in-law, has trained a number of my horses including Altmabrocky. Owning a racehorse and watching it run and talking to the trainer about its prospects is great fun. I have probably not made anything out of the exercise financially but I have met many interesting people, attended some great meetings and established an interest in racing form and bloodlines.'

Ballydoyle and the name O'Brien are synonymous. Aidan O'Brien is a worthy successor to the great Vincent O'Brien who, for half a century, reigned supreme in the world of horse racing. Vincent O'Brien was the true master of training, recognised and acknowledged as such worldwide. His record speaks for itself: three successive Aintree Grand Nationals, three successive Cheltenham Champion Hurdles, three successive Gold Cups and a fourth in 1952. In switching from the jumps to the flat he was no less successful: six Epsom Derbys, five Irish Derbys, three Prix de l'Arc de Triomphes, three King George VI's and Queen Elizabeth Diamond Stakes and one Washington International.

Vincent O'Brien was born in 1917 and was brought up on the family farm at Churchtown, Co Cork. His father, Dan O'Brien, trained and raced horses and was an expert at picking out a good horse and breaking it in. Soon the young Vincent was showing a fanatical interest in his father's horses and learning about horses. Dan O'Brien died in 1943. Vincent O'Brien's half-brother took over the farm and Vincent ran the stables and gallops. His first break came when Frank Vickerman a wealthy Yorkshire wool merchant moved to Dublin and began to send horses to the O'Brien stables. He had successes with Dry Bob, Good Days and in particular Cottage Rake, whose victory over Happy Home ridden by Martin Molony was his first success away from Ireland. Cottage Rake repeated the victory in 1949 and in 1950 defeated Lord Bicester's unbeaten Finure.

Vincent O'Brien was to be top of his profession until his retirement in 1993. However, in his early days as a trainer, even with the successes of Cottage Rake he had to gamble to survive; prize money in Ireland was poor. Vickerman suggested the sale of Cottage Rake, but the decision was made to keep him and he was trained at the Churchtown stables until 1953. O'Brien was good at training for a particular race and pulling off victories at often very good odds. He was to become the bookies' nightmare and he enjoyed it all. He had famous parties at the Adelphi Hotel in Liverpool and on the boat journey back to Dublin. It was not long before Vincent was secure in his profession and able to pay top money for his horses. Nor was it long before he was able to move into stables at Ballydoyle, Cashel, Co Tipperary. Having turned his emphasis to the flat, success came rapidly at the Ballydoyle stables. Ballymoss was his first major classic winner, pulling off the Irish Derby, the English St Leger in 1957 and the Prix de l'Arc de Triomphe in 1958.

At Ballydoyle, O'Brien established the perfect racing establishment; Robin Norris, the son of Paddy Norris, who was at one time the assistant trainer to O'Brien, became the vet. O'Brien was a man for detail and left nothing to chance, all the stable boxes were lined with rubber to prevent injury. The stables boxes were spacious, three boxes were made into two; wood shavings rather than straw were placed on the floor, these were changed every few weeks. The boxes were mucked out daily and each box had half doors, thus enabling the horses to look out and keep their interest in goings-on in the yard. In the big barn he installed starting stalls to allow the two year-olds to gain experience at this before they raced and background music was played to calm the nerves of any anxious horse! The best horses, the ones which had won the big races, were housed in a corner area near the actual house, although the boxes of Cottage Rake and Hatton's Grace were to become offices. Every day the stable lads would arrive at 8 o'clock and start work at 8.30; earlier at some times of the year. O'Brien would supervise the gallops which were set in the beautiful Co Tipperary country with the Galtees, the Knockmealdowns, the Comeraghs and the Slievenamon mountain ranges offering a spectacular backdrop. He would know the good and bad points of every horse that went by. He would be dressed in cavalry twill trousers, waterproof jacket and leather boots gleaming brown. Uppermost in Vincent's mind would be the well-being of each horse, but also he would be thinking about their next race and the best tactics to win. He used to have tactical sessions with his jockeys, whether it be a jump or flat race. His talks with Lester Piggott and Pat Taaffe would leave no detail unturned.

As he passed his 70th birthday in 1987, Vincent O'Brien had already started to plan for the future of Ballydoyle. It was hoped that his younger son Charles would take over so he was sent to Australia and the USA to look at their techniques. The eldest son David, is a trainer in his own right and has won classic races with Assert and Secreto – the latter defeated his father's horse El Gran Senor in the Derby of 1984. Charles finally took over in 1993; in the years 1987-93 Vincent O'Brien continued to have his successes, but no classic winners. Charles ran the stables between 1993 and 1995 before Aidan O'Brien inherited the keys to the Ballydoyle stables. A.P. O'Brien is no relative of the Vincent O'Brien family but is a worthy successor and has already established himself as the leading trainer in Ireland and possibly in Europe. ▪

The 1990s and early 2000s continue to bring success to the Irish racing industry. There have been many horses that have given great pleasure to their jockeys, trainers, owners, spectators and, of course, the bookmakers. To mention just a few: Danoli, the popular hurdler-chaser trained by Tom Foley retired at the end of the century. He won 17 of his 32 starts and was the top-rated novice over hurdles in the 1993/94 season. His big race wins included the 1994 Sun Alliance Novices Hurdle at the Cheltenham festival, two Martell Aintree Hurdles and the Hennessy Cognac Gold Cup at Leopardstown in 1997. Two previous winners, Jodami and Imperial Call, finished second and third respectively in that 1997 race. However, perhaps his greatest achievement was coming third to Collier Bay in the Irish Championship Hurdle since it was his first race since fracturing a fetlock.

Looks Like Trouble, bred in Scava, Northern Ireland, but trained in England by Noel Chance won the James Nicholson Champion Chase against two of my favourite horses: Doran's Pride and Florida Pearl in November 2000. Doran's Pride has won 30 races and over half a million pounds whilst Florida Pearl has won nine races and £440,000 and is regarded as Ireland's top chaser. He is a fine big upright old-fashioned type of chaser but he will find it hard to reverse the result of the 2000 Gold Cup when he was beaten by Looks Like Trouble. Florida Pearl is trained by Willie Mullins, the son of Paddy Mullins and is perhaps the most accomplished of Ireland's new generation of trainers. He also has Alexander Banquet in his yard, which was unlucky to come second to Lord Noelie in the Royal and Sun Alliance Chase at Cheltenham in March 2000. The year 1996 saw two Irish horses, Collier Bay and Imperial Call win the Champion Hurdle and Gold Cup respectively.

Aidan O'Brien has had a string of top-class flat race horses at his Ballydoyle stables including of course, Giant's Causeway, Ciro, Toroca, Mozart, Minardi, Endless Summer, Hemmingway, King Charlemagne, Galileo, Imagine, Black Minnaloushe, Rock of Gibralter (owned by Sir Alec Ferguson, Manchester United's manager), Landseer, Tendulkar, Milan, Sophisticat, Mozart and Castle Gandolfo.

The last year of the century was to see a fairytale victory by an Irish horse in the Martell Grand National held on the 10th April 1999 at Aintree, Liverpool. Bobbyjo, so named after its owners Bobby and Jo Burke, won by ten lengths from Blue Charm. Bobbyjo started the race at 10-1, having been 50–1 three weeks prior to the race and 22–1 on the morning of the race but money in Ireland and in England particularly north London, made Bobbyjo a well-backed horse and one of the fancied horses for the race. Omens were promising; Bobbyjo had won the Irish Grand National in 1998 at Fairyhouse. He had plenty of support including ten coach-loads of regulars from Bobby Burke's chain of pubs in north London and the horse had an impeccable Irish background.

Bobby Burke was in County Galway in the West of Ireland near Mullaghmore, the place of his birth, to play golf with his friend Liam Shehan, a local accountant. Later in the pub and after a few jars, Bobby Burke was persuaded to buy six horses, 'I can't remember how much I paid' – one of which was Bobbyjo. This later was to prompt the story, 'Did you hear about the Irishman who went to the pub and bought a horse'. Bobbyjo was reared on Bobby Burke's brother, Eugene's farm in County Galway and then handed over to Tommy Carberry for him to train in Ratoath, Co Meath near Dublin. Bobbyjo was in good hands; Tommy Carberry, a trainer since 1980, was the last jockey to win a Grand National on an Irish horse. In 1975, riding L'Escargot, trained by his father-in-law Dan Moore, he beat the great Red Rum. The family connection continued, Bobbyjo was ridden at work by Tommy's wife, Pamela and daughter Nina, and a son Philip won a two-mile hurdle on Bobbyjo, but it was the elder son Paul who was to have the ride in the Grand National.

Paul Carberry is an outstanding jockey, taller but similar in style to his father and like his father, he likes to enjoy himself. However, on the eve of the Grand National of 1999, he was

ABOVE ▪ 1999 Grand National. The celebrations start; Paul Carbery leads Bobbyjo, with police escort, into the winner's enclosure.

ABOVE ■ Celebrations continued from the Adelphi Hotel, Liverpool to Hawthorn's Bar in Co Galway via Rory's in Ratoath and here Bobby Burke and Bobbyjo are outside Keary's Lounge.

in bed by 9.00 pm The next day, 49,000 spectators witnessed Paul Carberry with a memorable ride on Bobbyjo, win the 1999 Aintree Grand National. 'He's big and bold and he's a fantastic jumper. He cleared Becher's (arguably the toughest jump) at Aintree without even touching it', said Paul and his father Tommy said, 'This was a prouder moment than when I was a jockey'. Celebrations at the Adelphi Hotel in Liverpool continued until 5.00 am. Fifteen friends had flown in from Co Meath and 19 jockeys, including Charlie Swan, flew over that night to join the party. 'We gave it a fair old craic', said Paul. Lorcan Wyer on the runner-up Blue Charm summed up the race by saying 'I had a look round and saw the wizard – Paul Carberry – and he just whizzed by me'. The craic continued in Ronny's Bar, Ratoath, Co Meath and Hawthorn's bar in Mountbellow, Co Galway and in Bobby Burke's pubs in north London for many days. Paul Carberry's comment, 'I don't think I'll be going home for a week,' was confirmed!

But the year 2000 was a landmark year for Irish racing. Papillon, Giant's Causeway, Istabraq and Sinndar were the horses that won the glory; a neat division between flat and jump racing. On Saturday 8th April, 2000 Papillon, trained by Ted Walsh at Greenhills, near Naas, Co Kildare and ridden by his son Ruby, won the Martell Grand National at Aintree for Ireland. Quite extraordinarily, it was Ireland's second successive Grand National and equally extraordinarily, an Irish father and son combination had won. It was just as amazing that the winning team comprised a horse subjected to one of the most dramatic gambles in national history. For much of the week prior to the race and up to the Friday, odds of 40-1 could be got from the bookmakers; on the day, Papillon was to start at 10-1. My visit to the local bookmakers early on the Saturday, offered 28-1 and that was where my modest each-way bet went. The winning team also comprised a teetotal Irish trainer and his accident-prone young son having his first ride in the race. To complete the team was a female American owner whose wealth was matched only by her anxiety over the perils of Aintree.

ABOVE ■ Papillon and Bobbyjo winners of the 2000 and 1999 Martell Grand National. Mrs. J. Maxwell Moran (the owner), Ted Walsh (the trainer) with Papillon and Ruby Walsh (the jockey) and Bobbyjo with Paul Carberry (the jockey) and Bobby Burke (the owner) and Tommy Carberry (the trainer) at the Royal Dublin Society showgrounds at Balls Bridge before the Nations Cup Competition, 2000.

However, Papillon was the right age: nine years old and carried an attractive weight. Ruby Walsh might be only 20 but in the previous year he had been Ireland's champion jockey in his first year as a professional with 96 winners. By the time of the National, Ruby had recovered from his injuries of a broken collar bone and a leg which he broke twice but, above all, he had a wisdom and maturity beyond his years. His father Ted had been champion amateur jockey of Ireland eleven times and had won at Cheltenham four times besides training a Cheltenham winner in Commanche Court in the Triumph Hurdle. Papillon and Commanche Court have brought great joy to the family-run, twenty-horse stable. Prince Ri (means Lord of the Dance in Irish) is another bright prospect. Ted Walsh is a loquacious man and good company – his talents are recognised by RTE for whom he commentates. He needed these skills to calm Papillon's owner Mrs. Betty Moran when she arrived by Concorde from America.

The memory of the race will be Ruby Walsh in his green silks riding over the line and standing up in the saddle in triumph. It had been a hard race but Papillon had been balanced and soared at jump after jump. His jockey with his long legs and his hands threading and re-threading the reins drove Papillon forward. As he jumped the last fence and the straight run to the finish began, the roar of the crowd unnerved him momentarily. A similar roar in a previous National had caused Devon Loch, the Queen Mother's horse, to makes its phantom leap and lose the race. Mely Moss, ridden by Norman Williamson, was within a length but Papillon recovered and in a sustained duel to the line found reserves of energy and resolve sufficient to triumph. In another coincidence, Williamson and Ted Walsh were brought up in Fermoy, Co Cork where both their fathers were publicans. Bobbyjo was nearly brought down at Becher's Brook but went on gamely to finish eleventh, whilst Micko's Dream owned by the 24 Irish Prison Officers at Portlaoise had fallen at the first and lost many of the inmates their cigarette money. ▪

Giant's Causeway crowned a magnificent year with a defeat in November in the Breeders Cup Class C in Kentucky, USA by Tiznow. Some unkindly blamed Ireland's top jockey, Michael Kinane for allowing the reins to slip while switching his whip to his right hand when 100 yards away from the winning post. The Irish colt renowned for its audacity, bravado and talent had drawn level on the dirt track so much favoured in America but now he faltered. Tiznow was able to regain the advantage and won by a neck. Kinane admitted the mistake but said that it had 'no bearing on the result – the whip just got caught in the rein. If you put it down, he just starts to fade. I put it down just to switch it. I thought the winner was stronger in the closing stages. My horse had given everything. He ran his heart out.' He never flinched in an epic duel and in defeat emerged with his reputation enhanced. Giant's Causeway will now be retired, aged three, after a really glittering career and this son of Storm Cat is expected will make a great stallion. He will be remembered for his five consecutive Group 1 victories in three

ABOVE ▪ 9th September 2000. Giant's Causeway ridden by Michael Kinane gets ahead of Best of the Bests ridden by Frankie Detori to win the Irish Champion Stakes.

months including two photo finishes over Kalanisi at Sandown and York, his defeat by Observatory at Ascot in the Queen Elizabeth Stakes but again in defeat his reputation was not diminished. The race was only over a mile and made Giant's Causeway vulnerable to a speed horse. Observatory, trained by John Gosden and ridden by Kevin Darley specially for the race, came late and wide and unseen to Giant's Causeway who always preferred the thrill of defeating his rivals in close proximity.

Istabraq, bred for the flat, by Sadler's Wells out of Betty's Secret (the dam of Secreto), which won the 1984 Derby, proved a moderate horse on the flat. Istabraq was purchased for 38,000 guineas by J.P. McManus in 1997 for the jumps. The plan was for John Kurkan, a young promising trainer in England, to look after Istabraq. Fate intervened when Durkan was struck down with leukaemia and Istabraq came to Ireland and to the stables of Aidan O'Brien. He won his first hurdle in December 1997 with Charlie Swan as his jockey. In 2000 Istabraq, by now eight years old, won his third successive Champion Hurdle at Cheltenham. Istabraq owned by J.P. McManus, trained by Aidan O'Brien, ridden by Charlie Swan; this team reads like a Who's Who of Irish racing.

Sinndar was born at the Coolmore Stud, his sire is Grand Lodge and he is owned by the Aga Khan, trained by John Oxx at The Curragh and ridden by Johnny Murtagh – a truly Irish horse and one in whom all Ireland is proud. In the words of the Aga Khan, Sinndar is 'among the best I have seen'. His credentials as a two year-old were sound but unspectacular. It was the year 2000 which was to be Sinndar's annus mirablis. His form at training gallops disguised his immense ability. Basically he was lazy but once in competition his true potential emerged – he had speed, stamina, determination and ability in abundance. These attributes were to carry him to triumph as a three year-old in the three major classics of the European scene; the English Derby at Epsom, the Irish Derby at The Curragh, the Prix de l'Arc de Triomphe at Longchamp. No other horse has ever won these three races in one season.

In the English Derby, Sinndar surged past Satchee ridden by Richard Hills to win narrowly with Bent Hollow third. In the Irish Derby he had a comfortable nine-length victory over the Aidan O'Brien trained pair, Glyndebourne and Ciro. In the Arc de Triomphe the dual with Montjeu never quite materialised. Montjeu, another Irish-bred horse, but by now trained in France at Chantilly by John Hammond, came with a record of 13 races and eleven wins. These included

ABOVE ▧ 14 March 2000 Cheltenham. Charlie Swan celebrates winning the Champion Hurdle on Istabraq.

victories in the French and Irish Derbys and the Prix de l'Arc de Triomphe as a three year-old and as a four year-old unbeaten in four runs. Montjeu was attempting to emulate the achievement of Vincent O'Brien's Alleged (1977 and 78) by winning the Arc in successive seasons. However, Montjeu was left trailing in fourth place – seven lengths adrift with two French trained horses occupying second and third place. Johnny Murtagh, Sinndar's jockey, described the day as 'the greatest of my life'. For Murtagh it was the climax of a great year and the confirmation of a lost soul vibrantly restored.

On the same day, Sunday 1st October 2000 at Longchamp, Murtagh won on Namid for John Oxx and on Petruskka for Sir Michael Stoute the renowned Newmarket trainer. Johnny Murtagh joined Oxx's stables in 1986 as a 16 year-old straight from apprentice school and has remained under Oxx's wing since. The only blip in their relationship came in 1993 – Murtagh had become overweight and drinking had caused his temporary dismissal, but once restored to good health he was quickly reinstated as the No 1 jockey at the stables. His fine qualities, his outstanding horsemanship, his will to win, his calm approach and his good nature could not be allowed to languish. On Saturday 21st October 2000 in the last Group 1 race of the British season, Murtagh riding Dilshaan for Sir Michael Stoute and deputising for the injured Kieren Fallon, won his tenth Group 1 race – an unprecedented achievement. On 5th November he won

ABOVE ■ 2nd July 2000. Johnny Murtagh winning jockey of Sinndar with winning trainer John Oxx, after victory in The Budweiser Irish Derby.

the Breeders Cup Turf on Kalanisi in Kentucky USA – his eleventh Group 1 win. However, in the long-term Murtagh prefers to ride in Ireland, as does Michael Kinane; not for them the English grind and the likes of trainer A.P. O'Brien and John Oxx are unsurpassable. ■

John Oxx runs a 120-horse stable at Creeve, near the Kildare golf club on The Curragh. He took over the stables, bought by his father in 1950, in 1979. John Oxx has become the principal Irish trainer for Sheikh Mohammed and the Aga Khan. In the year of Sinndar's trimphs, Oxx passed his 50th birthday; a man of receding hairline, of almost clerical look and above all a decent, wise and modest man. He is a qualified vet and believes this qualification helps him to understand his horses and pleases his owners. His composed authority and dedication attracted Sheikh Mohammed and the Aga Khan. Since 1988 the Aga Khan has sent 25 yearlings each year to the Creeve Stables where John Oxx, dressed often in cords and workaday sweater, keeps a concerned eye on his horses. He has earned a reputation of a thoroughly professional trainer who runs an impeccable establishment; a calm man with no showmanship and with no affectations but when Sinndar races 'I get a bit anxious'. The previous best horse he trained was the underrated Ridgewood Pearl. She had won the Breeders Cup on heavy ground and broke the course record at Ascot in winning the Coronation Stakes.

What of the future for Sinndar? Should he race on or go to stud? The decision faced by the Aga Khan and his team is not an easy one. They have the examples of Storm Cat, Grand Lodge and the bloodstock market in general to look at. Storm Cat is probably the most sought after stallion by the bloodstock industry. He was not particularly successful on the racetrack nor was he that handsome, but when his first crop of colts and fillies hit the track in the 1990s, it was realised that Storm Cat's progeny could run. They could run at two, three or four years old, they could run long or short, on turf or dirt, in Europe, Japan or America. It was remembered Storm Cat had lost races he should have won, that he had a blistering turn of speed and that he retired prematurely after injury. His stud fee rose from £14,000 to command a fee of £285,000 a time. He is introduced twice a day to the most desirable mares during the four and a half month breeding season. At the last count he had 714 children. The Coolmore stud paid £4.5 million for a Storm Cat colt at the September sales at Keeneland, Kentucky USA and in 1999 his offspring earned £8.5 million on the track.

To conclude as to Storm Cat's potential, he has at least another 12 years in the stud business and his job is safe as the bloodstock industry will not allow artificial insemination, but it is a risky business. Cigar, American bred and raced, who was exceptionally successful on the racetrack proved to be infertile as a stallion. This blow was somewhat lessened by an insurance policy which realised £17.5 million. No policy however, covers a horse that fails to produce a winner.

The bloodstock industry depends on colts like Minardi for whom £1.25 million was paid as a yearling in the USA and who has won races for Michael Tabor. Also there is the danger of injury to the stallion whilst with the mare, to the staff in the breeding shed, of fire and of sabotage as in the case of Shergar. Perhaps above all the Aga Khan and his team will be swayed by the lure to prove Sinndar's true greatness as he moves into a four year-old. Dubai Millenium, Montjeu and Giant's Causeway are already booked for stud duties; horses are for racing and to bring enjoyment to others. John Oxx is a dependable trainer but the decision to send Sinndar to stud has been made.

The Aga Khan succeeded his father, Ali Khan, when his father was killed in a tragic car accident in 1960 in Paris. At first the Aga Khan was not particularly interested in his equine empire in Ireland, but as time went by, a tremendous enthusiasm and energy was fired and now his knowledge and love of horses is exceeded by few. Racing and the bloodstock industry in Ireland owes its undoubted gratitude to the Aga Khan; he is the leading owner and breeder and his daughter Princess Zara has made her home in Ireland. However, none of the Aga Khan's and his Grandfather's nine Derby winners ran beyond their classic season; assets must be realised and there is the example of Sendawar, who was not a success as a four year-old. Recent bloodstock sales in the USA, England and Ireland point to the huge demand for the right bloodstock; for instance at Keeneland, Kentucky, USA, 225 horses changed hands for £66 million. The whole bloodstock industry is enlivened by the intense rivalry between the Tabor/Magnier team at Coolmore with Sheikh Mohammed and the Godolphin team.

In September 2000 the Coolmore Stud paid £3.4 million for a son of Sadler's Wells out of the dam of Grand Lodge, sire of Sinndar. This one, out of Darara, is now named Diaghilev. At the same sale Tabor/Magnier paid two million guineas for the Sadler's Wells half-brother to Grand Lodge who, unusually, was already named Sorcerous — he was an easy winner of his only start to date. Both Grand Lodge and Sadler's Wells stand at Coolmore. Grand Lodge has been regarded as a relatively unfashionable stallion but the policy of mating him to choice mares in both the northern and southern hemisphere at £10,000 a go has worked well. One of his progeny won the Australian Derby and using him in both hemispheres has increased his breeding output. Sadler's Wells charges £150,000 for his favours. Due in large part to Sinndar's successes Grand Lodge's fee for 2001 was raised to 35,000 Irish guineas. His fee for 2002 is private. The breeding rights to Grand Lodge for the southern hemisphere season are owned by John Messara and he stands at the Arrowfield Stud. Sadler's Wells' fees for 2002 are also private, but will be considerably above the £150,000 previously mentioned.

The Coolmore Stud was established in 1975 with a partnership which consisted of international owner and breeder Robert Sangster with Vincent O'Brien as trainer and John Magnier as stallion master. They took over a 350-acre existing stud with the objective of creating a world-class stallion operation. In 2000, Coolmore stallions sired over 150 Group winners worldwide and in 2001 there were over 50 stallions under Coolmore management on five continents (Europe, Japan USA, South America and Australia). In Ireland, the Coolmore team is led by John Magnier and Michael Tabor with Aidan O'Brien as trainer and the stud has over 20 stallions under its control, the latest recruits being Giant's Causeway, Montjeu and Monasheee Mountain. It is probably the pre-eminent stallion station in the world. ■

The racing season 2001 has continued the trend of Irish successes, perhaps not with the outstanding achievements of 2000 but the special atmosphere and excitement associated with Irish racing has again been prevalent. It appeared as if Istabraq would be thwarted in his preparations for a fourth win at Cheltenham by the bad weather at Leopardstown for the Christmas Festival; already he was an odds-on favourite to win his fourth Champion Hurdle. The Leopardstown Festival took place – Istabraq fell. Was this the end of the great Istabraq? Clearly the bookmakers did not think so and he was installed as odds-on favourite for the Irish Champion Hurdle, to be held again at Leopardstown in January 2001. This time there was no mistake. Was this to be the prelude to his fourth Champion Hurdle? The abandonment of the Cheltenham Festival due to the foot and mouth removed this possibility for 2001.

ABOVE ■ Aidan O'Brien gives some words of encouragement to some of his horses in training.

Istabraq fell again in April at Leopardstown and again at the last hurdle. Once more doubts were raised as to whether he would have won at Cheltenham, however the intention was to race Istabraq, now ten years old, in the Champion Hurdle in 2002. Would the brilliant but fragile and ferociously complicated Istabraq win in 2002? Istabraq did run in 2002 but was pulled up early in the race and has been retired, to live in memory, as one of Ireland's sporting heroes.

To continue the racing season of 2001, Papillon was unexpectedly allowed to run in the Grand National at Aintree and finished fourth. Giant's Causeway and Sinndar are no longer racing but Irish racing continues to be a dominant force. Aidan O'Brien is firmly established as Ireland's leading trainer. What qualities had John Magnier, the landlord at Ballydoyle and sponsor of O'Brien, recognised before giving Aidan O'Brien the keys of Ballydoyle 'He was winning lots of races'. He has continued to win a phenomenal number of races. On the breeding side the stallions at The Coolmore Stud, Grand Lodge and Sadler's Wells, are world renowned. Mick Kinane, O'Brien's No. 1 retained jockey, is spoilt for choice. He came third in both the Irish 2000 and 1000 Guineas on Minardi and Toroca respectively behind Johnny Murtagh whose run of good fortune continued from the 2000 season, with rides on the less favoured of the O'Brien horses, Imagine. In the Oaks, Kinane made no such error and rode Imagine to victory over Flight of Fancy, who was bidding to give the Queen a first classic since 1977 and Relish the Thought; all three horses were sired by Sadler's Wells.

At Royal Ascot another twist in the Johnny Murtagh and Mick Kinane rivalry had occured. Murtagh, the builder's son from Co Meath and the jockey with the errant past confirmed that his successes of 2000 were no flash in the pan and that a sunny, open personality was his true personality, by being the leading jockey with five winners. One of Murtagh's winners was again, Black Minnaloushe, a Storm Cat sired horse. Mick Kinane was eighth on Minardi, which Aidan O'Brien had asked him to ride. Another Murtagh winner had been Sahara Slew, owned by Lady O'Reilly, the wife of Sir Tony O'Reilly and trained by John Oxx. Grand Lodge may be the more unfashionable stallion but he sired Sand Mason who won the Hardwicke Stakes over 1 mile and 4 furlongs at the meeting.

In the Derby, Kinane was in the saddle of Galileo, whose sire was, again Sadler's Wells who previously had no Derby winner on his c.v. Galileo's time for the 1 mile, 4 furlong race was the second fastest in the history of the race. 'It was a race I could really enjoy, because I was always in control,' said Mick Kinane. 'When we quickened, unless something had got wings, they were not going to pick me up.' Golan, trained by Sir Michael Stoute, trainer of Shergar in 1981, was a gallant second. Victory in the Irish Derby followed. In the King George VI and Queen Elizabeth Diamond Stakes run at Ascot, Galileo had another brilliant win. This time Fantastic

ABOVE ■ 20th April 2001. Istabraq ridden by Charlie Swan falls at the Leopardstown Races.

Light ridden by Frankie Dettori gave Galileo a real battle: a furlong out from home it seemed as if Fantastic Light would win, for about a hundred yards the two horses raced neck and neck; Kinane had to crack Galileo's quarters six times with the whip in his left hand and this with the horse's strength and determination led to a two-length victory.

Mick Kinane might never have had the ride – the Irish Turf Club had banned him for careless riding. In an audacious move he obtained in the Irish High Court an interim injunction which allowed him to race in the Diamond Stakes. Somewhat ironically if Mick Kinane had missed the ride, his substitute would have been Johnny Murtagh. Galileo's ultimate goal for the 2001 season was the ten furlong Breeders Cup Classic at Belmont Park. It had been expected that Point Given, the outstanding American three year-old horse, trained by Bob Baffert and ridden by Garry Stevens and Galileo would fight out the race and give the Ballydoyle team a chance to revenge Giant's Causeway's defeat in the race in 2000. But the unpredictability of racing won the day. Point Given was retired to stud; it was regarded as too great a risk to chance a damaged suspendory tendon for a potentially lucrative breeding career. And at Leopardstown in the Irish Champions Stakes run over ten furlongs, Galileo lost his unbeaten record by a head to Fantastic Light. Suddenly the wisdom of running over ten furlongs and on a dirt track began to be

ABOVE ■ 26th May 2001. Black Minnaloushe with Johnny Murtagh after winning The Irish 2000 Guineas.

questioned. In the event Tiznow won the Breeders Cup again, from Fantastic Light ridden by Frankie Dettori and Galileo finished out of the places. ■

I wanted to end this chapter with an insight into the working life and a career of a young bloodstock agent. Johnny McKeever lives in Newmarket, England; he has followed his father Peter into the bloodstock industry, thus furthering the family tie-up which is so prevalent in Irish racing. It was Tuesday 12th December 2000 that I found myself driving into Newmarket. You know you are in racing country. 'It only comes truly alive on race days and when the sales at Tattersalls, Houghtons are on,' says McKeever.

After leaving Trinity College, Dublin, Johnny McKeever worked on various stud farms in America, Ireland and England. In 1985 he joined The Curragh Bloodstock Agency, working first with David Minton at Newmarket and then with Paul Webber, who is now a noted National Hunt racehorse trainer. However, in 1990 with the bloodstock industry facing economic problems, he was made redundant. This led to the formation with his wife, Susie, of the Johnny McKeever Bloodstock

Agency. The bloodstock market started to improve in the early 1990s and the reputation in the industry of his father, Peter particularly in Ireland, helped establish a reasonable business.

In 1995 Harry McCalmont, Chairman of The Curragh Bloodstock Agency, bought the McKeever Bloodstock Agency and Johnny found himself working once again for the CBA. In August 2000 McCalmont bought the McKeever shares and indeed all the shareholders' holdings in the CBA and Johnny left and set up a new agency in Newmarket with Oliver Gatesford St Lawrence, called McKeever St Lawrence. The new agency has gone well. Public auctions of bloodstock have become bigger in recent years. Johnny told me that he spends about half his working life attending auctions in Britain, Ireland, France or America and even as far afield as Australia and Hong Kong. Attending auctions is both competitive and time-consuming. The large agencies, such as the British Bloodstock Agency and the CBA are competing with many individual agents who advise clients on the selection and purchase of bloodstock. Gone is the day, as in Peter McKeever's time, when the bloodstock agent dealt with trusted stud farms with whom there had been established a friendly relationship.

The racing season 2000 was a successful one; yearlings were purchased for some major trainers in England, including Brian Meehan, an Irishman who trains at Lamborne. Bad As I Wanna Be was purchased for an American called Joe Allbritton and won a Group 1 race in France – the Prix Morny, which is the first Group 1 race of the year for two year-olds. It was Johnny McKeever's first Group 1 winner and coincidentally it was related on the female side of the family, to Right Tack, who was his father's first Group 1 winner. Johnny said: 'When I first started buying on behalf of clients in the middle '80s, I was confined more or less to National Hunt horses. I bought a number of fairly decent ones, some for trainers such as David Nicholson and Jenny Pitman who were at the top of their careers. However I slowly drifted away from the National Hunt racing business side of things and became more and more orientated to the flat mainly through the necessity to make money when I started the Johnny McKeever Bloodstock Agency. The reason being that the jumping industry is fairly one denominational in that it is purely horses that are bought and sold for racing; the breeding side of it is very much a secondary part. Whereas with flat racing you have the opportunities, not just for buying racehorses, but also for buying breeding stock and stallions which gives you three dimensions. Flat racing stock is worth, on a global basis, an awful lot more than jumping stock. This is where my interests now lie.'

Johnny went on about the life of a bloodstock agent. He obviously loves the life; it involves visiting stud farms, seeing training stables, visiting clients all over the world and spending a lot of time at race meetings but it is a seasonal life. Thus it's Cheltenham in March, Newmarket in

April and May, Royal Ascot in June, Goodwood in July, French yearling sales in August and then to the sales which could mean Kentucky, USA or Melbourne, Australia. A bloodstock agent meets many interesting characters; often they are wealthy such as Joe Allbritton, who is Chairman of Riggs Bank, the largest private bank in the USA and owns a stud farm in Virginia, or Edward St George who is Chairman of the Bahamas Port Authority. He has bought a number of yearlings for Johnny or Paul Roy of Merrill-Lynch or the Arab princes who are racing fanatics. Perhaps, though, the most rewarding is the one horse that is bought for the lawyer, doctor, schoolteacher or small syndicate that wins and gives such pleasure.

Johnny finished by telling me that his brother, Andrew, was also heavily involved with horses. 'Andrew worked as an assistant trainer in England, firstly for Oliver Sherwood who trained jumpers and then for Peter Walwyn who trained horses for the flat – his best horse was Grundy. Andrew then moved to America where he worked for Neil Drysdale, perhaps America's most famous trainer, and Bill Shoemaker, the well-known jockey who after a major accident was left paralyzed from the neck down. He is currently a racehorse trainer at Churchill Downs, Kentucky.' The McKeevers are an Irish racing family.

Irish racing? I think it is the craic for the likes of me: the companionship, the thrill of the race. The expertise and class is there; outstanding horses and jockeys, dedicated and gifted trainers, knowledgeable bloodstock agents, interested owners, honest bookmakers and fanatical spectators. Ireland has all of this. Once in the blood, racing seems to grip a family and go from grandfather to father, from son to brother, from wife to daughter.

These pages applaud not only those families like the O'Briens, the Walshs, the McKeevers, the Oxxs, the Mullins, the Taaffes, the Swans, the Carberrys, the Molonys, the Robinsons and so the list could go on, but also all who have contributed to Irish racing.

Michael Bowler has spent most of his life involved with motor racing – as a driver, as a collector of classic cars and as a journalist including editor of Motor Magazine and Classic Cars. He was Historic Cars of the 1950s and 1960s European Champion in the early 1980s. He has worked in Milan at Zagato (1987-89) and in Milton Keynes for Yamaha (1990-93) where he was General Manager as part of the development team; later he was a director of Aston Martin. He is currently chairman of the FAI Historic Committee and is re-writing the rules for historic cars. ∎

The editor reflects: It was R.M. Foster (St Columba's, Dublin, pre-First World War) and his friend, McDonald Hobley, the BBC commentator, who roused my interest in motor sports. My 'Uncle Rex' and the Board at Cheshire Car Circuits developed Oulton Park into a fine racetrack. Motor racing and motor cycling to me meant Mike Hawthorn, Stirling Moss, Fangio, Geoff Duke, Old Hall Corner, the Cascades and Esso Bend.

I was brought up with motor cars. My father used to race at Brooklands with a 3-litre Bentley before the war. After that, he was a leading light in the Vintage Sports-Car Club, so I went to all their events from the forties onwards. Since then, motoring and motor sport has been my life, through motoring journalism into the industry – Aston Martin and Yamaha – and back to journalism. I only caught up with motorcycling in the seventies, so readers of this chapter will have to forgive the 4-wheeled bias.

My Irish connection is, at best, tenuous. My uncle, Sir Ian Maclennan, was the British Ambassador in Dublin 1959-64 in the days when this was the preserve of the Commonwealth Relations Office. I attended a Dublin Horse Show or two and sundry related liquid-fuelled functions during that period. It was a time of relative peace, but Sir Ian still had a couple of portly minders who accompanied him everywhere regardless of their suitability for the job in hand on the day. He was a noted cross-country runner, which included surmounting such obstacles as impenetrable country hedges, ideally suited to catching the triggers of holstered weaponry; it was his insistence that guns were not to be worn by the perspiring guardians however far behind they lagged. In the end they just stopped following as long as he promised to return to their car. Based at Glencairn, the ambassadorial residence in Sandyford, 6 miles south of central Dublin, he played golf at nearby Carrickmines; what elements of my swing that are still traceable are due to the professional there.

It was only when I was editing Classic Car magazine that I returned to Ireland; August 1978 was the 50th anniversary of the first Ards TT but I went over for the preview in June. We were taken round the old Newtownards course and royally entertained at one of the many pubs overlooking the old circuit, after which I was driven up Craigantlet hill-climb by Ian Titterington, the cousin of Jaguar racer Desmond. It was then that I appreciated that freedom of the roads which has shaped Irish motor sport throughout the 20th century.

ABOVE ▦ Paddy Hopkirk, who had great success on the road and track, is seen here in his finest hour winning the 1964 Monte Carlo Rally in a Mini-Cooper.

It is small wonder that it is motorcycling has produced the greatest Irish impact on world motor sport over the years. From Stanley Woods to Joey Dunlop, the two-wheeled Grand Prix scene has had more than its fair share of Irish riders since the twenties. The Irish advantage has been that it has always been possible to close public roads for motor sport – tight, narrow country lanes that demand a high degree of skill to stay alive; this has produced a breed of road racers that have been very much at home on the European race circuits.

This freedom of the public highway also helped the rally drivers in the past in the days before rough tracks and forestry roads became the norm for world championship rallying. Ronnie Adams and Paddy Hopkirk starred on the road rallies of Europe in the fifties and sixties. But the reliance on road-racing has worked against the four-wheeled racers of today. After the 1955 Le Mans disaster, when motor racing became almost universally confined to closed tracks with ever-increasing safety measures, Ireland was ill-prepared. They had two tracks in Phoenix Park and Kirkistown and no handy Second World War airfields ripe for conversion. Now, only the latest, Mondello Park which opened in 1968, is up to staging international car events.

ABOVE ▪ Ireland's foremost Grand Prix driver John Watson (left) presents a golfing trophy to Michael Bowler, the author of this chapter.

While Irish motor racing can provide as good a grounding as anywhere, budding stars have to leave its shores to climb the rest of the ladder before they stand a chance of international acceptance. Irish motor cyclists were more fortunate as the old road circuits have continued to be used for two-wheeled sport. But there is no shortage of enthusiasm and determination amongst the four-wheeled racers as the successes of John Watson and Eddie Irvine, Ireland's most famous Grand Prix stars, bear rich testimony. ▦

ON FOUR WHEELS

World motor sport (the four-wheeled variety) is controlled by the Federation Internationale de l'Automobile (FIA) because it was the Automobile Club de France (ACF) who first started to organise international motor racing with agreed competition formulae in 1906. To control the sport, the FIA runs the many different commissions who create the international rules for the various motor sport disciplines – broadly, racing and rallying. National bodies and their affiliated clubs run events within an overall FIA framework to these rules or adopt their own. Any country that has a motor sporting interest is represented on the World Motor Sport Council of the FIA.

In Great Britain it is the Royal Automobile Club and in Southern Ireland, the Royal Irish Automobile Club (RIAC). Before Edward VII granted the royal handle in 1907, the RAC was the Automobile Club of Great Britain and Ireland, founded in 1897. The Irish Automobile Club was formed as a separate entity in 1901, becoming the RIAC in 1918, in honour of the club's war efforts. From 1922, Northern Irish motor sport has been controlled by the Royal Automobile Club in England and Southern Irish events are run under the RIAC, although border crossing is taken for granted.

Ireland can trace its motor sporting history back to 1901 when the Irish Automobile Club ran a 1000-mile tour. However the first motoring competition in Ireland was the 1903 Gordon Bennett Trophy. In 1902, this international contest had been a part of the Paris-Vienna race; it was won by S.F. Edge's Napier. The rules stated that the defending champion's country (the British Isles) had to organise the following year's event. The law didn't allow racing on the public highways of the mainland but the Irish MPs pressed hard for it and the event was finally run in July 1903 over a figure-of-eight course in Leinster. Starting from Ballyshannon, the first loop headed clockwise from Kilcullen to Carlow and back to Athy and Ballyshannon then the second loop went anti-clockwise through Kilcullen, Monasterevan, Ballydavis and Athy – three of one loop, four of the other to make a total 327 miles; it was won by Jenatzy's Mercedes at 49.2 mph, an impressive speed on the poorly surfaced roads of the day.

Competitor Charles Jarrott wrote of practice for the event: 'There was one thing we found out very quickly, and that was that the high roads in Ireland were used more or less as farmyards for the breeding of chickens and other birds and beasts. The result was that the greatest care had to be exercised to prevent disaster occurring; occasionally, however, all the skill in the world would not prevent an unfortunate chicken being run over. We always made a rule on these occasions to find out the owner and recompense him or her for the loss. On no occasion did we find the owner displeased; a price was put on the bird, you paid your money, the owner retained the carcass, and you went on your way – if not rejoicing, at least satisfied that you had done the right thing. After this became known it was extraordinary to notice the increased number of chickens on the road. I do not suggest that they were turned out purposely, but the fact remains. The increased number was balanced to a certain extent by the increased intelligence displayed, as the chickens after a time seemed to understand that the proper thing to do was to clear out quickly when a car appeared in sight.' This event was followed by an 'Irish Fortnight'. The first ever Irish speed trials were held two days after the Gordon Bennett in Phoenix Park; two French Mors beat the French Panhard of Hon Charles Rolls (Royce's other half). Two hill-climbs followed. Rolls won at Killorglin, near Killarney but was beaten by Campbell-Muir's Mercedes at Ballybannon, Co Down. Hill-climbs were to become a major feature of Irish motor sport over the ensuing years.

A consequence of the Gordon Bennett races was to have a considerable effect on Irish racing some 20 years later with the arrival of the Tourist Trophy. James Gordon-Bennett, proprietor of the New York Herald, had followed the Continental inter-city races of 1894-99 with considerable interest and offered the ACF a trophy for an annual international contest between national clubs. These were represented by a team of three cars of which every component had been made in that country. Each would have national colours, ascribed as white for Germany, red for America, yellow for Belgium and blue for France; the British weren't represented in the first year, but when Charles Jarrott borrowed a Panhard for the 1901 Paris-Berlin race, the French had painted it dark green (a lucky colour for them) to counteract the fact that he had been given No 13 to wear on the car. Green then became the British national colour – British Racing Green. Of the other colours red was annexed by Italy, so America became blue and white and Germany adopted silver when Mercedes had to take the paint off at a thirties race to get under a weight limit. ▪

After 1904 the Gordon Bennett races were falling out of favour as the French in particular wanted to run more cars in the actual event and thus do away with the need for eliminating trials – the British had used the Isle of Man for these. While the 1905 event took place, the French went their own way and ran the first Grand Prix in 1906. But the British preferred to see contests between regular touring cars, so they instituted the Tourist Trophy in 1905, run in the Isle of Man until 1914 and then on a single occasion in 1922, after which it lapsed. It was due to Harry Ferguson, tractor magnate and 4-wheel-drive exponent that it was revived and taken to Northern Ireland for 1928. Although events were run on closed roads before, this had to be formally recognised in 1922 when the separate parliaments passed appropriate laws; Harry Ferguson had lobbied strongly for this in Stormont. Born in Ulster in 1884, Ferguson was an early racing driver and had won the inaugural Craigantlet hill-climb in 1913. It was Ferguson who set the wheels in motion for the Ulster government to approach the RAC; the TT duly ran on the 13.7-mile Ards circuit (Dundonald - Newtownards - Comber) from 1928 to 1936 when a car skidded into the crowd at Newtownards and eight people died. Two more races were then held on the closed circuit at Donington Park in England before the war. While the RAC remained the organisers of the TT, the Ulster Automobile Club took over the running of other events in the six counties.

Meanwhile the Irish Free State had run its own races. Encouraged by the success of the TT, the RIAC organised the Irish Grand Prix for sports cars from 1929-31 in Phoenix Park; these consisted of two 300 mile races for the Eirann cup for big engine sizes and the Saorstat cup for engines up to 1.5-litres. Although the races were well supported by international entrants, the RIAC lost money on them so they abandoned race organisation and ceded control to the Irish Motor Racing Club. The IMRC ran Grands Prix for racing cars in cooperation with the townships of Cork (1936-8), Limerick (1935-6), and national races with Tallaght (Leinster Trophy), Bray and Phoenix Park.

After the war, racing started again in 1946 at Ballyclare with the Ulster Trophy which then used Dundrod until 1955; it became quite a popular non-championship Formula 1 event in the 1950-54 period. Cork's Carrigrohane circuit (1954-55) had a few races too and the army barracks at The Curragh (1949-54) saw Stirling Moss take HWM's first international victory in 1951. Ulster managed to recapture the TT from 1950-55 but over the 7.4-mile Dundrod circuit (Rushyhill - Leathemstown - Cochranstown - Jordan's Cross - Tornagrough). Bobby Baird, Joe Kelly, Desmond and Ian Titterington, Cecil Vard and Dickie Odlum were just some of the Irish drivers who were to take part during the six years alongside such motor racing greats as Moss, Fangio and Hawthorn.

The TT became part of the World Sports Car Championship for 1953, 1954 and the 50th anniversary event in 1955; sadly that was the swansong. John Mayers' Cooper, which he was sharing with Jack Brabham, crashed and caught fire killing the driver; it was probably the high banks that hid the disaster from oncoming drivers but six more cars were involved and Bill Smith also died. Occurring in the wake of the terrible June 1955 Le Mans accident in which a number of spectators were killed when a car flew into the crowd, this marked the end of the open road TTs. It was the last truly international open road race in Ireland too, although the 100-mile Leinster Trophy continued as a handicap race for a few more years in Wicklow and from 1958, at Dunboyne. I well remember escaping from the rigours of polite conversation on horses and watching the whole 70 minutes of the 1962 event from half-way up a tree overlooking a railway bridge – it was won by Bobby Olthoff's Austin-Healey.

Although the 2.1-mile Phoenix Park circuit in Dublin continued to be used for many years it is now only suited for historic car racing as it does not have the full panoply of modern safety features. Ireland's only other closed circuit at that time was Kirkistown in Cloughey, Co Down, tucked away on the Ards Peninsula. This 1.5-mile ex-airfield circuit is owned by the 500 Motor Racing Club of Ireland; the club was founded in 1948 based on the old 500 cc Formula 3 cars. They have moved with the times progressing through the 1959-64 Formula Junior to Formula Ford and Formula Atlantic. They have had Ford special clubman cars and international Formula 3 events too. People like Paddy Hopkirk, John Crosslé, John Watson, Tommy Reid, John and Jay Pollock, Eddie Jordan, Derek Daly, Michael Roe, Kenny Acheson, Brian Nelson cut their track teeth on this little circuit; some went on to bigger things abroad, others stayed at home to become local household names. Another race circuit was set up at Bishopscourt, Co Down but this was only operational in the sixties. A fourth circuit came along in 1968. Mondello Park near Naas was just 1.24-miles long when it was opened but can now offer 1.14, 1.73 or 2.16 mile laps. Since then it has hosted many international events. It has all the usual paraphernalia of a modern circuit with a racing school and facilities for corporate entertainment. Under its new management headed by Martin Birrane it will be developed further and nurture many more Irish racing drivers. However, closed public roads can still be used for sprint hill-climbs which helps to relieve the pressure on the two circuits. There are nine venues in the south, of which six make up the annual RIAC Hill Climb Championship and eight in the north, of which Craigantlet is still used for the RAC Hill Climb Championship.

Ireland has Midget racing too. In England, Midget racing is buried within the overall ambit of stock-car racing and Ireland, too, has stock-car racing, but the Midget Racing Car Club of Ireland (MRCCI) stands on its own, affiliated to the RIAC. To quote the RIAC rule book: 'The Midget Racing Car Club of Ireland was formed in 1936 by Dudley Colley, Count Cyril McCormack, Cyril Murray, George Reddy and Leo Manthorpe. They were a group of well respected gentlemen in the motor and horse trade and one of their main ideals was to keep the sport inexpensive… they enjoyed many seasons racing in front of large crowds on cinder surfaced tracks in Raheny, Santry, Chapelizod, Portmarnock and Shelbourne Park… After the war a son of one of the founder members returned from the USA with a Bantam car. This was quickly adopted for Midget Car Racing and with a group of already organised competitors from Co Wicklow the basics were laid for the sport as we know it today.'

The original cinder tracks disappeared in post-war industrial development and the sport moved to compete on grass which is how it survives today. All the cars use rear wheel drive which ensures the classic tail-sliding driving technique that is a feature of this form of sport worldwide. Front engines can be as big as 1200 cc but rear engines are limited to the 850 cc Mini. These are mounted in a single-seater car which is shorter than a Mini; just a 6ft wheelbase and a maximum length of 9ft. The MRCCI holds some 8 meetings a year between April and September and there is also a Junior championship.

However the majority of the Irish motor sporting calendar and by far the greatest number of RIAC licence holders are involved with rallying of one sort or another. World rallying dashes around the Finnish forests, the rough roads of Africa and public roads in countries where this is allowed; each rally has slow road sections and flat-out special stages. Until the RAC came to an agreement with the Forestry Commission to use the Scandinavian-style forest tracks, the major UK rallies had to make do with private roads on stately home estates, ex-War Department property or the fringes of established race circuits. British drivers were poorly prepared for the international scene until the forests became available.

Because Ireland can close road sections, drivers such as Ronnie Adams (fifties), Paddy Hopkirk and Rosemary Smith (sixties), Cahal Curley, Adrian Boyd and Billy Coleman (seventies), Bertie Fisher (eighties) became expert on this terrain – the tarmac rallies – and competed successfully overseas until the loose surface events predominated. Like mainland UK, Irish rallies, north and south, are divided into three categories, Forests, Stages (closed roads) and Navigation. Navigation rallies are run against the organiser's route cards which may have map references or arrowed diagrams; the co-driver or navigator has to ensure that each control is visited exactly on time with an overall average speed of no more than 30 mph – a lot harder than it sounds. ▪

The major Irish event has been the Circuit of Ireland, organised by the Ulster Automobile Club under the authority of the Royal Automobile Club. First run in 1931, the Circuit takes three days around the island using closed road sections. Multiple winners from overseas include Russell Brookes (7 times), Roger Clark (three times in a row), Jimmy McRae father of twice world champion Colin while, for the honour of Ireland, Paddy Hopkirk won it five times, and Adrian Boyd and Billy Coleman twice each. It was a round of the British Open

ABOVE ■ Ronnie Adams throws his Jaguar Mk.VII around an Alpine hairpin on his way to victory in the 1956 Monte Carlo Rally, with Irish co-drivers Derek Johnston and Frank Biggar.

Rally Championship during the eighties. Nowadays it is part of the Irish Tarmac Championship which includes four events under the RIAC: Galway, Killarney, Donegal, Munster-with-Cork, plus the Manx rally; all are run over two or three days. Because the venues for UK rallies are so restricted, these Irish Internationals are very popular with the mainland competitors; Russell Brookes won the 1989 Tarmac championship.

Other off-road events are Rallycross, with six racing against each other on grass, tarmac or mixed tracks; Autocross where cars run individually to get a best lap time and Autotests with single runs round pylons against the clock. Winners of the long-standing 15-event RIAC Hewison Autotest Trophy include Cecil Vard (international rally-driver and Le Mans competitor) in 1950 and 1958 and Paddy Hopkirk 1955 and 1957. And for those who like to pit their cars against slippery inclines, there are Sporting Trials. Irish motor sport is certainly rich in variety and enthusiasm. In the north, it is still controlled by the Royal Automobile Club through its subsidiary MSA (Motor Sport Association) and the Royal Irish Automobile Club runs the southern events through MSI (Motor Sport Ireland). ■

FOUR-WHEELED HEROES

So who are Ireland's motor sporting heroes? No one can have a definitive list but those that follow have all achieved a level of recognition on the international stage in world championship racing and rallying. John Watson, born in Belfast in 1946, worked his way through from club racing in an Austin-Healey Sprite into Formula 2 (driving for Belfast's Gerry Kinnane) to Formula 1 by 1973 in a Brabham-Ford driving for Bernie Ecclestone. His first GP win came in 1976 driving a Penske-Ford at Austria. Four more wins came during 1981-83 while he drove for McLaren, including equal second in the Championship to Keke Rosberg in 1982. By the time he retired in 1985 he had competed in 152 GPs and earned 169 championship points – Ireland's senior driver. He is now a motor racing TV commentator and, like many race drivers, also plays golf with just as much intensity as he used to display on the track.

ABOVE ▪ Eddie Irvine from Newtonards has won four Grands Prix for Ferrari but joined the Jaguar Grand Prix team for 2000.

Eddie Irvine from Newtonards, Co Down may well challenge John Watson's record before he hangs up his helmet. Born in 1965, Irvine was a generation on from 'Wattie' so went through the now traditional route of karting, Irish then British Formula Ford racing, Formula 3 to Formula 3000, this last with Eddie Jordan Racing, for whom he finished third in 1990. Not finding a Grand Prix seat he then raced F3000 in Japan, but returned to Jordan in 1993 to join the GP team before going to Ferrari for 1996. He already has more points than Wattie but still only four victories obtained in the Ferrari years; Michael Schumacher's British GP accident allowed Irvine to lead the Ferrari team for the latter half of the 1999 season and he finished second to Mika Hakkinen in the championship. He moved to lead the new Jaguar team in 2000 but they still have some way to go before they have a chance of winning a Grand Prix.

So who was Eddie Jordan, Irvine's mentor? Like many racing team owners, EJ started as a driver himself. Born in 1950 in Dublin, he was the Irish karting champion in 1973; in 1978 he won the Formula Atlantic championships in both north and south Ireland moving on to take part in the 1979 British Formula 3 championship. But he realised he wasn't going to make the Grand Prix grade and formed Eddie Jordan Racing in 1980; Jean Alesi won the British Formula 3 championship for him in 1987 and then the International Formula 3000 in 1989. The team took third in F3000 with Eddie Irvine in 1990 and set up Jordan Grand Prix for 1991. The new Jordan 191 was designed by Gary Anderson (born 1952 near Coleraine, Co Antrim), now back with Jordan after a spell with Jaguar and the first person to drive it was John Watson; Eddie Jordan waves the flag for Ireland whenever he can and there was a fair amount of Irish green on the car in 1991. That year Bertrand Gachot was one of EJ's drivers; the Belgian driver's imprisonment in September for spraying a taxi driver with CS gas the previous year left EJ without a driver for the 1991 Belgian GP, so he drafted in Michael Schumacher from the Mercedes team of young sports-car drivers. Although Schumacher fried the clutch on his debut start he had impressed all by putting the Jordan into seventh place on the grid during practice, after just a handful of shake-down laps the previous week. EJ thought he had this new rising star firmly tied to his team till the end of 1992, but somehow the Benetton team contrived a fresh deal with Mercedes, and Schumacher switched camps for the next race, leaving EJ older and wiser to the ways of Formula 1. 'Welcome to the Piranha Club' said a rival team manager the next day.

Since then progress has been slow but steady and to some extent, dependent on the engine supplier. The first victory came in 1998 when Damon Hill won the Belgian Grand Prix with team-mate Ralf Schumacher second; the engine was a Mugen-Honda. The same engine was also used to power the Jordan team to its best year in 1999, third in the Constructors championship with two GP victories for Heinz-Harald Frentzen. For 2000 and 2001 the team had full Honda backing and took fourth in 2001, a demotion largely because BMW power brought Williams back into the podium frame.

If a near-privateer like Jordan achieves a World Championship title it will be a remarkable feat in these days of major investment by such as Mercedes, Ferrari and BMW, but the impossible doesn't figure in the EJ vocabulary. As he said to journalist Alan Henry in 1991 when the Jordan 191 made its debut: 'It (starting a GP team) was massively high risk. On reflection, I wouldn't even think of doing it again today. It was the craziest risk-taking moment of madness you could consider. It had a tiny chance of survival, tiny.' But he's still there over a decade later. ■

For every star that prospers in Formula 1 there must be a thousand who started racing with a Grand Prix drive as their ultimate goal; that they never got there was often due to finance, the lack of sponsorship, failing to materialise at a critical time or simply that the next stage up was beyond their ability. Some reach the Grand Prix platform but don't impress enough people to stay there; so often they have accepted a drive in an unreliable tail-ender, hoping someone will spot their latent talent, but they never get any chance to shine. Ireland has had its share of near misses; those who go through all the usual ropes but just don't get the right breaks once there.

ABOVE ■ Ken Doherty, Padraig Harrington and Eddie Jordan during the Pro-Am event at the Benson & Hedges International Open held at the Belfry in May 2001.

Derek Daly (born Dundrum in 1953) almost made it. He won the important British F3 championship in 1976, the year James Hunt won the World Championship; his F1 career started in 1978 with Hesketh, the team that had given Hunt his first break, but the team packed up half-way through the season. He switched to tail-ender Ensign for 1978/9 but that team ran short of money too, so he changed again in mid-season to Tyrrell who were going through a bad spell. He drove for March in 1981 and was hardly able to qualify a bad car. He started 1982 with another tail-ender, Theodore, run by Macau-based Teddy Yip and Dubliner Sid Taylor. After half the season, Reutemann retired from Williams and Daly was offered the chance he had been waiting for, a drive in a decent car. Keke Rosberg had also arrived in the Williams team that year and went on to win the championship; although Daly got 8 points (four, fifth places) which put him 13th in the drivers championship, it wasn't enough to keep his seat. He retired from the Grand Prix scene and went to race in America where he was successful in Indy cars and sports machinery. Daly was the classic case of a Formula 1 'nearly-man'. He now lives in Indianapolis and includes a racing school in Las Vegas as one of his business interests.

Curiously Daly's last year in Formula 1 had seen three Irishmen on some of the grids; it was the year that John Watson had come second in the championship in a McLaren. Tommy Byrne (born in Drogheda in 1958) took the Theodore seat vacated by Jan Lammers and Daly. From five attempts in that latter half of 1982, Daly qualified twice and crashed in both of those – too anxious to succeed in an uncompetitive car. Byrne had gone straight into Formula Ford from the Mondello Park racing school and improved each season to take two British Formula Ford 1600 titles in 1980. In 1981 he won the major Formula Ford 2000 championship, the year before Ayrton Senna, working for the championship sponsor, Pace Petroleum. I used to drive the winners round in the back of an Aston Martin and well remember the intense little Irishman. For 1982 he moved on to drive a Formula 3 Anson, did development driving for McLaren but took a wrong turning with Theodore and that was that. Like Daly he went off to race in the USA, where he still lives, working at a race driver's school in Atlanta.

Martin Donnelly from Anderstown, Belfast was another who might have made it to GP stardom. He had won the Irish Formula Ford championship and went on to race for Eddie Jordan in Formula 3 and Formula 3000. He joined Lotus in 1990 just when they had changed engines from the reasonable Judd V-8 to the heavy and unreliable Lamborghini V-12. Although he took one seventh place that wasn't enough to earn any points. Then came the Spanish Grand Prix towards the end of the season and a practice accident left him badly injured. Although he eventually recovered, he didn't race again and went on to form his own team in the grass roots of motor sport – Formula Ford – giving others the chance which he was never able to fulfil. He may even be another Eddie Jordan in the making.

Three more had a brief crack at Formula 1 but always in uncompetitive cars. Damien Magee from Belfast, Scottish Formula Ford 1600 champion in 1970, had a single drive in 1975 in a Williams-Ford. Frank Williams' star had yet to rise and he had a spare seat for the Swedish Grand Prix; Magee finished 14th but then went back to race in Formula 5000. Kenny Acheson (born Cookstown, Co Tyrone in 1957) won the Northern Irish Formula Ford championship with a Crosslé in 1977, won 29 races in England including three championships in 1978. The next two years saw reasonable success in Formula 3 and he went on to Formula 2 for 1981 but an accident in mid-season put him out for the rest of the year. He had a handful of Grand Prix drives for the poorly funded RAM team in 1983 and 1985 but had already established a reputation in Sports Car racing in the USA and Europe. He was part of the Mercedes Group C racing team in 1989, switching to Nissan for 1990.

David Kennedy (born in Sligo 1953) was another to make a more lasting mark in sports cars. After two years of shoestring racing he won the Irish Formula Ford championship in 1974. Over that winter he and Derek Daly went to Australia working 16 hours a day in outback iron ore mines to earn enough money to repay previous racing debts and start with a clean sheet for 1975. Although that wasn't a good season he fared better in 1976; with backing from fellow Irishman John Hynes, he used a converted bus as a base and entered three Formula Ford 1600 championships, winning two British ones and taking second in the European one. Formula 3 for 1977 and 78 saw some results before Sid Taylor entered him in the British Aurora F1 series for 1979 with a Wolf-Ford to get a championship second. That took him into a Shadow seat for the 1980 GP season but the car was uncompetitive and he only qualified once before the team quit in mid-season. After that Kennedy concentrated on sports cars and became lead-driver for the Mazda team racing in Japan and the World Sports Car championship from 1984 to 1991, the year the team finally won the Le Mans 24 hour race. Today he is a Grand Prix commentator for RTE and a director of Mondello Park circuit.

Sports car racing also proved to be the forte of Michael Roe (born 1955 in Naas). Having won the Mondello-based Irish Formula Ford championship, he took off to England to win another Formula Ford championship, then on to America in 1981, where he repeated the feat. There he was up against Michael Andretti, whose father Mario (former World and Indianapolis Champion) was not at all pleased to see his son being beaten by a foreigner. Roe then moved into central seat 5-litre sports cars racing from 1983-85 with Count van der Stratten's team, becoming Can-Am champion in the latter year; he also raced in the Indianapolis-style CART series alongside Jacques Villeneuve. In America's premier sports car IMSA series, he drove a private March GT Prototype and did much of the test-driving for the Nissan team that dominated the series in 1988. For 1989 he continued to drive in America but joined the new

Aston Martin team for the World Sports Car Championship; while this only lasted for a year, Roe made his mark on the world stage and the team finished sixth in the championship. He went back to racing Nissans in the US and at Le Mans 1990 before retiring from racing and returning to Naas. Michael was a good test driver when we were both in the Aston Martin racing team, so I brought him in to help in the development of the Yamaha Grand Prix supercar over 1992 – a sort of racing sports car for the road; sadly it never reached production.

Sports cars and big saloons also appealed to Martin Birrane. Born in Ballina, Co Mayo in 1935, his racing didn't start until 1967, after which he became a successful saloon car racer in England with the big V-8 engined Ford Fairlanes and Mustangs. He had some single-seater drives in the seventies and also ran at Le Mans on 10 occasions, including entering his own Ford C-100 with David Kennedy as one of his co-drivers in 1983. He was also an Irish Land Speed Record holder; this is now held by Brendan O'Mahoney who took a Porsche 962 down the closed Kilcock-Maynooth by-pass (the N7) at an officially-observed 179 mph – probably the only current national record to be taken on public roads!

ABOVE ■ Martin Birrane raced saloon and sports cars in international events; he now owns Mondello Park and Lola Cars and is seen alongside a new Lola.

Martin Birrane set out to be a big business success but got involved in motor racing along the way. Having made his fortune in property he is now very much involved in motoring. In 1987 he bought out the RIAC Consortium's interest in Mondello Park race circuit whose facilities he is now expanding with the added intent of helping young Irish drivers to get to the top; one of his directors is David Kennedy whom he had helped during his racing career. Grand Prix involvement was limited to a brief association with the Pacific team in 1994/95, but Birrane then switched to making cars for others. In 1997 he bought race car manufacturer Lola Cars of Cambridge out of receivership and has returned the company to a thriving business supplying single-seater and sports cars for international racing around the world. Since then he has become involved with the Phoenix consortium that took over Rover Cars from BMW and relaunched the MG marque. It was the combination of these interests that led to the entry of two Lola-MGs at Le Mans in 2001 with two young Irish co-drivers, Kevin McGarrity and Jonny Kane, among his more established stars. While most of Martin's activities have been England-based, he has a house in Killiney, not too far from Mondello Park.

If there is one thing that stands out in this brief resume, so far, of Irish achievements on the modern international motor racing scene, it is the willingness to help other Irishmen. People like Eddie Jordan, Sid Taylor, Martin Donnelly and Martin Birrane as well as a host of private sponsors have done a lot to promote Ireland on the world stage. Those above are a part of the modern generation. But Ireland had stars in the fifties too. Almost forgotten among Ireland's Grand Prix contenders was Brian Shawe-Taylor who seemed destined for higher things in the early fifties. Born in Dublin in 1915 of Anglo-Irish land-owning parents, he sadly lost his father in a Sinn Fein ambush in 1920. His childhood was spent at Moore Park in Athenry, Co Galway but he was educated at Shrewsbury. His first ever race was to co-drive Bob Ansell's ERA in the Nuffield trophy at Donington in 1939 – he had met Ansell while living in Stratford-on-Avon and they finished fourth. Having served as an anti-aircraft gunner in the war, he emerged as Major but couldn't find a job, so went to work for the garage that was looking after Ansell's ERA, which had been stored through the war years. Although the ERAs were pre-war cars, the new Grand Prix formula happened to match their engines, so they had a renewed lease of life post-war. He had a few drives in that car in 1946 and 1947 and again in 1948 when Ansell's cousin Geoff acquired it. Geoff and Brian shared the wheel in the 1949 British Grand Prix to finish ninth. Shawe-Taylor bought the car in mid-1950 at which point he started to figure in the results of major meetings – fourth in the 1950 British Empire Trophy was the best. He didn't get an entry at the 1950 British Grand Prix as the RAC said the car looked too old, so he co-drove Fry's Maserati into 10th place. At the end of the season he bought Cuth Harrison's ERA which had a new front suspension and more modern-looking bodywork. The other ERA was sold to an Irishman, Ernie Wilkinson, who continued to use it in Irish sprints and hill-climbs.

With the new car, Shawe-Taylor began to show his talent and beat the ERA establishment, finishing close up behind much more modern machinery and winning minor events. He was third in the 1951 Ulster Trophy at Dundrod behind one of the all-conquering Alfa Romeo 159s and a Ferrari; this was followed by eighth in the 1951 British Grand Prix and he won a Formule Libre event at Boreham. He also had two drives for Aston Martin that year in a DB2, finishing fifth at Le Mans with George Abecassis, and seventh at the Dundrod TT. And he nearly had a Grand Prix drive for Vanwall when they entered the big Thinwall Ferrari Special at Rheims in July 1951, but he was displaced at the last minute by Reg Parnell; obviously his ability with the ERAs was beginning to be noticed. However, at Goodwood at the end of September, his promising career came to an end. He had come fourth in a minor race but in the feature event, he had a bad accident after contacting another car; he was thrown out and was unconscious for many weeks. It took him a long time to recover and he never raced again. He spent the rest of his working life at GCHQ Cheltenham, retiring in 1980 at 65. He died in 1999.

A similar Grand Prix nearly-man was Belfast's Desmond Titterington. Born in Cultra in 1928, he started racing in Ireland in 1951 and co-drove Ernest McMillen's MG in the Alpine Rally that year. He drove his own Allard J2 to win the 1952 Leinster Trophy and the 1953 Phoenix Park race. That year saw him drive Bobby Dickson's private Aston Martin DB3 into sixth place at the Dundrod TT. At the end of 1953 he had driven a Frazer Nash into fifth place at Charterhall in Scotland and met David Murray, the owner of Ecurie Ecosse, who normally only chose Scottish drivers. On applying to join the team, Titterington's justification was that his mother was Scottish and he had been educated at Glenalmond and St Andrews. He joined the team's Jaguar driving squad for 1954 and 55, the latter his best year with the Jaguar D-types including wins at Dundrod (not the TT), Charterhall and a second place with Ninian Sanderson in the Goodwood 9-hour race. He had a Vanwall Formula 1 drive at the 1955 Oulton Park Gold cup and finished third behind Moss and Hawthorn.

On his home ground he had teamed up with Ulster's Joe Kelly for the 1954 TT driving a 3-litre Ferrari, but they didn't finish. However Jaguar put him into a works car for the 1955 event with Mike Hawthorn; at one stage they were in the lead but the engine blew up near the end, handing victory to Mercedes. Given his Irish road-racing experience, Titterington was invited by Mercedes to drive in the Targa Florio at the end of 1955; teamed with American John Fitch, they finished fourth, which would have been good enough to earn him a regular seat had not Mercedes promptly withdrawn from racing. Although he had an offer to drive sports cars for Ferrari in 1956, he chose to drive for Ecurie Ecosse with reasonable success and also drove for the Connaught Formula 1 including the 1956 British Grand Prix; he got it as high as ninth before the engine packed up and Connaught were beginning to run out of money, so that drive evaporated too.

ABOVE ▨ Desmond Titterington in the Jaguar D-type which he shared with Mike Hawthorn in the 1955 Tourist Trophy at Dundrod.

Although his sports car performances are best remembered, Titterington was twice runner-up in the Circuit of Ireland (1955 and 56) in a Triumph TR2 and emerged from retirement to take a third place in the sports car class in the 1958 Alpine Rally with a Triumph TR3. He had hung up his racing helmet at the end of 1956 to return to the family wool business in Belfast; when he sold this in 1972 he retired to Scotland where he still lives.

Almost an honorary Irishman by virtue of his successes on Irish soil was the English amateur Anthony Powys-Lybbe. Having learnt his craft in sports cars at Brooklands, he bought an Alfa Romeo Monza two-seater in 1936. He finished second to Reggie Tongue's ERA in the 1936 Cork Grand Prix, then won the County Down Trophy at Bangor; he was second again at Cork in 1937. After the war he bought a single-seater more powerful Alfa Romeo; despite its 1933 vintage it was still very fast. He won the Wakefield Trophy at the Curragh in 1949, the Ulster Trophy at Dundrod in 1950 as well as the racing car section of the Leinster Trophy. He was back again in 1953 with the 20-year-old car at the Curragh circuit where he won the Wakefield

Trophy scratch race from the Irish stalwarts, Joe Kelly (Jaguar) and Dickie Odlum (Frazer Nash), and also took the Frank O'Boyle handicap award. By then he was 44 and retired the following year. Although he had raced in England and on the Continent it was the Irish races that he had most enjoyed. ■

While most of our listed heroes have been from the post-war period, Irish stars were shining before the Great War. No story of Irish motor sport could be complete without mention of the Guinness family, many of whom served on the RIAC committees and two of the Earls of Iveagh were presidents. Sir Algernon Lee Guinness won the touring car class in the 1904 sand races at Portmarnock; he went on to drive for Darracq before and after the Great War, and won the TT in 1922. His younger brother, Kenelm Lee (Bill) Guinness, had acted as his riding mechanic but became a driver in his own right as well as an engineer – he founded the KLG spark plug company. He won the TT for Sunbeam in 1914 and raced for the same company after the war winning three major races in a row in 1922. That year he also held the World Land Speed record in a Sunbeam powered by an 18-litre aero engine, reaching 134 mph at Brooklands.

ABOVE ■ Sir Algernon Lee Guinness (Bart) was the first of the famous family to go motor racing. Here he is seen achieving 120mph in a 200hp Darracq on the Saltburn Sands in 1908. His passenger is his younger brother Kenelm 'Bill' Lee Guinness who went on to race Sunbeams and founded the KLG spark plug company.

A fellow Sunbeam driver was Henry Segrave; his father Charles from Co Wicklow had married an American and Henry O'Neal de Hane Segrave was born in Baltimore in 1896. The family was soon back in Ireland and Charles Segrave was on the IAC committee in the early days. After war service earned him the rank of Major, young Segrave joined the Sunbeam team in 1921 and went on to become the first British driver to win a Grand Prix in a British car in the 1923 French Grand Prix. It was due to Segrave and Bill Guinness that the Irish Grand Prix was established in Phoenix Park; they had proposed the venue back in 1925 but it took four years to reach fruition. Although he continued to race until 1927, Segrave had been caught by the record-breaking bug; still driving for Sunbeam he held the Land Speed Record at 152 mph in 1926, was the first man to break 200 mph in 1927, but switched to Napier power to achieve 231 mph at Daytona, Florida in the Golden Arrow in 1929. By then he had developed a passion for high speed boats and, on the same trip, won an international boat championship in Miami, using his own 'Miss England'; he was knighted on his return. The following year he lost his life at Lake Windermere while attacking the World Water Speed record in 'Miss England II'. It is a fitting tribute to Segrave and the two racing Guinness brothers that the family has endowed the Guinness-Segrave library at the RIAC. ◼

While circuit racing is more likely to catch the headlines, rallying is the major part of Irish motor sport; this has bred many stars who have done well in Ireland and the mainland, but these have generally been confined to the tarmac surfaces on which the Irish rally driver is predominantly brought up. Modern world championship rallying demands the different skill of driving on loose surfaces, an ability which was the preserve of Scandinavian drivers until relatively recently. But it was not always so. In the days of open rallying on the public roads of the Continent, Ireland held its own.

One such rally star was Ronnie Adams, born in Ulster in 1914 and remembered as the man who won the 1956 Monte Carlo Rally in a seemingly unlikely Mark VII Jaguar. In those days many entrants used three-man crews to help with the driving and navigation, so big high performance cars were well suited to most of the event, although it needed particular skill to go fast in the snowy Alps. That was actually the fourth Monte Carlo Adams had run in a Mark VII. Driving his own car, albeit with some works preparation, he had finished 15th in 1953 and sixth in 1954, the latter with fellow Ulsterman Desmond Titterington as one of his crew.

Those two years had also seen Dubliner Cecil Vard in the team; Vard had driven a Mark V Jaguar into third in 1951 and fifth in 1953. Actually the car was his aunt's and he had borrowed it in 1951 under the pretext of taking it for a Continental tour. For 1954 he was lent a works Mark VII and finished eighth. Vard and Adams were both in Mark VIIs for 1955 with Ian Appleyard making a third; they won the team prize, Adams finishing highest in eighth with another Irish racing driver Ernest McMillan as co-driver. Then came victory in 1956; in winning, Ronnie Adams, with Frank Biggar (another Irish resident) and Derek Johnston, defeated the Mercedes 220 of Schock and Moll who were going on to win the European Rally Championship that year. Although Adams drove the Monte for Jaguar he won his class for Alvis in the RAC Rally in 1954 and 1955; he had finished second in the 1952 RAC in a Sunbeam Talbot. He also drove for Rootes in 1953, and he was in the winning Triumph team in the 1956 Circuit of Ireland.

ABOVE ■ Cecil Vard, circuit racer and rally driver, seen here in his aunt's Jaguar Mark V on his way to third place in the 1951 Monte Carlo Rally.

Adams did the Circuit of Ireland 15 times but the only time he was in the winning car was in the very first event in 1931 when he was still a schoolboy – he had been given a driving licence at 13. He had just returned to Ireland for the school holidays when he was offered a ride in an Austin 16 alongside Basil Clark and Clifford Holmes; it was an icy year and Adams drove much of the 1000 miles including the driving tests. He is still the youngest-ever winner although his name does not figure on the winners' lists.

Adams' rallying career continued after his Jaguar period. He was driving for Ford in 1957. Driving for Mercedes in the East African Safari he would have won in 1959 if he hadn't given his team-mate the spare can of fuel which he would shortly need himself. He was in Africa again in 1962 driving a Rover 3-litre which he had taken to third place until the steering broke. Before that he was in one of the works Austin-Healeys that won the team prize in the 1960 RAC. He retired from rallying at the end of 1962, and returned to the family linen business. He was actually offered a works drive in the 1963 Monte Carlo rally with a Mini-Cooper but decided it was too small – he was used to big cars. One of the 1963 Mini drivers on the Monte was Paddy Hopkirk who developed an amazing affinity with the little car that Adams had dismissed as 'a little box on wheels'.

Paddy Hopkirk was born in Belfast in 1933. It is said that the he used a motorised bath chair to practise autotests in his parents' driveway at the age of 9; apocryphal or not, he certainly took to motoring while he studied engineering at Trinity College, Dublin. He started co-driving with Michael O'Flaherty, son of the Republic's VW and Mercedes importer. He bought a Beetle and competed in Autotests so successfully that he led the winning Northern Irish team in the 1954 British Autotest Championship using a Triumph TR2. He won the Irish Hewison Autotest Trophy in 1955 in the Beetle (and again in 1957); the Beetle also gave him a class victory in the Circuit that year. The next step was a Triumph works drive during 1956 Rally of the Midnight Sun in May with a TR3, Alpine Rally in July with a TR3, gaining a Coupe des Alpes and second in the class to team-mate Maurice Gatsonides, the inventor of the radar speed traps; the season ended with an impressive debut in the RAC rally driving a Standard 10. The first Circuit of Ireland victory came with a TR3 in 1958, at the end of which year he changed over to drive Sunbeam Rapiers for Rootes. This added another Coupe des Alpes in 1961 (third overall), a third in the 1962 Monte Carlo, fourth in the 1961 RAC and two more Circuit victories in 1961 and 1962. He switched to BMC in time for the 1962 Liege-Sofia-Liege where his big Healey broke its rear suspension, but the RAC Rally saw a fine second place. After that it was Minis all the way as far as rallying was concerned. He came sixth in the 1963 Monte Carlo with a 997 cc Mini-Cooper, winning it the following year in the hotter 1071 cc Cooper S. It should have been Paddy who won the Circuit that year but the honour of driving the first Circuit victory in a Mini went to Ronnie McCartney – Hopkirk's time came in 1965 and again in 1967. Other outright victories, all in Minis, included the Austrian Alpine rally in 1964 and 1966, with the Acropolis and (French) Alpine rallies in 1967, but there were a string of podium finishes throughout the sixties.

In between, Hopkirk also drove works MGs on the racetrack when required. He had been to the Le Mans 24-hours with the Sunbeam Alpines in 1961 and 1962 but failed both times. He returned for the next three years with an MGB and finished each time winning the class in 1963. He drove MGs in the Targa Florio and MGCs at Sebring where first in class in 1968 was the best finish. He took part in the two great marathons, the 1968 London-Sydney (second overall in Austin 1800) and the 1970 London-Mexico (fourth in Triumph 2500). By 1970, British Leyland were cutting back on their competitions budget and concentrating more on racing; Paddy's final Mini fling was a second place in the 1970 Scottish Rally. By then the days of the Mini were over as the Ford Escort had arrived. Paddy retired from active competition that year to concentrate on his motor accessories business, but he still drives in historic events with all the old panache which made this autotest expert into such an accomplished controller of the little box on wheels. ▨

While ladies generally have achieved little notable success on the international racing scene, there is something about rallying that seems to justify equal opportunities. Stirling Moss' sister Pat was a front runner through the early sixties and won three major rallies outright; 'blonde Dublin dress-designer' (the standard tabloid description) Rosemary Smith wasn't quite as effective but still won the 1965 Tulip rally outright in a Hillman Imp and also drove Sunbeam Tigers for the Rootes Group, collecting a number of Ladies' Awards in both cars; like every successful Irish rally driver she had proved her ability on the Circuit of Ireland and 1965 saw her take her third successive Ladies' Award in that event. She now runs a driving school near Dublin. ▨

ON TWO WHEELS

The world ruling body for motorcycles is the FIM, Federation Internationale de Motocyclisme, founded in 1904. As with the FIA, this delegates the running of international events to the National clubs. However, unlike the four-wheeled equivalents, Irish motorcycle sport is run by a single body, the Motor Cycle Union of Ireland (MCUI), founded in 1902 with its first president John Boyd Dunlop, the inventor of the pneumatic tyre.

As an aside, Dunlop was actually a Scottish vet but settled in Belfast in 1867; he patented the first pneumatic tyre in Belfast in 1888 as a result of trying to make his son's tricycle more comfortable to ride. Cars had yet to arrive so it was the bicycle world that was the first to adopt the patented 'chamber of rubber or other suitable material to contain air under pressure or otherwise, fastened to the rim by the most convenient method'. The Dunlop Pneumatic Tyre Company was set up the following year by Dubliner, Harvey du Cros of the famous cycling family; Dunlop had sold his patent to them for £700.

The first event for the new MCUI was a social run from Dublin's Phoenix Park to Bray in 1902 with the first race meeting on a dirt track in Ashtown, Co Dublin later the same year. Sand racing, hill-climbs and reliability trials were the main events over the early years. As Ireland's largest city at the time, Dublin was and has remained the headquarters of the MCUI; however the need for expansion was rapidly evident and a Belfast centre was set up in 1903. Since then the Southern and Ulster Centres have cooperated to run motorcycle sport on a voluntary basis throughout Ireland. While the MCUI joined the FIM in 1906, it opted out the following year and didn't rejoin until 1927; despite that Dublin's Charlie Franklin became the first Irish rider in the Isle of Man TT races in 1908, a year after their foundation. After the First World War, off-road trials and road-racing became the popular two-wheeled events; the 1921 Patland Trial is still run in Leinster and the first Ulster Grand Prix was held in 1922, the first southern road race was the Leinster 100 in 1923 at Dunshaughlin, Co Meath and the first North-West 200 ran in 1929. Meanwhile racing on the sandy beaches had been replaced by grass-track racing which was kinder to the machinery; major meetings were held at such horse racecourses as the Maze, Co Down, Windy Arbour, Co Dublin and Cobh Junction, Co Cork.

In 1926 four Irishmen made up the works Norton team, Joe Craig and Jimmy Shaw from Ulster, Stanley Woods from Dublin and naturalised Canadian Alec Bennett, a function of the persuasive powers of Norton's Dublin agent Dene Allen. Craig had already won the Ulster Grand Prix three times in succession. Woods had won the 1923 Junior TT on a Cotton and would go on to win many Continental Grands Prix and TTs for Norton; in 1935 he won both the Senior and Junior TTs to give Guzzi their first international success. He clocked ten TT wins. Joe Craig was working as an engine designer for Norton in the pre-war period but moved over to BSA in 1939; he rejoined Norton in 1947 and was responsible for the Norton 500 cc engine that was to form the basis of the Grand Prix Vanwall unit. ▩

By the arrival of the Second World War, the Ulster Grand Prix and the North West 200 were well established. The first Ulster in 1922 was over 7 laps of a 20.5-mile circuit at Clady, Co Antrim close to the site of Belfast airport and famed for its 7-mile straight from Muckamore to Clady, now the B39; it became an international event in 1926, by which time they were doing 10 laps. With such a big circuit all entrants would run in the same race with staggered starts for each class.

After the war, the Ulster started again on the Clady circuit reduced to 16.5 miles. When the road-racing world championships started in 1949, the Ulster was one of the rounds. However the Antrim County Council decided they didn't want to close so much road every time the race and the preceding practice were held, so the event moved to the 7.5-mile Dundrod circuit a few miles south in 1953. On the smaller circuit the classes had separate races. The fifties and sixties were the heyday of the Ulster Grand Prix. John Surtees on MV scored double victories in 350 cc and 500 cc races in 1959 and 1960. Mike Hailwood won his first world championship event at the Ulster on a 125 cc Ducati. Giacomo Agostini won his first 350 cc Ulster GP in 1967 with 350 cc and 500 cc double victories from 1968-70. The troubles intervened in the seventies when the Ulster lost its world championship status, but this returned in the eighties with the introduction of the road-based TT Formula world championship classes. Since then the event has had its ups and downs but is now in the hands of the Coleraine and District Motor Club seeking to regain former glories.

The Coleraine Club has also been in control of the North West 200 since 1964. Because the original 1929 event was planned by the Derry and District Motor Club for a circuit near the City of Derry in the North West corner of the province and the circuit was later changed to a 11.1-mile Portrush - Portstewart - Coleraine triangle, the name was retained out of respect for the Londonderry intentions. The North of Ireland Motor Club took over the running in 1930 through to 1962. Over the years the original circuit has been shortened to just under 9 miles. Although it has never been used for world championship events, the North West has been a major event in Ireland and attracts many competitors and spectators from the mainland.

After the Second World War, Artie Bell, Reg Armstrong, Cromie McCandless and Ernie Lyons were the Irish stars of the forties and fifties, all well-known on the world road-racing scene. The Belfast trio of Tommy Robb, Sammy Miller and Ralph Bryans notched up many more road-racing successes. Bryans, born in 1941, was Ireland's first world champion, riding a Honda in the 50 cc class in 1965; as a works Honda rider from 1964-67 he won 10 world championship Grands Prix. Robb, born in 1935, won five times in the North West races and, as a new works Honda rider, once in the Ulster, beating Jim Redman in 1962; that year he finished second in the 350 cc World Championship and third in the 125 cc category. And Sammy Miller, born 1934, won the 1954 Cookstown 100 on an AJS 7R, and, on a 250 cc NSU was just pipped by John Surtees in the 1955 Ulster GP; for 1957 he was a Mondial works rider and took third in the 250 cc World Championship, also winning the North West 200 from 1956-58. He then turned to trials; twice European trials champion, 11 times British trials champion, he also won the Scottish 6-day trial six times and the more local Hurst Cup International trial at Clendeboye on 13 successive occasions. An amazing record.

He wasn't an Irishman but Giacomo Agostini had a strong Irish following. Between 1966 and 1975 he was World Champion eight times in 500 cc and seven times in 350 cc; he had ten TTs to his name but he still came to the Ulster GP where he picked up seven trophies from 1967-70 and the crowds still loved him when he turned up for the classic parade at the 1998 Ulster GP.

And then there was Joey Dunlop, sadly killed in 2000 at Tallinn, Estonia. Born in 1952 in Ballymoney, Co Antrim, he spent most of the seventies learning the tricks of the trade in Irish club racing. His sponsor, John Rea, was behind him in 1976 when he finished third in the 250cc class at the Ulster GP and second in the 500cc class at the North West 200. He took part in the Junior and Senior TTs that year but finished well down on a 350cc Yamaha. He was back the following year and won the 50th anniversary Classic TT on Rea's 750cc Yamaha and he won again in the Isle of Man in the 1980 Senior Classic TT. This attracted the attention of Suzuki for whom he rode in the 1980 Ulster GP, helping his team-mate Graeme Crosby take the TT Formula 1 World Championship.

He signed for Honda for 1981 and stayed on their machines for the next 20 years of incredible success on the road circuits of the Europe. He was the TT Formula 1 champion from 1982-86; he won 26 TT races including treble victories in 1985, 86 and 2000. He won 24 Ulster GP races and 13 at the North West 200. But there was much more to the quiet, modest man from Ballymoney than his skill in the saddle. In 1986 he received an MBE for services to motorcycle

ABOVE ■ Joey Dunlop at the Skerries 100.

sport, an award echoed by the presentation of a Silver Medal by the FIM world congress in 1993. And in 1996 he was awarded an OBE for humanitarian aid trips to children's orphanages in Romania. He was a lot of things to many people and he was still winning races in the year that he lost his life at the age of 48.

Future stars may match his pace on the track and Ireland has a number of regulars in world championship events: Tom Herron, Norman Brown, Gary Cowan, Eddie Laycock, Jeremy McWilliams, but none are likely to displace his fans' claims that Joey Dunlop was the greatest road-racer ever. ▪

THE IRISH MOTOR CAR INDUSTRY

While the emerald isle no longer has a road car manufacturing industry, it has produced a fair number of motor cars over the years and has, even now, some 10,000 people producing components for the world's manufacturers. Probably the first Irish vehicle manufacturer was Chambers which produced a few hundred cars in Belfast from 1904-25; Jack Chambers worked for Vauxhall and sent a car over to his brothers who had an engineering business in Belfast. They improved the Vauxhall and decided they could do better themselves. The first cars were unorthodox with a transverse flat-twin driving a rear mounted epicyclic gearbox via chains. They proved their reputation for rugged reliability in trials. Their later cars were more conventional but the company ran out of money during the twenties.

Far more significant though was the Ford factory set up in Cork. William Ford had been a farmer in Clonakilty, 30 miles south-west of Cork. Suffering in the potato famine, he emigrated to America in 1847 following his brothers who had left in the thirties and settled in the village of Dearbornville, Michigan. Working as a carpenter, William met and married Mary, the adopted daughter of a fellow Irish exile, Patrick O'Hern from Cork. Their eldest son Henry was born in what was to become Dearborn in 1863. It was 1903 before Henry Ford established his own company. Only four years later the first Ford was imported into Ireland and a dealer appointed. The first overseas Ford factory was in Manchester in 1911 to build the model T which had been launched in 1908. However, very conscious of his Irish roots, Henry Ford visited Cork in 1912 and announced that he would build a factory there; although this eventually happened in 1917 complete with its own wharf, the initial production from 1919 was of tractors. Model Ts were built there from 1922-27 to be replaced by tractors again until 1933. From then until 1982, the Irish factory assembled the various models of Ford, only ceasing with the introduction of the Sierra whose robotic assembly was incompatible with the old plant.

While Ford were not noted for producing competition cars, there were some sporting models that were used in competition in the thirties. My 1936 Cork Grand Prix programme carries an advertisement for Henry Ford and Son Limited of Cork, extolling the successes of the Ford V-8 in the Monte Carlo rally 'finishing 1st, 4th, 6th and 9th – ask your dealer to demonstrate one of the Irish-built V-8s, from £215 at Works'. What was as important, though, was that Ford components were used as the basis for many home-built cars which were used in competition – racing and trials. J. Toohey's 933 cc Ford 8 special won the Leinster Trophy on handicap in 1935 and 1936.

Ford in particular were to benefit from the 1932 post-depression government's imposition of very high taxes on imports, which effectively meant that only cars built in Southern Ireland could be sold in that market. By 1934, there were ten assembly plants. After the war, the Beetle was among those assembled in Ireland along with a number of early Japanese cars. This protectionism was only finally overturned in 1972 with the arrival of the EEC, although Irish assembly of overseas models continued to the end of the decade.

ABOVE ■ The Crosslé Car Company is now Ireland's major manufacturer. In the driving seat of a Crosslé 9S with John Crosslé is Arnie Black the present owner of the company.

In the north, the decline of the shipbuilding industry in Belfast was behind the misguided agreement of the British government to provide finance for the DeLorean project. This rear-engined sports coupe was the brainchild of former General Motor's vice-president John DeLorean and subsequently received further development by Lotus; with funds channelled through the Northern Ireland Development Agency a new factory was built at Dunmurry on the outskirts of Belfast. It was unfortunate that the car was only half developed when put on sale in 1980 and that some of the funds went missing; the factory closed in 1982 after just 8,583 had been built.

Apart from Ford's 65-year presence during which around half a million vehicles were built in Cork, the longest-serving car manufacturer has been Crosslé (pronounced Crossley), founded in 1961 and still producing racing cars. It all started with John Crosslé building his own Ford-engined special in 1957; the following season he won the Irish Ford championship. He won again with a new car in 1959. When he moved to Holywood, Co Down in 1960 it was the start of a growing business. Over the years they have built cars for almost every formula outside the mainstream Formula 1,2,3 exporting them all over the world but particularly to America. Stars who have cut their teeth on them include Nigel Mansell, Peter Gethin and Mario Andretti as well as every one of Ireland's Grand Prix drivers. Two American racing schools use Crosslé cars exclusively.

John Crosslé retired from the company in 1998 and it is now run by Arnie Black, a long-standing Crosslé racer who tackled European Formula Ford championships in his youth. He still drives one of the older F2 cars and won the British Historic F2 championship two years running. Recently he has instituted a one-make Crosslé championship using an updated version of the 1966 9S sports car with a Ford Zetec engine. Crosslé seems set to continue for ever. A few others have taken a leaf out of the Crosslé book. Mondiale Cars have been built in Bangor, Co Down from 1984 mostly single-seaters for Formula Ford racing. Sheane have been building Formula Vee cars in Wicklow but launched Formula Sheane in 2000 using a 2-litre Rover engine. Leastone have been quietly building Formula Vee cars since 1993 in Lowtown, Co Kildare.

Road car manufacture may have disappeared from the Irish shores but the racing fraternity have more than made up for the loss with sheer enthusiasm. ▪

Not all sports have been mentioned in this book and this section does a little to rectify that omission. Whatever the sport, the Irish will play it and indeed have been responsible for initiating their own sports. Sometimes the sport is played with success, sometimes it is played with apparent failure, but always the aim is to enjoy the craic. For instance, success has come in show jumping with Seamus Hayes, a long list of Army officers and more recently with Peter Charles on Traxdata Carnavelly, Dermott Lennon on Liscalgot and the riders Kevin Babington and Cian O'Connor.

Ireland's coastal and inland waters have provided a natural environment for sailing. Sailing has produced its champions in the likes of Harold Cudmore who has been a leading light since 1975 for various Irish and British yachts from Irish Mist to Indulgence. Cudmore has taken part in America's Cup and Admiral's Cup campaigns and Maria Coleman sailed in the Sydney Olympics 2000.

Michelle Smith burst into prominence in the world of swimming at the 1996 Atlanta Olympics. Sensationally she won three gold medals, including the 400 metre individual relay. Sadly the celebrations turned to despair when FINA, the swimming world governing body, found her guilty of tampering with a drug test and imposed a four-year ban from the sport. Michelle de Bruin (nee Smith) lost her appeal against the ban and announced her retirement from swimming in June 1999. Swimming is a popular sport. It is promoted by Swim Ireland formed in 1998 and is supported by the Irish Sports Council and the Sports Council for Northern Ireland. Swim Ireland is comprised of over 120 affiliated clubs with over 10,000 members. Its aim is to encourage swimming both in competition and for enjoyment. A number of Irish swimmers including Nick O'Hare and Niamh Cawley have done well at international level since the formation of Swim Ireland.

LEFT ▨ 8th August 1998 Nations Cup. Peter Charles on Traxdata Carnavelly.

BELOW ▨ Members of the Irish Olympic Equestrian team prepare for the 2000 Sydney Olympics.

ABOVE ▪ 2000 Sydney Olympics. Maria Coleman.

BELOW ▪ 1996 Atlanta Olympics. Michelle Smith celebrates after winning the gold medal in the 400 metre individual medley.

The particularly demanding three-day eventing competition has a long tradition in Irish sport and the Irish countryside is well suited to hunting, shooting and fishing. Snooker produced its unforgettable moment when Dennis Taylor, from Northern Ireland, beat Steve Davis on a re-spotted black in the finals of the world championship. The 35-frame final had been locked at 17 frames each and the 35th frame ended with the scores equal. Taylor's triumphant smile and celebrations were matched by Davis' gracious acceptance of defeat. Today's Irish leading snooker players are Ken Doherty, Joe Swail and Fergal O'Brien.

However, it is perhaps in the sports of cycling and squash that Ireland has had some of its most memorable moments. On July 28th 1987 when Stephen Roche from Dublin became the first cyclist from the British Isles to win the Tour de France. He also became the fifth man to achieve the grand slam of cycling by winning the Tour of Italy and the Tour de France in the same season. Roche, aged 27, was honoured by the presence on the Champs-Elysees of Charles Haughey, the Irish Taoiseach (Prime Minister), as well as thousands of Irish supporters who had filled every Paris-bound plane or cross channel boat to be in Paris to see Roche record his victory in the 74th Tour de France.

ABOVE ■ 1987 Tour de France. Sephen Roche celebrates winning the tour.

John Wilcockson in an interview with Stephen Roche in 1987 wrote: '"It was a real thrill to see many faces in the crowd I recognised", Roche said. "In the Alps last week, I saw a friend I raced with when I was a teenager. I never thought then that I would be a professional cyclist, let alone a Tour de France winner." Only continentals had won the Tour de France in its first 72 editions before Greg LeMond, of the United States, broke the sequence last year. Yesterday it was the strains of the Amhran na bhFiann that succeeded the Star Spangled Banner over the Champs-Elysees.

'Roche was always in contention for the yellow jersey in this 74th Tour de France. He finished third in the prologue stage in West Berlin 26 days ago and always rode like a champion. He confirmed his role of favourite by winning the 54-mile time-trial at Poitiers on the tenth day, maintained his challenge through the Pyrenees and wrested the yellow jersey from Jean-Francois Bernard, of France, at Villard-de-Lans last Monday.

'Despite losing the lead 24 hours later to Pedro Delgado, of Spain, Roche fought back when Delgado went on the attack again at the mountaintop finish in La Plagne on Wednesday. By conceding only four seconds to Delgado after being one minute behind him four miles from the summit, the Irishman drained himself and collapsed on the finishing line. "I had absolutely no energy left in my body," Roche said, "But I knew that I had to make such an effort. That wasn't the day I won the Tour, but the day I knew I wouldn't be beaten." The Dubliner recovered to launch several attacks himself the next day, resulting in a gain of 18 secs over Delgado on the downhill finish to Morzine. This left Roche with a deficit of 21 secs going into the 24-mile time-trial at Dijon on Saturday.

' "I was only concerned with beating Delgado," he said. "I put everything into the first ten miles, which were into the wind, and once I had more than a minute's lead on him, I eased back." Despite taking it easy, Roche still finished second in the time-trial, 1 min 44 secs behind Bernard, but a vital 61 secs ahead of Delgado. Yesterday, Roche wore his yellow jersey with dignity on the final stage of 119 miles from Creteil to Paris and was content to allow a group of eight riders to move clear during the last six miles.

'Jeff Pierce, an American, broke clear from this group to earn an unexpected stage victory, Pierce's stage success and Roche's overall victory emphasise the growing stature of cycling worldwide. "The youngsters have ambitions to follow Sean Kelly and me," the Tour de France winner said. "But it's not as easy as they think. Until they have been on youth hostel weekends, riding a bike with a fixed wheel and a saddlebag, they don't know what cycling is all about." The $80,000 he earned in prizes yesterday will not affect Roche. He will remain as he was described

ABOVE ■ The Nissan Classic 1988. Stephen Roche and Sean Kelly.

on Saturday by Jacques Goddet, aged 82, the Tour director, as "a man of dignity and intelligence who is not only a tremendous athlete but a most charming young man". '

Sean Kelly, Stephen Roche's friend and fellow cyclist from Ireland, in a career lasting from 1972-94 achieved 22 classic wins, including winning the Green Jersey of the Tour de France four times. Kelly is the fourth most successful cyclist of all time. He was regarded as an outstanding sprinter.

In squash, Jonah Barrington achieved the ultimate goal. After leaving Dublin University, Barrington committed himself totally to a spartan regime designed to build both skill and stamina; he won the British Amateur Squash Championship in 1966, 67 and 68, and the British Open Championship six times between 1967 and 73. He also captured the Australian, South African, Pakistan and United Arab Republic (Egyptian) titles. By 1970 he had turned professional and had broken the Pakistani dominance of world squash. His success, dedication and enthusiasm did much to promote the game of squash in Ireland and the British Isles. ■

ABOVE ■ Between 1967 and 1973, Jonah Barrington won the British Open six times. He broke the Pakistani dominance by fitness and the sheer force of will.

HURLING

ALL-IRELAND HURLING CHAMPIONSHIP – WINNERS 1887-2001

Cork (28)	1890, 1892-94, 1902-3, 1919, 1926, 1928-9, 1931, 1941-2, 1943-4, 1946, 1952-4, 1966, 1970, 1976-8, 1984, 1986, 1990, 1999
Kilkenny (26)	1904-5, 1907, 1909, 1911-13, 1922, 1932-3, 1935, 1939, 1947, 1957, 1963, 1967, 1969, 1972, 1974-5, 1979, 1982-3, 1992-3, 2000
Tipperary (25)	1887, 1895-6, 1898-9, 1900, 1906, 1908, 1916, 1925, 1930, 1937, 1945, 1949, 1950-1, 1958, 1961-2, 1964-5, 1971, 1989, 1991, 2001
Limerick (7)	1897, 1918, 1921, 1934, 1936, 1940, 1973
Dublin (6)	1889, 1917, 1920, 1924, 1927, 1938
Wexford (6)	1910, 1955-6, 1960, 1968, 1996
Galway (4)	1923, 1980, 1987-8
Offaly (4)	1981, 1985, 1994, 1998
Clare (3)	1914, 1995, 1997
Waterford (2)	1948, 1959
Kerry (1)	1891
London (1)	1901 (London were given the right in 1900 to play in championship.)
Laois (1)	1915

(There was no championship in 1888 because of the 'American Invasion'.)

NATIONAL HURLING LEAGUE – WINNERS 1926-2001

Tipperary (18)	1928, 1949-50, 1952, 1954-5, 1957, 1959, 1960-1, 1964-5, 1968, 1979, 1988, 1994, 1999, 2001
Cork (14)	1926, 1930, 1940-1, 1948, 1953, 1969, 1970, 1972, 1974, 1980-1, 1993, 1998
Limerick (11)	1934-8, 1947, 1971, 1984-5, 1992, 1997
Kilkenny (9)	1933, 1962, 1966, 1976, 1982-3, 1986, 1990 1995
Galway (7)	1932, 1951, 1975, 1987, 1989, 1996, 2000
Wexford (4)	1956, 1958, 1967, 1973
Clare (3)	1946, 1977-8
Dublin (2)	1929, 1939
Waterford (1)	1963
Offaly (1)	1991

(There was no competition in 1927)

GAELIC FOOTBALL

ALL-IRELAND FOOTBALL CHAMPIONSHIP – WINNERS 1887-2001

Kerry (32)	1903-4, 1909, 1913-14, 1924, 1926, 1929, 1930-2, 1937, 1939, 1940-1, 1946, 1953, 1955, 1959, 1962, 1969-70, 1975, 1978-81, 1984-6, 1997, 2000
Dublin (22)	1891-2, 1894, 1897-9, 1901-2, 1906-8, 1921-3, 1942, 1958, 1963, 1974, 1976-7, 1983, 1995
Galway (8)	1925, 1934, 1938, 1956, 1964-6, 1998, 2001
Meath (7)	1949, 1954, 1967, 1987-8, 1996, 1999
Cork (6)	1890, 1911, 1945, 1973, 1989, 1990
Wexford (5)	1893, 1915-18
Down (5)	1960-1, 1968, 1991, 1994
Tipperary (4)	1889, 1895, 1900, 1920
Kildare (4)	1905, 1919, 1927-8
Louth (3)	1910, 1912, 1957
Mayo (3)	1936, 1950-1
Offaly (3)	1971, 1972, 1982
Limerick (2)	1887, 1896
Roscommon (2)	1943, 1944
Donegal (1)	1992
Derry (1)	1993

(There was no championship in 1888 because of the 'American Invasion')

NATIONAL FOOTBALL LEAGUE - WINNERS 1927-2001

Kerry (16)	1928-9, 1931-2, 1959, 1961, 1963, 1969, 1971-4, 1977, 1982, 1984, 1997
Mayo (10)	1934-9, 1941, 1949, 1954, 1970, 2001
Dublin (8)	1953, 1955, 1958, 1976, 1978, 1987, 1991, 1993
Meath (7)	1933, 1946, 1951, 1975, 1988, 1990, 1994
Cork (5)	1952, 1956, 1980, 1989, 1999
Down (4)	1960, 1962, 1968, 1983
Galway (4)	1940, 1957, 1965, 1981
New York (3)	1950, 1964, 1967
Laois (2)	1927, 1986
Cavan (1)	1948
Longford (1)	1966
Monaghan (1)	1985
Roscommon (1)	1979
Offaly (1)	1998

RUGBY

1958 IRISH SIDE

P.J.Berkery (debut 1954 v Wales and 11 caps), A.J.F. O'Reilly (debut 1955 v France 29 caps) and a career which ended in 1970 v England. Last played in 1963 against Wales. N.J. Henderson (debut 1949 v Scotland and 36 caps), A.C. Pedlow (debut 1953 v Wales and 31 caps), J.W. Kyle (debut 1947 v France, first full International since the war. 46 caps), A.A. Mulligan (debut 1955 v France and 22 caps), P.J. O'Donoghue (debut 1955 v France and 11 caps), A.R. Dawson (debut 1958 v Australia and 27 caps), B.G.M. Wood (debut 1954 v England and 29 caps), J.B. Stevenson (debut 1958 v Australia and 5 caps), W.A. Mulcahy (debut 1958 v Australia and 35 caps), J.A. Donaldson (debut 1958 v Australia and 5 caps), R.J. Kavanagh (debut 1953 v France and 35 caps) and N.A.A. Murphy (debut 1958 v Australia and 41 caps). S.V.J. Quinlan, D.C. Glass, T. McGrath, S. Millar (37 caps), J.G.M.W. Murphy, F.L. Brown were to play in one match in the season and M.A.F. English began a long career (16 caps) when Jack Kyle retired.

1965 COMBINED UNIVERSITIES V SOUTH AFRICA

Ireland's side was: A. Hickie (U.C.D.), M. Lucey (U.C.C.), J.C. Walsh (U.C.C.), M. Grimshaw (Queen's University), W. Glynn (U.C.D.), J.B. Murray (U.C.D.), M. Whiteside (Queen's University), M. Carey (U.C.D.), M. Argyle (Dublin University), A. Moroney (U.C.D.), M. Leahy (U.C.C.),* O. Waldron (U.C.C.), J. Davidson (Queen's University), H. Wall (U.C.D.), (*O. Waldron was to play also for Oxford and Dublin Universities).

1969 IRISH SIDE V ENGLAND

Ireland's side was: T.J. Kiernan, full-back and captain, A.T.A. Duggan and J.C.M. Moroney, wings; F.P.K. Bresnihan and C.M.H. Gibson, centres; B.J. McGann and R.N. Young, half-backs; S. Millar, K.W. Kennedy, P.O'Callaghan, W.J. McBride, M.G. Molloy, J.C. Davidson, K.G. Goodhall and N.A.A. Murphy constituted the forwards. Others to play for Ireland in this period were B.A.P. O'Brien, R.D. Scott, W.M. McCombe, B.F. Sherry, J.T.M. Quirke, L.M. Hunter, J.J. Tydings, H.H. Rea – backs. A.M. Brady, M.G. Doyle, T.J. Doyle, O.C. Waldron – forwards. M.L. Hipwell, Kiernan, Bresnihan, Millar, Kennedy, McBride, Molloy played in every match in that unbeaten period.

1983 IRISH SIDE

H.P. MacNeill, T.M. Ringland, D.G. Irwin, M.J. Kiernan, M.C. Finn, S.O. Campbell, R.J.M. McGrath, P.A. Orr, C.F. Fitzgerald, G.A.J. McLoughlin, C.G. Lenihan, M.I. Keane, J.F. Slattery, W.P. Duggan and J.B. Driscoll. The only replacement was A.J.P. Ward, who came on for O.S. Campbell at the end of the English game.

FIVE NATIONS RUGBY RECORDS

FRANCE	Won	Drawn	Lost
1950s	5	1	4
1960s	1	1	8
1970s	3	2	6
1980s	1	1	8
1990s	-	-	10
Played 51	10	5	36

ENGLAND	Won	Drawn	Lost
1950s	1	2	7
1960s	4	3	3
1970s	6	-	4
1980s	4	-	6
1990s	2	-	8
Played 50	17	5	28

SCOTLAND	Won	Drawn	Lost
1950s	9	-	1
1960s	4	-	6
1970s	4	1	4
1980s	5	-	5
1990s	-	1	9
Played 49	22	2	25

WALES	Won	Drawn	Lost
1950s	1	1	8
1960s	4	1	5
1970s	2	1	6
1980s	5	-	5
1990s	6	1	3
Played 49	18	4	27

WORLD CUP

1. 1987 (AUSTRALIA and NEW ZEALAND)

v Wales (Wellington)	Lost 6-13
v Canada (Dunedin)	Won 46-19
v Tonga (Brisbane	Won 32-9
v Australia – Quarter-final (Sydney)	Lost 15-33

2. 1991 (BRITISH ISLES)

v Zimbabwe (Lansdowne Road)	Won 55-11
v Japan (Lansdowne Road)	Won 32-16
v Scotland (Murrayfield)	Lost 15-24
v Australia (Lansdowne Road)	Lost 18-19

3. 1995 (SOUTH AFRICA)

v New Zealand (Johannesburg)	Lost 19-43
v Japan (Bloemfontein)	Won 50-28
v Wales (Johannesburg)	Won 24-23
v France (Durban)	Lost 12-36

4. 1998 (BRITISH ISLES)

v Georgia – Qualifying Round (Lansdowne Road)	Won 70-0
v Romania – Qualifying Round (Lansdowne Road)	Won 53-35
v South Africa (Lansdowne Road)	Lost 13-27

CRICKET

INTERNATIONAL CAPS (50 OR MORE)

Some players listed received caps prior to 1950

121 caps	D.A. LEWIS (1984-97)
118	G.D. HARRISON (1983-97)
114	A.R. DUNLOP (1990-2000)
114	S.J.S. WARKE (1981-96)
93	M. HALLIDAY (1970-89)
87	O.D. COLHOUN (1959-79)
87	P.B. JACKSON (1981-94)
86	I.J. ANDERSON (1966-85)
76	J.D. MONTEITH (1965-84)
74	P. McCRUM (1989-98)
73	S.C. CORLETT (1974-87)
72	A.J. O'RIORDAN (1958-77)
69	M.F. COHEN (1980-94)
64	S.G. SMYTH (1990-99)
62	W.K. McCALLAN (1996-2000)
60	J.C. BOUCHER (1929-54)
59	J.D.R. BENSON (1993-97)
56	G. COOKE (1994-2000)
56	J.F. SHORT (1974-84)
55	G.A. DUFFY (1953-74)
53	S.F. BERGIN (1949-65)
52	B.A. O'BRIEN (1966-81)
52	M.P. REA (1985-96)
50	R.L. EAGLESON (1995-1999)
50	P.G. GILLESPIE (1995-2000)

RUNS (1500 AND OVER)

	M	Inns	NO	HS	Runs	Ave	100	50
M.A. MASOOD (1982-88)	40	55	5	138	1940	38.80	4	11
I.J. ANDERSON (1966-85)	86	141	25	198*	3777	32.56	7	13
S.J.S. WARKE (1981-96)	114	151	10	144*	4275	30.31	4	28
M.P. REA (1985-96)	52	71	3	115	2044	30.05	2	11
A.R. DUNLOP (1990-2000)	114	128	20	150	3164	29.29	4	16

J.F. SHORT (1974-84)	56	91	5	114	2515	29.24	3	15
J.D.R. BENSON (1993-97)	59	60	7	79	1528	28.83	0	9
D.A. LEWIS (1984-97)	121	145	20	136*	3579	28.63	4	20
M.F. COHEN (1980-94)	69	96	8	118	2519	28.62	2	17
S.G. SMYTH (1990-99)	64	76	9	102*	1912	28.53	1	10
S.F. BERGIN (1949-65)	53	98	7	137	2524	27.73	2	15
G.D. HARRISON (1983-97)	118	132	26	105*	2765	26.08	1	12
M.S. REITH (1969-1980)	44	81	2	129	1838	23.26	1	11
J.S. POLLOCK (1939-57)	41	73	3	129	1506	21.51	1	9
B.A. O'BRIEN ((1966-81)	52	86	9	72	1636	21.24	0	9
J.D. MONTEITH (1965-84)	77	99	16	95	1712	20.62	0	9
E. INGRAM (1928-53)	48	84	3	83	1628	20.09	0	10
A.J. O'RIORDAN (1958-77)	72	121	17	119	2018	19.40	3	6
D.R. PIGOT (1966-76)	44	79	1	88	1515	19.39	0	

* Not out

WICKETS (100 AND OVER)

	M	Overs	Mdn	Runs	Wkts	Ave	10M	5I
J.C. BOUCHER (1929-54)	60	1597.1	371	4684	307	15.25	7	31
J.D. MONTEITH (1965-84)	76	2414.1	886	5664	326	17.37	7	27
E. INGRAM (1928-53)	48	1394	514	3038	151	20.11	1	7
S.S.J. HUEY (1951-66)	36	942.5	293	2314	112	20.66	1	7
A.J. O'RIORDAN (1958-77)	72	1950	621	4503	206	21.85	1	7
D.E. GOODWIN (1965-75)	43	1125.4	420	2551	115	22.18	1	6
S.C. CORLETT (1974-87)	73	1892.2	440	5387	233	23.12	-	8
M. HALLIDAY (1970-89)	93	1961.2	474	5819	192	30.30	2	5
P. McCRUM (1989-98)	74	938.4	147	3426	106	32.32	0	1
G.D. HARRISON (1983-97)	118	1332.5	218	4714	140	33.67	0	3

R.D. Lambert (1893-1930) was a fine all-rounder. He scored 1995 runs and 4 centuries at an average of 27.70 and took 179 wickets at an average of 18.35. He played in 52 matches for Ireland.

HIGHEST SCORES

198*	I.J. ANDERSON	v Canada	Toronto	1973
150	A.R. DUNLOP	v Scotland	Ayr	2000
148	A.R. DUNLOP	v MCC	Malahide	1996

147	I.J. ANDERSON	v Scotland	Hamilton Crescent, Glasgow	1976
144*	S.J.S. WARKE	v Scotland	Clontarf, Dublin	1985
138	M.A. MASOOD	v MCC	Lord's	1985
137	S.F. BERGIN	v Scotland	College Park, Dublin	1959
136*	D.A. LEWIS	v. Wales	Kimmage, Dublin	1990

* Not out

BEST BOWLING

9-26	F. FEE	v Scotland	College Park, Dublin	1957
9-113	G.D. HARRISON	v Scotland	Myreside, Edinburgh	1990
8-44	J.D. MONTEITH	v MCC	Lord's	1973
8-48	S.S.J. HUEY	v MCC	College Park, Dublin	1954
8-60	A.J. O'RIORDAN	v Holland	The Hague	1970
7-18	J.C. BOUCHER	v Scotland	Perth	1950

OTHERS OF SPECIAL NOTE

6-13	S.S.J. HUEY	v Scotland	Beechgrove, Londonderry	1963
6-13	J.D. MONTEITH	v Denmark	Clontarf, Dublin	1973
5-6	D.E. GOODWIN	v West Indies	Sion Mills	1969

HIGHEST PARTNERSHIPS FOR EACH WICKET (INCLUDES THOSE ESTABLISHED PRIOR TO 1950) FOR IRELAND

1st	224	M.P. REA & S.J.S. WARKE	v Wales	College Park, Dublin	1992
2nd	207	M.A. MASOOD & D.G. DENNISON	v MCC	Lord's	1985
3rd	206	A.R. DUNLOP & A.D. PATTERSON	v MCC	Malahide	1996
4th	224*	D.A. LEWIS & G.D. HARRISON	v Scotland	Hamilton Crescent, Glasgow	1994
5th	175	J. HARRISON & A.J. O'RIORDAN	v Denmark	Clontarf, Dublin	1973
6th	201	A.D. COMYN & W.D. HAMILTON	v I Zingari	Phoenix Park Dublin	1896
7th	150	W. HONE Snr & W.S. ASHTON	v I. Zingari	Vice Regal Dublin	1868
8th	150	S.C. CORLETT & A. McBRINE	v Scotland	Coleraine	1987

9th	96	J.W. HYNES & W.D. HAMILTON	v Gents of Canada	Rathmines, Dublin	1887
10th	96	D.G. DENNISON & M. HALLIDAY	v MCC	Clontarf, Dublin	1986
11th	100	P. McCRUM & J.O. DAVY	v Scotland	Malahide	1997

* Not out

MOST CATCHES (50 OR MORE)

	M	Ct
A.J. O'RIORDAN (1958-77)	72	57
S.J.S. WARKE (1981-96)	114	54

WICKET-KEEPING DISMISSALS

	M	Ct	St	Total
O. D. COLHOUN (1959-79)	87	148	42	190
P.B. JACKSON (1981-94)	87	103	30	133

QUICKEST CENTURY

51 balls, 51 mins – J.A. PRIOR (119) v Warwickshire, Rathmines, Dublin. 1982

HORSE RACING

SOME EXAMPLES OF WINNERS BRED BY MAJOR HALL

Nasrullah, Khaled, Noor, Hairan, Tulyar, Gino, Badruddin, Rustom Pasha, Felicitation, Claro, Bahram, Theft, Nilo, Pherozshah, Rivaz, Teresina, Udaipur, Gallant Man, Poona, Palariva, Hafiz, Toro, Masaka, Yia, Amante, Taboun, Petite Etoile, Saint Crespin III, Ginetta, Diabletetta, Palestine, Sheshoon, Venture, Charlottesville, Silver Shark and Zeddaan.

VINCENT O'BRIEN'S RECORD

Aintree Grand National – Early Mist (1953), Royal Tan (1954), Quare Times (1955)

Cheltenham Gold Cup – Cottage Rake (1948, 1949, 1950), Knock Hard (1953)

Champion Hurdle – Hatton's Grace (1949, 1950, 1951)

Epsom Derby – Larkspur (1962), Sir Ivor (1968), Nijinsky (1970), Roberto(1972), The Minstrel (1977), Golden Fleece (1982)

Irish Derby – Chamier (1953), Ballymoss (1957), Nijinsky (1970), The Minstrel (1977), El Gran Senor (1984), Law Society (1985)

Prix du Jockey Club – Caerleon (1983)

Epsom Oaks – Long Look (1965), Valoris (1986)

English Two Thousand Guineas – Sir Ivor (1968), Nijinsky (1970), Lomond (1983), El Gran Senor (1984)

English St Leger – Ballymoss (1957) Nijinsky (1970), Boucher (1972)

English one thousand Guineas – Glad Rags (1966)

Prix de l'Arc de Triomphe – Ballymoss (1958), Alleged (1977 and 1978)

King George VI and Queen Elizabeth Stakes – Ballymoss (1958), Nijinsky (1970), The Minstrel (1977)

Washington International – Sir Ivor (1968)

3. AIDAN O'BRIEN AND CHARLIE SWAN WINNERS 1995 – 1998

Royal Mountbrowne in the Pierse Leopardstown Handicap Chase (1996), Morris Oil Chase (1996) and in the Hotpower Chase (1996). Private Peace in the Baileys Arkle Challenge Cup (1998) and the Chiquita Drinmore Novice Chase (1997). Istabraq in the A1B Europe Champion Hurdle (1998), in the Deloite & Touche Novice Hurdle (1997), in the Stanley Cooker Champion Novice Hurdle (1997), the Avonmore Waterford Royal Bond Novice Hurdle (1996), the Avonmore Waterford Hatton's Grace Hurdle (1997), the A1B Agri-Business December Festival Hurdle (1997), and the John James McManus Memorial Chase (1997). Theatreworld in the Red Mills Trial Hurdle (1997 and 1998) and in the AIB Agri-Business December Festival Hurdle (1996). Idiots Venture in the Oliver Freaney and Co Dan Moore Handicap Chase (1997) Hotel Minella in the Country Pride Novice Hurdle (1995). Life of a

Lord in the Compaq Galway Plate Handicap Chase (1996) and in the Guinness Kerry National Handicap Chase (1995). Just Little in the Murphy's Irish Stout Handicap Hurdle (1997). That's My Man in the Auction Novice Hurdle and in the Avonmore Waterford Royal Bond Novice Hurdle (1995). Urubonde in the Lizmullen Hurdle (1996). Rainbow Warrior in the Derry Three Year Old Juvenile Hurdle (1997). Double Symphony in the Derry Gold Medal Novice Chase (1995. King of Kerry in the Kevin McManus Bookmaker Novice Hurdle (1996).